CW01237908

ns and Memories

Histories and Memories

Migrants and their History in Britain

EDITED BY
KATHY BURRELL
&
PANIKOS PANAYI

TAURIS ACADEMIC STUDIES
LONDON • NEW YORK

Published in 2006 by Tauris Academic Studies,
An imprint of I.B.Tauris & Co. Ltd
6 Salem Road, London W2 4BU
175 Fifth Avenue, New York NY10010
www.ibtauris.com

In the United States of America and in Canada distributed by
St. Martins Press, 175 Fifth Avenue, New York NY10010

Copyright © Kathy Burrell and Panikos Panayi 2006

The right of Kathy Burrell and Panikos Panayi to be identified as the editors of this work has been asserted by the editors in accordance with the Copyright, Design and Patents Act 1988.

All rights reserved. Except for brief quotations in a review, this book, or any part thereof, may not be reproduced, stored in or introduced into a retrieval system, or transmitted, in any form or by any means, electronic, mechanical, photocopying, recording or otherwise, without the prior written permission of the publisher.

International Library of Historical Studies 37
ISBN 1 84511 042 0
EAN: 978 1 84511 042 0

A full CIP record for this book is available from the British Library
A full CIP record for this book is available from the Library of Congress

Library of Congress catalog card: available

Printed and bound in India by Replika Press Pvt. Ltd.
from camera-ready copy edited and supplied by the editors

Contents

List of tables	*vii*
List of illustrations	*vii*
Acknowledgements	*ix*
Preface	*xi*

Part I: Introduction: Immigration and British History

Immigration, History and Memory in Britain *Kathy Burrell and Panikos Panayi*	3
Great Britons: Immigration, History and Memory *Tony Kushner*	18
Historical Practice in the Age of Pluralism: Educating and Celebrating Identities *Kevin Myers*	35

Part II: Histories and Narratives

Italian Immigrants in Britain: Perceptions and Self-Perceptions *Lucio Sponza*	57
Narratives of Settlement: East Europeans in Post-War Britain *Inge Weber-Newth*	75
The Migrant at Home in Spitalfields: Memory, Myth and Reality *Anne J. Kershen*	96
Reinventing the Myth of Return: Older Italians in Nottingham *Deianira Ganga*	114

Part III: Memory, Metaphor and Material Culture

Migration, Memory and Metaphor: Life Stories of South Asians in Leicester 133
Joanna Herbert

A Journey Through the Material Geographies of Diaspora Cultures: Four Modes of Environmental Memory 149
Divya P. Tolia-Kelly

Hidden Objects in the World of Cultural Migrants: Significant Objects Used by European Migrants to Layer Thoughts and Memories 171
Caroline Attan

Part IV: Irish Remembrances and Representations

Passing Time: Irish Women Remembering and Re-telling Stories of Migration to Britain 191
Louise Ryan

Family History and Memory in Irish Immigrant Families 210
John Herson

Marginal Voices: Football and Identity in a Contested Space 234
Joseph M. Bradley

Notes and References 253
Notes on Contributors 299
Index 303

List of tables

Stafford Irish: Interviewees and Families   232

List of illustrations

Goan Palms, by the artist Melanie Carvalho   167

Acknowledgements

This volume originates from a conference which occurred on the subject of 'Immigration, History and Memory in Britain' at De Montfort University on 6-7 September 2003 convened by the editors. The event was made possible with the help of a number of individuals and organisations. First, David Sadler, then Head of the School of Historical and International Studies, who supported the idea from the outset. Other members of the School who demonstrated their support included Ian Jackson. Most important, however, we must single out Margaret Barton of the Conferences and Short Courses Unit of De Montfort Expertise, who organised and publicised the conference with immaculate efficiency. In addition, we would also like to thank the bodies who supported the event, including the British Academy, the Royal Historical Society and the School of Historical and International Studies of De Montfort University.

Preface

This book, originating from the 2003 De Montfort University conference on 'Immigration, History and Memory in Britain', is inspired by wide-ranging debates on the relationship between immigration, history and memory. It incorporates contributions from a variety of academic disciplines and perspectives (five from History, two from both Geography and Modern Languages, and one each from Politics, Social Policy, Education, Sports Studies and Art and Design), and carries work done by both new and more established researchers. While it endeavours to cover a range of different views and experiences, it cannot include all immigrant groups in this coverage. What this book does offer, however, is a genuinely interdisciplinary attempt to work through the issues of immigration, history and memory in Britain on a variety of different scales, ranging from the national to the individual.

The first section of this book, 'Introduction: Immigration and British History', begins with an overview chapter 'Immigration, History and Memory in Britain' by Kathy Burrell and Panikos Panayi. This chapter considers three broad ways in which the experiences of immigrant groups have been 'remembered' in Britain. Firstly, it charts the development of an academic historiography on the topic of immigration history, highlighting, in particular, the continued strength of Jewish history writing. While there is a growing field of immigration history, however, it is noted that in mainstream British history writing, immigration still tends to be a peripheral topic. Secondly, the popularisation of immigration history and memory is addressed, using examples ranging from local heritage projects to the construction of ethnic minority 'communities'. It finds that while this increased interest in remembering is to be generally welcomed, the presentation of ethnic memory is not straightforward, and can be distorted or contested. Finally, the importance of personal memories of home and migration is explored, showing how oral history interviewing especially can reveal, and even create, a different type of immigration history, and a different type of remembering. The subsequent chapters in this section focus specifically on the larger scale issues of remembering immigration in British history. In the first of these contributions, 'Great Britons: Immigration, History and Memory', Tony Kushner openly confronts the problems associated with the production of immigration histories, noting the two opposing traditions of immigration and native racism in British history, and underlining the difficulty of introducing counter narratives to established notions of Britain's liberal attitude to newcomers. While progress has been made in questioning these assumptions, he focuses on the recent production of the 'Great Britons' list to show how marginalised immigration and ethnic minorities remain in the wider sweep of British history and the historical imagination of the British public. Including a discussion on the role of Black History Month, his chapter raises interesting questions about how Britain sees itself and its contemporary ethnic profile. Kushner also discusses the recording of community history by the Jewish population, demonstrating the difficulties that arise from creating histories from within immigrant groups, and highlighting similar issues of representation, silencing and dissent. Concluding this section, Kevin Myers, in 'Historical Practice in the Age of Pluralism: Educating and Celebrating Identities', continues with a similar stance, warning both of the narrowness of accepted narratives of English national identity and history, and of the dangers of misrepresentation in public constructions of immigration history. Although an increased interest in heritage and minority history projects is to be welcomed, he observes that a wider understanding of immigration can be undermined by overly celebratory depictions of immigrant life, exemplified here by the case of the Irish in Birmingham, influenced by the desire to produce comforting, easy histories that fit a prevailing political purpose. He also highlights the problem of overdependence on history and the desire to use it to stabilise contemporary identities, a pitfall of heritage projects that can inadvertently work to trap young people especially in a past that lacks present relevance.

The second section of the book, 'Histories and Narratives', concentrates on case-studies of different groups and orientates around the themes of settlement and establishment, change and 'home' in the histories of immigrant communities. In his contribution, 'Italian Immigrants in Britain: Perceptions and Self-Perceptions', Lucio Sponza offers an insight into the changing characteristics of the British Italian community from the nineteenth century onwards, highlighting the internal regional, class and occupational divisions within the population, the relationship of the community with Italy, but also charting the different perceptions and attitudes which have been historically directed at Italian immigrants. Italian settlement developed in the face of both popular and official suspicion – a hostility which culminated in the internment of British Italians during the

Second World War, and a history which does not fit comfortably with the narrative of Britain as a historically inclusive nation. Using both original and pre-recorded interviews with East European wartime 'Displaced Persons', in her chapter on 'Narratives of Settlement: East Europeans in Post-War Britain', Inge Weber-Newth focuses predominantly on the difficulties faced by post-war European Volunteer Workers during their settlement in Britain, while also drawing attention to the politically motivated nature of the selection of traumatised labour immigrants, chosen for their perceived assimilability in British society. Here another type of history is unearthed – that provided by the interviewees themselves as they narrate their experiences of adjusting to life in a new and strange environment, trying to embrace the present without forgetting the past. This desire to hold on to what came before forms the central strand of Anne Kershen's contribution on 'The Migrant at Home and in Spitalfields: Memory, Myth and Reality', examining Huguenot, Jewish and Bengali reconstructions of 'home' in Spitalfields. Using the 'cultural tools' of language, religion and food, all three groups have been able to transport some of the surroundings of their respective homelands into their everyday lives in London – a phenomenon both important internally and visible externally. By using pieces of the past to furnish their new lives, not only did these immigrants manage to ease, with varying success, some of the emotional dislocation caused by migration, they also forged a new identity for the Spitalfields area. The final chapter of this section, 'Reinventing the Myth of Return: Older Italians in Nottingham', by Deianira Ganga, focuses on some of the ambiguities of this pull back home and the issue of Italian return migration. Caught between the need to succeed in Britain and the often unrealised expectation of an eventual return to Italy, the respondents in this chapter illustrate the difficulty in dividing 'history' too neatly along national lines. Here the life-histories of the interviewees effortlessly span the two countries, bringing British and Italian history together. The transnationalism of the Nottingham Italian community serves as an important reminder that settlement in the UK does not necessarily signal the end of the migrant journey, and that immigrant histories and realities are as much about 'there' as they are about 'here'.

The penultimate section, 'Memory, Metaphor and Material Culture', takes this last concept further, investigating the uses and mechanisms of remembering the migrant past. In her contribution on 'Migration, Memory and Metaphor: Life Stories of South Asians in Leicester', Joanna Herbert illustrates how life-story interviews collected with South Asian immigrants in Leicester reveal not only the details of migrant histories, but also hold messages about how these histories are viewed and how they are represented, offering an indication of how different people frame and 'tell' their lives in contrasting ways. Seemingly straightforward narratives of food and descriptions of home, therefore, are fused with other meanings of gendered identities, social standing, migratory expectations and issues of inclusion and exclusion in Britain, harnessing memory and metaphor to reconnect the past with the present. For Divya Tolia-Kelly in 'A Journey Through the Material Geographies of Diaspora Cultures: Four Modes of Environmental Memory', the British South Asian past is communicated less through chronologies, and more through the material cultures of home, film and landscape and the stories attached to them. In her chapter, she uses interviews undertaken with South Asian women in North London to show how remembering is an intrinsic part of the home environment, from the woman who keeps a suitcase full of memories from India and Kenya, to the African elephant foot used as a telephone seat in the home. By embedding these artefacts in the everyday, the home and the past together, as signifiers of life before migration, are safely incorporated into the current context of Britain, again easing the possible disjuncture between the two. Continuity and rupture are also important themes in the final chapter of the section, 'Hidden Objects in the World of Cultural Migrants: Significant Objects Used by European Migrants to Layer Thoughts and Memories', by Caroline Attan. Here these themes are investigated through the objects which are kept by European, predominantly Jewish, migrants in their homes, objects which are often either purposely hidden away, or have hidden meanings attached to them. For survivors of forced migration in particular, the ownership of certain objects holds a powerful ability to invoke painful memories which are not always easy to confront on a daily basis. While material reminders of traumatic migration experiences can be put aside, however, they also form an important part of the transmission of cultural memory to the next generation, allowing younger family members to build a picture of their parents' lives.

The book concludes with 'Irish Remembrances and Representations', a selection of chapters which incorporate many of the themes already discussed, considering them from the perspective of Irish immigration to England and Scotland. In the first chapter of this section, 'Passing Time: Irish Women Remembering and Re-Telling Stories of Migration to Britain', Louise Ryan discusses the different narrations offered by Irish women of their journeys to England and their lives before migration. Just as with the material culture of the previous contributions, the life stories produced by these women work to reconnect their Irish lives with their English ones, allowing them to move, metaphorically, more easily between the two, and to use one to justify the other. The process of talking about remembering is considered here too, with the interviewees offering a variety of stories and 'memories' which on the one hand appear to be well rehearsed, and on the other fail to conform to standardised life-cycle chronologies. If these women's memories seem omnipresent, in his chapter on 'Family History and Memory in Irish Immigrant Families', John Herson investigates the apparent loss of Irish memory in Stafford. While the presence of an Irish population dating from the nineteenth century is clear from historical records, there appears to be little folklore or family history left to accompany it. It is this significant, if unfashionable, discovery that reminds us of the fragility of memory. The transmission of cultural knowledge is not automatic, and ethnic remembering is ultimately a pragmatic endeavour, strongest when the memory of the past has a designated use in the present and weakest when the here and now does not seem to need any historical reinforcement. Joseph Bradley, in the final chapter 'Marginal Voices: Football and Identity in a Contested Space', explores a different manifestation of Irish memory again – that of the role of Celtic Football Club as a symbol and mainstay of Irish cultural identity in Scotland. As the interviews used in his contribution demonstrate, Celtic provides a means of talking about being Irish in Scotland that allows wider issues of hostility and marginalisation to be discussed indirectly. The trust invested in Celtic and its historical and contemporary relevance to Irish identity is made very clear: the continued popularity of the football club, moreover, has ensured that a cultural space has been created where Irish memory can be safeguarded, a resource for future generations to use in remembering their Irish ancestry and an enduring marker of the Irish presence in Scotland.

The contributions as a whole therefore introduce scholars and students to the various ways in which immigration has been remembered in Britain. This has happened in tangible ways, through academic writing, community and heritage projects and the establishment of institutional structures such as churches, schools and clubs. Just as importantly, it has happened through the individual transportation of memories to Britain by the migrants themselves, who have then gone on to nurture these memories through the personal spheres of home and family. One thing all of the contributors make clear is that this remembering of immigration history can never be neutral. While on the one hand it is vulnerable to simplification or neglect in its public and academic construction, on the other, the histories and memories that are commemorated by immigrants are also inevitably distorted, this time by the migration process itself.

Part I

Introduction: Immigration and British History

1

Immigration, History and Memory in Britain

Kathy Burrell and Panikos Panayi

Introduction

In his impressive work on 'sites of memory' in France, Pierre Nora makes a distinction between history and memory. In his words:

> Memory is life, always embodied in living societies and as such in permanent evolution, subject to the dialect of remembering and forgetting, unconscious of the distortions to which it is subject, vulnerable in various ways to appropriation and manipulation, and capable of lying dormant for long periods only to be suddenly reawakened. History, on the other hand, is the reconstruction, always problematic and incomplete, of what is no longer.[1]

History and memory signal two different approaches to the uses and presentations of the past – the desire to write official historical chronologies, and the need to bring selected aspects of the past into the present to strengthen group and individual identities. The study of the place of immigration in British history and memory highlights this distinction. On the one hand, immigration history has been recorded to some extent in academic accounts of British history, providing a standard version of the history of inward migration movements to the nation. On the other hand, there has also been an increased desire to focus on the 'memories' of the immigrants themselves, to provide alternative histories of immigration, and to open up understandings of the past beyond official national narratives.[2]

It is generally accepted that the writing and production of ordered histories has been a foundation of nationhood and national identity in the modern era.[3] Since the emergence of history as an academic discipline during the nineteenth century, the most important identified 'groups' have been national, and history has been largely written, understood and recognised through the prism of the nation.[4] British historians, for example, have written mostly about their own history, partly due to the implicit influence of nationalism[5], and partly due to a lack of linguistic training which limits the possibility of a wider geographical focus. But, while these histories have often embraced historical aspects of the British Empire, with regards to immigration, the standard histories of Britain have, until more recently, tended to exclude minorities, whether based on class, gender or ethnicity. The combined influence of academic Marxism and the more recent 'turn' towards postmodernism, however, has ensured that this situation has altered. Within academic writing more generally there is now a much greater interest in 'alternative' histories that stress these previously neglected areas of class, gender and ethnicity[6] – in short a focus on multiple *histories* rather than one overarching *history*.

But attempts to uncover and commemorate the past are not only restricted to an academic process of producing scholarly publications. Historical recovery can also involve public heritage initiatives designed to record local histories[7], often in collaboration with migrants who actively contribute to the collective remembering of their own communities. In addition to this, immigrants nurture their own individual memories, passing on stories to future generations and making histories which are ultimately destined never to reach any sort of academic or public arena. With all this remembering taking place, it could be argued that the influence of various academic and heritage projects, combined with a growing recognition of the evolution of a multicultural Britain, have worked together to give the experiences of immigrants a heightened presence in everyday national discourse.

This chapter will focus on three different ways in which the history of immigration in Britain is 'remembered' – that is researched, recorded, selected and presented for current and future consumption. Firstly, it will focus on the development of 'professional' immigration history, a process dating back to the nineteenth century, and a movement largely led by historians with immigrant roots themselves. Secondly, it will trace the more recent popularisation of the experiences of immigrants and their memories, assessing the positive attributes of this development, but also the potential dangers of misrepresentation. This section will also consider how the reconstruction of ethnicity itself can be viewed as a means of conserving immigrant group memory in Britain. Finally, this chapter will investigate a further area where immigration, history and memory coincide – the increased interest in memory studies and oral history and how individual memories of migration are constructed and communicated.

The Emergence of Immigration History

In Britain, the study of immigrants has only recently begun to concern 'mainstream' historians. Nineteenth century historical writing was characterised by the production of glorified histories of England in the Whig tradition, whose central argument focused upon a progression away from the arbitrary power of medieval monarchy towards liberal democratic freedom. Two central characteristics of such writing consisted of its belief in progress and its tendency to ignore the position of the working classes, whose fate improved gradually as a result of the democratisation process consequent upon industrialisation.[8]

In opposition to such writing, a distinct working-class history began to develop during the first half of the twentieth century, especially under the influence of scholars such as G. D. H. Cole,[9] and J. L. and L. B. Hammond.[10] A major turning point came with the publication of E. P. Thompson's *The Making of the English Working Classes* in 1963, after which less ambitious books appeared on individual aspects of working class life and particular geographical locations. At the same time, the development of social and economic history in British universities allowed the creation of a large number of lectureships, often taken up by scholars writing about the working classes, a process that continued until the 1980s. This development was also fundamentally influenced by the working class origins of many of the individuals taking up the new posts, who had made their way up the educational ladder through the grammar school system implemented by the 1944 Education Act. Essentially, by writing about the working classes, they were reconstructing the history of their parents and grandparents.[11]

Few of the historians appointed during the 1960s and 1970s ventured into the field of immigrant history. But this could not remain the situation for long, primarily because of the early impact of post-war immigrants from the Empire and Commonwealth. Social scientists such as Michael Banton[12] and Ruth Glass,[13] immediately focused upon them, ensuring that the contemporary concern with race would eventually seep through to historians, whose methodology and areas of interest change less quickly than those of social scientists. The admittedly small number of historians with immigrant origins, who often write about the group from which they originate, has helped the growth of the history of migrants.

As the different historiographies of immigrant groups illustrate, the study of immigrants in British history was not simply instigated as a reaction to post-war influxes. The two largest groups in Britain at the end of the nineteenth century, the Irish and the Jews, had already begun to produce their own histories. Beginning with the Irish, an important starting point was John Denvir's informative *The Irish in Britain* from 1892, which gives an account of contemporary Irish settlements, as well as providing much detail about their history. The next contribution of equal academic merit did not appear until the 1940s, consisting of J. E. Handley's meticulously researched two volume social history of the Irish in Scotland.[14] In 1963 there followed J. A. Jackson's *The Irish in Britain*. The influx of over a million Irish into Britain after 1945 has led to an explosion of interest in this group. The leading scholars who have worked in this area have included Patrick O'Sullivan,[15] Roger Swift and Sheridan Gilley,[16] Mary Hickman[17] and Donald MacRaild,[18] most of whom have some Irish antecedents. Furthermore, an Irish Studies Institute has been established at the University of Liverpool[19] together with an Irish Studies Centre at London Metropolitan University,[20] each of which focus heavily upon Britain. In addition, an Irish Diaspora Research Unit exists at the University of Bradford.[21]

Anglo-Jewry has an even fuller history in Britain, dating as far back as 1738 with the publication of *Anglia Judaica* by D'Blossiers Tovey. The year 1851 offers a better starting point because it witnessed the publication of Moses Margoliouth's monumental three volume history of Jewish settlement in Britain from pre-Roman times to the Victorian era. The period leading up to the First World War also saw the publication of further scholarly studies.[22] More importantly, the Jewish Historical Society of England came into existence in 1893, one of the first immigrant history organisations in Britain, which has also published its own scholarly journal in the form of its *Transactions*.[23] Consequently, the groundwork was laid for Cecil Roth, the father of twentieth century Anglo-Jewish history, who began his productive career in the inter-war years and continued to write on numerous general and specific aspects of the Jews in England after 1945.[24] The only other figure who could really compare with Roth was V. D. Lipman, producing a series of books, most notably his *Social History of the Jews in England* in 1954.

The 1960s and 1970s witnessed a breakthrough in the historiography of the Jews in Britain, with the publication of three major social histories on the late nineteenth century influx from Eastern Europe.[25] Since then, Jewish history has witnessed the production of numerous studies, focusing especially upon antisemitism, ethnicity and relations between different ethnic groups within Anglo-Jewry. The leading figures in the field have consisted of British Jews, most notably Geoffrey Alderman, David Cesarani, David Feldman, David S. Katz and Tony Kushner, together with two American Jews, Todd M. Endelman and W. D. Rubinstein. Also included here should be Colin Holmes and Bill Williams, amongst others.[26] Most importantly for the future development of Anglo-Jewish academic history is the Parkes Centre for Jewish Non-Jewish Relations, established by Tony Kushner at the University of Southampton.[27]

Few other groups in Britain have a historiography as long and detailed as that of the Jews. The one exception consists of the Huguenots, as the Huguenot Society of Great Britain and Ireland, as well as the *Proceedings* published by this group, date back to 1885, preserving the memory of this now almost totally assimilated group. Although it is a scholarly body, much of its work is genealogical, used by people trying to trace their Huguenot ancestors.[28] This minority also has a detailed historiography.[29]

The study of Germans, like the Irish and Jews, dates back to nineteenth century, beginning with Karl Heinrich Schaible's *Geschichte der Deutschen in England* from 1885. The works of the next two authors on the subject, Ian Colvin and C. R. Hennings, however, can be considered to be unreliable because in both cases World War I coloured the perspectives of the authors.[30] Only from the 1970s has the history of Germans in Britain begun to attract close attention, with a focus upon refugees from Nazism, but also, in more recent years, on the nineteenth century and the immediate post-Second World War period. Although a couple of the early authorities who founded this subject consisted of non-Germans,[31] the history of this group is increasingly written by German scholars.[32] Furthermore, the history of German refugees from the Third Reich has taken on a life of its own,[33] most notably through the establishment of a Centre for German and Austrian Exile Studies at the University of London's Institute of German and Romance Studies, which now publishes a *Yearbook*.[34]

Italians have attracted serious academic attention since the end of the 1980s, with the two leading scholars consisting of Lucio Sponza and Terri Colpi, both of whom proudly display their Italian origins: the former was an immigrant himself (now returned to Venice)[35] and the latter described herself as a 'third generation Italian Scot'.[36] In addition, several smaller scale studies, usually written by people with Italian origins, have also recently appeared.[37] People of Eastern European origin have also received attention from scholars who usually originate from these communities, as the example of the Poles illustrates.[38]

When the focus is turned to the major migrant groups originating beyond Europe, it might appear that their historiography is in its infancy, but this statement applies to some ethnic communities more than others. Certainly, the study of black people in Britain is not a recent development, although most of the older volumes on this group had been written by white males,[39] a situation which is now changing.[40] The history of Indian groups, meanwhile, is a more recent phenomenon, with the standard work remaining Rosina Visram's volume originally published in 1986.[41] The best of the other volumes include Shompa Lahiri's, *Indians in Britain: Anglo-Indian Encounters, Race and Identity, 1880-1930* from 2000 and Katy Gardner's *Age, Narrative and Migration: The Life Course and Life Histories of Bengali Elders in London* from

2002. It is important, again, to acknowledge the role of social scientists in producing early accounts of black and Asian people who settled in Britain after the Second World War. In fact, most work on these groups has been concerned with the wider issues of diaspora and post-colonialism, important perspectives that are yet to infiltrate fully into the discipline of history and its approaches to immigration.

Clearly, immigrant historiography has made significant strides forward. Most books have been produced by individuals working on their own community, indicating the importance of history as one factor in the creation of group identity. But how have mainstream historians dealt with the history of immigrants in Britain? Despite the transformative impact of post-war immigration[42] and the fact that ethnic minorities now make up nearly eight per cent of the population,[43] as well as the centrality of immigration in the evolution of Britain,[44] mainstream historians continue to ignore them, a fact which experts on immigration have previously highlighted.[45] For the leading historian of Britain, David Cannadine, immigrants simply do not exist, even though he deals with core social history issues such as class.[46] With regard to mainstream British history it is still difficult to argue against Paul Gilroy's assertion that *There Ain't No Black in the Union Jack*.[47]

It is therefore necessary to rely upon a series of general studies that have appeared over the years to understand immigration as a phenomenon in British history. The first example of such a book was published as long ago as 1897.[48] In recent decades a series of historians have produced such general books, focusing mostly on the last two centuries.[49] Collectively these volumes help to ensure that scholars, students and the interested reader have a good awareness of the importance of immigration in the country's recent history, even if mainstream historians regard it as largely irrelevant.

The Popularisation of Immigration Histories and Memories

While the development of an academic historiography represents one aspect of the emergence of immigration in collective memory in modern Britain, immigrant experiences have also been remembered in a more popular manner, encapsulated in publicly constructed histories. This type of 'history-making' is important in two different ways. Firstly, it aids the formation and strengthening of group identity by establishing a common past which ethnic minority communities, first generation immigrants and their children, can commemorate and celebrate in the UK.[50] Immigrant groups, like nations, need their histories.[51] Secondly, it works to inform mainstream British society of the presence of such groups, opening up channels of communication between them, and promoting and conserving a range of histories which would otherwise remain excluded from the public gaze.

This process of historical construction has intensified in recent decades in Britain, mirroring an increased interest in history more generally.[52] Not only have migrants themselves reconstructed their life experiences for these projects, but mainstream organisations have also become engaged in these activities, using immigrant memories to illustrate Britain's increasingly multiracialised character. This effort to remember migrant experiences is not purely a post-war development of course. Contributions to a book edited by Tony Kushner have previously demonstrated that Jewish heritage was constructed largely before 1945.[53] Yet it is recent decades that have really seen the beginning of the construction of migrant identities, a process that has worked at all levels and in which oral history has played a central role. It is now possible to identify several examples of this remembrance of migrant experiences, involving both members of ethnic minorities and their representatives, as well as local government bodies, especially in areas where there are significant ethnic concentrations.

One key development in this public memorialisation of the experiences of immigrants is in the field of genealogy. While an interest in family history has gathered momentum amongst the ethnic majority,[54] it has also attracted attention amongst minorities, although this interest has largely arisen from members of the ethnic majority tracing their foreign roots. This is apparent in the evolution of two organisations in particular. First, the Anglo-German Family History Society, which has existed since 1987, has held annual meetings, produced publications about the history of Germans in Britain, and has, most importantly, offered genealogical information for Britons wishing to trace their German ancestry.[55] In addition, the much larger Jewish Genealogical Society of Great Britain, which has an international membership, 'encourages genealogical research and promotes the preservation of Jewish genealogical records and resources'.[56] As yet, probably because of the recent arrival of such groups to Britain, there do not seem to be any formally registered genealogical societies developed specifically by post-war Imperial and Commonwealth migrants.[57] The impetus for organisations like these clearly comes from people who have some sort of foreign ancestry essentially working as a group.

In addition, more recently, local authorities – above all libraries and archives – have also played a key role in the process of constructing migrant histories. An early project from the end of the 1980s and beginning of the 1990s, for example, organised by Hammersmith and Fulham Council, produced a series of introductory leaflets by an organisation called the Ethnic Communities Oral History Project on a variety of immigrant communities in London. These leaflets essentially consisted of members of particular groups recalling their experiences of migration to, and settlement in, Britain.[58] Since then, other libraries in areas with significant ethnic minority communities have also participated in the popularisation of the history of specific ethnic minorities, as Kevin Myers demonstrates with regard to Birmingham.[59] Leicestershire's Multicultural Oral and Pictorial Archive Project, a joint venture between Leicestershire Libraries and De Montfort University, resulted in the Highfields Remembered Project, a collection of interviews with a variety of ethnic groups who have lived in this inner city area of Leicester. All of these have been transcribed for the website of the project.[60] While ventures like these consciously work to promote and support a multicultural civic identity, they often embody a more particular purpose or carry a more overt political message. In Newham, for example, the Newham Monitoring Project, aided by local libraries, produced a history of the local black community partly in response to persistent racist attacks in the area, playing up links between the experiences of the black working class and the socialist traditions of the East End.[61]

Archives have also increasingly, although somewhat belatedly in many cases, been used to recognise the multiethnic past of the area they serve.[62] One of the most impressive indications of the memorialisation of migrant experiences is the development of the Moving Here website, supported by the National Archives and financed by the New Opportunities Fund of the National Lottery. It is a virtual archive of over 150,000 items on a variety of groups (although concentrating upon Caribbeans, Irish, Jews and South Asians) who have made their way to Britain over the past 200 years, from collections throughout the country.[63] Another important development has been the establishment of the Black Cultural Archives. Its website states that it was:

> ... established in 1981 by a group of educationalists, writers and other interested individuals who were concerned about the paucity of historical documentation and social data on black experiences in Britain. The BCA was thus set up to collect, document, preserve and disseminate materials concerning the history and culture of black people in Britain, and to make these resources available and accessible nationally and internationally.

It 'ultimately hopes to establish the first national museum of black history in Britain'.[64]

Museums have, of course, also played a role in the popularisation of migrant experiences. Perhaps the most important exhibition in this context consisted of the 'Peopling of London' which took place at the Museum of

London in 1993.[65] In fact, while the UK does not yet have a Museum of Immigration, the Jewish community has developed small Jewish Museums in Manchester and London, which hold exhibitions and act as a resource for those researching aspects of Jewish life in Britain.[66] However, perhaps the most spectacular indication of the popularisation of immigrant experiences can be found in the development of Black History Month (inspired by a similar event in the USA), begun in 1987 and now a truly national celebration of the history of the black presence in Britain, with much focus on contemporary experiences, held in October every year. In 2004 it hosted 1,400 events.[67]

A variety of developments are therefore increasingly commemorating the immigrant experience in Britain, mostly initiated by people with migrant origins. This can be partly understood in the wider context of the economic and social success of post-war migrants, as well as immigrants who arrived before that time, and seemingly corresponds with a growth in the media presence of people with immigrant origins. In fact, it could be argued that this coincides with a more general acceptance of 'alternative' experiences and histories in fiction, film and television, with the publications and productions of Meera Syal, Zadie Smith's *White Teeth*, Monica Ali's *Brick Lane* and Andrea Levy's *Small Island* as acclaimed recent examples.

This popularisation of ethnic history within the UK, however, is not without its problems. As Tony Kushner and Kevin Myers both illustrate in this volume, publicly constructed immigration histories carry all the same caveats and limitations that are acknowledged in large-scale national histories.[68] While these histories are invaluable in giving a voice to otherwise unheard experiences, the issue of this 'voice' has to be addressed. With any public history or heritage project it is crucial to think about who is constructing it, who is being asked to participate and collaborate, and why it is being done at all. If community leaders are involved, to what extent can these leaders themselves be considered to be representative of the entire group? To what extent are the interviewees selected by these leaders? These issues are so important because this type of project does not always acknowledge issues of gender and class, or experiences of hardship and racism. As Myers highlights with the portrayal of the Irish in Birmingham, there is a tendency, instead, to focus on the positive stories of integration and economic success, sidelining the less comfortable experiences of destitution and hostility. Above all, any signs of internal conflict along class, religious, gender or generational lines can be silenced completely, allowing a more harmonious image to be conveyed. When minority histories are constructed to try to create a sense of community that may be weakening or even non-existent, or to encourage the outside recognition of an ethnically distinct group, there is a danger that they are not accurate histories at all.

While this does not necessarily denigrate their worth, it is important to be aware of their politicisation.

Although there is strong evidence to suggest that some degree of progress has taken place, immigrant history has remained largely absent from the ultimate form of mass media, the television screen, despite the increasing popularity of history in general. Even away from the forum of television, public histories have not managed to counteract the sense that immigrant history is a separate history. Black History Month, for example, is allocated one month for the commemoration of ethnic minorities, but what of the other eleven? Should we be worried that the need for Black History Month reflects a segregated national memory? As Kushner notes in his discussion of the Great Britons competition, there is still a real divide between national memory and immigration history.

Public histories and forums such as these are clearly an integral part of the process of remembering immigrant experiences. While not as obvious, the re-construction of immigrant ethnicity in Britain more generally is also fundamental to the preservation of migrant memory. The development of ethnic minority 'communities' in particular enables new spaces to be set aside for ethnic activities, whether they are religious, economic, political or social. As Anne Kershen has shown with different groups in Spitalfields[69], within these arenas certain aspects of 'home' can be rebuilt, and thus introduced into life in Britain, acting both as a powerful reminder for future generations, and a visible signal to the wider community.

Religion has always played a key role in this type of ethnic consolidation. One of the most successful ways in which the Irish in nineteenth century Britain continued their Irishness, for example, was in the practice of their religion, with the English Catholic establishment playing a large role in this process.[70] Similarly, the continuation of religion represented the principal way in which the Jewish immigrants of the late nineteenth century maintained a connection with their homeland in Eastern Europe, and, just as importantly, their ultimate place of origin in Israel.[71] The same could be said about Muslims[72] and Greek Cypriots, for whom the establishment of Churches as well as secular organisations in the post-war period allowed the reconstruction of many aspects of their lives in Cyprus.[73] For the Polish population in Britain Catholicism has proved to be pivotal to the continued strength of national and historical identity away from Poland.[74] The role of these institutions in sustaining ethnic memory is immense – not only do they provide an allocated space within Britain for the discussion and celebration of the homeland religion, but they also form a visual external marker of community presence. Adherence to an organised religion, furthermore, brings with it a whole host of associated trappings – value codes, social networks, cultural capital, collective rituals – ideal for preserving a forum where a shared ethnic memory can be held, and a useful tool for encouraging community solidarity in the present.[75] Even when followed independently, religious practices automatically relocate migrants back home on at least two levels – spiritually and temporally. The annual calendars of religion are a powerful, daily reminder of the life left behind.

'Remembering' the homeland, of course, extends beyond the remit of religion. A focus on the Jewish case study, for example, shows that even before the influx of the late nineteenth century immigrants, this community had developed a rich ethnicity. After about 1880 Jewishness became extremely complex because of the different types of Jewish ethnicity which existed according to place of origin, religious practice and class within Britain. This ethnicity encompassed a wide range of organisations from schools, to theatres, to literary societies and charities, as well as newspapers.[76] An examination of most other groups in recent British history would reveal a similar pattern, both before and after the Second World War.[77]

The various ethnic organisations established by immigrants in modern British history, whether they consist of churches, schools, charities, newspapers or even satellite television links, therefore represent another aspect of the memorialisation both of the homeland and the immigrant experience. Any way in which ethnicity is constructed provides a means for newcomers to Britain to remember their origins – this is implicit in all 'ethnic' activity. In fact, it is possible to argue that ethnicity is, for migrants and their offspring, memory in action, the perpetuation, but *recreation*, and all that implies (in terms of adapting to the new environment), of the homeland in new surroundings.[78] As Anne Kershen argues, the process of migration can easily turn these memories into myths. The powerful attachment felt towards everything associated with home, however, illustrates how important it is to fashion a sense of the past that is useful to the present, regardless of how out-dated or inaccurate these historical reconstructions are.

Personal Memories of Home and Migration

While much commemoration of immigration has found a national or community scope, an increased academic interest in the use of oral history and in-depth interviewing for migration studies has aided a better understanding of the relationship between memory, ethnicity and migration on an individual basis.[79] At a basic level, the use of interviewing allows a different history of migration to be recorded – one where the main protagonists are the migrants themselves, not the workings of the global economy, domestic immigration agendas, the policies of dictatorships, or the fallouts from natural catastrophes.[80] The lived experience of migration, and the emotions attached to it, takes centre stage, with the structural forces of change providing only the backdrop.[81] Migration movements are no longer nameless masses, homogenous and predictable, but are instead revealed as divided, complex, intensely human phenomena. This approach also helps to redress the imbalance of many community projects, allowing hidden histories to be heard, and class and gender differentials to be addressed.

Although interviewing is an integral research method in both the humanities and the social sciences, oral history is still viewed with suspicion by some historians.[82] Collected testimonies are often considered to be an unreliable source material for the reconstruction of the past, prone to historical inaccuracies and embellishments, or worse, unrepresentative, irrelevant anecdotal conversations that add little to historical knowledge. It is unfortunate that this sentiment persists, as it demonstrates a deep-seated misunderstanding of the aims and uses of biographical research, and the real value of oral history accounts. As Brian Roberts points out, 'oral history is not merely interested in "facts" but in the respondent's perception of what is "true"'.[83] Allessandro Portelli, furthermore, asserts that 'the credibility of oral sources is a *different* credibility ... the importance of oral testimony may often lie not in its adherence to facts but rather in its divergence from them, where imagination, symbolism desire break in'.[84]

While the debates over the methodological implications of the gathering of such testimonies, and their academic use, continue, there is some degree of consent about the nature of narrated memory.[85] Remembering is recognized as an ongoing process, ultimately more interested in serving the present than resurrecting the past, and prone to adapting past events so that they fit more easily with contemporary realities.[86] The narratives that are offered in an interview situation, therefore, may not be authentic memory at all. As the contributions of both Joanna Herbert and Louise Ryan demonstrate, they may incorporate ready-made stories, or alter the past slightly to fit better with the perceived demands of the interviewer.[87] This, however, is the different credibility that Portelli identifies – while these interviews might not be an accurate source in some senses, in others they are rich in social meaning and can offer an important window into the process of remembering itself.

With regards to immigration studies in particular, oral history is an extremely important research method, capturing stories and experiences that could not be accessed in any other way. Narrated memory can present an important way of reconciling the geographical realities of migration. For immigrants, questions of memory and history are particularly pertinent: migration compels a confrontation with the past that non-migrants might never have to face. The act of migration sees the colliding of a journey through space with the passing of time, forcing the past to literally become the foreign country that Lowenthal has coined. By talking and thinking now about what came before, the chance of a continued disconnection between the two can be greatly reduced – different places can easily be incorporated into the story of one life, as Divya Tolia-Kelly shows in her contribution.[88] These types of conversations really offer the only available insight into how migration can frame individual perceptions of time and place, and what migration does to personal relationships with history, memory and home.

Once collected, a closer consideration of the typical content of these types of narratives can inform a more rounded understanding of migration. As the more recent concentration on the transnational activities of migrants demonstrates, the everyday lives of immigrants frequently overlap national boundaries even after they are supposedly settled.[89] Through travel, satellite television, the internet, telephone calls, letters, the sending of remittances and political activism, immigrants in Britain, as elsewhere, maintain a strong interest in, and sometimes exerting influence on, the everyday happenings of the homeland and the wider diaspora. The enduring Italian focus on Italy, for instance, can be seen clearly in both Lucio Sponza and Deianira Ganga's chapters.[90] To take another example, since the end of the Second World War, Britain's Polish community has sustained extensive links with Poland ranging from anti-communist political campaigning through to a high incidence of subscriptions to TV Polonia.[91]

If migrant lives are so flexible geographically, crossing national borders with apparent ease, it should come as no surprise that the use of oral history interviewing has generally indicated that immigrant memory is also as concerned with life before arrival in Britain as it is with life since – something that is often lost in popular understandings of migration. While histories of community development in Britain are important, for many immigrants, and refugees especially, they can only provide, at best, half of the context of what it means to migrate. To take the Polish example again, oral history interviews undertaken with Polish immigrants are generally dominated by accounts of forced migration and deportation to Siberia or German labour camps – settlement, or exile, in Britain is of secondary importance.[92] In the current climate of anti-asylum seeker sentiment, more public emphasis on the circumstances of traumatic migratory journeys would go a long way to counter popular misconceptions of contemporary refugee movements. The lives of immigrants do not simply begin when they reach the British mainland.

Individual memory is an integral part of immigrant ethnicity. Less visible and obvious than other forms of ethnic and national reconstruction, it is in many ways more important – something that is personal, but also something that can be shared with, and reinforced by, family and community. Stories of migration establish themselves in narratives of betterment, of success and hard work, of tropes of survival, implicitly providing guides for life in the new environment, while simultaneously commemorating life before. Ethnic memory can also be understood as a concealed ethnicity, preserved in the stories told at home, the tales passed on to grandchildren, the photographs kept in the attic. The memory of migration is pervasive – ordered and encapsulated in ready-to-tell legends, but also embodied in food, domestic objects, in conceptions of 'home'. As several of the contributors demonstrate, the vestiges of homeland memory are everywhere: hidden away or celebrated, the memory of migration does not easily dissolve. Caroline Attan and Divya Tolia-Kelly both illustrate that even the smallest fragments of a past life can reappear as reminders – 'memory' after all, unlike history, does not always work in a coherent, chronologically sound manner.[93]

Cultural memory is able to provide a legacy that can be transmitted through the generations: the presence of ethnic memory, in fact, is a good antidote to notions of assimilation. The way migrants talk about their lives, and the mnemonic practices they use, work to keep the past firmly in the present, in many cases affording an unseen barrier against the total loss of ethnic identity.[94] When ethnic memory is forgotten, as John Herson has found with the Irish in Stafford, there is usually a reason – either it is no longer needed, or it is too painful and divisive to sustain.[95]

Conclusion

This chapter has considered three different ways in which the history and memory of immigration in Britain have been remembered: professionally through the growth of academic historiography; popularly through community and heritage history initiatives; and finally by individuals themselves.

Two important points in particular stand out. The first is that immigration has been, and remains, neglected in both national history and public memory. While some progress has been made, immigration is still largely viewed as a peripheral area of academic concern within the discipline of history itself. In fact, of all academic disciplines, history has been one of the slowest to recognise the importance of immigration to British society. In society at large, immigration history is still perceived as something separate and different, outside of the accepted scope of popular historical memory. When it is embraced, furthermore, there is a danger that in the rush to create positive, attractive histories the complexities of immigrant experiences are lost. Heritage projects, for example, while undeniably valuable on many levels, demonstrate how vulnerable the histories and memories of immigrants are to simplification and distortion.

The second point is a wider observation that in most aspects of remembering immigration there has been some misunderstanding of where exactly history and memory fit into the wider experience of migration. In both academic and popular works there has been a tendency to see immigrant history as something which starts in Britain; as the increased use of oral history has illustrated however, for many migrants, Britain marks the end of a journey, or at least the middle stretch, not the start. Migrants need to be recognised as being both *im*migrants and *e*migrants if understandings of migration at an academic and public level are to be deepened.

However imperfect all these rememberings have proved to be, there is no doubt that the histories and memories of immigration in Britain are strong, and are probably growing stronger. Technological developments have helped migrants preserve their own ethnic memories through closer connections with their homelands, and have simultaneously given impetus to community history projects that work with these memories. Immigration history may in some respects still be a marginalised history, but it is undeniably a dynamic one, and one which shows no signs of diminishing.

2

Great Britons: Immigration, History and Memory

Tony Kushner

Reading Brick Lane: From Rushdie to Great Britons

Salman Rushdie's *The Satanic Verses* may seem an odd place to start a chapter on social inclusion sub-titled 'Immigration, History and Memory'. But lost in the polemic and tragic violence associated with this notorious novel and its alleged blasphemy against the prophet Mohammed[1] is a celebration of Britain's ethnic diversity in the past and its diasporic connections in the present, as well as a chronology of the country's racist traditions. Appropriately, given the more recent presence of Professor Gunther von Hagens' *Bodyworks* exhibition in a former brewery in the street,[2] Pinkwalla, one of the principal characters in Rushdie's novel, enters the Club Hot Wax in Brick Lane. In a classic moment of magical realism, Rushdie has his literary creations dancing between the waxwork figures representing what is labelled starkly 'History':

> See, here is Mary Seacole, who did as much in the Crimea as another magic-lamping Lady, but, being dark, could scarce be seen for the flame of Florence's candle; and over there! One Abdul Karim, aka The Munchi, whom Queen Victoria sought to promote, but who was done down by colour-barring ministers. They're all here, dancing motionlessly in hot wax: the black clown of Septimus Severus, to the right; to the left George IV's barber dancing with the slave, Grace Jones [and ...] with the slave's son, Ignatius Sancho, who became in 1782 the first African writer to be published in England. The migrants of the past, as much the living dancers' ancestors as their own flesh and blood, gyrate stilly while Pinkwall rants toasts raps up on the stage, *Now-mi-feel-indignation-when-dem-talk-immigration-when-dem-make-insinuation-*

we-no-part-a-de-nation-anmi-make-proclamation-a-de-true-situation-how-we-make-contribution-since-de-Rome-Occupation ...

British history, however, has another side, and Rushdie continues 'from a different part of the crowded room, bathed in evil green light, wax villains cower and grimace: Mosley, Powell, Edward Long, all the local avatars of Legree'.[3]

Brick Lane in the East End of London is Britain's most famous, or, for some, infamous, multi-ethnic street. It has been and is a place of settlement for refugees, immigrants and their children from the Huguenots in the eighteenth century through to the Irish and the Jews in the nineteenth and twentieth centuries to the Bengalis after the Second World War and Somalians today.[4] Ethnic mixing and ethnic succession have combined to give it its unique character. The monumental masons at one end and the twenty four hour bagel shop at the other are reminders that this was once the heart of the Jewish East End. That there is little in between functioning in everyday use, other than as ghosts of the past, shows how much has changed. Even the relics are fast disappearing. Reflective of this change is the frantic journey through the East End of Nazneen, the heroine of Monica Ali's *Brick Lane* (2003), towards the end of her epic novel: '[she] pressed on, past the Sylhet Cash and Carry, the International Cheap Calls Centre, the open jaws of a butcher's shop, the corner building run to ruin and bearing the faded legend of a time gone by, Schultz Famous Salt Beef.'[5] As early as 1974 the writer Arnold Wesker and artist John Allin had produced a text and painting memoir of the East End, its buildings and people, entitled *Say Goodbye: You May Never See Them Again*.[6] Taken as a whole, there are probably only one or two thousand Jews in the East End today, representing largely the elderly and straitened remnants of the former community which, in its heydey, numbered well over a hundred thousand who crowded into its slums.

The building at the corner of Brick Lane and Fournier Street is the most obvious and reproduced symbol of ethnic succession – from Huguenot chapel to synagogue to Mosque, 'stand[ing] today as a symbol of centuries of immigration to Britain'.[7] Against this somewhat cosy image of continuity and diversity in action one can point to another side of Brick Lane's history – that of collective and individual violence and hostility against the newcomers taking in riots or organised movements, whether the British Brothers League in the 1900s, the British Union of Fascists in the 1930s, and the National Front and British National Party and their murderous attacks in the area since the 1970s.[8] Superficially, it is not surprising that the demented neo-nazi nail bomb murderer, David Copeland, should choose Brick Lane, alongside Soho and Brixton, as sites of hatred reflecting his xenophobia and homophobia in his 1999 one man terror campaign.[9] In many ways, however, Copeland's paranoid and dystopian metropolitan imagination was out of date. Brick Lane is not what it was. Chanu, husband of Ali's character, Nazneen, comments 'All this money, money everywhere. Ten years ago there was no money here'. Looking at the 'little shops that sold clothes and bags and trinkets' in between the Bangladeshi restaurants, Chanu looks in a shop window: 'Seventy-five pounds for that little bag. You couldn't fit even one book in it.'[10] Gone, at a surface level at least, is the poverty and exploitation that prompted Prince Charles to comment after a visit in 1987 that 'something needs to be done'. The day after the nail bomb explosion in Brick Lane, the owner of one of the new generation of upmarket Bengali restaurants, Cafe Naz, stated a reality that had escaped Copeland: 'If [we] had been open, 99 percent of our customers are white. Who are they [sic] targeting?'[11] Cafe Naz itself reflects neatly the changing patterns of Brick Lane life. In the 1930s it was the Mayfair Cinema catering for a largely Jewish clientele. In the 1960s and for the next two decades it became the Naz Cinema and a major focal point for the local Bengali community.[12] Now it caters for city workers as the reach of the financial hub of London stretches ever eastwards as well as to visitors sampling the restaurants, boutiques and nightclubs that are beginning to dominate Brick Lane.

As the artists and yuppies move in, and the streets around Brick Lane are redeveloped, with wonderful irony, as luxury accommodation, one site that perhaps might be mourned less than others was a converted portacabin previously located in Bethnal Green police station and moved to Brick Lane in November 1978. The timing of its transfer reflected the vicious racist attacks on Bengalis and the street battles developing between the neo-nazi National Front and the forces of anti-fascism fighting for ownership and control of the street. The hut, as it became known, was in the middle of the front line, a shelter and mini-headquarters for the police. Replaced later by Britain's first permanent community police station, the hut has recently been demolished, too bijou even for today's property speculators and estate agents to market. The police's own narrative of the hut's history is itself revealing of wider tendencies. First, a comfortable image of the East End as a place of immigrant succession is presented

> an old synagogue has been transformed into a mosque; the kosher butcher is now a halal butcher and salt beef has been superseded by tandoori chicken. It's still a centre for the rag trade, though, but black leather coats are now stacked in the spaces where the Huguenots did their weaving.

Second, the racial motive for attacks on local Bengalis is denied and the media and 'political factions' blamed for 'fann[ing] Asians' fears'.[13] The refusal of police to accept that racial violence was an everyday part of minority life fuelled minority distrust throughout the period from the late 1970s through to the Stephen Lawrence Enquiry in the late 1990s. This was particularly true in the East End which had experienced so much 'blood on the street'.[14] Yet the official police narrative has not been able to dominate the subsequent battle over memory. In 1998, twenty years after the racist murder of Altab Ali, a young East End Bengali, a park was named in his honour with an archway entrance designed as a memorial to this young clothing worker and to all victims of racist violence.[15]

Rushdie and Brick Lane point to two traditions – that of immigration and of native racism – which have run counter to the dominant narratives of Britain's past, especially state versions of it, as ethnically homogeneous and essentially tolerant. In the last quarter of a century a conscious effort has been made to break up such complacency and to tell different stories of British history. Educators and historians have, at a national and grassroots level, from within and outside ethnic and religious minority groups, attempted to challenge dominant assumptions. Books such as Peter Fryer's *Staying Power: The History of Black People in Britain* (1984) and Rozina Visram's *Ayahs, Lascars and Princes: The Story of Indians in Britain 1700-1947* (1986) were written to show the longevity and depth of African Caribbean and Asian settlement in Britain as well as the hostility these groups faced.[16] Both, significantly, were endorsed on their covers by Rushdie. He said of *Staying Power* that 'For his retrieval of the lost histories of black Britain Mr Fryer has my deep gratitude. This is an invaluable book ...'. Similarly

> *Ayahs, Lascars and Princes* is a lively – and timely – survey of two and a half centuries of British Indian history, from the earliest slaves to the cricketer-princes, from the first ayah to the first-ever woman law student at a British university, from Queen Victoria's Munshi to the nationalists. I found it fascinating and useful.[17]

As Sukhdev Sandhu has argued in *London Calling: How Black and Asian Writers Imagined a City* (2003), Rushdie, through the 'Club Hot Wax' attempts 'a black literary London hall of fame'. In fact, Rushdie's evocation is much wider, incorporating many aspects of past black British presence from his close reading of Fryer and Visram amongst others, and not just those notable for their writing. Sandhu is correct, however, in suggesting that:

> This attempt at historical connection signals a living, *felt* tradition of black metrography – one that infuses the imagination of today's writers. They are engaged in constructing a heritage, one that makes the city more navigable.[18]

The growth of black and Asian historical consciousness from the 1970s onwards postdated that of Jewish historiography in Britain by a century.[19] Nevertheless, it coincided with new social history perspectives on the British Jewish past. This 'history from below' approach, incorporating the experience of previously ignored groups and experiences including poor immigrants, children, women, antisemitism and radicalism,[20] provided the intellectual foundation for projects such as the Manchester Jewish Museum and the Museum of the Jewish East End to come into existence in the mid-1980s.[21] A similar development occurred in the Afro-Caribbean and Asian communities, resulting in the creation of Black History Month.

It has been suggested that 'Black History Month was conceived in the US in the 1920s and taken up by the UK in the 1980s'.[22] The American example and influence should not be dismissed, but nor should the importance of the local context. In Britain, Black History Month had its roots in the national politics of the 1980s, and, as Yasmin Alibhai-Brown suggests, was a 'rebellion, a declaration of defiance against [the] monstrous, narrow nationalism' represented by Thatcherism. 'Anti-racists, the Inner London Education Authority and the GLC found small ways of keeping warm the alternative truths about slavery and colonialism. We met in cold, dusty halls, empty school classrooms and kept our hopes up.' Now, she argues, in the early twenty first century 'In Mr Blair's inclusive Britain, Black History Month has been mainstreamed ... too safe perhaps. Worse, it has had little impact on the popular consciousness'.[23]

Alibhai-Brown's evidence for this failure is the absence of one 'single person of colour' on the list of the hundred Great Britons voted in 2002 in its first stages by 33,000 viewers in a highly successful BBC television initiative. Alibhai-Brown was right in focusing on the programme – it generated widespread debate about British national identity, both past and present, in the media and amongst the public. Echoing Rushdie in reverse, Alibhai-Brown provided her own list of exclusion from 'Great Britons':

> Not even Magdi Yacoub, the brilliant heart surgeon, or Mary Seacole, whose nursing of the wounded in the Crimea was so effective that she was more valued by soldiers than Florence Nightingale. For a country still consumed by the two world wars, they didn't even rate Noor-un-Nisa Inayat Khan. Who? I hear you ask. The beautiful daughter of one of the men who founded the Sufi movement and an American mother, she volunteered to join the British secret service. Under the code name 'Madeleine', she went to France and worked as a vital link until she was arrested by the Gestapo, tortured and then shot dead at Dachau.[24]

Alibhai-Brown doubted whether 'David Starkey and, say, Simon Heffer ...

will be participating in Black History Month. These are the men whose views reassure millions of white Britons that all is still well with their world'.[25] Heffer, not surprisingly, as a leading right wing 'little Englander' commentator and biographer of racial nationalist, Enoch Powell, did not subsequently contribute to Black History Month.[26] Yet through his column in the *Daily Mail* Heffer was an important commentator on the 'Great Britons' debate. His attack on the failings and lacunae of the top one hundred matched Alibhai-Brown's for passion and anger, denouncing some of those included, particularly the Princess of Wales and John Lennon, and decrying the non-appearance of John Milton, William Gladstone and Adam Smith. The ignorance of such figures, argued Heffer, was the result of forty years of educational and cultural policies, leading to a political culture 'which hates the past and devalues greatness - particularly if those people who achieved such status were what the Left sneeringly calls "white middleclass males"'.[27]

It seems curious that even within his apoplectic 'angry of Tunbridge Wells' rage, Heffer did not spot the fact that the top one hundred included no-one who was black, very few women, and an equally small number from working class backgrounds. Where such views easily lead was provided by an editorial in his own newspaper entitled 'The distortion of a proud history'.[28] At this point in the 'Great Britons' competition, Churchill was trailing the national poll in third place and had been smeared by a German historian as a war criminal who killed civilians 'through indiscriminate wartime bombing'. Aside from an opportunity to air its Germanophobia, the *Daily Mail* decried New Labour's ignorance of British history, especially its imperial past. It was such ignorance, argued the *Mail*, which explained why Tony Blair was unable to safeguard the sovereignty of Britain. From here it was a small step for the *Mail* to point out that 'the most disturbing symbol of this loss of national identity is the fact that we have lost control of our own borders'. What followed was its usual sustained diatribe against asylum seekers, continuing the newspaper's vicious campaign against the Lottery Community Fund that had had the audacity to work for asylum seeker detainees awaiting deportation.[29] The battle was still on, it warned its readers: 'So long as the liberal elite is ashamed of our past and obsessed by minority rights, there is the risk that the common sense and decency of ordinary people will be brushed aside.'[30]

Six months later, other elements of the right wing tabloid press developed the theme of history further, this time blaming asylum seekers themselves for destroying British tradition. In a totally fabricated story, the *Sun*, the highest circulation daily newspaper (3.5 million), accused asylum seekers of 'barbecuing the Queen's swans'. Rather than an appalling opportunity to illustrate its 'wit' – the front page was headlined 'Swan Bake' – the story was used to contrast the elegant bird, a 'symbol of Britain as powerful as Windsor Castle' with undesirable immigrants and immigrant gangs. Such 'sickening behaviour' was, according to a *Sun* editorial, 'an insult to our nation's civilised traditions'.[31] The *Express*, the most intensively anti-asylum newspaper in Britain, joined in the campaign. It showed the fluidity of the hostile labelling process of 'outsiders' and provided a new definition of those described in the 1951 United Nations Convention as 'Any person [with] a well founded fear of being persecuted for reasons of race, religion, nationality, membership of a particular social group or political opinion'. Rather than confront the human misery as well as legal complexity reflected in that definition the *Express* simply stated that 'Refugees Eat Swans'.[32] A month later the *Sun* denied that it, or the British public could in any way be tainted by racism in its hostility to asylum seekers. It stated that asylum seekers 'who abuse our hospitality are stealing not just our money but our character and our culture'.[33]

In her critique of Black History Month, Yasmin Alibhai-Brown also referred to asylum seekers, but within a somewhat different frame of reference:

> Black History Month has tended to focus mostly on Caribbean stories - reclaiming the black label as meaning only that. Why are British Asian stories kept to a minimum? Yes, slavery was confined to Africans, but, after abolition, Indians were taken as indentured labourers to places as far-flung as Fiji and South Africa. And, to be truly daring, the month should also include the histories of asylum-seekers. We have a fine body of work on Jewish exiles and it is right that we should forever be reminded of the Holocaust, but with such obnoxious attitudes fostered by the press and politicians against those seeking refuge, Black History Month should have made these narratives the core of the programmes.[34]

The perspectives offered by Alibhai-Brown and the tabloids the *Daily Mail*, the *Sun* and the *Express* offer extremes within mainstream British society, culture and politics, though the influence of the latter, with their millions of readers should not be underestimated. What they have in common, however, is a belief that history, however constructed and distorted, matters in the formation of individual and national identities. The forces of exclusion in Britain, as represented by Simon Heffer, are still as alive and well as when Black History Month was first instigated. Yet what Alibhai-Brown bravely acknowledged were the silences and hierarchies that have developed *within* the writing of minority histories and heritage production and the dangers inherent when inclusion is attempted - the potential for tokenism as well as an approach that highlights the role of famous people and their positive contributions.

In a rather naive but revealing editorial, the *Guardian* praised the BBC's 'Great Britons', defending it against the charge of dumbing down and proclaiming that 'it was clearly coming to a novel and immensely successful way of reminding us of this nation's glory'. It was great because it 'provoked arguments – the best engine for increased knowledge; it spawned offspring, like the Greatest Black Britons or the Greatest Women'.[35] However appealing in its Whiggish optimism for the future, there is a misleading equivalence suggested by the *Guardian* between the main list and those forced into existence purely because of exclusion. They can only be discussed as equal if power relations and subsequent influence are totally ignored. It was also left to others, for example, to provide minor footnotes outlining the xenophobia, racism, antisemitism and genocidal acts related to the career of Winston Churchill who won the competition.[36] Indeed, those shortlisted had little problem with their co-greats. The pop star Sir Cliff Richard (56 in the list), for example, when questioned about the man above him, Enoch Powell, said that he was well-meaning and a great statesman.[37] Such comments were also common from leading politicians of both left and right at the time of Powell's funeral in February 1998.

Great British Jews

From the general level, I want now to turn to a specific case study from the 'Great Britons' debate – that of the heritage and memory work of British Jewry – to examine how a particular minority has responded to the various pressures outlined by Alibhai Brown in the reproduction of its own history. Michael Gilkes has commented that 'John F. Kennedy spoke proudly of the United States as "a nation of immigrants". To say that today about Britain might give offence'.[38] The relative longevity of British Jewish historiography and heritage production compared to other minority groups in Britain provides an opportunity to examine the opportunities as well as the dilemmas of producing such memory work in what was, until very recently, a hostile climate.

In a column in the *Jewish Chronicle*, the self-proclaimed organ of British Jewry, Brian Viner pointed that one thing those on the list of the top one hundred 'Great Britons' had in common was 'the glaring omission ... of a single Anglo-Jew. Goyim, the lot of them!' He added that it was 'like looking at the lists of certain venerable golf clubs, although the Jewlessness here is arguably attributable less to anti-Semitism than to anti-Haroldism; no Harold Pinter, no Harold Abrahams, no Harold Laski. Nor is there any sign of any of the Rothschilds, Tom Stoppard, Lucien Freud, Lew Grade, Zangwill or Siegfried Sassoon'.[39]

Viner's alternative 'Great Britons' list was rather predictable and with one or two exceptions, those named and the reasons for their inclusion have the feel of 1930s Jewish defence literature which, in an atmosphere of violent antisemitism at home and abroad, documented the worthy contribution of Jews to British politics and culture. Indeed, Sidney Salomon, secretary of the Board of Deputies of British Jews' Defence Committee, in his *The Jews of Britain* (1938) gave great emphasis to the same figures as listed by Viner, aside from the latter's post-1945 entries. Salomon's book was divided in two parts – the first designed to answer 'The Allegations', the second to outline 'Some Jewish Contributions'.[40] Viner included Jack Cohen and Michael Marks for their impact on retailing; Benjamin Disraeli and Leslie Hore-Belisha in politics and Lucien Freud, Harold Pinter and Isaiah Berlin in the arts and culture. Two women were included – Lilian Bayliss who helped form the Old Vic Theatre Company and Viner's Auntie Bertha, 'a woman now into her 80s yet still of redoubtable wit'. Finally, Viner's first choice was 'Harold Abrahams, who, in 1924, became the first European to win the Olympic 100 metres title, set a British long-jump record that lasted 30 years, and showed that Jews could run as well as think'. Aside from Auntie Bertha, included because 'all top 10s need a left-field choice', the list is noticeable only for its very predictability. The inclusion of Disraeli, for example, shows the desire for success stories even, in this case, when the individual concerned was a practising Christian and buried in a churchyard. Normally Jewish Christians get little shift in the Jewish world, but Disraeli is simply too good a historical figure to disown.[41] Abrahams featured at the top presumably to give Viner's list a touch of masculinity, providing some machismo steel in the absence of Anglo-Jewish cigar chomping heroes such as Churchill or Brunel who ultimately came first and second in the national competition. Abrahams was thus a 'tough Jew', and one who also featured prominently in Salomon's defence tract sixty four years earlier.[42]

Inevitably, such lists are individual and have peculiar quirks. Nevertheless, its mixture of assertiveness of ethnic pride and apologetica has a wider resonance within the collective identity of contemporary British Jewry. In October 2003 Michael Howard was elected as leader of the Conservative Party. The *Jewish Chronicle* responded with a front page headline 'Son of Refugee Set to Lead Tories'.[43] It was, as one commentator suggested, 'like a grandmother bursting to announce that her golden boy has won a place at university'.[44] But to test out its broader applicability, the study of the self-representation of the British Jewish heritage is well-illustrated through the development of the Jewish Museum in London.

The Jewish Museum was originally opened in 1932 at Woburn House. The building in which it was housed became the most focused point of British Jewry at a communal level during the Nazi era and beyond, dealing with national and international crises in this troubled and tragic period. After 1945 Woburn House became symbolic of the drabness of official British Jewry. The Jewish Museum had become literally part of the furniture, 'ensconced in cramped and dispiriting rooms'. In it was an elite collection of Judaica, especially ornate silver ware. Although a small example and late, it was typical of the approach to Jewish museums across Europe – Vienna, Danzig, Prague and Warsaw had opened before 1914.[45]

The small size and late date of the Jewish Museum in London reflected the stifled nature of British Jewish historiography and heritage preservation. Although starting off impressively with the Anglo-Jewish Historical Exhibition at the Albert Hall in 1887, it was a further six years before the creation of the Jewish Historical Society of England (JHSE). Many distinguished historians, including Lucien Wolf and Cecil Roth, were closely connected to the JHSE, but its communal influence and level of support was always marginal.[46] The subject matter of the early JHSE was often defensive – its overall aim was to show the longevity of Anglo-Jewry, and the progress from persecution to toleration to full acceptance of the Jews in Britain; that is from medieval to early modern and finally to modern Britain. As David Katz puts it: 'Anglo-Jewish historiography has always been patriotic, conservative and Whig, that is, ends-oriented, written with one eye on the final destination of the history train, the End of Anglo-Jewish History – "Emancipation".'[47]

Heritage preservation was limited to the formation of the Anti-Demolition League, set up in 1886 to preserve Bevis Marks Synagogue from destruction at the hand of its elders. That British Jewry was willing to demolish its oldest and most prestigious synagogue reveals the indifference and antipathy that existed towards its own past as well as the vision of those who tried to preserve it.[48] Within those that were concerned, Jewish history was largely interpreted as Jewish religious history, or at most within the secular world, the history of great men within Anglo-Jewry who had played a major part in British politics, society and culture. Within the Jewish Museum at Woburn House, a similar perspective was shared. David Clark, the historian of the Jewish Museum, has commented that its founders

> sought the most impressive and aesthetically pleasing pieces, with memorabilia associated with leading Anglo-Jewish families featuring strongly. The list of exquisite objects is endless: an imposing 16th Century synagogue ark from Venice, elaborate silver-ware Torah crowns, Shabbat and Hanukah lamps ...

He adds that internationally the approach for such collecting 'had been set by the 1878 exhibition of the Isaac Strauss collection at the World Fair in Paris, and it became the most common template for a Jewish Museum'. It was, argues Clark, 'essentially top down. The aim was to marvel at the individual objects'.[49]

Whereas the writings of those linked to the JHSE were aimed at both a Jewish and a non-Jewish audience, the latter to correct some of the imbalances that had occurred in the representation of Jews in British historiography, the Jewish Museum was more insular. Hidden away in a Jewish communal building (visitors were scarce) it might be argued that its purpose was partly to give reassurance and a sense of permanence to its organisers in the bleakest days of world Jewry and to provide a place of shared ethnic interest to Jewish visitors from abroad. Just as the JHSE avoided any mention of and indeed deflected attention from east European immigration and settlements in Britain, so the Jewish Museum had a collection policy of obtaining and displaying items of high artistic merit that were normally at least one hundred years old. It thereby excluded the great westward migration by default.[50]

The strengths and weaknesses of the Jewish Museum in its early years very much reflected the nature of contemporary historiography and museology in Britain and beyond in its narrow, elite focus. Admittedly, the general world of history and heritage tended to either ignore or problematise the Jewish presence, especially with regard to the medieval period where Jews in England were presented as a 'problem' to be solved – hence the apologetic approach of Jewish historians in response.[51] On the Jewish side, the marginality, even within Jewish circles, of Anglo-Jewish history and heritage is notable. That so much was rescued is a tribute to the individuals involved. Nevertheless, a somewhat warped view of the British Jewish experience emerges from what they collected. Immigrants/refugees from eastern Europe and later those from the Third Reich were not absent, but they were presented largely as objects to whom things were done rather than subjects/historical actors in their own right.[52]

This, then, was the background to the revolution that occurred in the world of Anglo-Jewish historiography and heritage preservation from the late 1970s. The maxim what 'Manchester does today, the world does tomorrow', yet again proved correct. Out of the Manchester Studies Unit of Manchester Polytechnic Bill Williams assembled a team of talented young people who were to open up British Jewish history. At the forefront of and influenced by the History Workshop movement, oral history, alongside the collection of photographs and artefacts of ordinary life from home, work and leisure, were at the heart of the Manchester Studies Unit, leading eventually to the creation of the Manchester Jewish Museum.[53] For the first time, sensitive issues such as class, ethnic, gender and religious differences within Anglo-Jewry were explored as were non-Jewish responses including the antisemitism of exclusion and what Williams referred to as the antisemitism of toleration – the pressure on Jews to conform and remove their difference.[54]

In total contrast to the collecting policy and overall approach of the Jewish Museum of London, its Manchester equivalent aimed to be 'by the people, for the people and about the people'. The Manchester Jewish Museum opened its doors formally in 1984, a year before that of its sister museum in London, the Museum of the Jewish East End whose curator, Rickie Burman had worked in Manchester.[55] Alongside her in London was Bill Fishman and others who, from the 1960s onwards, did their best to preserve what remained of the physical and written heritage of the former Jewish East End.[56] It is nearly two decades since the forming of these Jewish social history museums. Now (at the beginnings of a new millennium, and especially as for the first time it is planned to have an integrated and wide ranging Jewish Museum in London) is a good moment to take stock in a critical engagement of what has been achieved so far with these new approaches and museum/heritage projects.

The first area to be explored is the surviving physical heritage. Taking part or leading walking tours of former Jewish immigrant areas, what is increasingly notable is the absence of sites. In Cheetham Hill, Manchester, there no longer survive houses that were inhabited by the immigrants and only a handful of the major religious and secular buildings have not been demolished. In the East End, a similar process has occurred – a marked contrast, for example, to the Lower East Side in New York.[57] The facade of the Soup Kitchen for the Jewish Poor now fronts luxury flats. Most tellingly the one major heritage preservation project, the Heritage Centre in Princelet Street, Spitalfields, has been a 'museum of immigration' in making for several decades. The failure to find the financial resources for it reflect the failure of British society, including its minority populations, to take a tradition of immigration and settlement seriously, which takes us back to the limitations of the 'Great Britons' listing. There is a marked and obvious contrast here to the spectacular development as site, museum, resource and research centre of Ellis Island, or, on a smaller scale, the Tenement Museum in the Lower East Side.[58] As British oral historian, Rob Perks, presciently remarked in 1991 after visiting New York: '[I doubt] if £8,000 could be raised in Britain for a museum about immigration, let alone the £80 million raised for Ellis Island.'[59] The antipathetical cultural background has forced those currently in control of the Heritage Centre to resort to myth making to sell their project – conjuring the memory of the Battle of Cable Street, the *Kindertransport* and the *Diary of Anne Frank*, none of which has a direct connection, to elicit financial and moral support.[60]

The physical British Jewish historical heritage is thus either largely abandoned, destroyed or at risk. The dangers of this neglect are powerful both to the Jewish minority and to society as a whole. As the black British artist, Lubaina Himid, has suggested with regard to memorialising slavery, 'when something is there you can talk about it, write about it, paint about it, but when something isn't there what can you say, how can you make something of it[?]'.[61] More progress has been made with archives: the University of Southampton, the London Metropolitan Archives and local repositories across the country have played a major role. Even so, there is still a dire shortage of material generated by, rather than about, ordinary people, making the oral history projects that have developed especially important.

Returning to the Jewish museums, the focus of both social history projects was initially on those from eastern Europe. The emphasis was understandable on numerical grounds: these were the largest group of Jews to come into Britain – it has been estimated that half a million settled in this country for at least two years between the period of 1870 and 1914.[62] Moreover, it was justifiable given that their settlement had previously been ignored or seen somehow as unsavoury by both British and British Jewish historians. The permanent displays at both museums were thus largely devoted to immigrant trades, housing, religion and politics linked to the east Europeans. The climax of the early focus was the Celebration of the Jewish East End in 1987, the quality and range of exhibitions and events far outweighing anything previously attempted. It included David Mazower's superb representation of the Yiddish theatre. Overall the 'Celebration' was in marked contrast to the silence on east European Jewish culture in previous national events such as the Anglo-Jewish Exhibition in 1887 and the Tercentenary Celebration in 1956. In spite of its title, the 'Celebration of the Jewish East End' was hard hitting and explored many areas of everyday life that would have been unimaginable to the practitioners of Anglo-Jewish heritage just a few decades earlier, including anti-alienism in a comparative framework, poverty and radicalism, and conflict within Jewish communities.[63]

Since the 1987 Celebration, however, attention has focussed elsewhere. One of the major triumphs of the London Museum of Jewish Life, formerly the Museum of the Jewish East End (which in 1995 merged with the original Jewish Museum), has been the incorporation of some of these lost stories through major exhibitions, most obviously with those focusing on refugees from Nazism. Of equal importance are those devoted to the Jews of Aden and the Jews of Iraq.[64] Such inclusivity is crucial and justifies the change of title from its original focus on the Jewish East End. The emphasis on refugees from Nazism parallels the growing interest and awareness on the Holocaust in Britain. Both Jewish social museums played an important role in that process with exhibitions in Manchester and London.[65] There are many positive aspects to the rediscovery of refugee and survivor stories and their integration into wider narratives of Jewish and British history. There are, however, potential and real dangers that need also to be considered.

First, there is a danger of being market driven. At the Jewish Museum site at Finchley, school visitors, who are the majority, focus almost solely on the displays relating to refugees from Nazism and to Holocaust survivor, Leon Greenman.[66] The other materials, relating to the earlier Jewish settlement from eastern Europe, are relatively neglected and ignored. Crude interpretations of the national curriculum could lead to the Museum being used only to focus on the Holocaust or Judaism, thereby ignoring much of the Jewish experience that is or could be displayed which is either secular or not about persecution (potentially the case of Brian Viner's Auntie Bertha would be a good case in point). Further north, the Manchester Jewish Museum has increasingly struggled financially and more recently has become limited generally to the safe territory of teaching about the Jewish religion to local school children. For now, the wider, inclusive and challenging vision of its founders has been marginalised.

Second, there is the danger of saturation with regard to those that came to Britain escaping Nazism. To give a blunt example: the British Library's National Sound Archive has over seven hundred interviews with British based Holocaust survivors.[67] This is probably well over half of the potential sample. Should national and international bodies put even more resources into recording these groups when there are whole and larger immigrant and refugee movements that have been left utterly untouched? Third, there is a danger that focusing on the refugees from Nazism, rather than connecting us to today's asylum seekers, does the reverse. The refugees from Nazism are now packagable as a neat, self-contained group the legitimacy of whom now is, in the light of the Holocaust, indisputable. In the rhetoric of politicians, most of the media, and a large proportion of public opinion, the genuine refugees of the past are used as a weapon against contemporary asylum seekers. They are seen as genuine, people that have contributed, as opposed to those who are perceived as bogus and scroungers on the already overly stretched welfare state.[68] 'Continental Britons' (2002), the Jewish Museum's last major exhibition on the theme of the refugees from Nazism, allows for negative responses to the entry and settlement of Jewish refugees during the 1930s, but ultimately it is a celebration of achievement, positive reception and contribution to British society. No link is made to the refugee crisis today and rather than being seen as part of a never ending narrative of the persecuted seeking refuge, it is self-contained.[69] To give a specific example, internment in the Second World War is portrayed in 'Continental Britons' as unnecessary, but something in the end stopped by the reassertion of 'the British liberal tradition of fair play and freedom'.[70] Yet internment of aliens and refugees has never stopped in Britain – the huge reception camps for asylum seekers planned by the government the same year as this exhibition were not a new development.[71]

Towards a Conclusion: Future Models

To conclude and to return to the 'Great Britons' debate: the case study of British Jewish heritage and memory work suggests that there may be a price to pay for inclusion, especially the limitations of a 'contribution to Britain' school of thought. It is particularly present in relation to the historiography of refugees from Nazism who came to Britain. This 'remarkable contribution to their adopted country'[72] has been marked by one major book with the title *Hitler's*

Gift and another with the subtitle *The Cultural Impact on Britain*.[73] The negative sides of this experience such as loss and disorientation, shown through the experience of persecution and refugee/alien status are in danger of being ignored in such celebratory approaches – ones which extend way beyond this particular case. In 1996, for example, the Commission for Racial Equality put much energy into a travelling exhibition, publication and related material entitled *Roots of the Future: Ethnic Diversity in the Making of Britain*. Indeed, it was described as 'the most ambitious project ever undertaken to breathe life into [multiculturalism]'. The emphasis throughout was on the 'contributions of Britain's ethnic minorities' and the hope that by recognising that those making them, past and present 'are an integral and invaluable part of the British nation'.[74] We are not far here from Sidney Salomon's *The Jews of Britain*. In stressing the national, the global diasporic networks which are integral to migrants and their descendants are downplayed in order to establish the primacy of local patriotism. In relation to refugees specifically, entry to Britain becomes dependent not on need but on potential contribution. Rather than 'Refugees Eat Swans', the alternative headline reads 'Refugees create jobs, art, learning, science'. The arguments of both sides are, however, irrelevant to the international legal and moral obligations towards the persecuted.

Yasmin Alibhai-Brown wants a Black History Month that has the courage and confidence to confront African participation in the slave trade.[75] A similar approach is needed to all minority history so that it can be studied and valued warts and all but also incorporate those who have been marginalised by the mainstream – the disabled, women, the elderly, gays, criminals and so on. It also needs to return to the radical focus emerging in the 1970s in which conflict *within* minority groups was acknowledged and explored without embarrassment. Moreover, to be true to its inclusive roots, taking the black history and Jewish history examples, it needs to study those who have not 'made it' as prominent politicians, artists, sports figures and other 'heroes' and figure heads. In the book of the 'Great Britons' series, Mark Harrison comments that were the poll to be carried out a hundred years later the absence of a single non-white face would be unlikely to be repeated.[76] Well over a century of British Jewish historiography and heritage work and the absence of a Jewish figure would suggest that such optimism might be misplaced.

The fight for historical inclusion is still ongoing and the 'white English male' preserve of much of the heritage and history world in Britain, reflecting much broader tendencies, has to be recognised. It cannot be dismissed as a past problem. Where black and other minority experiences have been incorporated there is still the danger of tokenism – what one museum director in America has described as '"One night stands" rather than a true commitment to equality'.[77] The American folk singer, Tom Lehrer, satirised this danger in relation to 'National Brotherhood Week' during the 1960s:

Be nice to people who
Are inferior to you
It's only for a week, so have no fear
Be grateful that it doesn't last all year![78]

More seriously, the black British writer, Vanessa Walters, outlines how:

> the fact that [Black History Month] takes place only one month of the year undermines the positive benefits. The school curriculum should aim to give pupils a year-round, broad view of British history – a view that does not confine itself to a Eurocentric perspective. Black history month cannot do this, not only because it is time-restricted but also because it ghettoises black experience.[79]

Even the limited inclusion that has taken place has led to a backlash, most recently manifested in Michael Collins' *The Likes of Us: A Biography of the White Working Class* (2004). A study of Southwark, it concludes with an elderly man, Jo, confronting a glossy brochure promoting the borough and highlighting its cosmopolitanism 'with a rich mixture of communities going back centuries':

> 'They don't mention us English', Jo says. 'You would't think we'd ever existed would ya?' Jo sees himself as part of a long-established tribe that dominated the urban working class within the area from the beginning of the nineteenth century and earlier. It has been airbrushed from the history of the area as reported in the brochure.

Collins, whose book has been widely reviewed and positively received, argues that in the future it is likely 'the story of the urban white working class here and elsewhere is to be erased by multicultural rebranding'.[80]

In Britain in the early twenty first century even a little minority history can still be too much. Equally, there has been only limited success in acknowledging a tradition of racism within Britain. The ahistorical perspective was neatly encapsulated by the liberal *Guardian*. To mark Black History Month in 2004 it commissioned an article entitled 'Remember the Riots of 1919?'. The author, Jane Morris, editor of the *Museums Journal*, pointed out that 'Far more children learn about the American civil rights movement than the 1919 riots in Liverpool and South Shields'.[81] The following day the newspaper ran a feature on remembering and forgetting the 1950s which commented critically on the nostalgia of 'The generation raised in the era of secret nuclear tests, London razor gangs and the *first* (my emphasis) race riots'.[82] The failure to connect is not simply historical laziness – it is a reflection of how much of the collective memory of Britain as a tolerant and decent society is at stake.[83]

Finally, within ethnic minorities themselves the key to, and challenge of, memory work is to ensure that the desire to incorporate the diversity of the British past does not in any form replicate the elitism that led to exclusion in the first place. Thus the later '100 Great Black Britons' competition, with its eventual winner, Mary Seacole (Rushdie's 'magic lamping lady') has the potential of all such ethnic cheerleading.[84] On the one hand, Seacole provides a role model – a source of pride and affirmation of a positive sense of identity for contemporary generations of Afro-Caribbean background. On the other, a focus on the famous can lead to a failure to consider that figures such as Seacole were extremely rare and untypical as a whole of contemporary minority experience. In this respect, there is a necessity to follow the model of women's history which, after its initial desire in the 1960s to show the *presence* of women as major players in British history, has matured more recently to show also their *absence* and marginality through the forces of patriarchy, as well as its general move towards an inclusive study of gender as a social and cultural category. As Natalie Zemon Davis suggests, 'Our goal is to explain why sex roles were sometimes tightly prescribed and sometimes fluid, sometimes markedly asymmetrical and sometimes more even. Unlike the compilation of Women Worthies, this is a relatively new goal for historians'.[85] It should be remembered that after nearly half a century of women's history, there were only two women in the 'top ten' of 'Great Britons' and both were part of the Royal Family (Elizabeth I and Diana, Princess of Wales). The chances of Mary Seacole appearing in 'Great Britons', 3002, are put into sharp focus when it is considered that Florence Nightingale herself only managed to come fifty second, one of just thirteen women in the whole list.[86] 'Great Britons', as well as subsequent alternative minority rivals to it, show how much memory work and re-thinking still needs to happen.

3

Historical Practice in the Age of Pluralism: Educating and Celebrating Identities

Kevin Myers

Introduction

This chapter is concerned with possible connections between specific forms of historical practice and the ubiquity of racism in contemporary England. It is a historiographical chapter; an attempt to think critically about the ways in which social and political conditions in given historical moments shape what has been called elsewhere 'public history'.[1] Public history is an expansive term, potentially concerned with all the myriad ways in which ideas about the past are constructed in contemporary society, but space necessitates a more specific focus. That selected is the increasing amounts of 'professional public history' concerned with notions of national and cultural identity. This 'popular presentation of the past to a range of audiences' can be found in a great number of different guises[2]; in community histories and social exclusion projects, in tourist literature and town planning documents. The focus is on how a kind of public history specifically interested in notions of identity is shaping historical consciousness.[3] Its purpose is to register a concern about how that history is facilitated by a relatively novel set of socio-political conditions and to begin a preliminary investigation on how these are impacting on popular representations of the past. There are three substantive aspects of the argument.

The first is to suggest that contemporary historical practice has been significantly shaped by the gradual emergence of a particular (and limited) form of pluralist politics over the past three decades. This pluralism can be captured in the phrase 'community of communities' and in the idea that the nation – in this case, England – consists of a number of communities that may overlap and be interdependent, but are also distinctive because of their religion, race, ethnicity, culture and history.[4] In this changed political landscape – in the shift from a broadly nationalist to pluralist model of politics – history has become an increasingly important tool for all those who claim to form communities. It can act as a guarantee of community identity. It can help develop a sense of dignity and esteem. Importantly, it can also provide access to material resources.

The second aspect of the argument is to observe that in the conditions set by this version of pluralism, it should not come as a surprise that there has been a significant return to forms of historical practice that are genealogical and celebratory. In the increasing number of affirmative narratives that more or less implicitly set out to describe 'who we are', the story-telling capacity of history has come to dominate over its explanatory potential. Underpinning this shift from analysis to description that is characteristic of so much contemporary public history is an important philosophical change; history is increasingly granted the power to determine our identities in a manner that constrains action in the present. As Frank Furedi argued in 1992, the purpose of much contemporary 'history is to confer a sense of distinctness, to differentiate and exclude'.[5]

The third and final aspect of the argument presented here is that though these professional public histories may have laudable aims and though they may provide short-term benefits in terms of community recognition, their impact over the longer term is likely to be much more ambiguous. In fact, there is sufficient anecdotal evidence to suggest that the developing tendency to retreat behind historically determined ethnicities is at best failing to challenge, and at worst aiding, the further development of racism in contemporary England.

Public Histories: Contexts, Developments and Debates

Historical knowledge is contingent. It is produced in concrete time and space and so inevitably has connections, complex and elusive though these might be, with the wider social world in which it is produced. As Mary Fulbrook has recently and succinctly put it 'the discipline of history is in considerable measure shaped by the circumstances in which historical knowledge is produced and received'.[6] It follows that any analysis of contemporary historical practice must begin with that wider social world and its circumstances.

Arguably the most significant change in post-war England was the transformation of the economy. The slow and painful decline of industrialism was accompanied by the rise of what has latterly become known as the 'knowledge economy' and all that this entailed. Whereas industrial economies produced heavy goods in urbanised factories and plants, the new knowledge economy is geographically mobile and its products are largely symbolic and informational. It is an economy made up of financial services, hospitality and tourism and it is characterised by conspicuous consumption for a wealthy elite. This economic transformation set in train a whole series of very significant social and political changes; a transformation in urban landscapes across Europe; a shift in both the nature and the patterns of work; an associated, and loudly proclaimed, death of the manual working class and the emergence of what are supposed to be more open, plural and mobile societies. These profound changes in economic and social life were experienced as a series of recurrent crises in 1970s and 1980s England and they contributed to that pervasive sense of national decline that Margaret Thatcher exploited to such effect. In the lexicon of the New Right, national decline was attributed to a bloated and inefficient state, to an archaic and obstructive class structure and to an allegedly permissive liberalism that had encouraged the growth of divisive social movements; anti-racism, women's liberation and gay rights amongst them. Immigration also became a potent source of political debate and mobilisation. Enoch Powell became the respectable figurehead of an anti-black immigration movement that demanded repatriation on the grounds that it was damaging to national culture.

For the purposes of this chapter on historical practice there are two really significant political responses to the (perceived) crises of the 1970s. The first was the development of a restrictive immigration policy that sought to, and largely succeeded in, preventing the further arrival of black immigrants in Britain. This was accompanied by a series of policy shifts, played out over decades, on the management of those black immigrants (and their families) who remained in England. According to some writers at least, assimilation slowly gave way to integration and in the 1980s and most prominently at the local level, to multiculturalism; a form of governance where the assumed autonomy of ethnic communities was to be recognised and respected and their cultural difference celebrated.[7] In these developments it is possible to discern a rather reluctant and uneven development of what has been called 'liberalism 2'.[8] Put simply, the state has gradually committed itself both to the protection of individual rights whilst also actively recognising specific 'community rights' and legislating for them. The result is a geographically uneven, far from popular, but nevertheless still significant, multiculturalism where cultural diversity and race equality are officially recognised and respected.[9] To use the current language of government, a 'multiethnic and multiracial nation' may only be emerging piecemeal and with considerable difficulties, but it represents a qualitative shift from the monoculturalism of even three decades ago.[10]

The drift to multicultural Britain also witnessed a novel emphasis on the idea of culture in political discourse. The slow emergence of political pluralism has been characterised by what Kenan Malik has called a series of ongoing 'cultural wars' in states across Europe and in the United States of America. The conflict can be understood, if a little simplistically, as the battle between 'entrenched pluralism' and 'assertive nationalism'. Pluralists utilise 'culture' in pursuit of progressive political struggles and in order to articulate the diversity that constitutes modern England and render problematic racialised and hegemonic notions of national identity. Nationalists employ the same term to resist or limit this diversity and insist on the necessity for a dominant culture that will act to secure social harmony.[11] These cultural wars are likely to remain a significant feature of contemporary political life because they can accurately be regarded as a tension that is integral to the (limited) pluralist settlement currently prevailing in England. In fact, in the conditions set by pluralism these wars are likely to escalate as culture becomes increasingly important in social policy decisions. Culture is already a key element of the criteria by which claims on redistributive support strategies, affirmative action programmes and publicly funded compensatory grants are judged.[12] As such the incentives for being recognised as a cultural or ethnic group are considerable and gaining recognition is a critical element of contemporary politics.[13] As Nancy Fraser has argued, 'we are witnessing an apparent shift in the political imaginary' where the 'most salient social movements are no longer economically defined "classes"' but 'culturally defined "groups" or "communities of value" who are struggling to defend their "identities", end "cultural domination" and win "recognition"'.[14]

The second significant political response to the crises of the 1970s was the adoption of an economic policy that accepted what were called the realties or the disciplines of the new global economy. As manufacturing and production headed for the developing world, and unemployment and social deprivation accelerated, successive governments liked to preach the importance of enterprise. Amidst recurrent recessions, rising unemployment and spiralling social inequalities, there was one source of new economic activity generating both jobs and income; public history. Put simply, from the 1970s onwards there was a quite astonishing explosion in the numbers of museums, galleries, exhibitions, displays, theme parks and shopping experiences that were concerned in some way with the presentation of the past.[15] This was the case at both the national level, where the National Heritage Act of 1980 acted as a further stimulus to the preservation of selective elements of the built environment, and at the local level where, as Raphael Samuel noted, heritage was one of the very few areas where municipal authorities were able to create jobs.[16] By the middle of the 1980s public history had become an important economic resource, a promoter of tourism, a provider of jobs and a key element in urban regeneration schemes.[17]

Public history is, however, much more than an economic resource. It is, as Brian Graham has recently argued, 'a knowledge, a cultural product and a political resource [that] possesses a crucial socio-political function'. Arguably the most important of these functions is that it helps to 'construct popular interpretations of the past', or 'narratives of inclusion and exclusion' that define communities and provide validation of selected identities in the present.[18] Of course, such an observation is hardly novel, but it is worth being clear about what is at stake in the presentation of public history.[19] It is precisely because it has the power to include or exclude that make it such an important site of contestation. From below, it was, and it remains, a site where opposition to the systematic racism encountered by post-war migrants and their children can be articulated. From above, public history was and remains, a useful tool of governance, providing opportunities for economic growth and the promotion of particular visions of social harmony whether these be the monoculturalism espoused by the New Right or the multiculturalism now advocated by New Labour. In short, public history increasingly became a search for roots that made visible claims to cultural, ethnic or racial identity in the present.

It is clear from all this that by the so-called 'New Times' of the 1980s it was commonplace to argue that the politics of class was an inadequate response to the economic and cultural changes of post-1945 Britain.[20] The shift from a Fordist to a post-Fordist economy was supposed to have weakened the conditions that had previously given meaning to the politics of class and bound different immigrant groups together in shared experiences of racism and exploitation. Alongside these structural changes in the economy came a new society characterised by 'diversity, differentiation and fragmentation' and the expansion of the available identities that subjects could adopt, particularly in terms of culture, ethnicity and gender, and over which successful political battles could be fought. In fact, the development of these battles over identity was bound up with a changed form of politics over the past twenty years. One result of the 'hollowing out' of the state is that it increasingly acts as an enabler for communities who may be defined through their locality, their cultural identity or their shared interests. As Clarke and Newman put it, the new politics imagines a civil society 'populated by a citizenry which is active but particularised (spatially or culturally)' and where 'the proper role for the state in such circumstances appears as investor, enabler, empowerer'.[21]

In summary, these were the significant social and political conditions underpinning some significant developments in historical practice in the post-war period. Two such developments require fuller exploration here; the emergence of professional public history explicitly concerned with questions of identity; and the adoption in this work of specific notions of culture and ethnicity as organising conceptual tools.

It has already been argued that the last three decades have witnessed a phenomenal growth in professional public history concerned with questions of national and cultural identity. This is a public or applied history sector that focuses on non-academic arenas for history and is usually written or presented by professional historians based either outside or only partially within universities. Its work is normally associated with museums, preservation agencies and the like. In Britain it has been argued that at a national level this professional public history was largely bound up with nostalgia for the past caused by that sense of national decline that was a characteristic feature of 1970s Britain.[22] It was also an important element of Margaret Thatcher's political response to the perceived decline and her nostalgia for old times and old values found expression in the active promotion of a selective and conservative national heritage in a diverse number of ways.[23] Yet, as Bhattacharyya has argued, there have been more liberal versions of public history that have challenged more conservative renditions of the past.[24] Sometimes these have been based on a politics of class – on the demand to include working classes – and sometimes on a struggle for ethnic recognition and sometimes a mixture of the two. These struggles were valuable and it is important to insist that they did have an impact. Admittedly, this has not been, even in a self-proclaimed progressive city like Birmingham, extensive, but the importance of 'reshaping collective memory' is now recognised in policy discussions and marginalised histories of the city are slowly beginning to make a public appearance.[25] Cultural diversity is now regularly marketed as a defining feature and strength of urban cities whose history is cast as one of growth and change. Different communities arrive and 'uplift the City' and cultural diversity is now officially seen as a powerful asset. Moreover, and whilst the extent of this should not be overestimated, this more positive view of diversity is at least beginning to appear in the history national curriculum.[26] Even if the concrete results of this shift towards embracing diversity in local governance are still few, it is an important element of commonsense understanding in the city, a kind of cognitive heuristic that works to publicise the benefits of a multicultural history and, in doing so, to promote social harmony. More or less explicitly, the aim has been to convince a sometime sceptical public that a diverse cultural history is a valuable resource. Malcolm Dick accurately represents the central message; 'without migration, Birmingham would not have emerged as a significant industrial and commercial centre, secured a range of retail and leisure opportunities or staffed its health and welfare services'.[27]

Discussed in these terms the development of professional public history may be welcomed as a sign of a more representative history, but its consequences for critical historical study may be rather less benign. For the incorporation of previously subordinated experiences and histories into strategies of either national or local governance may have significant consequences for the content and meaning of these histories. Both Barnor Hesse and Gargi Bhattacharyya hint at this when they refer to the 'exotic tendencies' of a project that Hesse characterises as ethnographic and contrasts with the historiographic.[28] Similarly, David Parker and Paul Long have recently noted in the case of Birmingham, public history may have helped to recast the city's 'identity as a modern and progressive and cosmopolitan city' but much of it has become 'too steeped in nostalgia to encompass serious critical analysis of the local economy and social structure'.[29] Too often the celebration of difference or the records of the achievements of particular immigrant groups have little or nothing to say about continuing economic and social inequalities. Moreover, the absorption of a formerly oppositional people's history into an official public history changes not only content and meaning but also the implicit philosophy of these histories. Where once they may have emphasised historical agency and were designed to direct a class based political strategy in the present, a softer version – a good intended for passive consumption and uncritical celebration – has been enabled and co-opted by the new pluralist politics.[30] Of course a more critical version of this history continues but it has been marginalised in the public sphere by a partial, celebratory and often tokenistic discourse of diversity.[31] Furthermore, this injunction to celebrate diversity in either the national or local past raises some difficult theoretical issues for historians.

For some writers the 'postcolonial moment', when former colonial nations were forced to confront their pasts and their citizens, encouraged the understanding of just how commonsense contemporary culture – including both academic and popular history - articulated gendered and racial hierarchies.[32] In academic history, this moment contributed to what became known as the cultural turn and the increasing emphasis placed on issues of culture, language and representation as explanatory factors in historical analysis. Lawrence Stone was an early commentator on the change when, in 1979, he recognised the revival of narrative in historical writing. Stone characterised this work as descriptive rather than analytical, less concerned with economic and social structure than with culture, a history of man [sic] rather than circumstances.[33] And Stone embraced the change with studied neutrality by declaring that this was a modest shift and that history has always been a house of many mansions. Others have not been so dispassionate. Writing recently in his autobiography, Eric Hobsbawm saw in this apparently stylistic change a shift in the very purpose of history, so that it became less a means of interpreting the world and more a method for 'collective self-discovery'. Hobsbawm argued that such a move undermined the essence of history as a scholarly and intellectual discipline, blurred boundaries between fact and fiction and heralded the 'great age of historical mythology'.[34] This kind of alarmist claim undoubtedly put the matter too strongly but it does raise some important issues too rarely discussed by historians. These issues are concerned with whether, how and in what ways historians should consciously seek to respond to a changed social world with new kinds of professional practice. If we are indeed living in a postcolonial epoch, in what ways can new kinds of history correct or effectively respond to patterns of representation and communication that have aided the exclusion and domination of immigrant groups in British society?

A popular response to these issues is to argue that singular and exclusionary renditions of national history need to be replaced with a British history of flux and fluidity and where change, diversity and immigration become characteristic features of the national story. As the recent response to the Runnymede Trust Report into the *Future of Multiethnic Britain* showed, there is still some way to go before such arguments receive widespread assent.[35] Yet whilst this debate on the principles of national history is at least advancing, discussions about the practice of this history receive relatively little discussion. In fact the real challenges involved in articulating the diversity of national history are barely recognised by historians. This becomes clear when one considers the use of culture and ethnicity in responding to what Dilip Hiro rightly called in 1971 the 'grotesquely partisan account of British history'.[36] The terms appear in various guises – as the Irish community or the Black experience for example – but are all are at least designed to signify just how differently histories can be experienced as a result of particular ethnic, cultural and religious identities. In a political and pedagogical sense it can also be convincingly argued that the terms have been successful and played a key role in unpicking racist constructions of the English nation. Yet whilst the adoption of the terminology of ethnicity, culture and community has been a matter of continuing debate in sociology, historians have given rather less thought to its utility as a concept for historical study.[37] In fact, notions of culture and ethnicity tend to get used in a fairly loose way in historical study so that contemporary discourse gets projected back into the past. In itself this is not problematic because devising or employing conceptual tools is an integral part of historical study. However, this is a process that requires critical thought and judgement about their suitability both for analysis and for contemporary political aims. Against these criteria notions of culture, ethnicity and community may be judged negatively because they tend to be employed in ways that are vague, essentialist and subject to reification. Popular examples of this follow in the second half of this chapter but it is worth noting in passing that the casual use of this terminology has also shaped the presentation of important and otherwise critical historical work. Here, for example, are Jagdish Gundara and Ian Duffield introducing *Essays on the History of Blacks in Britain*:

> 'Black community', a phrase which recurs through these essays, is in our view a fundamental point about the history of Blacks in Britain, since it is clear that virtually as soon as they were established in sufficient numbers, they developed their own *social* as opposed to purely individual and atomized responses to the pressures they faced in a generally hostile society.[38]

Such a definition has a certain commonsense value and there is no reason to oppose the assertion that immigrants and their families developed collective responses to hostility. Indeed, some of the excellent studies in their book demonstrate just this. What is more problematic is the framing assumption that being Black (however that term might be defined) necessarily constituted membership of a community that should take the privileged point of departure for historical studies.[39] As is well established in sociology, this, and other chapters in the book that speak of the Black experience, offer a problematic position for several reasons.[40] First, it is vague since no definition of Black is offered and the boundaries of the term are not specified. Second, it is essentialist because it assumes that there exists a Black identity that is relatively fixed and forms the basis of Black community and experience across time. Third, it has the tendency to flatten class, gender and political divisions in the Black community and so privileges fixed cultures or ethnicities over other forms of social unity. Ultimately, if historians were to consider their use of these conceptual tools in more detail they would find it difficult to escape the circular argument that 'what makes our history common is our racial or ethnic identity; what defines our racial and ethnic identity is our common history'.[41] The challenge for historians remains, Azoulay has argued, to 'recognise difference without reifying it'.[42]

Culture, ethnicity and community are used in historical research and may now be taken to constitute a historical paradigm not because of their theoretical rigour, but to a considerable degree because of the political demands made of history in contemporary societies. This is not to underestimate the academic arguments made against other ways of writing history, and nor is it to ignore the fact that immigrant and minority groups have been and remain marginalised in national histories. Yet remedying those omissions through the deployment of culture and ethnicity was as much about the development of political pluralism as it was about the utility of those concepts for historical study and representation.[43] As Robert Colls has recently noted,

> A language of multiple cultures, once hopeful of ensuring mutual respect, began to turn into a language of claim and counter-claim. As 'race' became synonymous with 'culture', multiracial became synonymous with multicultural, and multicultural could become the site for any culture, white or black or Asian, that saw itself as embattled and didn't want to change.[44]

As Colls suggests, a pluralist society is one defined by difference and that difference is guaranteed by a deterministic and historically defined culture. So even in sophisticated accounts of ethnic groups, where the experiences of minorities were placed within wider processes of class formation, there is still the tendency to insist on the significance of a transcendent common ethnic experience. In public histories, the need becomes both more acute and more obvious; it is a history that is owned by the group, an essential part of their claim for contemporary distinctiveness. Put simply (and far too briefly here) the politics of public history in a multicultural society raise important theoretical and philosophical questions for historians. Arguably the most important of these is to do with the relationship between notions of race and ethnicity, the discipline of history and the construction of identities.

The Practice of History: Celebrating Diversity

This necessarily schematic survey has indicated some of the social and political conditions underpinning historical practice generally, and notions of nationhood more specifically, in the post-war era. Broadly, it has argued that the shift from mono to multiculturalism helped to politicise history in ways that were at once newly explicit and potentially damaging for critical historical practice. The second part of this chapter elucidates these claims in more detail and brings them up to date by briefly examining three works of professional public history that engage in some way with the relationship between history and identity. Two are texts by avowedly popular historians – Richard Weight and Carl Chinn – and the third is a national history project, *Young Roots*. These examples have been chosen in an attempt to indicate how the new pluralism has shaped the production of history at a number of different sites. Weight's *Patriots* is used to demonstrate how problematic conceptions of nationhood are reappearing in pluralist Britain under the guise of accessible and populist versions of the national past. Chinn's account of the *Birmingham Irish* is used to critically examine how the diverse communities that are now held to constitute the nation come to be articulated both in public discourse generally, and in the rebranding of multiethnic cities more specifically. It might be that at least some of the celebratory tone of the text can be explained by its source of publication. Birmingham Library Services is ultimately subject to the regulation of the Department for Media, Culture and Sport, as is the Heritage Lottery Fund which is responsible for the third and final work of professional public history examined here; *Young Roots*. An exploration of the *Young Roots* programme examines how the enabling state operates in practice and how, in setting the project parameters and defining outcome measures, specific assumptions about the purpose of history find articulation in the public sphere.

One recent indication of the shift from a narrow nationalist politics to a more pluralist model is the proposal that 'ethnic and religious pride' should be encouraged in all the communities of Britain.[45] Like a number of other commentators, Alibhai-Brown is keen that the English (along with the newly ethnicised Irish) rediscover themselves, remember a core identity and develop confidence and pride in that Englishness. The result has been the re-emergence of some of the favourite themes of national history. Celebratory histories of empire, biographies of monarchs and national narratives of progress are back. In an echo of the debates of the late 1980s, it is regularly argued that the history curriculum should buttress conceptions of national identity that might be multiple and accessible, that would stress temporal and thematic connections between ethnic minorities and England, but which should remain explicitly committed to the transmission of a national heritage. According to one particularly active lobbyist, Prince Charles, the primary purpose of history is to teach 'social, political and moral values'.[46] And the way to teach these values is, David Starkey argues, to articulate the excitement of history, the sweep of narrative or the drama of character.[47] Above all argues the former chief adviser on the curriculum, Nick Tate, history should give children 'a narrative in which to live their lives'.[48]

Historian and broadcaster Richard Weight provides one possible narrative in *Patriots*. It is just one of the many recent texts on national identity and it traces the demise of Britishness and associated emergence of specific English, Welsh and Scottish identities.[49] The Englishness that has emerged in recent decades should be welcomed as a sign of 'progress and renewal' because it is at once more inclusive, meaningful, and popular than the moribund sense of Britishness that it is replacing. This rediscovery of core and happily benign national identities proceeds in a chronological fashion. It discusses what Weight calls both popular and elite culture, and, aiming to be entertaining and accessible, adopts an emphatically narrative approach; it begins 'it is time now to begin our journey through the national identity of modern Britain. The story begins in the June sunshine over the fields of Kent in the south of an island threatened with invasion'. Seven hundred breathless and certainly entertaining pages later the English are emerging, 'dazed and confused, but need[ing] a sense that their own unique nationality is respected'. It is also worth noting in passing that Weight presents his method in terms strikingly similar to Simon Schama in his *History of Britain*. Schama is also hostile to theory, attacking the 'inadequacy of dismissing nationality as a deluded anthology of patriotic fairy tales' and committed to a narrative method that is clearly signalled and eloquently defended ('the votaries of Clio sworn to tell stories in order to make the journey easier').[50]

Whilst it would be possible to debate issues of selection, emphasis and detail in Weight's text (and in Schama's), it is more important for the purposes of this chapter to concentrate on its implicit philosophy. Firstly, the corollary of the commitment to narrative appears to be hostility to any kind of theory, particularly if it is (or it can be labelled) 'Marxist'. Weight dismisses Benedict Anderson's influential ideas on *Imagined Communities* in just half a page because he is convinced that national consciousness existed long before the 16th century, and because, he does not believe nations are artificial constructs. The two objections are tactically significant; the first designed to project Britishness so far back into the past so as to naturalise it and deny its historical character, the second reliant on a personal insistence, on what Ian Craib calls a truth, on the organic authenticity of nations that is difficult to challenge through rational debate.[51] The effect is to close down possibilities for debate and understanding because this Englishness is, in the end, something natural, deeply felt and needed.

Secondly, Weight's book is an explicit response to what he sees as 'the decline of Britishness' and in common with most other histories of identity, he turns to history for the remedy to this decline. Yet, despite the (welcome) emphasis on the flux and fluidity of national identity there is, after all, continuity as long treasured but hidden national characteristics are found in the rubble of history; the English are 'breathing life into a narrative of liberal democracy that had never been fully realised' and 'legitimising an extant identity rather than going back to the drawing board'. As well as finding an identity that had gone missing, history answers the contemporary need for a respected nationality in the present because whilst England has changed, and whilst all 'metaphysical depictions of a national community are not strictly true', a 'cultural continuum is apparent'.[52] It is a rather calming conclusion and one, whether by design or accident, that leaves the reader feeling something close to relief. It is also, despite the declared novelty of the interpretation, a rather old story. For the assumptions underpinning this kind of work have remained basically unchanged for a century or more. They are seen both in the bald assertion that the English have a need for a unique nationality, and in the claim that the metaphysical idea of national community is 'partly true'.

Weight's concluding assurances are entirely typical of a way of viewing history that domesticates it, internalises it and helps to secure identities, but does not seek to analyse it, interpret it or use it as a resource for critical action. Carolyn Steedman has written admiringly about this attitude to the past as a 'politics of the imagination' in which the past has

> become a place of succcor and strength, a kind of home...which is searched for something (someone, some group, some series of events) that confirms the searcher in his or her sense of self, confirms them as they want to be, and feel in some measure that they already are.[53]

Drawing on Raphael Samuel's work, she suggests that the cultural meaning of the past has changed, and that history in post-war Britain has increasingly become a site for pleasure, and importantly, for identification. History is primarily a resource that helps define and sustain identities. It may be that this historicist turn in British culture achieved much that was valuable, but the effects of abandoning a more critical mode of historical thinking have been underestimated and too little discussed. For history is increasingly written about, as Catherine Hall has done so recently, as though 'it is lived', as though it offers 'answers to the questions as to who we are' and tells us 'how we are produced as modern subjects'.[54] The problem with this is that it can be, and frequently is, read as though people are the passive spectators of a history that deterministically makes them, tells them who they are, and gives them myths to live by. This kind of historicism denies the politics of history and obviates what Schwarz has called the 'active construction of conceptions of the past as a continual and defining moment in political practice'.[55] Rather than engage in the politics of history, this kind of historicism contends itself with a naturalised history that insists on the continuity of past with present. For confirmation of this it is time to turn briefly to a professional public history account of the Birmingham Irish.

Carl Chinn, known locally as the 'people's professor', is Community Historian at the University of Birmingham and author of the recently published *Birmingham Irish: Making our Mark*. The text consists of some solid empirical work and some fascinating oral history material on Irish migration to Birmingham over the two centuries since 1800 and it is published by Birmingham Library Services whose divisional plan for 2003-04 speaks of building 'community identity and of developing community cohesion and citizenship'.[56] The title of *Birmingham Irish* speaks precisely to those multiple identities, to the different ways of belonging that is stressed in so much contemporary academic debate and political discussion. Indeed, the public articulation of this kind of Irish identity has been celebrated as a sign of progress in the struggle against myths of national homogeneity. Yet it is a peculiarly sanitised account of Irish migrants and their ancestors. There is no consistent discussion of the very significant differences of class and culture within the 'community'; little exploration of gendered experiences; little violence, alcoholism or mental health difficulties; no recognition of any racism within it and a curiously benign view of the process of settlement that comes, in the second half of the book, directly from the testimonies of the migrants themselves; 'I've never experienced prejudice at any time'; 'received with kindness and courtesy and successfully integrating'; 'grateful to Birmingham and its friendly people'; 'how tolerant and kind hearted the Birmingham people were to the Irish and other immigrants who came to the city in great numbers'.[57] In fact, apart from some very brief references to racism in the 1950s and 1960s, the only exception to the happy story is some uncomfortable experiences in the aftermath of the IRA bombings in 1974 from which the Irish community is now recovering. As Chinn concludes, 'Irish people have played a leading part in the building of a successful multi-cultural city in which people can be proud of their distinct communities but can also be proud of that which we share in common: our humanity and our belonging to Britain'.[58]

What is at stake here is not the facts of the past. Both Weight's text on Englishness and Chinn's on the Irish bear all the hallmarks of conventional historical scholarship and neither are demonstrably false. This is particularly the case in the Birmingham Irish because so much of it is from the people themselves and in describing these testimonies in almost reverential terms ('precious words' on which he should not 'intrude'), Chinn makes very strong (but disputable) claims for the authenticity of the text.[59] In that sense both might be praised as popular histories that are appropriate given the intended audience. The implication is that history of this kind might be criticised by academics but since it is not demonstrably false and since it draws on apparently authentic memories it is valid scholarship and, to the extent that it evokes a degree of civic pride, 'useful knowledge'.[60] This is superficially attractive but it is dangerous not because these histories are false but because they employ a rather naïve empirical method and a historicist philosophy. The latter, in particular, is becoming increasingly apparent in public debate and social policy implementation with some troubling results. For evidence of this it is time to turn to a brief consideration of the Heritage Lottery Fund's *Young Roots* programme.

Young Roots is a national grants scheme launched by the Heritage Lottery Fund (HLF) in October 2002. Operating until 2007 and with an annual budget of some £5 million, the scheme is central to the HLF's strategic aim of promoting young people's involvement in heritage.[61] In the period to March 2004 more than 240 projects had been awarded funding and according to the official evaluation of the national scheme, *Young Roots* projects has provided some excellent examples of heritage learning for the 'young people participating in them, the project workers managing them and the communities that have benefited from them'.[62] It is certainly the case that the scheme has made possible some interesting, important and critical historical work throughout England, Scotland and Wales.[63] It should be stressed that the purpose here is not to criticise actual examples of this work, but to locate the project in a wider social and political context and in doing so, to make explicit some of its assumptions and limitations.

The operation of the Heritage Lottery Fund provides a salient example of the new pluralist politics at work. Heritage Lottery is officially 'a non-departmental public body' since it is removed from government but it cannot realistically be considered autonomous since it is reliant on the Department for Culture, Media and Sport for funding and is therefore subject to its scrutiny, guidance and review processes.[64] As a result the funding priorities, evaluation criteria and the presentation of successful heritage projects frequently echo government policies in policy areas like education and culture. In fact, the influence of government policy on *Young Roots* is spelt out in the recent and aptly named document *Practical Partnerships*. This makes clear the importance of both the Social Exclusion Unit and the linked Policy Action Teams that were established to develop strategies for combating social exclusion. It also helps explain why Black, minority and ethnic young people are a particular target group for *Young Roots* projects.[65] It is worth tracing this policy background because a key working principle of both the DCMS generally and the Social Exclusion Unit more specifically is that cultural activity promotes social cohesion. Aside from the benefits of job creation, cultural activity, that is participation in the arts or sport, helps to develop 'a sense of identity and community'. However, whilst policy documents routinely and quite rightly indicate the range of benefits accruing from such activity Buckingham and Jones have argued, that 'there is a risk that cultural production will be seen as means of social control or ... a way of letting off the steam that is created by other social pressures and tensions'.[66] In reading through some of the presentation and evaluation literature associated with *Young Roots*, and in observing a *Young Roots* project in development, this is precisely the impression created. Too often history appears as a method of compensation and consolation, a way of imposing self-discipline for those at risk of social exclusion. Whilst the recent evaluation document emphatically demonstrates that some young people certainly benefit from the opportunities afforded by the scheme, it also articulates the benefits of historical study in a conservative and historicist fashion:

> A sense of pride emerges as young people gain knowledge and respect for the areas in which they live and for the histories of the people that live around them. This has encouraged and improved inter-generational relationships.
>
> Some of the Guides were able to express the responsibility they felt in keeping the traditions alive and passing them on to younger generations. One saw how she was part of a family tradition (her grandmother, her mother and she were guiders) and therefore a conduit for Guiding heritage. [67]

Young Roots may be a useful way of developing conversations about the past but the prominence of a discourse of generations helps to indicate one of the key purposes of this form of historical education. The emphasis here is on history as personal and familial testimony, as a set of experiences and testimonies that are to be passed down to a younger generation. Yet, and as Graham Carr has recently argued in the case of Canada, this more personal, empathetic and affective form of historical practice can entail a suspension of critical distance, and is often overdetermined by a larger social agenda that wants to 'pay homage to history by binding children deferentially to the past through the ties of affection and family'.[68] At the national launch of *Young Roots* Liz Forgan, the Chair of the Heritage Lottery Fund, made this more explicit:

> Young Roots' great strength is that young people can decide what is important to them and what they'd like to celebrate about their heritage. The scheme will create not just a greater awareness of their community history, and therefore of their own identity within it, but enable them to be active in restoring, sustaining and cherishing it.[69]

What is particularly striking in a programme designed for young people is the absence of any concept of critical engagement or generational change. The young people imagined here seem to be torchbearers of sacred stories whose only activity is a highly circumscribed choice about what to celebrate. Like the other two examples of public history examined in this section, the basic assumption is that history is a source of identity, a resource that is to be restored, sustained, cherished but above all celebrated. However, and as

Furedi has argued, this attitude to the past is itself historically specific and can be contested.[70] As Tom Paine realised in his dispute with Edmund Burke over the French Revolution, identities can just as easily be based on reason rather than tradition, principle rather than precedent, on breaking with history rather than being captured by it.[71]

Reasons for History

The production of identity history responds to, and possibly encourages, what appears to be a real and widespread desire in contemporary England. In a society and an age characterised by insecurity, it is often argued that there is a desire for identity, roots and a sense of belonging. This demand for identity is historically specific and is a product of social and political conditions. In particular, it has been argued in this chapter that the obsession with identity that is such a feature of late modernity is at least partly the result of the political settlement called multiculturalism. Settlement is used advisedly here. It refers to the process by which the different aims and interests of formal political parties, pressure groups, professional interests and so on are reconciled in sets of arrangements which are fairly lasting. Multiculturalism can be viewed as such a settlement.[72] It has inbuilt tensions which cause conflict but which are managed effectively. As Chris Haylett has argued

> ...the idea of the British nation as predominately constituted by multiple ethnic differences in a culturally hybrid whole is useful to the extent that it can be accommodated into the workings of a late-capitalist economy. Where cultural hybridity exceeds the presentational and challenges that economic organisation it becomes problematic, but the dominant discourse of multiculturalism is not pitched to make that challenge...[73]

In multicultural societies individuals belong to communities that are predominately defined by their culture. Practically the term culture is frequently conflated with ethnicity and increasingly both are guaranteed or shored up by an objectified history. It has already been argued that this has had important consequences for both academic and popular historical practice. More important than this, however, is the possibility that this kind of history facilitates or encourages the development of discrete and historically determined cultural identities. There is certainly some evidence to support this. For example, and whilst it should be treated with some caution, data from opinion polls does suggest that increasing numbers of the public make a clear distinction between the terms British and English and identify with the latter rather than the former. No doubt some of those expressing this opinion are also supportive of the current campaign to celebrate St. George's Day as a national holiday, and are already marking that day with public parades and concerts that, according to some commentators, 'will help to solve the nation's identity crisis'.[74] Similar trends can be discerned in Britain's Muslim communities and Irish communities. A recent poll found a significant minority (41%) of Muslims aged under 34 describing themselves as exclusively Muslim, compared with 30% of over 35s. The young were also more likely to say that their community was too integrated.[75] According to Holohan there has also been 'what some would describe as a revival of Irish ethnic identity, amongst the older generation, their children born in Britain and the 80s wave of emigrants'.[76] This turn to ethnic and cultural identities can, of course, be read in positive terms. These diverse identities can be taken as evidence of the increasing acceptance of diversity, of a growing tolerance to public displays of difference and, for writers in cultural studies, the emergence of new ethnicities or postcolonial identities that are fluid rather than fixed, negotiated rather than imposed. Yet even leaving aside the fact that hybrid ethnicity is itself a problematic concept,[77] this kind of optimistic reading ignores or fails to adequately understand both the structural conditions that severely limit the construction of cultural identities, and the consequences of their growth.

In some respects at least the turn by young people to questions of culture and identity is an indication of how the new pluralist politics works. Young people in particular are being encouraged to celebrate their cultural identity, but there is little recognition or discussion of how these identities have come to be constructed in a society characterised by racism and inequality. Kenan Malik has recently argued that in celebrating 'cultural difference, we are in danger of celebrating the differences imposed by a racist society, not identities freely chosen by those communities'.[78] It is important to be clear that this is not an argument for integration or assimilation. Nor is it some version of a social control thesis. It is rather to suggest that the recourse to cultural identities is not necessarily an indication of a successful pluralist nation but one where cultures of difference are used to make sense of continuing educational and economic inequalities. Indeed, both the fragility and the limits of the current pluralist politics of diversity can be gauged from the fact that even self-declared 'progressive' commentators are already wondering whether there is 'too much' diversity. Writing in the left wing journal *Prospect* about the future development of immigration policy the economist Bob Rowthorn has argued for a strategy that does not 'devalue the history of a nation'. This turns out to be an argument for a highly restrictive immigration policy because nations have 'historical roots' and are based on a 'historical continuity' that provides coherence and stability in present society.[79] More recently, the editor of the same journal David Goodhart has argued that Britain is becoming 'too diverse' to sustain social cohesion. To a considerable degree these arguments rest on a deterministic view of history; Alan Wolfe's aphorism – 'behind every citizen lies a graveyard' – is quoted to illuminate how British citizenship and values arise out of a shared and specific history that is somehow threatened by the arrival of 'too many' strangers. [80]

Such sentiment speaks to the fatalist position of popular historical practice under the conditions of political pluralism. Instead of using history as a resource for critically understanding contemporary identities, as a necessary stage in changing themselves and society, history all too often becomes a celebration of tradition, an affirmation of identity, the definition of who we are. Yet the purpose of historical study should not be celebration or denunciation, it should not aim to bring relief and comfort but understanding. In the so called postmodern age perhaps there is something to learn from Walter Ralegh who, five centuries ago at the birth of modernity, was humanising history and helping prepare the ground for its secularisation. Christopher Hill said of Ralegh that he helped turn 'history into a science' because 'he thought that men [sic] could control it'.[81] It seems appropriate to recall that and to think about forms of historical practice that might not simply produce identities but understanding.

Part II

Histories and Narratives

4

Italian Immigrants in Britain: Perceptions and Self-Perceptions

Lucio Sponza

The perception of foreign people (from Latin 'foraneous' < 'foris' = out of doors) presupposes the concept of 'otherness', which assumes some awareness of one's own identity. The building of nation-states and the development of their commercial, military and political contacts is accompanied by the sedimentation of sub-cultural strata of curiosity, fear, envy, admiration. All such sentiments are influenced by historical events. The result of this century-long process is that some sort of generalised and undifferentiated collective images of foreigners have taken shape and are hard to change, thus producing prejudices and stereotypes.

Of course, those consolidated collective perceptions have also been influenced by political calculation in the past and can be manipulated for the same purpose in the present. Against a well-established abstract and vague perception of a foreign country, the real and direct contact with immigrants from that country contributes to form that view. Depending on the size of the immigrant community, its social and cultural characteristics, and the degree of its separateness from the host society, the image of immigrants may strengthen the pre-existing perception, but may also result in a degree of revision of that perception. As the immigrants are exposed to such perception, their own sense of identity and self-perception is also influenced.

I will first sketch a historical profile of Italian immigration to Britain; I will then deal with six distinct and particularly significant instances and periods of that history: the early 1840s and Mazzini's free school; the 1870s and a confused Italian identity; the 1890s and racism; the 1930s and the age of Fascism; WWII and the Italians as 'enemy aliens'; the changing views in the post-war years. An epilogue will offer some considerations on the last thirty years.

Within those periods I shall broadly distinguish three axes: the perception of the Italians as expressed by writers, authorities and members of the public; the view of the immigrants as manifested by their fellow countrymen in some position of authority; the self-perception of the immigrants themselves.

Historical Profile

Although an Italian presence in Britain can be traced back centuries (monks, bankers, artists and artisans), a small community of what we would now call 'economic immigrants' was first noted in London in the second decade of the nineteenth century.[1]

This early settlement consisted of three main groups in terms of skills, occupations and regional origins. The most skilful section included the makers of small precision instruments (barometers and thermometers), picture-frame makers, glass and looking-glass makers. These artisans came from the mountain area of Como, north of Milan. Semi-skilled craftsmen were the plaster-of-Paris statuette makers, who came from the Apennine district of Lucca, in Tuscany.[2] The third, rapidly growing unskilled group was that of the itinerant musicians (mainly organ-grinders), who came from the Apennine valleys around Parma and Piacenza (between Milan and Bologna).

Most of the young apprentices, street vendors and itinerant musicians were sojourners rather than settlers. They were recruited by 'masters', back in their respective villages. The very young were, as it were, leased out for a few years by their parents as part of their precarious strategy of economic survival. Many Italian immigrants settled in a few dilapidated streets and courts in the London district of Holborn, where shabby lodging-houses provided them with cheap accommodation. The 1861 census (the first to indicate the foreign place of birth) recorded the presence of 4,600 Italians; nearly half of them lived in the Holborn district.

1861 was also the year of the unification of Italy, but emigration continued in the following decades to become a mass phenomenon at the turn of the century, when the main destinations were the United States, Brazil and Argentina. As for Europe, France was the main recipient of Italians. In 1911 some 25,000 Italians were recorded in Britain – now with significant numbers also in Scotland and Wales. A few London districts still accounted for nearly half that total figure. There were still several street musicians, but the dominant groups were now the ice-cream makers and street vendors, the waiters, the small food dealers and the domestic servants. Large numbers still came from the valleys around Parma and Lucca, but a new major district of provenance was the Liri Valley, between Rome and Naples. Most people from that southern area were involved in the ice-cream business.

In the inter-war period, notably from the early 1920s, Italian emigration to Britain virtually ceased. By now, the Italians were fairly well integrated into – yet isolated within – British society, as more and more of them were now engaged in food-shops, cafés and restaurants, thus consolidating the stereotype image of Italians, which is still with us.

When Mussolini's Italy entered the war, in June 1940, the Italians became 'enemy aliens'. Many men (aged 16 to 60) were interned. Several hundreds were deported to Canada and Australia. Tragedy struck when the liner *Arandora Star* was torpedoed and sank: 446 out of 717 Italians who were being transported to Canada drowned. Italian POWs began to be brought to Britain in late 1941. By the end of the war there were 155,000 in this country, mostly employed in agriculture. POW camps and their dependent hostels were located throughout Britain. Many prisoners were billeted in farms as living-ins, thus becoming a pervasive thread in the fabric of British rural society. Never before had so many ordinary British people become acquainted with so many ordinary Italians. This resulted in mutual appreciation, but also in the strengthening of reciprocal prejudices.[3]

Nearly 1,500 POWs were allowed to stay in Britain at the end of the war as agricultural labourers – thus turning into immigrants. On the other hand, shortage of manpower in post-war Britain led into inter-governmental agreements for the recruitment of Italian workers, both men and women. Men were mainly employed in metal and brick-making industries; women in textile mills, pottery factories, but also as orderlies in hospitals and for domestic service. In addition to those mass recruitment schemes, many Italians immigrated through the traditional mode of individual 'work permits'.

Two important features were revealed by the 1951 census apart from the expected confirmation of increased numbers (34,000): for the first (and only) time there were more women (61%) than men in the Italian community. Secondly, many of the new immigrants came from southern regions, notably Campania, Calabria and Sicily – a tendency consolidated in the 1950s and 1960s.[4]

By the early 1970s this economic immigration virtually ceased, but the Italian community in Britain expanded in the next three decades. This was partly because, once Britain had joined the European Economic Community, all restrictions to the movement of people within the Community were removed. The stronger trade and financial relations, and the availability of relatively cheap flights between Italy and Britain involved a growing inflow of newcomers: students, employees of Italian firms and public bodies, business people, managers and professionals. In the 2001 census, around 100,000 Italians were recorded, over half of them living in the London area. Let us now look into the mentioned six specific periods and instances.

The Early 1840s and Mazzini's Free School

In early November 1841 a free school for the Italian poor was opened at 5 Greville Street, in the heart of the Italian colony in London. It was the brainchild of Giuseppe Mazzini, the Italian visionary patriot and political exile. The young illiterate organ-grinders and statuette vendors were the main target of the initiative. As Mazzini expected, a strong opposition to the enterprise came from the Roman Catholic priests of the Sardinian Chapel (which belonged to the Legation of the Kingdom of Sardinia). Mazzini was profoundly religious, but equally forcefully anti-Roman Catholic. The school was to provide not only basic education in reading, writing and speaking Italian, but aimed also at instilling the love for a united and republican Italy, i.e. for subversion of the contemporary political condition of the peninsula. The episode reveals a full spectrum of perceptions and self-perceptions of the Italian immigrants.

The self-perceptions can be considered only indirectly. Mazzini himself wrote to a friend in Florence that:

> I will tell you that I have found here streets full, from top to bottom, of Italians from all districts, trying to earn a living in all sorts of occupations, in a condition of total barbarity. I will not say that they could not read; I will say that they could not speak, that in their company for a long time I could not make sense of what they were saying, as they were talking in a jargon which was half *comasco* [from the Como valleys] – for most of them are from Lombardy – and half English. Italy to them was the name of a foreign country; nothing more.[5]

The Italians identified with their mountain villages and only knew to which particular State they belonged, because that was indicated in their one-sheet passport: the Duchy of Parma, the Austrian-ruled Kingdom of Lombardy and Venetia, the Kingdom of Sardinia, the Grand-Duchy of Tuscany, or the Duchy of Lucca.[6] It was said that some potential pupils from the Parma valleys did not want to go to the school because they thought that people from the Como district were foreigners (which, of course, they were!).[7]

Out of this mass of isolation, parochialism, prejudice and ignorance, Mazzini wanted to mould a new and united 'Young Italy'. The teaching of reading, writing and arithmetic was complemented by courses on Italian history and geography – or, as Mazzini used to put it: 'History of the Motherland and National Geography.' The teaching of reading and writing was of great importance, Mazzini wrote, but 'the National Idea, the idea that we are all Italian brothers – not Genoese, Piedmontese, Lombards – is equally important'.[8] These principles were anathema to the London representatives of the various Italian states and a spanner in the works of the school was soon thrown from Roman Catholic quarters. Possibly acting upon instructions from the Sardinian Legation, the head of the Sardinian chapel (one Rev. Luigi Baldacconi) began to thunder against the school, by arguing: that the principles which were being taught were immoral, irreligious and anti-social; that it was the 'Devil's school'; and that the director and teachers were 'impious, liberals, philosophers and lost souls'.[9]

Mazzini was energetically supported by such diverse English newspapers as the liberal-minded *Weekly Dispatch*, the *Examiner* and the *Morning Chronicle*, but also by the *Sun* – a Tory paper. The only voice to speak in favour of the priests was the Roman Catholic the *True Tablet*. The *Weekly Dispatch* set the whole episode in a clear context:

> Dr Baldaconi [sic], a priest of the Sardinian chapel, with what seems to us the truly infernal spirit of bigotry, tried to preach the school down. His efforts were vain ... until the 10th of April, when he proclaimed that those who persisted in attending the school should be refused the sacrament and the priestly-offices on their death-beds. It is well known that Catholics are so wretchedly superstitious as to believe that the fate of their souls depends upon their receiving the services of the Church on the bed of the death. In consequence of the terrors of this denunciation, the school is understood to be on the decline or, at least, many terrified parents have refused to let their children any longer attend it ... But is it not most insolent that this foreigner, Baldaconi, a servant of a foreign ambassador, should dare to interfere with such a subject in our metropolis?[10]

The issue of the immigrants' identity, therefore, should be seen against the background of the debate on the position of Roman Catholicism in Britain and, more generally, of the role of religion and society. The episode of Mazzini's free school occurred between two important events regarding Roman Catholicism in Britain: the Catholic emancipation granted in 1829 and the restoration of the Catholic hierarchy, in 1850. Consequently, in those decades there was a resurgence of the entrenched No-Popery mood, together with Evangelical revival.

In 1835, the London City Mission was established, to fight against 'Popery, Infidelity and Ungodliness'. Their journal (the *City Mission Magazine*) reported on 'The Italians in London' in November 1844, and on the merit of educating them. It was written:

> Who can calculate the blessing which might result from their return to their land of superstition with a knowledge of the way of salvation? If the Italians in London were but brought to know and love the Redeemer, who shall say the effect which might be produced by those who are continually going back to that land of darkness on their degraded countrymen?[11]

As far as the Italian immigrants were concerned, the outcome of the controversy and prejudicial attacks was that there were soon three free schools available to them, instead of one. After the priests of the Sardinian Chapel opened one to compete with Mazzini's, an Evangelical British woman also started one, hoping to convert the young Italians.

The concern over the education of the Italian immigrants did not last for long. What went on for several decades were – intermittently – the outcry for the 'white slave trade' and cruel conditions to which the organ-boys were subjected by their *padroni*, and the everlasting protest against the torment imposed on the industrious classes, in their own houses, by the persistent organ-grinders. It is also true, however, that some sympathy for the peripatetic musicians was expressed by patronising members of the House of Lords, who thought the Italians offered some musicality to the London poor.

The 1870s and a Confused Italian Identity

On 29 December 1874, at 17 Eyre Street Hill, in the heart of the Italian quarter in London, one woman – Domenica Valenti – was allegedly stabbed to death by another Italian woman – Mariana Tortolani. The case produced great excitement within the Italian community, not least because the local reporter had written that 'Italians' were involved. Here is what he then wrote in the next issue of the newspaper:

> A mistake was made last week in the publication of the hearing of this case ... The murdered woman and the prisoner were described as Italians, whereas they are Neapolitans proper, and the Italian

women ... are so annoyed that they have determined to wear bonnets instead of covering their heads with handkerchiefs and shawls, as is the case with the Neapolitan women ... It was further stated that though the Italians proper and the Neapolitans reside in the same street, it is very rarely that they reside in the same house.[12]

In the 1870s a major change was taking place in the Italian immigrants' community. New categories of unskilled labourers came from the north-east of the peninsula, to be mainly engaged as paviours, bricklayers and asphalt workers; but much more numerous were the arrivals from the Liri Valley, who found their expanding niche in ice-cream making and street selling.[13] This change can be observed by looking at the make up of the virtually all-Italian dwellers of 17 Eyre Street Hill, which consisted of only three rooms and a basement (the kitchen where the fatal affray took place), at the time of the two censuses of 1871 and 1881.

In 1871 this was an unofficial lodging-house for Italians. The 'head', a 'bird fancier', lived there with his wife (housekeeping) and three sons, the eldest being himself a 'bird fancier'. There were also 19 'boarders', including two young couples, who were all 'street musicians', except two young children and one 'general servant' – who happened to be Domenica Valenti. If she was really just one of the boarders in 1871, she must have quickly improved on her status: by the time she was murdered her occupation was said to be that of an 'artists' model', while she was also subletting to lodgers, who therefore regarded her as their landlady. At the origin of the altercation which ended up with her death, there was an argument over unpaid rent. In 1881, at 17 Eyre Street Hill, the 'head' and his wife were 'coffee house keepers'; they had four children, of whom the eldest – a 17-year-old girl – was a 'street musician'. There were also four 'lodgers': one couple, both 'ice-cream sellers', and two 'street musicians'.

The hostility towards the 'Neapolitans' manifested by other components of the Italian colony did not reflect so much a regional prejudice, as antagonism towards newcomers who kept to themselves, while effectively competing with the 'Italian proper' in the most thriving of the itinerant trades. It is also worth mentioning, in passing, that in the 1870s Italian scholars began to investigate and theorise on the social backwardness of the southern regions, compared to those in the north of the peninsula. What they then called 'the social question', was to develop in the following decades into a racist-tainted prejudice – of which more in the next section. As far as the perception of Italians was concerned, the 'Leather Lane murder' reinforced the view that those foreigners were a quick-tempered lot, who easily resorted to the deadly use of the knife to settle their quarrels.[14]

The 1890s and Racism

In June 1891, two articles on the 'Italians in London' appeared in the *St. James's Gazette*. Those immigrants – it was written – could be divided into two broad categories: the 'superior' Italians and the 'itinerant' lot, obviously regarded as 'inferior'. The 'superior' Italians were the artisans, the shopkeepers, restaurant managers and their employees (cooks and waiters). Their 'inferior' fellow countrymen were themselves divided into two sub-groups: the ice-cream sellers – the largest component[15] – and the organ-grinders. The former, it was stated, 'are chiefly from the north of Italy and characteristically industrious' (thus their 'inferiority' was partly condoned); the organ-grinders, it was also written,

> are not quite so numerous as the penny-ice men, but even more objectionable. They possess all the vices of the latter, and laziness into the bargain; for they are from the south of Italy to a man, and especially from Naples. The point is worth noting. Italians from the north and centre are naturally industrious ... those from the south are the reverse.[16]

Another point worth making is that, contrary to what was written in the article, the vast majority of the much despised organ-grinders were from the north (from around Parma), whereas the majority of the less despised penny-ice men were from the south (from the Liri Valley). On the other hand, there were some who accused the ice-cream vendors to be worse because their lack of hygienic norms turned their product into poison (in fact a few cases of death were attributed to the eating of ice-cream purchased from Italian street sellers).

But a more vehement accusation of 'inferiority' was raised in a contemporary account by W.H. Wilkins:

> The Italians ... mostly come from Naples and the vicinity, where they live in pauperism, filth and vice, with no higher ambition than to get cheap food enough to keep them alive. Uneducated and slovenly when they come, they never improve ... They are ineradicably bad ... The degraded habits of this class of immigrants, innate and lasting as they are, stamp them as a most undesirable set, whose affiliation with our own people must in time work great injury.[17]

There was not only a fear of moral 'injury', but also – and worse – a fear that such an 'immoral, illiterate, vicious ... low [and] degraded class' caused social subversion, since, as Wilkins added, the Italians fell 'as easy prey to one of the secret socialistic or revolutionary leagues which abound in the metropolis'.[18]

The Italian diplomatic and consular authorities in London were also concerned that the then numerous Italian clubs were nests of 'socialistic and revolutionary' subversion – which was incorrect. It was true that some well known Italian anarchists were sheltering in London (including the famous Errico Malatesta).[19] And it was also true that violent actions by Italian anarchists were at the time quite frequent. In the same June of 1894 – for instance – the Italian Prime Minister (Francesco Crispi) escaped an assassination attempt; not so lucky was the President of the French Republic (Sadi Carnot), who was stabbed to death by Sante Caserio. Two months earlier, two Italian anarchists (Francesco Polti and Giuseppe Fornara) were implicated in the case of the French anarchist (Martial Bourdin) who blew himself up in pieces in Greenwich Park, when the bomb he was carrying exploded prematurely. But by and large the Italian immigrants had no political education and were indifferent to the dozen or so of their revolutionary compatriots in London.[20]

It is ironic that at the very apogee of the British Empire – Queen Victoria's Diamond Jubilee of 1897 – involving the domination and subjugation of a quarter of the world's population, there was growing fear that the presence of relatively few, racially 'inferior' immigrants threatened the political stability and the moral basis of society.

At the time of the dispute around Mazzini's school, the spirit of progress and freedom was pitched against the reactionary presence of intolerant foreigners – the Roman Catholic priests. Now the outcry was based on intolerant, reactionary – indeed racist – premises. The large-scale labour unrest in Britain during the 1880s, the emergence of Socialism, the agricultural depression, and the threat of Home Rule for Ireland – all this dented the vigour and self-esteem of the imperial ruling class. (Indeed, it has been argued that – up to a point – the ethos of Imperial rule was the façade to justify the desire of domination, which was now perceived as insecure at home.) In addition, the increasing number of poor Jewish immigrants from Russia contributed to precipitate xenophobic attitudes.

A racist discourse was then developing also in Italy, not so much connected with the indigenous population of the African colonies the Italians were trying to extend, but projected within the peninsula: southern Italians were regarded as racially inferior – and 'scientific' efforts were made to prove it. While northern Italy had begun its industrial revolution, the south had remained rural and archaic. At the time of the unification of the country it was thought that once the reactionary and backward domination of the Bourbons in the Kingdom of Naples was swept away, general economic and social progress would follow, as the day follows the night. But now, in the last decade of the century, the southern regions appeared as backward as ever, and only emigration seemed to offer a chance for survival. The reason – according to the positive sociologist Alfredo Niceforo – was that southern Italians were feudal, semi-civilised, barbarians, who lacked the superior sense of social organisation of the north.[21]

Indirect evidence suggests that even among the Italian immigrants their 'Neapolitan' fellow-countrymen continued to be looked down with a degree of contempt. They were still not recognised as 'Italians' at all. The fact is that even toward the end of the century, for most of the immigrants the concept of 'Italianness' was very confused. They continued to identify with their local culture. The only effective unifying agency was their common religion. As the largest Roman Catholic church in Britain, completed in 1863, St Peter's 'Italian Church' was built at the centre of the Italian community in London. By the 1890s it had become the focal point for all Italians in Britain, when a major yearly event was first organised. This was (and still is) the Festival of Our Lady of Mount Carmel, which involved a long procession and a parade of decorated carts moving around the Italian quarter.

The 1930s and the Age of Fascism

On 3 October 1935, Mussolini's generals started the invasion of Ethiopia and four days later Great Britain had the League of Nations impose economic sanctions on Italy. It was a useless move (if only because oil supplies were excluded from the ban and the Suez Canal was not closed to military traffic), but 'effective enough to make the war popular in Italy'[22] – and among the colonies of Italian emigrants around the world, not least the Italians in Britain, the country most determined that Mussolini's Italy be punished for the intolerable act of aggression. Thus, the Italians in Britain found themselves in the front line of a diplomatic and propaganda war, and had no hesitation in supporting *il Duce* and his empire-building project. Many of them had been very slow to embrace Fascism.

Even before taking power Mussolini had conceived the idea of extending fascist propaganda abroad by targeting the colonies of Italian emigrants. The *Fascio di Londra* was one of the first sections of the Fascist Party to be established abroad, in June 1921. Between 1923 and 1924 (by which time Mussolini had become – at 39 – the youngest head of government in the history of united Italy) other *Fasci* were established in Glasgow, Edinburgh, Liverpool and Manchester. They aimed at mobilising an emigrant community with a weak sense of national identity by appealing to patriotic unity and self-esteem. Sceptical at first of any political and ideological proclamation, the Italians were gradually induced to appreciate the politically motivated initiatives organised by the Italian authorities in the fields of education, welfare, health and leisure. These were promoted with vigour after Dino Grandi became ambassador in London, in July 1932.[23] The support of Fascism was the sign of a generic patriotic sentiment, which had to do more with the nostalgia for the lost original village life than with the manifestation of a national conscience.

Other factors contributed to this new self-perception. Some sort of national pride must have been stimulated by British acquaintances, praising the vigorous young head of the Italian government, who had succeeded in ending the climate of feuding, unrest and violence that had characterised post-WWI Italy (not to mention that 'under Mussolini trains ran on time'). Furthermore, much impression on the immigrants was made when the famous scientist and inventor, Guglielmo Marconi, was chosen 'by the unanimous vote of our Fascist comrades in London to be the Honorary President of the *Fascio di Londra*, to which he belonged since its inception'.[24]

But much more important in the development of a favourable attitude toward Fascism among the Italians in Britain, whose strongest common value was their religious faith, was the enthusiastic support that Pope Pius XI gave to Mussolini in 1929, at the time of the 'Conciliation' between the Italian state and the Vatican. It has been written that: 'Conciliation was probably the most important contribution to the consolidation of the Fascist government in power on a wider basis of support and consent'.[25] Now, at St Peter's Italian Church black shirts and fascist insignia were openly displayed during mass. Some traditional Catholic holidays became occasions for religious, political and social events. For instance, the feast of the Assumption (15 August) was chosen by the Italian Fascists in Britain for their annual reunion. The *Fascio* took over any private institution of the community, as well as controlling the public agencies.

Thus, the *fascistizzazione* – the fascist transformation – of Italians in Britain was awaiting completion when the invasion of Ethiopia was launched. Against the 'iniquitous' sanctions a formidable campaign was set off by the Italian embassy in London, in which emotional appeals to national pride and patriotism had the effect of mobilising virtually the whole community in support of Mussolini's action. To people who had for so long been looked down as an inferior race by their British neighbours, those appeals touched sensitive nerves. The collection of monies and valuables, to be sent to Rome to counter the alleged stranglehold caused by the sanctions, organised by the *Fascio di Londra*, was highly successful. As a mild-mannered, pious and family-centred café owner wrote many years later:

It was not just the wealthy and the well-to-do who gave their gold to the motherland, but the humblest workers, too, contributed some items of that precious metal: a brooch, a pair of cuffs-links ... In those stormy circumstances it was obvious that Italians in Britain were behind the Fascist government. Such solidarity had never been shown before to any Italian government ... With the victorious conclusion of the Abyssinian war, the Italian community in London became more united than ever before; even those who had had little sympathy for Fascism, now appeared to have changed their minds and began to participate in all patriotic activities which were organised every now and then.[26]

The Second World War and the Italians as 'Enemy Aliens'

A consequence of Germany's sudden invasion of Denmark and Norway, in April 1940, was the growing concern about the role of potentially disloyal people in case of an assault on Britain. The ensuing 'fifth column panic'[27] was fed by alarmist and xenophobic articles in the popular press. In April 1940, John Boswell wrote that:

Every Italian colony in Great Britain ... is a seething cauldron of smoking Italian politics. Black Fascism. Hot as hell. Even the peaceful, law-abiding proprietor of the back-street coffee-shop bounces into a fine patriotic frenzy at the sound of Mussolini's name.[28]

The tone changed into derision after Mussolini declared war on Britain and France, on 10 June, and many Italians were swiftly rounded up and interned as 'enemy aliens'. 'Laughter was the commonest reaction to Italy's entrance into the war' – the 'London Diarist' wrote in the *New Statesman and Nation* – 'Why was this? Partly, no doubt, because owing to a silly British convention Italy suggests macaroni and ice creams and is funny in itself'.[29]

Laughter was not the only reaction, but contempt as well. A. P. Herbert had a satirical little poem published in the *Sunday Graphic* (30 June) entitled 'Wopships', in which the protagonists were 'Captain B. Spaghetti' and 'Admiral Vermicelli'. On the same maritime note a cartoon in the *Daily Mail* (12 June) showed a wretched mustachioed ice-cream street vendor saying: 'Me – I tink I scuttle da barrow.' And in the same paper, the day before, another mustachioed, paunchy Italian – a waiter – told a customer: 'Sorry, sir, no spaghetti, only tripes and onions now.'

Only two days after Italy's entry into the war, Mass-Observation carried out a survey on 'attitudes to Italy'. It was noted that 'before Italy declared war, there already existed a large contempt for the Italians' and that 'leadership has actually increased and augmented this contempt, with the ready response of mass rationalisation'.[30] In the *Daily Mirror* of 11 June, the Report remarked:

> the Italians are referred to as aligators, baboons, 'The Italian Monkey' doubters, hoverers, foopads, clumsy louts, borgeas [sic], jackals, peanuts, etc. Most pages of the paper contain such crack, and Victor Emanuel [the king of Italy] is referred to as a 'Regal Peanut, falsely credited with a mind of his own', dwarfed and stunted, pint-sized, little more than knee high, less than a 'decent sized snake', and with conscience, like 'a spreading yellow stain'.[31]

To boost morale the authorities may have openly concurred in the peddling of a contemptuous image of the Italians and their king for home consumption, but in a directive to the BBC on British propaganda against Italy the Italian Section of the Ministry of Information instructed to 'use sarcasm, irony and wit, but never insults, taunts or vulgar abuse. Avoid political speculation on the King, crown Prince, royal family, Pope, Vatican and regular army'.[32] And at the end of the document the Ministry stressed that the BBC should bear in mind:

> That the Italians have a keen sense of humour – especially of the ridiculous;
> That they are logical;
> That they are jealous;
> That they are 'touchy';
> That they are impressionable;
> That they are unsentimental, except in intimate private and family affairs;
> That such sentiment is then really a passion;
> That it has its expression in nostalgia for home – and for peace to enjoy the home.[33]

Public opinion throughout the war appears to have manifested an ambiguous perception of Italians as a whole, as the outspoken early contempt was mellowed by a degree of condescension and even sympathy. It is, once again, Mass-Observation that gives us glimpses of this. Two surveys on attitudes to some foreign nationalities were carried out in January 1941 and April 1943. In the former, 20 per cent of the interviewees thought that Italians were 'cowards', but a close 19 per cent regarded them as 'peace-loving'; 12 per cent thought they were 'lazy or easy-going', but they were also considered 'attractive or likeable' (11 per cent) and 'cultural or artistic' (7 per cent).[34] In April 1943 many of the same individuals interviewed in 1941 were asked to express their views on the allies, but – oddly enough – also on the Italians. The purpose of the new exercise was to monitor any change in perceptions during the past two years. Here are the synoptic responses on the Italians: 'Favourable', 21% in 1941, now at 41%; 'Half and half', 23% then, against 26% now; 'Unfavourable', 37% then, against 19% now; 'Vague', 19% in 1941, 14% now. Mass-Observation commented:

> Favourable opinion about Italians has doubled since 1941 and unfavourable opinion halved. They are now relatively popular compared with some of the allied groups. In 1943 people no longer look upon them as dangerous enemies, sympathy comes to the fore and those who made generalisations about them two years ago can now consider them as individuals without feelings of disloyalty. Many regard them with great sympathy and liking, feeling sorry for them and their fate in Libya and Tripolitania.
> The Italians are mostly pictured as a peace-loving, lazy sort of people, dragged into the war by Germany ... Those whose feelings are mixed are often not hostile to the Italians, but feel that Italy has betrayed the traditional friendship between herself and this country. They often look on the Italians as incompetent fighters though pleasant enough socially.[35]

These mixed perceptions of Italians were probably also influenced by the direct experience a growing number of British people had of Italian POWs: some 40,000 of them had been brought to Britain by the time of the 1943 Mass-Observation survey. The prisoners were often appreciated for their hard-working qualities and their bright side (at least until their spirits deteriorated in the last stages of their captivity), but prejudices were also enhanced when the POWs were judged as spineless men, only too happy to have been taken far from the battlefields.

As for the Italians' self-perceptions during the war, the picture is much more complicated because the issue of divided loyalties was dramatically sharpened. Most first-generation immigrants, even those who had shown sympathy and support toward Fascism, were now confused and despondent. The sense of elation and pride they experienced when Mussolini was feared and respected was now destroyed. Their traditional pessimistic and resigned attitude to events concerning their lives resurfaced, eager to find some relief within family bonds and affections. Unfortunately, most family networks had been shattered by the policy of internment and deportation and many families had suffered terrible losses. In any case, but particularly for those who were suffering most, religious faith provided a degree of consolation and hope.

On the other hand, the self-esteem that Mussolini's success in building an empire and in challenging the United Kingdom had engendered in young British-born Italians, could not be easily brushed aside. This sentiment was entangled with their resentment not to be fully accepted as members of British society. As the Italian-Scot (as he defines himself, rather than as a Scottish-Italian), Joe Pieri has recently written:

> Despite my almost purely Scottish lifestyle, I just did not feel British. Almost daily I was reminded of the fact that I was an Italian ... Italy's invasion of Abyssinia and Mussolini's intervention in the Spanish Civil War had created a wave of ill feeling against Italy in the general population. The childhood taunts of 'dirty wee Tally' had given way to more frequent, forceful and insulting remarks about my nationality ... 'Dirty wee Tally' had given way to 'Tally bastard' ... These remarks bothered me no more than the weather did, they were part and parcel of my environment.[36]

The Changing Views in the Post-War Years

Early in 1948 there was a frequent correspondence between the Home Office and the Ministry of Labour (and Social Security) on the subject of employment of foreign labour. This is what an official of the Home Office's Aliens Department wrote:

> I have been given to understand that the order of intake of foreign labour is approximately Poles, Balts, Ukranians, other DPs (Displaced Persons), *Volksdeutsche*, Italians and finally Germans [ex-POWs]. I have never been at all happy about the proposal to take in male Italians in preference to Germans and I had it in mind that at a suitable season some representations might be made on this subject.[37]

The 'suitable season' did not take long to arrive. Five months after that exchange, the Permanent Secretary of the Home Office (Sir Alexander Maxwell) wrote to the Permanent Secretary of the Ministry of Labour:

> If some 10,000 or more able-bodied Germans of proved usefulness are sent back to Germany willy-nilly and there is subsequently an importation of Italians, such a policy would, I think, be difficult to defend. The Home Office experience suggests that Italian immigrants do not, generally speaking, make any valuable contribution to the economy of the country. May I take it that the recruitment of Italians is unlikely?[38]

The answer from Sir Godfrey H. Ince was as follows:

> I quite appreciate the embarrassment which would be caused if Italians were imported after Germans had been sent back, and you may certainly take it that we have no present intentions of recruiting Italians, apart from a small number of highly skilled Italians which we might recruit for special industries such as foundries.[39]

In fact, between 1948 and 1968, some 150,000 Italians came to Britain, in what can be referred to as the only true mass emigration from Italy to Britain. At first most were recruited through intergovernmental bulk schemes to provide labour to particular sectors of the economy. Later, individual immigration through 'work permits' prevailed. Despite the early requests for northern workers, the vast majority of the newcomers were from the south, thus introducing an important differentiation in the regional and cultural make-up of the Italian community in Britain.

1948, the year of the exchange of letters I have mentioned, was also the year in which the first post-war general election was held in Italy. It was a crushing victory for the conservative Christian Democratic Party against the left-wing alliance of Communists and Socialists. The Roman Catholic Church was now to influence all aspects of social life, as it had never done before.

As far as our immigrants were concerned, notably those who came under the bulk schemes, the new political climate of the Cold War saw the Italian and British authorities acting together in vetting the would-be emigrants. The Roman Catholic Church concurred in this by providing relevant information at the parish level. Meanwhile, the London-based Italian clergy and missionaries launched a newspaper, *La Voce degli Italiani* [The Voice of the Italians]. The leading article in the first issue – January 1948 – made it clear that patriotism and traditional faith went hand in hand. Its message was addressed to wherever 'there was an Italian heart still throbbing for the two loves of God and Country'.[40] The paper would not discuss politics, it was also stated; but only a few months later, as the result of the general election was known, it was written that: 'despite our poverty, we know how to resist the temptations of the devil in Communist attire'.[41] The paper warned the immigrants of the danger of living in a secularised, protestant country: their identity as Italians was at risk. Particular concern was expressed with reference to the many young women recruited for work in various industries and services.[42]

In the 1950s and 1960s, as the numbers of Italians increased and spread, Roman Catholic missions mushroomed: from Birmingham to Manchester, from Bedford to Bristol, from Peterborough to Nottingham, from Swindon to Leicester. In London a complex organisation was set up: the 'Scalabrini Centre', containing a church and the premises for various social activities. However, if religion acted as a major centripetal force to community life and cultural cohesion, centrifugal forces also came into play to undermine that cohesion: family and kinship bonding and *campanilismo* – i.e. the attachment and loyalty to one's birthplace: village, town or even region, which led the Italians to organise themselves into regional associations.

One common concern was for their children to learn the Italian language. Italian became a truly national language only after WWII. The vast majority of immigrants arriving in the 1950s and 1960s from southern Italy only spoke their local languages, but wanted their children to learn Italian for three reasons: to preserve a common cultural identity within the family; to make sure that the children would maintain family ties with relatives back in Italy; and to provide a useful insurance to enable the children to adjust to social life in Italy, if (when?) the family decided to return there. The Italian State did make an important effort to meet the emigrants' request: teachers were recruited in Italy and sent throughout Britain to integrate the children's education with tuition of Italian language and institutions.

What about the British authorities' and public opinion's view of Italians in the post-war years? The disparaging comments exchanged in 1948 by government officials were not followed by criticism and hostility – with the only notable exception of the coal miners who refused to work with Italians, and scuppered the initiative (in the early 1950s). Only isolated instances of annoyance by members of the public were noted, for instance by the *Bedfordshire Times* on 25 November 1960,[43] when it was reported that Italians were 'voluble and highly excitable people' and 'ear-shattering neighbours'. The fact was that precisely when the ill-judged prophecy by government officials was made – in the summer of 1948 – an event took place, which was to shift the attention from the undesired but necessary Italians to the larger and more controversial inflow of immigrants: the *Empire Windrush* brought nearly 500 immigrants from the Caribbean to Britain. Since then, the growing number of West Indians, Africans, Indians and Pakistanis became the central issue of political and social life in Britain. The Italians became mere 'invisible immigrants'.

Epilogue

The Italians remained a largely self-contained, distinct group within British society. Their children became integrated – and even assimilated – in the host society. Some of them attained success and acclaim in many professions, but never lost sight of their ethnic origins. The overall image of the Italian community benefited from the economic and commercial success of its mother country, especially in the highly significant sectors of the motor-car and fashion industries, cinema and design. Italian food and drink were elevated to sophisticated status symbols – and became a bonus to Italian restaurants and cafés – thus renewing and invigorating the most traditional perception of Italians in Britain. While all this has been occurring over the past thirty years or so, the old-time immigration of poorly educated Italians came to an end. The newcomers have been mainly students, business people, clerical personnel for Italian private and public institutions, managers and professionals.

The *Voce degli Italiani* is still the main newspaper of the community. It caters chiefly for the older strands of Italian immigrants, but has widened its scope and now also promotes a more critical notion of Italian identity – that of a community which ought to push to strengthen its citizens' rights *vis-à-vis* the Italian State. By insisting on this common purpose, the newspaper is participating in – and reacting to – the debate on national identity which has been developing in Italy over the past ten years or so, wherein regional loyalties (especially in the north of the peninsula) appear to be undermining the very concept of a common Italian heritage.

These issues have raised the profile of both the old and new components of the Italian community in Britain, and reflect an important change of attitude and self-perceptions: the traditional vertical tensions between generations, regional origins and time of arrival in this country have been replaced by a horizontal differentiation among social and interest groups. The common note is no longer to be uniquely found in the three 'pillars' of religion, kinship and *campanilismo*, but also in the acknowledgement that people's ethnic roots are now intertwined with a sense of belonging to British society, in the wider context of European citizenship.

5

Narratives of Settlement: East Europeans in Post-War Britain

Inge Weber-Newth

> Well, I left the country, I can say for the only reason at all, because I thought I prefer to live in freedom, where I can live, work, think, and speak as I like, without any fear of persecution, and can say whatever I want to say, which in my opinion was not possible in the country where I lived. So, as Europe was divided, or going to be divided soon, we choose to go and seek freedom outside our own land. So in those days there were thousands upon thousands of people, mostly young and able to walk to get out.[1]

Since the fall of the Soviet Union in 1989 many East Europeans have left their home countries and come to Britain, some as illegal immigrants, some as seasonal workers, mostly to better their living standard. This east-west flow has increased since the accession of eastern European countries to the European Union. Their skills, diligence and preparedness for adaptation and to work for low wages have been widely appreciated.

Labour migration from eastern Europe to the UK is not a recent phenomenon: a relatively large number of East Europeans entered Britain as workers in the late 1940s, many of whom stayed and settled. The motivations for leaving their home countries was different to that for the current migration from the East, and are mainly linked to the political changes and circumstances at the time of the end of WWII.

This essay aims to provide an account of the life experiences of East Europeans who, at the end of the war, were living in camps in Germany and Austria as Displaced Persons (DPs) and were subsequently allowed entry into Britain under the European Volunteer Worker schemes 'Balt Cygnet' and 'Westward Ho!'. The main focus will be on how the immigrants reconstructed their lives in Britain within the framework provided by the

British Government. On the basis of written and oral sources, it will explore selected aspects that shaped the settlement process of this migrant population in the post-war period, with particular emphasis placed on the perspective of individual migrants. Taking their own perceptions into account, it will finally discuss whether the government's vision and its prognosis that Europeans were 'more easily assimilated than other foreign immigrants'[2] into British society proved applicable. However, the essay will begin with an outline of the political framework for the immigration of East Europeans and an assessment of the British Government's motives behind the decision to grant them entry.

Apart from a relatively small number of Jewish DPs it is estimated that about 10 million DPs from German occupied countries such as Soviet Union, Poland, the Ukraine, Yugoslavia, Czechoslovakia, France, Holland and Belgium found themselves in the occupied zones of Germany following the defeat of Nazi Germany. Most of the men and women categorised as DPs by the Allied forces had been deported from their home countries to work as forced labourers, mainly in agriculture and in heavy industry to boost the war production but also in private families. But certainly not all those classified as DPs were deported forced labourers. There were also tens of thousands of Ukrainians, Poles and Balts who had fled into Germany before the advancing Soviet armies in 1943 and 1944. Amongst the refugees were soldiers forced to join the 'Wehrmacht' and those who joined voluntarily, civilian collaborators with their families, and even suspected war criminals. Despite this diversity of background, the official DP status meant that all groups were subject to the same strategies and policies of the American and British occupying authorities.[3]

Extended repatriation programmes organised by the Military Governments and supported by teams of the United Nations Relief and Rehabilitation Administration (UNRRA), later superseded by the International Refugee Organization (IRO), did not have the anticipated results. Although nearly all Soviet DPs were repatriated by 1946, if necessary by force, only about 80% of the total DP population returned to their home countries. The remaining East Europeans refused, or were unable to return to their countries of nationality; their reasons ranging from personal experience of life under Soviet rule to traditional hatred of Russia or Communism, an uncertain economic future or fear of Soviet retribution for their political history. Thus, around 260,000 men, women and children from Eastern Europe stayed in the British Zone of Occupation until 1947 when both the possibility and assistance to emigrate were offered.

Britain initiated this process and was soon followed by Australia, Canada and the USA. Whilst defined resettlement schemes explicitly welcoming DPs as new settlers were announced by the USA, Britain was more cautious, initially not offering any prospects of naturalisation and reserving the right to return the immigrants – under certain circumstances – to the camp. The Government's decision to receive DPs from German camps was less intended as a resettlement scheme for the refugees but rather more an employment scheme which primarily served Britain's needs to overcome its economic and reconstruction problems in the post-war era.[4] Despite the employment of Italian and German Prisoners of War in agriculture and the return of millions of British soldiers, the need for additional labour was pressing and the lack of foreign exchange was severe. Rather than modernising old industries, the British government decided on a quick fix, namely to support the 'old' industries: mining, textile, steel and iron. Labour was also needed for auxiliary work in hospitals and the domestic areas, as the indigenous labour force was no longer keen to work in these low paid and unpleasant domains. They were promised a better life by the new post-war Labour Government which had indeed taken steps to improve social conditions, for example by reducing the weekly working hours and increasing the length of compulsory school attendance. The introduction of a comprehensive national health system was under way. British women who had so admirably supported the war efforts of their country were on the one hand no more prepared to extend their work beyond the immediate wartime efforts and on the other were officially encouraged to return to the traditional female domains and raise families. Thus, economic need coupled with a concern for a decline in the British population[5] made it possible to target a foreign work force for the identified 'undermanned industries'. After initial opposition from the Unions, the government received their final agreement in 1947, as the areas of recruitment, payment and working conditions were settled, ruling out any competition with the domestic work force. The contract for individual foreign workers was intended for a two year period and included a 'deportation clause' to allow workers to be sent back to Germany if they were in breach of their working conditions.

The government – influenced by contemporary ideas of eugenics – was keen to portray the DPs as 'ideal' and 'suitable' immigrants for Britain. Baltic women in particular were praised as 'good types', of 'good appearance', 'scrupulously clean', as an 'exceptionally healthy and fit body', in short, a group that would constitute 'a good and desirable element in our population'.[6] By implication, other potential immigrants, such as Jewish immigrants from concentration camps or West Indians and Asians from the British Empire were part of the less desired element that did not possess the right characteristics to assimilate well into British society. In fact, Black and Asian soldiers who had fought in the British Army were repatriated quickly after they had fulfilled their wartime duties.[7] Hence, by stating a clear preference for Europeans, the government's decision was not only a pragmatic decision to fill the gap in the domestic work force, but also a decision based on racial considerations.

The actual labour recruitment process was organised and carried out by officials of the Ministry of Labour mainly in the British, American and French zones of occupation. Following the government's policy, strict selection criteria based on suitability to work were applied. The decisive factors in the selection were the age (18-50 for men, 18-40 for women), physical fitness, manual skills and – due to the prevailing housing shortage – the single status of the recruits.[8] This process was supported by personal interviews and thorough medical examinations. Political screening was not given equal importance: checks were rushed and not carried out rigorously as Nazi supporters were able to slip through the net and enter Britain[9].

The first scheme, the so-called 'Balt Cygnet', targeted Baltic women for work in British hospitals, followed by the large 'Westward Ho! Scheme', which reached considerably more East European male than female workers for the 'undermanned industries'. On arrival in Britain the recruits received the new name 'European Volunteer Workers' (EVWs). Altogether the British government was able to recruit about 85,000 DPs under both schemes. This included more than 8,000 Ukrainian Prisoners of War of the 14th Waffen-SS, the so-called 'Galician Division'. They received permission from the War Office to enter the UK in 1947, directly from Italy where they were interned. In order to avoid their repatriation to Soviet territory they were officially given a status equivalent to European Volunteer Workers[10]. It was hoped that they would take the place of German Prisoners of War who were returning to Germany, mainly in agriculture.[11] The 115,000 Polish ex-servicemen who stayed in Britain as part of the Polish Resettlement Corps, although in a special position as non-labour migrants, added significantly to the post-war labour force. A fair proportion of the EVWs left Britain for other countries after their contractual obligations were fulfilled, although the majority stayed, usually in the region in which they initially took up their work.

Oral Sources

Whilst a number of publications have focused on policy, initial integration, welfare issues[12], and analysis of the historical-political contexts of the EVWs' recruitment and employment processes[13] there is very limited knowledge about the life-experience of the East Europeans in the specific regions or areas in which they worked and settled. An exception can be found in Bradford where thousands of East Europeans were recruited into the traditional textile industry. The Bradford Heritage Recording Unit (BHRU) was able to preserve interviews with East Europeans which had been recorded as part of a larger oral history project with different local migrant communities. Although carried out in Bradford, the interviews have a wider application for experiences made in similar areas of the textile region, as conditions were comparable. The next part of this essay includes an analysis of aspects of these recorded local life-experiences and also draws on the above-mentioned literature, archival sources and contemporary newspaper articles. Some interviews from other oral history projects[14] are also considered.

One obvious factor that most East European immigrants of the first generation in the BHRU sample have in common is the relative closeness of age: most were born between 1922-1926, meaning they were around 20 years old on arrival in the UK. The main body of the Bradford interviews with East Europeans were carried out in 1983 at a time when most immigrants were in their mid 50s and had spent about 35 years in the UK. Whilst it is not clear how the respondents were chosen for the project, they represent a cross section of the East European countries concerned. Reflecting the strengths of the communities in Bradford, the largest national group represented is from the Ukraine, followed by a smaller group of Poles and several individuals from Yugoslavia and the Baltic States. Not surprisingly, and in the nature of this local project, most interviewees are closely linked to their ethnic communities, though not necessarily presenting similar attitudes on all issues. We come across individuals who were formerly, or still were, active members of the communities, who played roles in churches, schools or in the wider community; individuals from outside the community – be it physically or intellectually – are not represented.[15]

Despite the diversity in terms of ethnic background the groups will be treated collectively as East Europeans – as they were subject to the government's programmes – though nuances in national background become apparent in the narratives on several issues. The obvious dominance of male voices in the interviews is a result of the gender ratio amongst the recruited EVW workers: only one in four of them was female.

It is noticeable that the interviewers on the project are members of the Bradford community, with knowledge of the culture and history of their respondents: they have an awareness of national references and the language in question. All interviews appear to have the same pattern: based upon a traditional oral history approach, they follow questions starting with childhood memories, and covering the subsequent main stations in life chronologically. Despite the obvious restrictions of this method, the interviews provide interesting insights into perceptions of past experience and contemporary community life. It is also noticeable that certain themes did not need much prompting to trigger memories and generate vivid accounts. The chosen structured approach does, however, allow for comparisons of common and diverse experiences amongst the interviewees. Thus the main focus is on the themes that are well remembered in the narratives and relevant for this context: initial experiences in hostels and at work, the private settling process, their perceived reception by the locals, community activities and the respondents' relationship with their countries of origin. The set of interviews carried out by the author of this essay with German women who were also recruited for work in the textile industry under 'Westward HO!',[16] followed a more open life-story approach. The aim was to generate narratives with little intervention from the interviewer during the main stage of the interview. Only in a second phase were specific questions aimed at clarification asked.

Irrespective of the methods applied, either in the Bradford interviews or those from the more recent study, they did not serve to establish 'objective' facts, but to explore how the settlement process was remembered by the migrants themselves. Despite the diversity of individually experienced lives, certain trends emerge. These are specific to this particular migrant population, which settled under specific historical circumstances.

Early Experiences: Life in Communal Accommodation

Initially life in Britain started for the newly recruited European Volunteer Workers in communal accommodation. Hostels were made available, often in the shape of Nissen huts, army barracks, ex POW camps, or even large converted Victorian houses. They were usually located near the work placements, mainly outside the local communities, and provided the essentials: a bed in a shared room, communal washing facilities and meals for a relatively reasonable weekly charge.[17] First impressions of Britain – mostly as a gloomy and dirty place – and the first accommodation were well remembered. However, responses concerning accommodation were mixed, obviously depending on previous experiences. A few expressed gratitude for what they were allocated: 'It was nice to see that [we were treated] as humans, not just as a crowd, homeless and helpless'[18] or 'I was very surprised in hostel, we got towel and lovely bed and bathroom and everything we never had for a long time'.[19] Others remembered everyday-life in communal accommodation more critically, even comparing the conditions with DP camps in Germany, as it was surrounded by 'big barbed wire, about six foot high, "oh", I said, "it's from one camp to another camp", you know, you're disappointed'.[20] The lack of electric light, fights over bathroom and toilets, crowded conditions in dormitories and a lack of privacy were also mentioned: 'three beds in one room, we could not turn …

no wardrobe ... everything in suitcase'.[21] 'We had a small room, which was four of us crammed in.'[22] According to Kay and Miles[23] conditions and standards in hostels were indeed the subject of serious and frequent complaints. Improvements were made after official criticism from organisations such as the Women's Voluntary Service and the International Refugee Organization as they were also in the interest of the Ministry of Labour and National Service. It was realised that full production could not be expected unless the standards of accommodation in camps and hostels were raised.[24]

Clearly, the accommodation in separate hostels for males and females (initially also for married couples) did not contribute to the development of the 'normal life' the government had anticipated.[25] Reaction to this strict policy on the part of the workers was to abandon the hostels and to move into privately rented rooms, particularly when closer relationships between men and women were formed. The many male-only hostels were faced with additional problems caused by violence after heavy alcohol consumption, apparently a well-known problem of hostel life and still remembered: 'We used to fight [...] a few times, police has come, you know because when foreigners fight, they really fight.' According to this Serb man the reason was mainly jealousy amongst the men, as it was 'all because of girls'.[26] However, a big obstacle to the smooth and swift assimilation anticipated by the government, was caused by the location of hostels outside small communities. This spatial segregation of the EVWs from the British population did not encourage any mixing with locals and led to a perception of separateness. A government official commented self-critically: 'So long as these men are segregated in hostels, making their own meals and talking their own language, they will continue to feel foreign and to be thought of as foreign.'[27] Tannahill holds the 'lack of sex-life, combined with isolation from the world beyond the hostel-gate' responsible for the reported excessive drinking and the relatively high rate of mental health problems and suicides amongst male EVWs.[28] Kino also relates occurring mental weaknesses to external factors such as adjusting problems, language difficulties and loneliness.[29] Problems related to feelings of isolation and segregation applied particularly to those EVWs who remained in hostels for many years. Due to the housing shortages in some areas, problems remained well into the 1950s, in some cases even longer. A few EVWs got used to this arrangement and seemed to feel quite content not having to care for themselves and being amongst their fellow countrymen.[30] Some even made this their home to which personal touches were added: 'Our camp was always kept nice and clean and flowerbeds appeared in front of the huts and a miniature castle was made with a moat and a draw-bridge.'[31]

Employment and Reception

EVWs were first placed in four undermanned economic sectors: about 55% of the men worked in agriculture and 18% in coal mining, while the majority of women worked in the textile industries (61%) and in domestic work (31%).[32] These were the areas identified by the government as difficult to fill with the local work force as they were physically strenuous, often hazardous to health or in uncomfortable environments: involving long working hours, little free time, with shift work and low wages.

Interviews confirm that these jobs were not seen as simple or easy. Work in spinning, for example, demanded a great deal of concentration, speed and skill. If the concentration lapsed 'the fingers got burnt'. The environment was hot and humid, the machines produced a lot of dust, sometimes it 'snowed cotton-flakes'.[33] A male worker from the Ukraine describes his work environment in wool combing:

> It was a dirty job, smelly job, you know and when the water is boiling and you are washing raw wool in that, so you can imagine how pleasant a smell it was. And especially when we got human hair from Korea, you know during Korea war, and it was filthy that hair. Some people were off for three or four weeks poorly with that smell.[34]

A Serb talks about the conditions in a Scottish coal mine:

> It was one of the old, old mines, probably that had worked for a hundred years before it, it was a bit wet. I remember that – cases where I started to work on the coal-face, it was only – less than three foot high, in some cases just twenty inch high, with maybe four or five inch of water lying on the ground.[35]

But work in agriculture was not seen as romantic either: 'There was a lot of milking cows and my hand was swollen from milking.' After he left this farm the Ukrainian worker was sent to another farm 'and I was working on that farm and I was sleeping in very damp room ... during winter time and I got flu'.[36]

Despite the fact that work was mostly described as unpleasant, even characterised as 'a form of serfdom'[37] working morale was high. As EVWs came here literally 'with only what [they] were wearing'[38] they were very motivated to work in order to achieve their material goals: they felt they had to 'get things together, and quick, so the only thing to do was to work, and to work hard',[39] and particularly when 'you have little children so you wasn't objecting to a little overtime. When you come home and three of them lifting up their feet and showing you holes in their shoes, you were glad to have an hour or two overtime'.[40] This, some realised themselves, was often misunderstood by the local people 'they thought we were workaholics ... bloody hell, have you got wedded to the job ... they joked'.[41] They certainly held a reputation as good workers as the voice of a British contemporary worker shows: 'We, the English people, were content to work five days a week all year round but some of the foreign workers would work Saturday, Sunday and they'd add another day. [...] The Eastern Europeans would work every hour that god sends.'[42] This had an effect on the general industrial relations and 'the antagonism started to creep in'[43] particularly with the introduction of piecework. EVWs were accused of ignoring the unions, not becoming members and threatening the negotiated productivity by overproducing. No wonder that 'the bosses preferred to employ these people who were willing to work dreadfully long hours'.[44]

In the following narrative a Ukrainian male mill worker, not unionised, gives an impression of the industrial relationship between the EVWs and the local workers and the relationship with their employer:

> George Garnett, of Apperley Bridge in Bradford, it was a very, very good firm ... they had a very good reputation, not only in England but in Europe, United States, Canada and the Middle East and Far East, as far as I know. [...] He employed more or less mostly Ukrainians, altogether about three hundred and twenty. Three hundred and twenty ... all DPs, Displaced Persons from Germany. [...] Sometimes ... specially the old people ... we had to understand the old people. As far as I know, we were younger than the others ... er, English friends, but after a few months, so they found ... we found the friends altogether. They understand us, very nice people, but in some cases, well, most every ... in every-day life we were involved ... just 'why, what are you doing here? Why don't you go home?' and then after discussing with him personally, so he understand, and took our view very nicely. And then what was the most important thing, you see, he told the truth about us among the British people. That was a good idea from his side of view, to get the knowledge from us first and then to make the so-called distribution all over the British people so they knew very well. As far as I know, the Ukrainians were very good workers. They never been late, they never been out of work or lazy, so they done a good job for the firm, and the firm, special George Garnett himself and his son, was very nice. They were very friendly at that time.[45]

And another quote which summarises the self-perception of the East Europeans as workers: 'of course, you see, our people, they have been very good workers and they keeped each day to come to work. No poorly, [they] know discipline and that was exactly wanted. They give very good production [...] they always satisfied with us'.[46]

Such eagerness, probably also coupled with the wish to be seen as diligent immigrants, made the British workers, who held strong traditional views on industrial relations, suspicious of their foreign co-workers; their attitudes were often seen by British colleagues as not showing enough solidarity with them.[47] In fact most EVWs were not used to industrial work at all. Apart from a few highly educated people from the urban elites, they came predominantly from families with smallholdings in rural, non-industrialised areas and were thus unfamiliar with unionisation. Processes like 'clocking in'[48] or having set breaks were initially unknown. Even 30 years later workers remember the strictly regulated work days with frequent breaks for tea and toilet as a cultural novelty of their early work experience in Britain.

The high proportion of foreign workers in the mills gave rise to some remarks amongst British workers who felt that the place was 'full of foreigners,'[49] and several interviewees say that there was a lot of talking behind their backs, but nobody mentioned open conflict. 'They used to not understand us, you know and a lot of people was not friendly at all [...] sometime they shout and tell you to go back home, you know.'[50] Others remember the work atmosphere as generally friendly and felt well treated.[51] Particularly the work atmosphere in the coal mines is remembered fondly, characterised by comradeship and friendship.[52]

Considerable effort was put into informing the local population about the reason for the arrival of the EVWs and stressing their economic value. This was generally supported by the press. For example, the popular magazine *Picture Post* published sympathetic articles on European workers. One reported on a visit to a German DP camp about Balts who are 'physically fine and hungry for work' just waiting to be admitted into Britain to 'help solve the manpower problems'[53], followed up in a second article after arrival in Britain. Ex-DPs are depicted as happy and content workers who 'don't grumble', who 'know their place in a long queue' and who are 'hardy, keen and cheerful', taking 'care of their huts, canteens and gardens' and 'keen to learn English'.[54] The *Yorkshire Observer* devoted a three-part series on EVWs after allegations of favouritism at work and in housing were made against them. It takes a clear stance on the side of the EVWs, asking whether 'Bradford's lack of understanding of the foreign workers in the city is threatening to corrupt the harmony with which the strangers from European countries who have tried to fit themselves into English life'.[55] Similarly, on issues arising over the EVWs entitlement to rations and accommodation, the

Government appealed to local communities to extend their 'traditional custom of offering friendship to people coming to live in this country'.[56]

Whilst stressing the economic benefits of the EVWs for society, it seems that government agencies did not provide the public with enough detailed information about the different national or political backgrounds, as general knowledge remained limited.[57] Colloquial speech reflected the ignorance: migrants were often uniformly referred to as Poles since they were amongst the first to arrive (as part of the Polish re-settlement scheme), but also as Russians, an image particularly offensive to those who had fled the Russians. Contemporary newspaper articles characterise the reaction of the local population towards the East Europeans generally as 'suspicious' and 'indifferent'[58] as 'apathetic' and 'without effusion'.[59] Interviewees also talk of distant relationships between them and their neighbours, mentioning that they have 'never been invited to the house of an English person'.[60] Other interviewees remember not being made welcome outside the workplace: 'Some of the pubs wouldn't allow us to go in for dinner and very often you could find, particularly in the Barnsley area, that the 'Poles' are not allowed in door of pubs.'[61] It appears that this form of hostility towards foreigners was not a rare occurrence and not restricted to this particular regional area or to East Europeans. Similar experiences were noted at the time amongst other national groups, such as the Irish or the Germans.[62] However, only a few years later, with the arrival of migrants from the Commonwealth, public attitude towards Europeans shifted. In the Bradford area the Pakistanis were now seen as the 'unwanted'. In this the locals were supported by the East Europeans who also identified the newcomers as 'the other'. This constructed division includes the perception that EVWs were treated differently by government agencies whereas

> Pakistanis, Indians, when they came to England, they had courses, they were helping them about informing them about way of life in England, but when we came to England the Ukrainian community, Czech community, Estonian, Latvian, Lithuanian, nobody help us. We had to find everything, we had to find ourselves, nobody did help us[63]

or, 'there were no special classes, special schools or something for us. [...] We had to do it on our own, without any help at all'.[64] In fact, government assistance for the EVWs was provided but ceased after their two-year contract came to an end and they were allowed to move freely on the labour market.

Getting Settled: Buying Their Own Home

The housing provided did not stop some female EVWs from leaving the communal living arrangements early in order to be more independent. They preferred to care for themselves, or to share with a girlfriend or boyfriend. Despite a general shortage of accommodation, certain regions – such as Lancashire and Yorkshire – were less affected. Here rooms to rent and old Victorian houses to buy were both available, due to pre-war industrial decline and a shrinking population.[65] Often a deposit of £100 was enough to secure a modest house in need of renovation (the average weekly wage for female workers being £4.50-5.50). Typically these were small terraced houses, two-up-two-down without an inside toilet. Sometimes old large houses were just right for a larger group of EVWs to buy jointly. Local and regional newspapers reported as early as 1949 on the immense interest of EVWs to buy their own property.[66]

> The mill folk of Oldham, England, thrifty people by nature, are rubbing their eyes in bewilderment at the financial wizardry of the European workers who were imported into town to learn the cotton trade and help the Lancashire exports. There are about a thousand of them in the Oldham area now. Eighteen months ago, they were arriving in the town in small, shepherded groups – confused, penniless, unhappy. They spoke little or no English, carried all they owned in the world in one small bag or paper parcel. Today they are acknowledged to be hard working skilful textile operatives. They dress well. They have plenty of money, sometimes carried about with them in sizeable rolls and wads, though a few have now agreed to trust the British post-office. Most amazing of all, they are buying their own houses at an ever-increasing rate. There have been many marriages amongst them and it is estimated that about one hundred houses have so far been bought in the Oldham area – for big cash deposits.[67]

Owning their home had a great significance for immigrants: It served as a visible expression of personal achievement and embodied financial security: 'when I first came to Britain I felt like the poorest man ... but the fact that you have a house ... you never felt penniless,'[68] says a Yugoslav. How the EVWs achieved their goals financially was hotly speculated on by the locals and rumours of favouritism flourished. The *Yorkshire Observer* tackled the question 'how they can get houses when we have been living in the same drab, back-to-back streets all our lives' by offering the following explanation:

So many of them scraped and saved every penny, sacrificing smoking, drinking, cinemas, and even bus fares when their destination was in walking distance. From estate agents, insurance men, solicitors and others in close contact with the foreigners, I heard remarkable tales of grit, thrift and cheap living with one thing in mind: a house of their own.[69]

This enormous frugality was linked to shrewd financial calculation, for example by buying large houses and renting out several rooms to pay for the loan, or as described in the words of a Polish worker:

We used to put my wage away in savings and we used to live on my wife's wage and whatever expenditure was to be made out of that. [...] We saved like mad and we got a back-to-back cottage in Walker Street, Green Lanes [Bradford], it cost £350, - we had to put down £150, - the rest was over fifteen or twenty years. To us it was a palace at the time.[70]

Many interviewees remember feelings of jealousy and envy amongst the locals towards their achievements[71] but – in the eyes of a Ukrainian worker – it was simply the result of contrasting life-styles between them and 'the English', as 'they just eat and drink and they don't save nothing'.[72] This emphasis on home ownership is indicated by the fact that by 1960 nearly all immigrants in the Bradford area had bought their own home.[73]

Family, Language and Identity

Marriages were usually entered within the first year of arrival, often after a very short period of courting. The most favoured choice of partner was within the individuals' own national group. However, the uneven gender balance within the East European migrant communities made marriages with other 'foreign' women recruited from Italy, Germany and Austria also very popular. Unions between some East European men and southern Italian women[74] were seen as a good match since both partners shared the Catholic religion and similar, more traditional family values with clearly defined gender roles. Generally 'marriages outside the community were frowned upon'.[75] According to Tannahill, unions between local British women and East European men proved less successful.[76] The different religions, a 'tendency of the British wife not to pay too much attention to cooking' and often 'excessive drinking' were blamed for the failure of these marriages. He also stresses an 'over-developed national feeling' on the part of the husband as the reason for the many break ups of these marriages.[77] His observation matches the comments made by some of the non-British women. They expressed feelings of isolation as their husbands would spend a lot of time amongst men of their own national background, either in clubs or at home. A German woman complained: 'He always brought home Poles. It was like a hostel here, always strangers around ... and they only spoke Polish.'[78] Another German woman claimed that: 'The Ukrainians liked to go out ... and when he wasn't too tired he went to the club.'[79] Apart from leading often separate social lives, interviews also suggest that wives – regardless of their nationality – were expected to adapt to 'his' lifestyle, by learning 'his' language[80] and learning to cook 'his' meals 'borscht, pyrohy, holuptsi, kapustniak, I make all sorts'.[81] The women interviewed did not seem to object and are in agreement that their husbands supported the family well, that they were very ambitious, diligent and after all that they 'achieved more than those who were married to the English'.[82]

The nationality of the spouse affected how well the East Europeans acquired English language competence which in turn impacted on the kind of job they were able to carry out once restrictions on their working were lifted. Generally, the integration of EVWs worked better where the spouse was British and where English became the family language. However, this often meant dropping the 'mother tongue'. For most East Europeans this was not the preferred choice as keeping the native language alive within the family became an important goal. A Ukrainian man acknowledges that 'Scottish girls who married Ukrainians speak not bad Ukrainian'.[83]

Equally, if not more important, was that the children would grow up speaking Ukrainian and being knowledgeable in Ukrainian history and culture. At the beginning of the 1950s Ukrainian communities started setting up Saturday schools in order to cater for the needs of the second generation at school age. By 1965 there were about 5,000 children attending 43 Ukrainian schools spread over the communities in Britain and supported by a European network of Ukrainian teachers.[84] An interviewee, involved in the foundation of Saturday schools and the local and national Ukrainian Teacher's organisation, explains the demands on the children and benefits of these arrangements:

> They have to spend five days in English school which is very, very hard job, and Saturdays and Sundays are the only free days to do their work for the English school [...] we chose Saturdays, so they had six days teaching. So they might say 'Oh, I've got a headache, we haven't got enough time to do our English study' [...] its probably just a few hours on Sunday [left] because they used to go to church, you see, and then, after twelve o'clock, they came back, have dinner,

have a chat with the family or friends ... and then they started again to have to do English work and to do Ukrainian work as well. You see, it's the most important thing, and ... er but the majority of our children realise that, never mind what we do we go to the Ukrainian school and we get better knowledge of Ukrainian life and better understanding of father and mother. [...] And then when years passed on, so our children went to training colleges and of course were educated in modern techniques in England and then we took them to teach the youngsters.[85]

Most community members followed this bilingual approach against the contemporary trend and ignored warnings that their children might suffer educationally by learning two languages simultaneously. Their tenacity was finally rewarded by very good school achievements: 'Children who attended Ukrainian Saturday school more or less passed 11+.'[86]

The theme of passing on language and identity to their children runs through nearly all interviews with East Europeans, not just the Ukrainians. Other national communities also established their Saturday schools and encouraged their children to learn Polish, Serbo-Croat, Latvian or Lithuanian and take classes in national history, geography and general culture.

Despite the willingness of many non-British women to adapt to their East European husbands' native language, several women seem to have used their native language as well. A particularly interesting, but not unusual, language situation emerged in mixed households where both parents were of different nationalities and children grew up with two different home languages using English only as the public language outside the home. A recruited German woman explains: 'Table-language was German because my mother came here and stayed for thirteen years. And my husband spoke Polish with his friends ... and my children learned Polish as well as they went to Sunday school.'[87] Or an Italian woman married to a Ukrainian husband speaks about the achievement of her son: 'I forced him to speak Italian and he passed at university level.'[88] In general children of EVW families grew up multilingual but, due to the strong orientation towards the East European side, members of the second generation regard themselves firstly as Ukrainian or Polish.

As for the first generation: ten years after their arrival in Britain nearly 80% of the immigrants spoke either no English, or in a limited or insufficient way.[89] The interviews, whether carried out in 1983, 1988 or in 1998 testify that language remained a problem for many throughout their lives and contributed largely to the restricted possibilities of economic progress.

Naturalisation and Nationalism

Despite the fact that labour controls were removed in 1949, a relatively large proportion (approximately 25%) of the EVWs did not settle in Britain but migrated further to North America within ten years of arrival. Countries like Canada and the USA had fewer restrictions on economic advancement and promised a generally higher standard of living.[90] Another important factor, particularly for Lithuanians and Estonians, of whom nearly 50% left, was the existence of large migrant communities overseas and the wish to join relatives there, because 'when you had connection with people ... there were better conditions, they treat you better, not just ... [there] you're Canadian or American. So they decided going there, all young people, healthy, plenty of work, they are buying of sorts of land'.[91] Political conflict within the own national organisations caused by the arrival of the ex-servicemen may also have contributed. A witness recalls:

> by 1949, the end of 1949, the Association of Ukrainians split in two, and another organisation was formed, the Federation of Ukrainians in Great Britain. The majority of people that came to the Federation were [of] Greek Orthodox [religion] and Eastern Ukrainian people ... and they were mostly intelligent people, elderly people, educated people. And then you see, many people emigrated. Most of the intelligent people that came to the Federation and split from the Association, they emigrated to Canada and to America. They were poets, they were actors, they were teachers, I know one judge from Eastern Ukraine. And we were left – the younger generation at that time – were left without seniors, without intellectuals, without leading persons, personalities.[92]

By 1951 a diminished but self-contained population of about 30,000 Ukrainians was left in Britain with the largest communities in Bradford, Halifax, Oldham and Manchester.

The extent of naturalisation by the mid 1950s across the East European communities was less than 5%.[93] Although more EVWs obtained British citizenship in the course of their lives, this figure remained low and is reflected in the interviews in which loyalty to national backgrounds is stressed. A Pole says: 'I don't think we can ever become English'[94]; a Ukrainian: 'We should retain our own identity as long as possible. When we pass away, well, I don't know how far the young generation will go, perhaps third generation [...] go to Canada, and the Ukrainians are there for almost two hundred years but have retained their identity.'[95]; a Serb: 'You can't change your nationality [...] I just can't change myself ... even if I get nationality ... I'll still be a foreigner, I'll still be a Serb ... they'll call me British but I won't be British.'[96]

In comparison, a minority voice of a Yugoslav who married a British wife and took up citizenship:

> I came to the conclusion [in 1952] that if I am to stay here I'd better become a citizen and also if I am to progress in that job I had just started I'd better take up [citizenship] and change my name by deed of poll. And I have become known as Mr. Peters [formerly Petrovitch] [...] I didn't like to be different [...] I always wanted to integrate [...] and wanted to be belong totally here, and I mean totally.[97]

The general refusal by the East Europeans to obtain British citizenship reveals a strong feeling of belonging and loyalty to their East European origin. After decades of life in Britain, nationalist sentiments are still prevalent in all interviews with East Europeans, and are particularly forcefully articulated within the Ukrainian group. Although the tragic history of the country's divisions and occupations can be held responsible, perceptions of the occupying forces – Nazi Germany and the Soviet Union – tend to be one-sided: despite the sufferings caused during Nazi occupation (1941-1944) the Germans are not judged as severely as the Russians. Several East Europeans talk about their deportation to Germany as slave labourers and their experience in Germany but the narratives vary, ranging from depictions of exploitation and abuse to those of 'normal' work relationships. A female Ukrainian who worked for a German family explains: 'I couldn't say they had been bad to me, I had plenty to eat', whereas other girls who worked in a factory 'had hardly anything to eat, only soup and soup'.[98] Several interviewees were spared the experience of forced deportation to Germany, amongst them obviously those who had welcomed the invading Nazi troops. It is clear from the interviews that they were soldiers who had voluntarily joined the 'Galician Division' of the SS.

Even though East Europeans have come with a variety of different political experiences to the West, they are united in their strong anti-Communism. Coercive measures carried out by the Soviets, such as deportation to Siberia, although experienced by just a few interviewees, run through the interviews as part of the collective hatred of Soviet rule. Stories of the gulag and the famine of 1932 have since become the symbol for the oppressive Soviet regime. In particular the so-called 'man-made' famine which, as a consequence of Stalin's politics of forced collectivisation, led to the death of millions of East Ukrainians, is firmly rooted in the national consciousness and often described as the 'Ukrainian Holocaust'. A witness remembered:

> My sister died in 1932, and then my father died in 1933, that was half-starvation, because in our town you can see in a morning thousands lie down on the pavement dead. So every morning is lorry and big trucks coming and picking them up and take them away to where they are buried.[99]

Memories like these contribute to their passionate belief for independence and 'political freedom', a conviction often expressed in simplified views on the Soviet Union, very much influenced by the politics of the cold war era.

Community Organisations and Political Convictions

As the main reason given for non-return to their country of origin was the rejection of life under communism many regard themselves as political exiles. 'We didn't come to the West as economic immigrants, we came as political immigrants'[100] sums up the self-perception of a substantial part of the East European communities. Based on this view, they felt it their mission to build a strong 'community in exile' which would keep the cultural heritage alive and support the independence movements of their occupied countries back home. The Ukrainian explains 'it was everybody's obligation to be a member of a Ukrainian organisation'.[101] Hence, within a short period after arrival the Association of Ukrainians was formed, soon followed by other organisations, such as the Ukrainian women's, youth and teachers' association, together with Catholic and Orthodox churches. This process was supported by a thriving community infrastructure with their own food and bookshops, newspapers and social welfare facilities and translation offices as well as clubs for social meetings and cultural events. Comparable developments emerged in other East European communities. Being able to organise themselves in national communities and building up a social network certainly helped to ease the newcomers' settlement process in Britain and probably also helped them to overcome the painful reality of not being able to have contact with friends and family left behind.

An important political organisation, which enjoyed wide support amongst the East European community, was 'The Captive Nations Association'. This organisation – originally joined by Latvians, Estonians, Hungarians, Lithuanians, Ukrainians, Belorussians and Poles – aimed at raising the public awareness about the 'oppressive nature in Soviet occupied' countries in the West. They produced and distributed publicity materials and organised political and cultural events. In the words of an interviewee, who is also the founder of the association:

> [We want] the British people and people all over the world to know our attitude, why we here, why we start ... fighting against ... against Russian Imperialism. [...] Organisation is very, very good, very spread all over. [...] Captive Nations, that's ... more or less the same as the Anti-Bolshevik block of nations[102]

For some the idea of 'fighting Russian Imperialism' was translated into targeted activities. Supporters of 'Captive Nations' staged frequent local political actions, such as the demonstration against the state visit of Nikita Khruschev in 1956 or against performances of Russian artists. Convinced that singers or dancers were sent

> as what they call here, cultural exchange, we thought we should express our view [...] why shouldn't we demonstrate if they come here, to propagate how good the Soviet Union is, and there are people enslaved there? Hundreds of thousands of our people are in concentration camps, in psychiatric institutions and so on, why shouldn't we demonstrate?[103]

He recalls a concrete example of their action, the occasion of Lenin's 100th birthday in 1970, which was supposed to be commemorated in Bradford's Textile Hall:

> We just went there and helped them to celebrate [...] we came to the Hall just before it supposed to start and we all had invitation cards, so nobody could stop us really. And two of our young lads went on stage and ripped all Lenin's pictures down, so they panicked, the organisers, and rang the police, and police came and, of course when we finished all, ripping portraits and pictures down, nobody was fighting with anybody, they were just torn down, that was all. And we sang the National Anthem and went out, and that was all. [...] It was well publicised, of course trouble is, it was on front page in *Telegraph and Argus* and my name was mentioned a few times, but somebody had to speak.[104]

Sympathy for the cause of 'Captive Nations' seems to be widespread across the interviews. However, the interviews also suggest that the most vocal support was given by ex-soldiers who had served in the German Army. When asked directly, interviewees claimed that they were not interested in politics and would reply like this: '[join] a political party? Why should I? I am a foreigner, so its no good me belonging to any party, I can't vote. I am not a British subject and anyway, what is the point?'[105] Nevertheless, the narratives taken as a whole reveal their political orientation, which are closely linked to their motivation for leaving their countries: 'I will always stand for the free ... free country, free government and free enterprise. [...] I will stand for Conservative all the way.'[106]

Over a long period of time the East European communities lived quietly, largely unnoticed and not politicised as a group of immigrants to Britain. However, the media exposure of the fact that thousands of Ukrainian ex-members of the Galician Division of the SS were able to enter Britain attracted much public attention. Even more shocking was the accusation that some ardent Nazis and wanted war criminals, who had allegedly collaborated actively with the Germans during the war, killing 43,000 Jews, were living amongst the East European communities in Britain.

The majority of the community members were neither directly affected by these accusations, nor did they take part in the political activism against the Soviet Union. Most felt content to be united in just keeping their national cultural identity alive by supporting traditional activities such as folk dancing and choir singing, or celebrating national festivities in their traditional form. Women played a crucial role in conveying these traditional customs to their children at home and to the wider community: egg painting at Easter, costume-making for classical dancing, cookery and embroidery. Some however, were content with only participating in cultural community events or simply enjoying the company of their fellow countrymen. The social life of most interviewees has been much more connected with their compatriots than with people from their host country – some even say they have never been invited to a British home or ever had British friends.

Despite local and individual variations building 'a community in exile' after the war meant a strong orientation of the whole family in their own culture. It included marriage within the community, maintaining the language and culture at home, establishing churches, setting up schools to teach East European languages and educate the new generation in their traditional national culture. It appears from the interviews that a large proportion of families succeeded in passing on a strong national identity to the next generation.

Conclusions

The independence of Poland, the Ukraine and the Baltic States which members of these communities in the UK had so wholeheartedly supported and not really expected to happen in their lifetime, enabled them to travel to their countries of origin after 50 years and to be re-united with surviving members of families. However, Tannahill's prediction in the mid 1950s that a considerable number of EVWs would return 'home' for good if they could, did not materialise.[107] For them it was too late. Having raised a family, created a home and having played an active part in community life they had developed deep personal roots which they did not want to sever. But, the 'easy assimilation'[108] into British society predicted by the government also did not occur. The interviews indicate that migrants, who were not always welcome and understood by the local population, often did not aspire to be assimilated. All they aimed for after a hard life, formed by the experience of war at a young age, occupation, flight or forced labour, life in camps and work as recruited labourers, was the chance to live in their own communities, following their own customs and political convictions.

6

The Migrant at Home in Spitalfields:[1] Memory, Myth and Reality

Anne J. Kershen

At the time of writing[2] immigrants are all too frequently perceived as a problem, unwanted individuals on the national landscape. Yet Britain, and most particularly London, has been a magnet for immigrants for hundreds of years. Economic opportunity and, until the twentieth century, an open door policy towards incomers, were major factors in keeping the beacon of welcome alight. Though the twentieth century has seen a gradual closing of that open door the migratory pull still operates. Immigrants and refugees are still looking to make their homes and their futures in Britain, most particularly in London. This chapter seeks to understand the way in which memory, myth and reality combine in the construction of the migrant home. It sets out to explore the way in which immigrants and refugees have sought to (re)build their lives in an alien land and discover how large a part myth and memory have played in the construction of home in the 'elsewhere'. The subjects of the study are; Huguenot refugees of the seventeenth and eighteenth centuries, Eastern European Jewish immigrants of the late nineteenth and early twentieth centuries and Bangladeshi sojourners of the second half of the twentieth century. The Spitalfields area of London, the traditional first point of immigrant settlement in the capital, provides the spatial and temporal framework within which this study is set.[3]

The Setting

Spitalfields has been peripheral to the mosaic of London since Roman times. It was then, and has remained ever since, a place on the edge, a bridge between the included and the excluded. A twilight 'zone of transition'[4] in which the culture and economy of the native and the stranger have evolved, at times merging, at other times competing. Through metaphor Spitalfields has been presented as deprived, dangerous and exotic. It has been called variously, 'the city of darkest night', 'a jungle', 'a bazaar', 'an abyss',[5] words which instantly conjure up images of poverty, violence and otherness. It is encrusted with diversity and a history of tolerance which has lived side-by-side with intolerance. Spitalfields has vibrated with the sights, sounds and smells of the minority groups who have inhabited it over the centuries and has been known in turn as Petty France, Little Jerusalem and, currently Banglatown. Yet it is also part of the cockney East End and home to Petticoat Lane market. An area on the edge, yet only minutes from the heart of the nation, it is a landscape composed of myth and reality, constructed from the memories of migrants who made the journey from their home over there in order to construct a home over here.

The area known as Spitalfields is within 30 minutes walking distance of the London docks and a stone's throw from the City of London. At the time of writing its boundaries are formed by; to the west, Bishopsgate/North Folgate/Middlesex Street; to the north, Shoreditch/ Bethnal Green/ Quaker Street/Buxton Street through to Vallance Road; to the east, southwards down Brady Street to Whitechapel Road, the latter forming the district's southern boundary. Though the street names may have changed the locale can be identified on maps dating back to the sixteenth century. By the mid-seventeenth century a group of Huguenot settlers, some of whom could trace their roots back to silk weavers who had arrived from Rouen as early as 1532, had established a small community, which, by the early decades of the eighteenth century, had grown to number almost 20,000 souls. As though anticipating the influx of refugees, the area bordering the City of London underwent intensive development and, by 1675, more than 1,366 two storey tenement houses, with frontages measuring no more than 12 feet across, had been constructed. These small, mean houses were crowded into narrow streets and alleyways at the southern end of Spitalfields, in and around Dean and Flower Street[6] and Thrall Street. At the same time, other small houses were built at the northern edge, in Hare Street and Browns Lane which bordered on Cock Lane, now known as Bethnal Green Road. Daniel Defoe, in his *Tour of England and Wales*, which was published in 1724, recorded the 'numberless ranges of buildings' which were to be found in the area, 'called Spittle Fields, reaching from Spittle Yard, at Northern Folegate, and from Artillery Lane in Bishopsgate Street ... to Brick Lane and the end of Hare Street, on the way to Bethnal Green'.[7] The upgrading of Brick Lane,[8] the area's main thoroughfare, provides an insight into the transformation of the space that was, and remains, the spine of Spitalfields. In the sixteenth century it was little more than a country track. As late as 1671 Christopher Wren deemed it almost impassable, 'an area remote and inaccessible'. One hundred years later it had become a major thoroughfare for coaches and a meeting place for radical weavers, many of whom were French, or of French origin.[9]

Change of century brought a change of ethnic minority but no variation in the district's role as a home for immigrants and refugees. This time the aliens came from eastern rather than western Europe and were Jews rather than Christians; their language (or dialect) Yiddish rather than French. Though there had been a constant trickle of eastern European Jews throughout the eighteenth and nineteenth centuries (with the exception of the period of the French Wars), the 'flood' of immigrants occurred in the 1880s, 1890s and early part of the 1900s. By the outbreak of the First World War estimates of the number of Jews resident in and around the Spitalfields district ranged from a conservative 60,000 to the anti-immigrationists' scaremongering 200,000.[10]

The Second World War resulted in the large-scale out migration of the East End's Jewish population. By the 1960s a new immigrant community was assembling. Bangladeshi[11] arrivals began taking up residence in the same streets and buildings as had the Jews and Huguenots before them. With insufficient money to return home, the sojourners eventually accepted that their stay would become permanent and a process of family reunification was initiated. In some cases it is still going on. The result has been a dramatic expansion in community size. What numbered barely 100 at the end of the 1950s had increased to 4,872 by 2001; a figure which represented more than half of the total population of the Spitalfields and Banglatown electoral ward.[12] The overt face of the most recent immigrant influx is to be found in Brick Lane where, at its most southern boundary, a banner which straddles the east and west sides of the street, 50 yards north of the junction of Osborne Street and Brick Lane, proclaims in large letters the entry to 'Banglatown'.

The Meaning of Home in Myth and Reality

For migrants, even more than for those who do not move far from their place of origin, home is a contested metaphor; a carpet bag of memories, emotions and experiences. It is now but it is then. It is over here yet over there. It is days filled with laughter, love and sunshine but it can be also darkness and threat. Real and tangible yet imagined and mythologised, home is deconstructed on departure and then constantly reconstructed as the migrant experience and life cycle evolve. Home is all about belonging. It is about being rooted, of having a focal point at which to direct hopes, fears, ambitions and, the myth of return. One of the tools used in the (re)construction of home in the diaspora is memory. Memory which is inevitably coloured by the journey from over there to over here; memory which is sifted and manipulated in order to create the new home and forge the new identity. The use of memory in the home-building process provides the opportunity for a rediscovering of the self and for its re-rooting. Using the past and the now, always with an eye to the future, the outsider constructs a visual narrative which tells the migrant story.[13]

The meaning of home is not easy to define, for in the game of semantics it has a multiplicity of connotations. In feminist literature home is frequently a private place, one concerned with the 'intimate, personal, emotional, domestic and familial'.[14] For some women it is a place of subjugation and exclusion where they live out their hidden and other lives. A place which those used to life in a liberal and egalitarian society may find shocking and oppressive. As for example young Bengali women from Spitalfields who discover on their (temporary) 'return' to Bangladesh that, rather than the dream relayed to them by their parents, home is a place where the female is marginalised and subservient. Both male and female Bengali teenagers are reported as having been disillusioned by what they have found on returning 'home'. As Gardner and Shukur revealed in the early 1990s, 'The myth of beauty, food and trees heavy with fruit' was not quite the reality, instead the young people were faced with 'a lack of privacy, insects and mud',[15] a place, where now, in the twenty-first century, many homes have no electricity or running water and television sets run on car batteries. Others, visiting for the first time have 'loved it absolutely … After this first trip I've changed, I don't know, it's like I've discovered new things about myself, about my roots, my identity…'.[16] Even the older Bangladeshis find on return that home, as they remembered it, no longer exists, both it and they have changed, and can never be the same again.

Conversely, there is the construction of home in the public space. A territorial concept, as for example, home(land) as a metaphor for nation or region, *mon pays* as the Huguenots would have recognised it. Thus home may become a fusion of myths accumulated in a remembered landscape which may itself be more Anderson-like than real. Following this theme it is possible to suggest that, for the Huguenots, *their* France was an 'imagined community', and as such one that could be deterritorialised and spatially and temporally transported elsewhere.

Other commentators have referred to home as the 'normality',[17] but this only begs the question which home and what normality? Is it that which has been left behind due to religious persecution, as in the case of the Huguenots, or as the result of the combination of economic and religious persecution as was the case for many late nineteenth century eastern European Jews? In this context the experience of these two groups necessitates further clarification. Is their normality to be defined as peace and security or threat and hardship? In addition, we must determine whether 'home' was the family collective recently departed or, as in the case of religious Jews, the mythologised spiritual homeland exited more than two thousand years ago. What is clear from the above is that there is no single, or simple, definition of home. (The *Shorter Oxford English Dictionary* provides nine alternative definitions for the noun and adjective and equally as many for the verb and adverb.[18]) It is a term of reference which is still under debate and, though all of us experience it, we cannot always, accurately, define what it means to us in either the real or the imagined world.

The common denominator in the experience of all emigrants is the departure from home that begins the journey from that which is familiar to that which is foreign. Stowed away in the baggage is a remembrance of that which has been left behind. Over time this becomes an edited memory which may soften, or eventually exclude, all that is harsh, cruel and disagreeable, leaving the gentle, the happy and the agreeable in the forefront of the mind. These memories are transported by the individual and, as home and community evolve, incorporated by the group.

Joly and Cohen, writing in 1989, suggested that 'Immigrants cherish the myth of return ... for refugees the possibility of returning home is less feasible'.[19] But this should not presuppose that refugees do not cherish the myth of return. For the dispossessed and persecuted the myth is based on a land free from persecution and persecutors. Who could doubt the Huguenot longing to return to *leur patrie, leur pays, leur foyer*,[20] their land, their hearth, their home, an idealised *pays* where Calvinists would not be persecuted for their religious beliefs. However, the Catholic French monarchy maintained its ban on Calvinism until the year before the Revolution. During this time the Huguenot myth of return faded and, as the decades passed, many French Calvinists living in London transferred their national and religious allegiance to the British crown and the English church.

For late nineteenth century eastern European Jewry, diaspora was a middle name. Accordingly the location and definition of home is not straightforward. Was it to be found in the towns, villages and cities of the Pale of Settlement or in the biblical land from which Jews were exiled almost two millennia before? Wherever they were in the diaspora, Jews prayed for a return to their spiritual homeland. Until the emergence of political Zionism towards the end of the nineteenth century, the myth of return was solely a religious construct. Even after Herzl had called for a Jewish state, ultra-orthodox Jews believed (and still believe) that the true 'return' would follow the coming of the Messiah; then, and only then, could a religious homeland be constructed. The orthodoxy gave little credence to the concept of a wholly secular political state. For them the myth of return was a sacred dream. Accordingly, the majority of eastern European Jews migrating westward carried two myths with them, one of return and one of home, the latter incorporating a selection of religious, domestic and economic ingredients which could be fused into a fulfilling existence in the elsewhere. Whatever the dreams of the emigrants, home, in its material and physical form, was the *shtetl*, for those who settled in East London, it became a *shtetl* called Spitalfields. As the journey west began, so did the construction of the myth, not from bricks and cobblestones but from:

> The people who live in it, not the place or the buildings or the street. 'My home is the family and the family activities, not the walls or the yard or the broken-down fence ... essentially the house remains a temporary dwelling, inhabited for a brief moment of history.'[21]

Once settled in the west, the myth of return became, for some eastern European Jews, a remote dream, for others it remained a religious imperative. For all, the myth of home was a building block in the process of assimilation and settlement.

The mythologised *desh* [22] was the space in which the material proceeds of the pioneering Bangladeshis' short sojourn in the *bidesh*[23] would become manifest. Land ownership is a vital status symbol for Bangladeshis and 'is held in an almost mystical regard'.[24] In the early years of their overseas settlement, for many migrants from the Indian sub-continent, the myth of home was inseparable from the myth of return. In his eponymous book,[25] Muhammad Anwar records that Pakistani immigrants initially perceived themselves as sojourners who would soon earn enough money to enable them to return home and 'buy land [and] build better houses and to raise their social status'.[26] For the Bangladeshis who came to Britain in the late 1950s and 1960s, the myth of return was structured with economic bricks. The commitment to send regular remittances to Bangladesh,[27] low wages and/or unemployment in Britain meant that few of the pioneers were able to transform the myth into reality. The *bidesh*, the elsewhere, became another home, a pluralised home. One which was at the same time, a stone built house in Sylhet, and an overcrowded flat in a high rise block, or multi-occupancy, in Spitalfields.

The Construction of Home

Each of the three groups under the microscope in this study had earlier links with Spitalfields. In the last quarter of the sixteenth century a small number of Huguenot refugees[28] settled in England and established a network of religious and economic activity in the east of the capital. This was to prove a lifeline for later arrivals. The impecunious eastern European Jews of the late nineteenth century entered a city within which earlier Jewish arrivals, some whom were a part of the 1656 readmission, had set up an infrastructure of charitable support in the East End of London which would provide for their co-religionists and keep them out of the English poor house. Bengalis could trace their association with the mother country back to the early years of Empire when, as lascars on merchant ships out of Calcutta they had landed – and at times jumped ship – in the East End of London.

In the history of Spitalfields, the Huguenots and the Jews[29] were the first migrant pioneers in modern history to settle in any numbers at the eastern edge of the City of London. Unable to live within the City's walls they elected Spitalfields to be their first point of settlement and their launching pad to socio-economic mobility. The Huguenots turned the cobbled streets and alleyways into 'Petty France', the eastern European Jews transformed them into a 'Little Jerusalem' whilst the Bangladeshis have facilitated the most recent metamorphosis into 'Banglatown'. Each designation broadcasts the presence of an alien culture in the heart of one of the essentials of Englishness, the East End, the home of the cockney.[30] As each wave of incomers marked out their ghetto boundaries, tensions at the edge, where the insider and outsider confronted each other, heightened as threats to native territory were constantly reinforced. The immigrant settlers in Spitalfields sought to construct homes within which they could eliminate that which was alien and threatening and surround themselves with that which was familiar, that which was reminiscent of 'home'. Home as a creative memory more often than home as it had been. To do so they used cultural tools. Given the limitations of space in this chapter we will explore just a selection, those of language, diet and religion.

Language

Language is one of the pillars of civilised society and a gateway to all levels of day-to-day interaction in the public and private spheres. However, as much as it produces union and community it separates, creating invisible barriers and alienating outsiders unable to communicate in the language of the receiving society. Over the centuries, immigrants with little or no English have been consigned to linguistic ghettos. Within those linguistic ghettos the language of home becomes part of the carapace of memory that comforts those in a strange land. In the early stages of their settlement in Spitalfields all three of the groups focused upon in this study used their mother tongue (or dialect) as a verbal building brick in the construction of a spatial location away from a previous home; a dwelling place where they could set down roots and accommodate change in an alien society. At the same time they sought to create a fortress within which they could exclude all that was strange and threatening. Using familiar linguistic sounds – songs and 'kitchen' talk – memories of childhood and mothering, tenderness, warmth and security could be conjured up. A fusion of the real and the imagined in the evolving myth of home.

Though some of the Huguenot aristocrats could speak English, initially French was the working and domestic language of the refugees. Whilst those at the upper social levels rapidly acknowledged the need to learn English in order to integrate commercially and socially, for the semi-skilled and unskilled, French remained the language of work as well as home. Records suggest that the Huguenots were the first to construct a linguistic ghetto in Spitalfields; in 1710 we find reference to their 'persisting in using their own language and tending to live together rather than disperse'.[31] It was said at the time that, 'the stubbornly insular could learn colloquial French there without setting foot outside.'[32] Such was the general use of French that, in the first decades of the eighteenth century, it was considered preferable for the clerk of the Weavers' Company, to speak French. Even as late as the 1780s, the 'conversation in the street [in Spitalfields] was often French'.[33] Not all the refugees were keen to retain a 'French' identity. By the early eighteenth century, in the register of *La Patente* Church in Spitalfields, the English word 'weaver' is seen to have replaced the French *Ouvrier en Soye*.[34] Within three generations – the passage of time considered the average for the assimilation of an 'outsider' group – English was beginning to replace French as the main language of communication for Huguenots in Spitalfields. Its passing was mourned, there being criticism from those who felt that the French language had become neglected, even suggestions that the descendants of the original refugees were ashamed of their ancestors. Further confirmation of the linguistic transformation of the Huguenot home can be found in comments made in 1894 by W. M. Beaufort who, when looking back at the records of the French Protestant School noted that, for a number of decades, many of the children attending had 'never been taught French previously'.[35] Yet, the many was not all, for until the middle of the nineteenth century the French patois could still be heard in Spitalfields. For some the sound of 'back there' still remained an important element of the construction of home over here.[36]

For late nineteenth century eastern European Jews home was where being Jewish happened, be it in the *shtetl*s of the Pale of Settlement or in London's East End. It was here that the *mammaluschen* (mother tongue) was spoken and tradition upheld. In the linguistic landscape home echoed through the streets of Spitalfields. Yiddish Theatre played to packed houses,

Yiddish newspapers covered the political spectrum and Jewish trade unions carried out their business and published their reports in Yiddish and English. However, though it is tempting to think that the constant use of mother tongue was one of the strategies of home building and a means of maintaining links with the past, its usage can also be defined as a bridge to assimilation.[37] Yiddish Theatre eased the immigrant into an understanding of the English and western European way of life; Yiddish newspapers devoted more space to contemporary British politics and events than to those taking place in *der heim*[38] and immigrant children, forbidden to speak Yiddish at school, imported English into their homes. As a consequence the linguistic lacuna narrowed, the language of home became a fusion, and at times a confusion, of Yiddish and English; as when mother told the family that she was going 'to the chicken to salt the kitchen'.[39]

The Huguenots (after their initial hopes of an early return to France had faded) and the eastern European Jews settled in Spitalfields for the long term. In contrast, the young Bengali men who arrived in the late 1950s and early 1960s came as sojourners, to earn enough money to return after a few years as 'rich men of high status'. Many felt that for them there was no need to learn English. In the clothing workshops of Hanbury Street and the restaurant kitchens of Brick Lane the linguistic interaction that took place was between Bengali/Sylheti speaking employers and their Sylheti-speaking labour. By the late 1970s the myth of return had become even more distant; wives and, where possible children, were reunited with their men folk, in other instances new and younger wives were imported whilst first wives stayed behind in the *desh*. Home was no longer grounded in a fixed location, for some it had become pluralised, being at the same time both over here and over there. Spitalfields now rang out with the chatter of Sylheti, the music of Bangladesh and the passions of Bollywood.[40] However, these were not simply the transported sounds of the third world, but rather a fusion of urban technology and the rural homestead.

Whereas the Huguenots and Jews were willing to forego mother tongue and readily adopt that of their new homeland, the Bangladeshi community esteemed Bengali – the language over which the bloody civil war of independence was fought between 1952 and 1971 – and sought to preserve it in the *bidesh*. In spite of the place of language in the fight for independent nationhood, few of the women and children that travelled from *desh* to *bidesh* could read or write in their own language let alone speak or read English. However, as a result of initiatives begun in Spitalfields in the mid 1970s[41] second generation Bangladeshi children are now taught to read and write mother tongue and, in its 2003 consultative document, the current government acknowledged the importance of mother tongue tuition in mainstream education by advocating bi-lingual teaching in primary schools.[42]

Yet Sylheti is still spoken and valued by the elders, many of whose wives have been discouraged from keeping up or learning English. As I was informed during my research, 'my mother used to speak English but she doesn't any more'.[43] For the generations born in Spitalfields, for whom English is a first language, the learning of Bengali has been encouraged by their parents because, as one young Bangladeshi explained, 'It is the language of home and also, because my parents are not literate, it enables me to deal with any correspondence they have with 'home'.[44] However, one might question for how many decades more, diaspora Bengalis over here will continue to communicate in Bengali with those over there.

For all three groups the language of their sending society was, initially, the linguistic bedrock of their new homes in an alien society. However, unfailingly, willingly or unwillingly, the language of the majority society infiltrated, resulting in confusions similar to those of the Jewish mother. As a result the linguistic landscape of Spitalfields has been enriched by both the authentic foreign and the, at times erratic, dovetailing of the language of one home with that of the other.

Diet

It has been suggested that 'language of origin may be abandoned before diet changes.'[45] Appealing to the taste and olfactory senses, food is one of the most powerful activators of memory. How often is it that the smell or taste of a certain food brings back memories of childhood – nursery tea times or school dinners? Newly arrived immigrants from all three groups in this study either sought to reproduce the diets of home, or create a nourishing substitute for that which had been left behind. In the days before refrigerated storage and jet flights, immigrants from overseas could only reproduce 'home cooking' using locally available ingredients. Meals were a compromise that became a fusion of the remembered and the local. It is impossible to calculate how many Huguenots ate oxtail stew in France, but we do know that it was a dish they prepared in their refugee status, together with stewed root vegetables and herbs.[46] It is significant that the basic ingredients for both dishes were cheap and affordable for refugees who had been pauperised by the rushed and secret nature of their flight from France. For them diet in Spitalfields was the outcome of survival economics. It should be added that whilst the oxtail stew may well have stimulated the olfactory senses and recreated something of the culinary odours of home, it is doubtful that the same could be said of boiled cabbages.

For Jews, wherever they are, one of the most powerful tastes of home was, and is, chicken soup, its place in the homemaking process highlighted by the fact that, in 1896, there were a recorded 126 kosher poulterers in and around Spitalfields.[47] In addition to these outlets, there were, clustered around Middlesex Street and Wentworth Street, Jewish grocery shops, fish shops and fried fish shops – one owned by a redoubtable Mrs. Polly Nathan[48] – greengrocers and bakers. Food which conformed to Jewish dietary laws played an intrinsic role in the creation of the Jewish home and in the maintenance of a 'Jewish' community. One of the mainstays of the Jewish diaspora, has been, and is, the family nexus. Sabbath and holy festival meals were at the heart of the Jewish family and inscribed in the history of the Jews of Russia and Russia-Poland. Memory plays an essential part in recreating the tastes of homes left behind. The transporting of family recipes handed down through the generations facilitated the continuity of home away from home. However, late nineteenth century transmigration necessitated the adaptation of recipes. For what had been available over there was not always available over here. There were inevitable breaks in the continuity as immigrants from the *shtetls* transformed what had been 'grandmother's specials' into dishes that fused Spitalfields and the Pale of Settlement.

Recent New Commonwealth immigrants, more concerned than their indigenous neighbours with the advantages of healthy eating as opposed to 'fast food', have called for the ready availability of the fruits, vegetables and fish of 'home'. Their demands did not go unanswered. Whilst the first ethnic Bangladeshi food outlets appeared in Spitalfields in the early 1960s,[49] it was not until the 1990s that, as the size of the community increased and with demands for the traditional foods of home, fish and 'exotic' vegetables from Bangladesh were flown in and made available both to the local Bangladeshi community and those prepared to travel from further afield. For this group of immigrants the taste of home has become a possibility rather than a memory. Indeed, research has shown that contemporary minority ethnic group demands for fresh food from 'home' has encouraged the opening of retail outlets[50] – a walk down Brick Lane and Whitechapel Road serves to confirm this. Thus determination to retain the food of home has led to health benefits and the creation of economic opportunities for immigrant entrepreneurs.

However, the association of immigrants and diet is not generally considered for its health and local economic benefits. It tends to be viewed in the context of the introduction of the alien diet to the indigenous population by way of high streets whose landscapes are overpopulated with ethnic eating places.[51] Whilst chicken massalas and baltis might have become British favourites, they and their counterpart Chinese, Mexican and Thai marketed cuisines are rarely authentic but rather created to satisfy British tastes and markets. Paradox also exists in the case of so-called Indian restaurants, the majority of which are owned and operated by male Bangladeshis. Nothing could be further from 'home' where, in the village homesteads of Bangladesh, it is the women who, in the quarters reserved for the female members of the household, prepare and serve the food, a tradition maintained in the homes of Bangladeshis living in Spitalfields today. And although pizza and pasta are everyday foods for the archetypical native 'Brit', consuming Italian, Indian or Chinese is still 'eating the other'. The practice works both ways, for even though immigrants from the Indian sub-continent may eat muesli or cornflakes for breakfast and burgers for lunch they are fully aware of the intrusive nature of the alien diet and the conflict it creates in perceptions of identity, 'just because I eat English food, it doesn't mean that I am English', being the view of one young Asian woman.[52]

Over the centuries the preparation of 'alien' food in Spitalfields has excited native hostility. The 'noxious' odours issuing forth from the Huguenots' stewed root vegetables, the Jews' fried fish and the Bengalis' curries provided ammunition for xenophobes, anti-aliens and racists who highlighted the invisible but sensually disturbing aroma of stewed root vegetables, fried fish and curry. Odours which were alien to the receiving society yet, for the immigrant in a strange land, evocative of home.

Religion[53]

I have included religion under the heading of 'cultural' tools. However this does require some explanation. A culture can be defined as a society or group distinguished by its shared customs, history, language and achievements. Within some groups religion is one of those shared characteristics; the Huguenots were all Calvinists, spoke French, came from one country and shared a common history, one common also to their Catholic compatriots. Eastern European Jews observed the same religion and shared the same sending society, language, diet (with certain local variations). Yet it must be remembered that there were other Jews, for example Sephardim from the Iberian peninsula and North Africa, who though sharing the same religion, had different customs, a different language and if, the temporal measure is taken from the fall of the Second Temple, a different history. Thus not *all* Jews share the same culture, even if they observe the same religion. The religion of Islam has now a global spread with adherents from all continents, thus not all Muslims have the same cultural background. At the same time, though the vast majority of Bangladeshi migrants have been Muslim, there were a very small number who were either Hindu or Christian. However, for the purposes of this essay it is assumed that the subject Huguenots, eastern European Jews and Bangladeshis, shared not only the same religion but also a common culture.

It was the refusal by Louis XIV to tolerate the practice of Calvinism in public or at home, that forced the Huguenots to seek refuge across the Channel. For more than two thousand years Jews have known religious persecution, but it was the combination of that and increasing economic hardship at the end of the nineteenth century that drove them in their hundreds of thousands westwards. The young men from Bangladesh did not make the journey across seven seas and thirteen rivers as a result of religious or any other persecution but Islam figuratively, and the *Quran* literally, travelled with them from one home to another. For all, home would not be home without its religious content. The imported bibles and prayer books, candlesticks, prayer shawls, prayer mats and transported traditional practices bridging the lacunae of time and space and enabling the creation of the religious home within the fabric of the temporal home, wherever that happened to be.

Huguenots offer an ideal Weberian paradigm, their traits being summarised as reverence, chastity, sobriety, frugality, industry and honesty. The ownership and maintenance of a 'clean and solid comfortable middle class home'[54] was a religiously sanctioned ideal and thus home as a place of warmth, comfort and conspicuous consumption was a means of glorifying God and of giving thanks for his provisions. As soon as they were able, economically successful Huguenots, built graceful 'homes' in the heart of Spitalfields, many of which have survived until the present day. Behind the elegant porticos and architecturally satisfying constructs, the structure of family life continued. For some this meant the retention of all that was French, for others, the realisation that return to a France as practising Calvinists was becoming a cherished myth, encouraged them to accelerate the integration process. Whichever, memory, myth and reality suffused the 'middle class' houses in Fournier Street, and the mean houses of Brick Lane. In addition to the private, there was also a need for the public, for a communal religious home, a church or chapel, in which the members of the community could join together in worship. In 1550 the Huguenots took over the Church of St. Anthony's in Threadneedle Street – just beyond the borders of Spitalfields – and established the first French Church in London. In the following century, as the numbers of Huguenot refugees increased there arose a need to augment the Threadneedle Church as it could no longer accommodate all the French Calvinists in the area. It was at this point that Calvinism made its spatial debut in Spitalfields. The church of *La Église Hôpital* was opened as a chapel of ease and annexe of Threadneedle Street, in Black Eagle Street in 1688. Even this proved inadequate and further French churches were opened. By 1739, there were nine French churches in

Spitalfields.[55] In 1742 it was decided to build an 'extension' to *La Église Hopital* on the corner of Brick Lane and Church Street. This became known as *La Neuve Église*. In the centuries to follow, that building would become a signpost for the religiosity of the local ethnic community.

For practising Jews, home and religion are inseparable, the daily, weekly and annual rituals, particularly those of the Sabbath and festivals, both requiring and enabling the construction of home anywhere in the diaspora. For the Eastern European migrants the tools were tangible as well as spiritual, often transported thousands of miles from the Pale of Settlement; brass candlesticks, religious table linen embroidered by mothers and grandmothers who would never be seen again, even Passover cooking utensils carried with aching limbs across borders and seas. There was also the imagined and mythologised; Passover songs sung to traditional tunes round the Spitalfields tables and the dream of next year in Jerusalem. The private face of Judaism in Spitalfields was to be found in every household where, on the Sabbath eve, the family would gather around a table upon which the Sabbath candles glowed and upon which the Friday night meal of chicken soup and boiled chicken[56] would be served. The public face of Judaism in Spitalfields was to be found in the synagogues and smaller *chevras*[57] that had been established in back rooms and attics in streets including Princelet, Hanbury, Wilkes and many others running off the spine of Brick Lane. It was here that private and public merged, home often serving a triple purpose, dwelling place, tailoring workshop and place of worship. It was not unusual for a synagogue to be established in a building that had previously been a church or chapel. The most well-known example of this is the synagogue established by the *Machzike Hadath*. In 1897, this ultra-orthodox arm of Spitalfields Jewry took up the lease of the building on the corner of Fournier Street and Brick Lane from the trustees of the French Church.[58] In 1922 they purchased the freehold and subsequently sold the building to the Bangladeshi community for conversion into a mosque in 1974.[59]

It was not until the reunifications began in the 1970s and 1980s, in some cases continuing even until today, that the bachelor existence of the young Bangladeshi sojourners was replaced by one of conforming domesticity. As 'proper homes' replaced all-male bed sits, there was a conspicuous return to religiosity. In the early days the young men had broken the basic Islamic codes by visiting pubs and gambling, as one Bengali elder admitted, 'I was a broken Muslim. I had a white woman. I never lost my religion but then I never really prayed or anything.'[60] He was not alone, for as another said, 'In those days people didn't observe religious things properly.'[61] However, with the creation of home in the *bidesh*, Muslim men have returned to their religion, as well as praying in the work place and at home, Spitalfields provides them with a choice of mosques. The *Jamme Masjid* or Great London Mosque now proudly straddles Brick Lane and Fournier Street. Known as the elders' mosque it provides no facilities for their womenfolk who, in the tradition of the *desh* always pray at home. Just over the border of Spitalfields, dominating the landscape further to the east in Whitechapel Road, is the East London Mosque – rebuilt in the 1980s at a cost of more than two million pounds. Here old meets new. A new generation of young Muslims find their religious beliefs heightened in a house of worship which also provides – separate – prayer and communal facilities for women.

Whatever cultural and architectural changes may have overtaken Spitalfields since the arrival of the Huguenots, there has been one constant on the landscape, that building which bestrides the corner of Brick Lane and Fournier (originally Church) Street. This edifice, perhaps more than any other on the Spitalfields landscape, encapsulates the migrants' presence and their need for the spiritual familiar, even if contained within the unfamiliar. For more than 260 years, with the exception of the patina of time, be it church, synagogue, or mosque, externally the building has remained unaltered. Yet as each new group sought religious succour, major transformations were imposed on its internal landscape, in order that this extended territory of home could, at the start of the settlement process, be something private, personal and recognisable.

Conclusion

There is no doubt that one of the first priorities of the newly arrived immigrant is the creation of a home which is familiar and safe. The use of mother tongue is a vital tool in the construction. Irrespective of the temporal setting, initially each of the three groups clung to the language of their sending society. However, the Huguenots and the Jews recognised that at some point the language of home, of the over there, would have to become that of the receiving society. By comparison, the Bangladeshi community has shown a reluctance to sacrifice mother tongue, rather it has sought to retain and encourage its continued usage and general acceptance. Yet, as acknowledged above, whether the incomers are keen to fully assimilate or determined to retain ethnic identity, the language of home changes as interaction by parents and/or children increases. Within the workplace, the school, in the shops and even in the streets, home and away mingle and cross-coding takes place. Elements of French crept into English and contributed to the Spitalfields 'Cockney' dialect. Once the children of the eastern European Jewish immigrants attended school they imported English to into a domestic sphere which often operated only in Yiddish. Of the three groups, the Bengali wives of the first generation immigrants led the most sheltered and cloistered existence. Many keeping (or kept) within the home, their husbands and children act as interpreters for all their needs, including the most personal medical problems. In spite of this English seeps in. I was told by one young woman that, 'listening to my mother on the phone I notice that, without realising it, she uses English words such as friend, shops and television.'[62] In this way, the language of home is constantly, and often unknowingly, being reconstructed and the linguistic landscape forever changing.

Even as the diet of home survives it undergoes transformation. Though the young woman acknowledges that her cornflakes are alien, they are still to be found on her kitchen shelves as much a part of the landscape of home as the spices and fresh vegetables purchased in Brick Lane. Strictly orthodox Jews may have conformed totally to the dietary requirements of their religion and used the recipes grandmother imported from *der heim*, but one hundred years ago there were limits to produce and preparation and a blending of over here and over there could not be avoided. At the beginning of the 21st century, fusion food is the fashion; now what is home and what is not? However, for immigrants food fusion is not new, it is just another word for compromise, combining what we have with what they have and calling it home. In the context of the visual landscape it is only since the late nineteenth century that the immigrant diet has impacted on Spitalfields. As the twentieth century dawned a walk through Middlesex Street made it impossible to avoid the kosher butchers, poulterers and fried fish shops that protruded onto its pavements. A 2004 meander along Brick Lane confirms that the nation's passion for eating the other now dominates the landscape. Banglatown, the pedestrianised section of Brick Lane, was created at the end of the twentieth century as part of the Borough's urban regeneration process and 'Rich-Mix' scheme, a supposed acknowledgment of multi-culturalism. Inititially, the dominant culture of Banglatown was that of the Bangladeshi community, but gradually, as the area has become a magnet for upwardly mobile youngsters from the City and other parts of the capital, the appearance of sophisticated bars and nightclubs is beginning to change that landscape, providing us with yet another reminder of the impermanency of the Spitalfields 'communities' and the short shelf-life of their 'homes'.

Finally, we looked at religion. For all three groups home plays a major role in facilitating religious continuity. For Huguenots and Jews in Spitalfields, elsewhere became less alien when religion at home, and in the proximate houses of prayer, was familiar. For the Bengali men, the process of family reunification and the creation of homes over here revitalised their religious activities, arguably strengthening the structure. Yet not every immigrant follows a moderate or religious path. Huguenots in the seventeenth century were cautioned about their excessive drinking too close to the French church in Spitalfields, 200 years later Jewish anarchists eschewed religion and flaunted their departure at their co-religionists in the local *chevras*, whilst in twenty-first century Spitalfields, some young Bangladeshis have taken a far more traditional and fundamental path than that of their parents and grandparents.[63]

It would seem evident that irrespective of time and place immigrants have employed language, diet and religion to help construct their diasporic homes. However, the processes cannot but be affected by temporal change and ethnic identity. For those who, under threat, flee 'home' the tangible is often sacrificed and all that can be exported are memories and dreams, the myths of return and home. The forward march of progress has meant that some of those memories which were previously carried in the mind's eye could be transported as camera images; but these are still only snapshots in time, a captured second – the memory may last but the reality will be gone as the shutter clicks. The second half of the twentieth century brought, for those able to afford them, television, audio-video equipment and now video links via mobile phones. Changes at home, the ageing process, disasters and developments can be monitored daily, the music and language of home retained through a variety of radio and television channels. Home becomes more real and closer yet, at the same time, more distant as those at home, both here and there, become conscious of constant change and the realisation that 'Migration is a one way trip, there is no home to go back to'.[64] Houses are built with physical labour and concrete materials on a developing landscape; for the immigrant, homes in the elsewhere start out as mental constructs on a virgin landscape. The result is a mixture of reality and imagination, of memories and myths, dreams and disasters. Embracing both longing and belonging, at once solid and secure at the same time they are metaphysical constructs which can be moved at will but never exactly reproduced.

What role has the landscape of Spitalfields played in the migrants' construction of home? Over the centuries our three protagonist groups have imposed their identity and presence on an urban landscape which, even before their arrival, had played host to range of outsiders. The Huguenots, with their hard work ethic and skills as silk weavers, optical instrument makers, silversmiths and goldsmiths, inserted their physical presence onto the landscape and built houses and churches, some of which have survived to this day. There was no particular French influence in the architecture, in fact Fournier Street is regarded as one of the finest examples of British Georgian building still standing in London today. The buildings did however reflect the Calvinists' prosperity and their owners' desire to glorify God through the manifestation of their material success. Material success is once again evident on the twenty-first century streets of Spitalfields as affluent gentrifiers migrate from the suburbs and, easing out the multi-occupancy migrants, make their take-over bid for the landscape.

In the late nineteenth century eastern European Jewish immigrants departed a landscape of poverty and hardship only to find another, the difference being that Spitalfields, in spite of its overcrowding and urbanity, offered them an opportunity to fulfil the immigrant dream. By the 1890s, on the edge of the City of London there had been a metamorphosis, where once there had been Petty France, there was now Little Jerusalem. By the 1980s, an architectural landscape that had been familiar to the Huguenots and Jews – one that had survived the blitz almost in its entirety – had changed yet again. Spitalfields's backcloth was now, as described by Monica Ali, 'Buildings without end … that crushed the clouds',[65] with Banglatown about to emerge. In jerry built tower blocks and in ageing terraces encrusted with low French and Yiddish, the Bangladeshis were making their homes. In common with their predecessors they would not recreate home exactly as they had known it, rather they would create the home they would come to know. For Spitalfields provides a metaphorical space within which newcomers can acclimatise to that which is strange. For a while, it assumes the mantle of 'over there' and then, for those with the perspicacity and tenacity it acts as a pointer for a further stage in the diasporic journey.

Spitalfields and its inhabitants represent the permanent and the transitory. The one a canvas upon which strangers in a foreign land can paint their preferred landscape, the other, part of the permanency for just a moment in time, the quotation at the outset of this chapter provides a last word on the topic: 'For my home is the family and the family activities, not the walls of the yard or the broken-down fence … essentially the house remains a temporary dwelling, inhabited for a brief moment of history.'[66]

7

Reinventing the Myth of Return: Older Italians in Nottingham

Deianira Ganga

Introduction

During their life abroad, most migrants day after day plan and pursue their definitive return home. This occurs because 'returning home or to the home-country is a *tópos* common to the collective unconscious and nourished by real needs of self-esteem and historical and geographical self-placement (*the roots*)'.[1] The migratory project of most migrants can be summarised in the following stages: emigration, accumulation of capital and return to the place of origin where it will be invested.[2]

The aspiration to return to the place of origin permanently is often expressed in the very moment migrants decide to leave their country. Indeed, going back 'home' is not an episode but has to be interpreted as a process, a development implicit in every migratory project, even in the case of the migrants who will never go back.[3] Migrants, in fact, might end up settling in the country of residence 'often without making a conscious decision to do so'.[4] This is a phenomenon that lies at the root of the development of large and growing ethnic minority communities in many European cities. The Italian community of Nottingham, England, is certainly among these.

According to the econometric theory, the migration duration of target earners is the result of a complex balance of benefits and costs involved in staying in the country of residence and moving back to the country of origin. It follows that for those migrants who settle in the place of immigration the cost of leaving it would be higher than the advantages they would gain by remaining in the place of immigration.[5]

The purpose of the present chapter is to shed some light on the sometimes unconscious reasons for 'not leaving' and to explore the existence of a link between the numerous motivations lying behind the choice of older Italians of Nottingham to remain in the United Kingdom. Using the words of local respondents from within the group, through their rationalisation of their non-return and the interpretation of the ethnographic materials collected, the chapter adds a new perspective to the econometric analysis of migration duration by referring to more personal and hardly measurable variables involved in the migrants' decision processes. In addition, the chapter points out that the older Italians of Nottingham have found new ways of overcoming their physical distance from Italy and the dualism of their attachments to both their country of origin and their family. In doing this, the paper also suggests a reconsideration of the classical 'myth of return' by adding a new perspective on international migration taking place after retirement.

The following paragraph provides a conceptual framework for the article. First a methodological section introduces the way respondents have been selected and how empirical materials have been collected and handled. This section is followed by an outline of Italian immigration to the UK, set within a wider context of labour shortage and supply involving the whole of Europe. This discussion also introduces some considerations on the sociocultural characteristics of the Italian presence in the United Kingdom and the hypothesis that, after a few years of permanence in the place of immigration, some immigrants might not go back home. In order to clarify what 'home' is, the subsequent section presents some ideas of 'home' derived from current debates on migration and multiple belonging. This is what introduces the empirical core of the paper which analyses the motivations for non-return presented by the respondents, which is constituted by two sections entitled, respectively, 'Non-return: Motives' and 'Attempted Return'. The chapter ends with the development of the hypothesis that the recent phenomenon of the circulation of the Italian immigrants represents a development of the 'myth of return'.

Research Methodology and Respondents

What appears in the following pages is part of a wider three-generational comparative study on cultural identity transmission and construction in individual families of Italian origin living in the Nottingham area. Of the thirty-five people interviewed, fifteen belonged to the first generation, ten to the second and ten to the third. Recruitment, mainly performed through snowballing, involved individual families, with one or more respondents from each generation. For the purpose of this chapter, the analysis comes from the interviews with the fifteen members belonging to the older generation. Within the families that took part in the study, the respondents of the first generation share many elements characterising Italian immigrants who arrived in the UK through the 'bulk schemes' (see the following section). These characteristics render them a group that is homogeneous enough for comparison with the second and third generation.

The empirical materials have been collected through an extensive amount of time spent on the field, using as main data sources semi-structured interviews and observational techniques. For the comparative nature of the research, the use of semi-structured interviews was considered suitable. The use of the oral history method, regarded as a possibility in the first phase of the research planning, was soon discarded in the light that a collection of biographies might have caused the data collection phase to be too 'free', too spontaneous, too lengthy and, therefore, difficult to compare. Moreover, the use of biographies appeared to be too open to the risk that some questions – *a-priori* defined as crucial to the research – might not have been addressed. The interview schedule consisted of a list of topics identified in advance, differentiated according to the particular generation of the respondents and containing questions of various natures: biographical, attitudinal and behavioural/experience-based.

This chapter develops on two different but parallel levels. This is due to the nature of the events that are being presented. In fact, as it deals with events taking place in the years following the Second World War, both published sources – referring to 'historical' events – and original ones – the respondents' words – have been used and quoted. This essay will be characterised by the use of a 'historical' approach, through the results of studies on the field of the Italian immigration in Great Britain that have taken place in recent decades, complemented by excerpts from the interviews conducted in Nottingham.

Historical Background

After the Second World War, Western Europe was affected by significant labour market imbalances.[6] More specifically, Britain was suffering a manpower need for the reconstruction and functioning of factories bombarded during the war.[7] At the same time many Italians decided to leave their country for various reasons, including: population growth; the scarcely profitable agricultural economy on which most of the South depended;[8] and the introduction to alternative ways of living experienced by some people either through the travels forced by their military service or, possibly, through the contact with British or American soldiers allocated in the South of Italy at the end of the conflict.

This scenario takes us back to push/pull theories of migration. In his study of Italian immigration to America between 1890 and 1930, John Briggs argued that Italians preferred emigration to the efforts to obtain a better social and economic position in Italy.[9] As a consequence, they '*chose* to come to this country [Britain]'.[10] This is confirmed by the words of some interviewees.

> Baldo[11]: My father was a contractor and I used to work with him. I also worked in our farm. We produced tomatoes.
> D.G.: Why did you leave Italy, then?
> Baldo: I went away from Italy because there was little to do after the war. I applied for a post with the 'Carabinieri' and for one in the railway here in England. I thought 'the first offer I get, I go'. The first one that arrived was the one from England to go and work at the railway. After 3-4 months I had been here, the 'Carabinieri' in Italy offered me to work with them. If the offer had arrived earlier ... but I was already working here.

Giordano was the only interviewee who gave non-economic reasons for migration:

> In 1955 I was working in my uncle's wood firm in the province of L'Aquila. Then the emigration adverts arrived. My stepmother told me that in England according to the statistics there were seven women for each man. So me and my brother went to the job centre and applied.

With the expression 'emigration adverts', Giordano refers to the British formal recruitment through adverts in Italian job centres or local newspapers. This phenomenon followed the establishment during the last years of the 1940s of an agreement between the Italian and British Ministries of Labour for the recruitment of workers to be employed mainly in the textile and iron-and-steel industries.[12] Workers recruited through this scheme were subjected to a compulsory health check and were bound by contract to remain with the same employer for four years.[13] Through their working permits the Italian immigrants of the post war period went to Bedford, Leicester, Peterborough, Derby, Nottingham, Chesterfield, but also to Bradford, Lancashire and Cheshire.[14] What characterises this type of employment is the recruitment of large groups of workers at the same time, for which it was denominated *bulk scheme*.

The employment of workers in batches inevitably transformed the character of the existing Italian community living in Britain, as from this moment onwards, the characteristics of the Italian immigration into Great Britain changed radically. The new immigrants, in fact, were socially and culturally different from the ones who arrived in Britain some decades before. Moreover, the new immigrants were characterised by several common elements, including: a similar period of arrival: they emigrated in the 1950s and the 1960s; similar social and geographical origins in Italy; similar destinations in Britain; and similar occupational groups.

Although the bulk schemes, with their impersonal recruitment of workers, might have represented the end of the old chain migration, this in reality did not happen. In fact, when the recruitment was no longer regulated by intergovernmental agreements, the employers had to rely directly on their employees, by asking them whether they knew any aspiring *émigré* in their towns or villages of origin.

The majority of Italian men, recruited through bulk schemes for the Nottingham area, were mainly foundry workers employed by either the Beeston Boiler Company or the Stanton and Staveley Iron Works in Ilkeston. Italian women who migrated to Nottingham within the bulk schemes were primarily employed in the textile industry as machinists or worked as maids, mostly in hospitals or care homes. At the end of their four year contract, these workers, having obtained the permission to reside in the country, were allowed to stay with the same company, to move to another one or to go back to Italy. At the time, many predicted that they would have remained in the country of immigration only on a temporary basis. The same immigrants were among these. Some invariably went back to Italy but the ones who remained in Britain represent those non-returnees who constitute the 'founders' of today's Italian community of Nottingham, including the interviewees for this study.

Home

Much current research is engaged in the description of what 'home' is and the definition of where it is. It also analyses the way individuals construct their sense of belonging, especially in relation to two or more localities.[15] As suggested by Ahmed, the process of migration from one country to another involves 'a splitting of home as place of origin and home as the sensory world of everyday experience'.[16] Nevertheless, this is not a passive phenomenon as migrants are often actively engaged in the development of strategies in order to cope with this separation.

The concept of home is not fixed.[17] Moreover, to the changeable nature of home corresponds a mutable sense of belonging. When individuals live between two places, in a transnational space, they often develop a different perception of themselves and construct innovative attachments to both the place of origin and that of immigration.[18] In particular, this transnational space becomes 'an institutional expression of multiple belonging, where the country of origin becomes a source of identity, the country of residence a source of rights, and the emerging transnational space, a space of political action combining the two or more countries'.[19] It is not just elite transmigrants who link within themselves the place of origin and host country/countries. By claiming the country of origin and that/those of residence as their own 'homes' all migrants may find new ways of belonging. Consequently, in this transnational milieu, the idea of family also develops and becomes a 'dynamic network of relationships that changes over time'.[20]

'Home' can be defined mainly through feelings of attachment. On the one hand, home can be interpreted as the 'homeland', the place of birth. On the other, the nature of home – or *Heimat*, according to Andreas Huber and Karen O'Reilly's definition – can be determined in relation to the familial and social relations taking place in the country of residence. Feeling 'at home' depends on the level of place affiliation, and this depends on a multiplicity of different variables, including the presence of friends and family members in the place of residence and the existence of emotional ties.[21] According to Lee Cuba and David Hummon, there is an inverse relationship between the significance of these dimensions and the age of the migrants at the time of their move: the younger they are, the more important these elements become for their self-affiliation.[22] This is particularly significant in the context of the present chapter as at the time of migration the respondents were in their twenties and thirties.

The Migration Project

As ascertained from the interviews conducted among the first generation Italians living in Nottingham, going back to Italy at the end of their four years contract was originally part of their migration project. Many of their friends, colleagues or *paesani* (people originating from the same town or village) left England and returned to Italy long ago. So-called 'birds-of-passage'[23] can, therefore, change their targets – for example, by deciding to postpone their return until they retire – and become settled. The presence in Nottingham of a substantial group of residents who, for a variety of reasons illustrated in the next few sections, did not manage to accomplish their migratory project in full is particularly significant and merits investigation.

Non-Return: Motives

The reasons the first generation interviewees attributed to the decision to remain in England can be summarised in the following points, which have been divided between those applying during working age and after retirement.

a) During working age

- The slow accumulation of sufficient capital
- The impossibility of taking children to Italy
- The undesirability of a 'false' return migration to the industrial areas of Northern Italy
- Considerations for the future of children

b) After retirement

- Concern about the possible need for care in old age
- The feeling of being better socialised in Britain

We can analyse these in more detail. The slow accumulation of the capital necessary to leave the country of residence represents one of the reasons delaying the return of Italians of Nottingham to their places of origin. On the other hand, the respondents never openly mentioned financial security as a prerequisite to their return home, even though the context of the interviews hints at this. During their working age, the first generation Italians of Nottingham found that it was more difficult than initially envisaged to return to Italy. In fact, it took them longer than expected to be able to leave the country (i.e. to earn enough money, although the respondents are never explicit about this), being therefore forced to postpone the moment of their return.[24]

There is a high cultural value attached to savings. Firstly, returning to the place of origin without being able to demonstrate to themselves and the people living in town that they have managed, through migration, to enhance their quality of life would be felt as a failure. Furthermore, saving enough money to invest in some kind of property – house or land – or in setting up a business would be perceived as having been able to transform their future and the circumstances that produced migration initially.[25]

Having deferred the moment for the return to Italy for a few years, many of the respondents realised that it was too late. Marianna and her husband are among these.

Marianna: My husband came here to work, but just for two-three years ... Two-three years, but then the children grew up and we ...
D. G.: Was the intention to go back?
Marianna: Yes, yes...

This leads to the second point. Their children, either born in England or brought up in the country since their early childhood became socialised within the English environment, attending school or already in a stable relationship. This made the parents realise that a return to Italy would have been impossible. This is due to the fact that the strong ties among family members involve for the respondents both spatial and emotional closeness. For this reason, the idea of moving back to Italy and leaving the children in Britain is strongly rejected.

At the same time, some parents realised that Britain might have offered their children better opportunities for linguistic and educational reasons:

Baldo: After Riccardo was born, grew up, got engaged and all the rest ... where could you take him anymore? He had studied here, his language was here, his job was here.

In addition, some interviewees were conscious that going back to Italy would not have implied a return to the town of origin, where the economy was still at an *impasse*. Leaving England during working age would have forced them to move to industrial areas of Turin or Milan to find a job in a factory, which is perceived as a *false return*. Indeed, for the respondents, 'going back to Italy' does not correspond to moving 'anywhere' in the Italian peninsula. Italy is associated with the village of origin, known neighbourhoods, rhythms, smells and practices. The village is the 'home' to return to, the place in which the 'roots' have been left and it is more likely that they might be recovered. In this sense, Marianna's phrase 'If we *returned* to Turin or Milan, isn't that like here? It would have been the same factory work ...' refers to the highly possible lack of improvement in their lives and in their working patterns.

Similarly, the idea of retiring to Italy, leaving the children in England, is dismissed. This is due to the parents' concern for the implications that this might have on them in the hypothesis that they needed care. This fear originates from the cultural practice that it is mainly the children who take care of the older parents, with little reliance on more formal support. The proximity of the children is perceived as fundamental for the assistance that they can provide for their older parents on several levels: moral, emotional, practical and bureaucratic.[26]

> Gioacchino: Today, one thing that we can't live without, because we have worked and we reached this age, are the children ... the children. What do you do if you've got a family? Leave a child here and go to Italy? And when you are in Italy ... I am not as I was yesterday, if anything happens to you, where do you go? Who comes to take care of you?

A recent study by Bolzman *et al.* on the wellbeing of Italian and Spanish older immigrants in Switzerland indicates that familial solidarity is at the basis of everyday behaviour and spans the life-course: parents make sacrifices for their children's security and comfort, but expect certain reciprocity later in life.[27] These patterns are typical of the sub-culture of immigrant families and relate both an urban popular culture and the migrant condition.[28]

It is apparent that at the basis of the plurality of reasons for remaining in England there is a deep anxiety about material security. On the other hand, equally significant is the process of socialisation undertaken through the years of residence in the country, which makes older Italians experience an unexpected sense of 'foreignness' while in Italy. Socialisation, customs and habits developed through the time of residence in Britain might result for the respondents in a sense of rootedness in the country of residence. This phenomenon might also be at the basis of their decision to remain in Britain, a country they feel they belong to, often more than the place of origin.

> Matilde: For me this is my home. Here I've got the children, here I have got the grandchildren, here I've got the people I love, here I've got my friends, here I have everything. In Italy I find myself a bit out of place, because, of course, when I leave I haven't got a circle of friends, we've got cousins, relatives, we've got some friends, a neighbour, but you haven't got a circle of friends of yours that you go out with, you go here, there, and enjoy yourself, we haven't got that.

Matilde feels out of place in Italy. Her home is Nottingham, the place where the people she loves are: children, grandchildren and friends. There are cultural qualities of the country she has been living in for almost half a century that she has appreciated and acquired. The immigrants' human capital, increased through the variety of skills, practical knowledge and cultural know-how developed through the years of permanence abroad, is for many of them the resource they draw from and which allows them to 'feel at home away from home'. The borders between remaining in the country of immigration as a necessity or as a choice therefore become blurred.

> Matilde: I have been here for a long time...
> Alberto: We've been here for ... it will be 45 years in July.
> Matilde: And then for the fact that we have got the children here, the family that 'recalls' you ... I have to tell the truth, the English haven't done anything wrong to me. They might be false, as many say ... but there are many false people in Italy too. So if I stay here, I got everything I got: I let the children do what they wanted. I like many things of the English. I like the order, I like the privacy, here, the freedom ... all things that in Italy are not that much at hand.

The importance of the family is also central in the discourse of Giordano and Rina. They also underline the feeling of inadequacy they would suffer if they went back to Italy. However, this feeling is different from Matilde's.

> Giordano: I don't like this nation that much, but I am forced to stay because I have got the children here, now married. If we go to Italy now we are emigrants, my wife and I. Many of my friends are deceased. We haven't got a house there. Even if you rent a house you are a foreigner.
> Rina: Even if I have got a brother and a sister, we are always in the family, but if you ...
> Giordano: Here, wherever I go, it seems normal. If I go to Italy ... in Italy you are afraid that they steal from you, that they rip you off ...

This quotation appears to be particularly significant as it is interlaced with themes contributing to the idea that a return to Italy is impossible. By saying 'If we go to Italy now we are emigrants', Giordano shows that he has acquired a very deep insight of his own circumstances. Indeed, generally, people do not consider the return to their own country as a form of migration. However, some research has demonstrated that going back home only rarely allows the migrants to re-occupy their initial position.[29] These studies indicate that migrants are usually unaware of the reasons that make their return difficult. In contrast with this, Giordano seems to be aware that returning to Italy would be for him and his wife like a new form of migration.

For Giordano and Rina the family plays a very significant role. Family means their children and, as they underline that their children are now married, their grandchildren. Their offspring seems to overshadow the importance of siblings. In fact, Rina has got a brother and a sister in Italy, but she introduces them starting the sentence with 'even if', so suggesting that, though they are part of the family, the attachment to them is not as strong as the one with her children. This is the most plausible reading as Rina did not manage to complete the sentence, having been interrupted by her husband.

The phrase 'in Italy you are afraid that they steal from you, that they rip you off' is a significant as much as an unpredicted one. A statement of this type would probably be expect from an individual having no familiarity with Italy whatsoever, who has been advised by others on how tricky Italians may be. Undoubtedly, this sentence could be used by people who would feel out of place in Italy because unaware of the language or the way of life, feeling therefore vulnerable. Assuming that Giordano is using a stereotype in order to justify his decision to remain in England would be misleading as, in reality, Giordano feels vulnerable: he has been away from Italy for such a long time that he now feels that he does not belong to it anymore. In contrast, England is different for him, as everything seems 'normal'. However, it is possible to provide another possible reading for this: it could be that Giordano is providing the others and himself with an explanation of the reason why he decided to stay in England, and this is because *Italy is not good as people try to rip you off*. This is, however, just an excuse. From other passages of the interview it is clear that Giordano wanted to return to Italy and he even tried to return, as illustrated in the next section.

Three of the six justifications for non-return previously exposed are strongly related to the immigrant parents' perception of their children's role and life. Undeniably, the significance that the older Italians interviewed attributed to their offspring is extremely high: *'I figli sono la vita'* [children are a person's life], as underlined on several occasions by the respondents. Among the motives for remaining in Britain, two others appear to be, to a certain extent, related to the migrants' children: the slow accumulation of capital and their feeling of being better socialised in Britain. Most of the Italian migrants who moved to Britain in the post-war period were unmarried. Through the time of permanence in the country, they set up their own families. If it could have been possible for a single worker to save capital within expected time limits and return to Italy, the same task would have been more demanding for a family person. Supporting a family, providing the children with housing, education, clothing and leisure activities caused most people to live under great economic pressure. Even though both partners might have been working full time, the adoption of new patterns of consumption and new life-styles often had as a consequence a slimmer chance of saving money for their return. At the same time, as a result of the activities of their children outside the family circle, many parents made contact with 'the British world', so different from that of their typically Italian neighbourhood or workplace.

Attempted Return

Two of the older respondents spoke about their attempted return to Italy during their working age. Although the motivations at the basis of the failure of their project are very diverse, one element links the three experiences: the idea of the centrality of the family. In the extracts from the interviews, family circumstances, often characterised by frequent contact and attachment between family members, appear to play a significant role in preventing the immigrants' definitive return.

In one case, the respondent found employment in a factory in Tuscany, while waiting for his family to sell the house in Nottingham and join him. During his time in Tuscany, he had to face the strong discriminatory frame of mind of his 'northern' co-workers. Feeling rejected, he ended up seeing England and its people in a new light.

> Giordano: I returned to Italy, near Firenze. I worked there one week; they treated me like a foreigner, a complete foreigner. I said 'how come? I am in England, a foreigner, an immigrant, and wherever I go, door open, they treat me with white gloves'. If I did the sacrifice to sell the house and we left all together, I would have suffered ... and my wife and my daughter. That's the mistake I made, I went on my own. I said 'I am going to try. Let's see, what is like'.

Giordano feels that in Italy he was treated like a foreigner, while in England, where he was expecting such treatment, he was not. His words summarise the difference between expectation and reality: he was expecting to be considered as an outsider in England and an insider in Italy – he probably was in both cases, but not as much as he thought – and he ended up with being disproved by the facts. However, he thinks that he would probably have been stronger – and therefore, would have succeeded in his attempt of going back to Italy permanently – if he had received the support of his family. Here the family appears to be the source for the strength necessary to face the problem of adaptation to a new environment. This case also illustrates the problems encountered by people who undertake a 'false return' to a region different from that of origin.

After fifteen years spent in Nottingham – three times the five-year period planned – Matilde moved with her husband and her teenage children to the husband's village of origin, after having bought a 'a nice little house, all furnished'. They also bought a lorry as the husband worked as a driver. As the economy of the village was mainly based on farming and the transportation of agricultural products was just a seasonal job, they faced financial difficulties:

> Matilde: Other people did tell us 'you are maybe frightened, but you have to suffer a little bit here, too, at first. You went to England and you suffered. Now, it's logical, you cannot find all the things that you left there.' For example, I was seeing so many things: the communities, what I was giving to the children, the whims, the small things. But my husband started thinking about some things 'these children when they'll be older, in a small town, they have to go out, take the train, the car, the university, the school ... how can we give these children ... some interests? an education?' And he became obsessed with this, nothing else. We spent there 3 or 4 years. 'That's it' he said 'let's go back!'.
> Alberto: I was thinking about the children ...
> Matilde: ... and we came back. We left again with ...
> Alberto: ... with just the suitcase ... because we had sold the house here. It can be that we maybe made a mistake. Because, after 3-4 years things changed in Italy too. The boom, uhhh, money ...

The village of origin, having lost its original appeal, appears as a small place whose economy would not enable the immigrants to keep up the standards of living acquired while in England and, furthermore, would possibly not provide a bright future for the children. The old village lacks both the economic basis for the returnees to prosper and the services and facilities of a big city. Matilde's and Alberto's concern for the children's future in such an environment was a further motivating force – or justification – for their decision to go back to England.

There are two particular elements of considerable interest in this interview extract. One of them is Matilde's refusal of further 'suffering'. This seems the reaction of a person who can accept suffering once but not twice, or who can allow a certain amount of hardship while residing in a foreign country – and with the prospect of leaving it, sooner or later – not in her own. The second element involves Alberto's words 'It can be that we maybe made a mistake'. This sentence seems to reveal that, in his progress as an individual, Alberto has become very 'relativistic'. Looking back to his experiences, he cannot establish whether leaving Italy for the second time was for his family the best option. Alberto's circumstances seem to summarise the condition of many of the people interviewed for this study.

The older Italians of Nottingham know two realities, the English and the Italian one, but it seems that none of them can be satisfactory if considered separately. This disappointment is what causes a hint of bitterness or resignation in their words. In this sense, it is possible to hypothesise that the 'myth of return' might lose its fascination as soon as it ceases to be a myth and becomes reality – a reality which is different from the one imagined while abroad or during the short visits to family and friends.

Circulation: A Development from the 'Myth of Return'

On the one hand the Italians interviewed did not succeed in moving back to Italy permanently, but, on the other, most of them tended to divide their time between England and Italy, sometimes even six months in each country. They constantly commute between the two countries. Being members of the two societies – being fully integrated or not is not relevant – they oscillate between them. It is just the point of reference that is different: England. This phenomenon demonstrates the 'portability' of their identity[30] which allows them to have the 'tendency towards claiming membership in more than one place'.[31]

Their commuting corresponds to a wish to provide both spatial and temporal continuity between the two countries: spatially, through the continuity provided by the frequent trips which bring them nearer, and, temporally, through the postponement of the decision to settle in one place 'for good'.[32] The Italians of Nottingham have, therefore, adjusted the 'myth of return' through shifting 'from a culture of roots to a culture of routes'.[33]

These kinds of movement are the sign that the global dimension has changed and that migrations are not to be seen within a mono-linear system of permanence in a certain place for a certain time. Consequently, the 'myth of return' still exists but seems to have assumed a certain cyclic nature. It is the return visit that represents for the migrants – as well as for their children – an 'integral experience of their life' in the form of a symbolic 'pilgrimage'.[34] The 'integrality' of this experience can be expressed in different ways. Baldo feels 'at home' both in Italy and in England, while, in Matilde's case, Italy and England have assumed a certain complementarity in her life, becoming one 'lived experience'.

> Baldo: I always say that my home is England *and* Italy because I have a house in Italy and one in England. I have two places. My real home is this [Nottingham] because I live here. There, yes, it's mine, it was left to me by my parents and I spent so much money on it to

renew it. So I have got two of them, one in Italy and one in England [my emphasis].

The concept of 'home' is, therefore, 'plural and evolving'.[35]

> Matilde: There's never been one year that we haven't gone to Italy. But as soon as it starts being colder, there's not so much life ... I start being bored and I think that I want to go home [Nottingham]. Because I feel free here. You might ask 'don't you feel free there?' No. I feel limited ... in that small town, you cannot do much. There are not these big shops, where you watch for a while, you buy something, you take a cup of coffee, meet a friend, chat for a while. You cannot do this. In brief, there comes a moment when I am tired and want to go home ...

The older Italians tend to spend the summer in Italy and the winter months in Nottingham, a period in which their children and grandchildren are involved in their activities. Within the sphere of international retirement migration, the case of the older Italians of Nottingham adds new perspectives. They are different from most of the northern European transnational migrants who 'seasonally migrate' to Southern Europe in order to take advantage of milder winter weather.[36]

For the older Italians of Nottingham, the possible reasons for spending the summer and part of the autumn in Italy also relate to a variety of other circumstances. Going back to their villages during the summer months allows them to meet long-term friends and acquaintances who have migrated to different areas. In this sense, 'the return visit may not be explicitly causal, but may instead be the means by which social relationships are maintained'.[37] It is also easier meeting and entertaining family members and friends during the holidays. Moreover, the end of the summer and beginning of autumn corresponds to the harvest period for grapes and olives. Many older Italians still possess, often with their siblings, plots of land inherited from their parents. The permanence in Italy during this period represents a way to affirm their presence in their village as more than just visitors as well as to allow them to take with them the wine and the oil produced for family use. This phenomenon seems to have a very symbolic value as they usually go back to England not empty-handed but with goods from their 'other' land, which might also be considered – and perceived – as symbols of wealth achieved through hard work.

Marianna's case provides a very interesting case of circulation. Marianna feels equally part of two societies: that of her Italian village and the immigrant one of Nottingham.

D.G.: You are going to your town soon, aren't you?
Marianna: Oh, I am thrilled at the moment. I need to go to my town. Last year I went twice, two years ago too, three years ago ... I think ... too. Because I have the houses that I rent to the students [in Nottingham], I have got properties. I worked really hard ... and we are all the same. I have just one house in my town ... I don't disturb anyone: I have got my house. And even if I don't disturb anyone, my uncles and aunts, my cousins, all the friends that I have got there say 'have you arrived? Come, come and see us'. In brief, for me ... even here when I go out and find either *paesani* or people from the province of Matera ... they are all my friends ....

Marianna owns just one house in her village, but several properties in Nottingham, rented to students. This aspect further reinforces the idea that people like her, who end up settling in the place of immigration, rather than spending their savings in the village of origin – common among migrants who intend to return – prefer to invest their money in the place where their close family lives. Although the older Italians of Nottingham regard both England and Italy as being within their range of action, the real 'home', the steady point of reference is incontestably identified with Nottingham.

The interviewees appear to follow trends which are specific to their condition of migrants who planned to return to their places of origin who are now settled in the country of residence with their families. It is for this reason that during their visits to their villages they would not fit into any of the various categories identified by Karen O'Reilly.[38] Indeed, they are neither returnees nor tourists, neither residents nor expatriates. Instead, they appear to belong to a sub-category of 'seasonal migrants' identified by O'Reilly[39] and King, Warnes and Williams, who tend to 'spend variable amounts of time at different times of the year in their countries of origin and "abroad"'.[40] On the other hand, as their main reasons for moving from one country to another are never strictly weather-related, they are certainly not definable as *snowbirds*.

Conclusion

A fundamental component of most forms of voluntary migration is represented by the 'myth of return'. Returning to the country of origin is for many migrants an implicit part of their migratory project. As illustrated in the previous pages, at the time of emigration – and for a few years after that – the Italians of Nottingham considered their experience abroad as a short parenthesis from their life in their village of origin. Returning to their hometown was, in fact, the envisaged, but never fully achieved, conclusion of their migratory project.

Through the examination of the rationalisation of the respondents' reasons for non-returning, it has been possible to show that the settlement in the place of residence has to be understood as a social rather than as a strictly economic process. The slow accumulation of capital, necessary for a successful return 'home', is just one of a multiplicity of issues – many of which appear to be closely linked to their children and their family life – which might explain their non-return to the immigrants' place of origin. The moral and material concern for the wellbeing of all the members of the family is, in fact, one of the typical characteristics of families of Italian origin in a diaspora setting.

Differently from the majority of 'amenity-seeking' older migrants from Northern Europe, the interviewees did not choose a specific destination, often away from their close family, in order to make it their 'home' at retirement age. It is through the exclusion principle that Nottingham was chosen as their 'home', as it is the place where their children and grandchildren live. Without these conditions, Nottingham would hardly be seen by them as the ideal place to reside. Instead, the city has 'grown on' them through time and life events. Yet again, differently from people from Northern Europe who are involved in retirement migration, the older Italians of Nottingham do not suffer from loneliness and isolation. If this is possible, it is thanks to the moral and geographical closeness of their family members and of the network of friends and acquaintances developed through the decades of permanence in the UK.

As a result, it is apparent that it is not possible to comprehend the living circumstances of the older Italians of Nottingham without taking into consideration the role of family relationships as an explanatory factor. Furthermore, having been unable to go back to their places of origin for good, the interviewees return there cyclically, so reconciling their desire of moral and geographical closeness to their offspring and to fulfil their need for a enduring 'pilgrimage' to their places of origin. Instead of wiping out the myth of return, this phenomenon transforms it, instead, into its contemporary and assertive version. Thanks to this original variation of the myth, the respondents are able to live in two worlds or, better, in their own transnational space, characterised by specific and often original networks, values and allegiances.

Part III

Memory, Metaphor and Material Culture

8

Migration, Memory and Metaphor: Life Stories of South Asians in Leicester

Joanna Herbert

The methodology of oral history allows a unique insight into how individuals themselves comprehend and invest meaning in their past. The aim is not to access the objective historical 'facts' but to gain an insight into human subjectivity, including the complex web of perceptions, emotions, visions and desires. In Portelli's words 'They tell us not just what people did, but what they wanted to do, what they believed they were doing, what they now think they did'.[1] Recently, academics have highlighted how subjective meanings can be gleaned not only through the content of the interviews but through a close reading of the form. The genres used to narrate stories, patterns of speech or recurring images and metaphors may all represent an attempt by the respondent to communicate certain messages to the audience.[2] Thus, seemingly mundane and inconsequential details can offer clues to hidden meanings and uncover rich and fruitful insights.

There is an established, significant, and growing body of literature which draws on oral history research to examine the histories of migrant groups, and academics within this field have noted the salience of metaphors in migrant stories.[3] This chapter will explore one of the dominant metaphors which emerged in interviews with South Asians who migrated to Leicester in the second half of the twentieth century, that of food.[4] The theme of food will be explored in three contexts: memories of 'home', experiences of work and stories of inclusion and exclusion. The aim is not to ascertain the cultural meanings of South Asian food per se but to unravel what statements about food reveal about the respondent's feelings and identities.[5]

Background to the Research

The research is based on over forty interviews drawn from existing oral history archives and fourteen of my own in-depth life story interviews.[6] The respondents occupied diverse positions shaped by a multitude of variables including gender, economic status (in the country of origin and Britain), ethnic origin, language ability, their place within the family hierarchy, education, religion, household type and so on. They were mainly adult migrants, but also included those who attended school in Britain. Some respondents had migrated two, three or even more times before arriving in Britain and approximately half of the respondents migrated from East Africa, namely, Kenya, Uganda, Tanzania and Malawi. This reflects the ethnic composition of Leicester as the city was an important haven for incoming East African Asians in the late 1960s and early 1970s. By 1983 22,477 people residing in the city were born in East Africa, compared with 22,414 from India.[7]

East African Asians exhibited a number of characteristics that distinguished them from earlier settlers who had migrated directly from the Indian subcontinent.[8] In particular, they were mainly of urban, middle class and Gujarati speaking background and having constituted the privileged minority within the colonial system in Africa they came to Britain with a myriad of transferable skills: business acumen, language capabilities, expertise in urban and bureaucratic institutions and familiarity with English lifestyle. In addition, as forced migrants, they arrived as complete family units and were more likely to invest in long term commitments in Britain. This contrasts with the majority of South Asians who migrated with economic and family ties in the homeland and often subscribed to the 'myth of return'.[9] Notwithstanding these shared characteristics, it is also important to appreciate the marked differences within the East African Asian category. For example, although the majority were Gujaratis, there were also Goans and Punjabis. The many layers of differentiation produced a spectrum of subjectivities, experiences and histories. For instance, the life story of Gheewala, a Gujarati Muslim who migrated to Britain in the 1980s to pursue his academic career was very different to Patel, who was compelled to leave Zambia due to political circumstances and arrived in Leicester in 1976 at the height of National Front activity.

My own interviews followed a life story method and rather than imposing a strict interview structure, the respondents were asked to discuss events and issues that they felt had been important in their lives. This approach reveals the importance of subjective perceptions and highlights pivotal points in the respondents' life trajectory. Life stories do not aim to yield generalisations; rather, the uniqueness of the subject is prized. Thus every person's story is unique. At the same time, life stories allow an insight into how social and structural forces penetrate and shape lives and, moreover, how people respond to and negotiate these forces.[10] This was most important considering women, in particular, have often been presented within migration literature as simply disadvantaged and disempowered.

Ethical issues were a key consideration throughout the interview process and my ethnic identity as a white 'English' female researcher undoubtedly shaped the research process and influenced the type of stories the respondents decided to tell. Although I was unequivocally positioned as an 'outsider', this was not experienced as a hindrance to establishing rapport and the women respondents in particular were often remarkably candid, with many revealing deeply private stories. Perhaps my location as an 'outsider' granted them the opportunity to talk freely and discuss issues without fear of repercussions. The cross-cultural context of the interview was, however, only one factor which underpinned the construction of the stories. The act of recalling past events is intrinsically revisionist.[11] It involves a simplification of reality and a process of editing whereby certain details are selected, prioritised and ordered and others suppressed and omitted. Some memories may be too painful to recall but they may also be censored if they conflict with the norms and expectations of society.[12] Events may be altered to reflect the respondent's desire for how their past should have been and as stories are always told from the standpoint of the present, the picture revealed by the respondent cannot be disentangled from their present-day concerns.[13] Ultimately, though, memories are related to the self and identity and recollections provide a sense of identity in the present. As Giddens has noted, self-identity is not founded on what we do, or the responses of others, but 'the capacity *to keep a particular narrative going*'.[14] In short, we need to know how we have become who we are. This does not impair the significance of oral histories; instead, an understanding of these aspects offers insights into the realm of subjective meanings and mentalities.

Memories of 'Home'

The interviews were replete with references to food and this has been observed in other studies of migrant groups.[15] Recollections of food can be traced throughout the stages of migration and settlement and were also typically triggered when the respondents reflected on growing up in their place of origin. When Sophina was asked to describe the village where she was born in Tanzania, she first recalled the market place and this evoked the powerful memory of a specific smell. She fervently exclaimed, 'you know I can still vividly, I can, this lovely smell of what used to be fried sort of, it was like sort of doughnuts, like bread, and I can still smell it you know?'[16] The smell of food clearly helped Sophina to actively recreate a particular location and this illuminates the importance of physical sensations in the process of reconnecting with the past.[17] Yet it also reveals how 'home' constituted not only inhabiting a specific place, but was essentially an embodied experience. That is, the locality was experienced through what one smells, touches, tastes and hears.[18]

Food was not simply used by the respondents as a sensory map to help guide them through their life story but was also used, mainly by the male respondents, to convey particular meanings about their country of origin. Karim worked as a bank clerk in Nairobi, Kenya and left in 1970 for Britain aged twenty nine. For him, East Africa in the 1960s and 1970s was a 'lovely country'. He elaborated,

> Well at the time of living in East Africa the life was much, much better than UK ... The availability of food was plenty. All kinds of food there meat, fish, no problem, vegetables, milk, butter everything. Some of the food used to come from Europe as well as UK because the white community who were living there were very fond of eating salmon, smoked salmon.[19]

East Africa was essentially remembered as a place where food was both plentiful and varied and included products imported from the West for the colonial British. Karim was therefore using food to highlight aspects of his former self-identity. In particular, to demonstrate his knowledge of the British way of life prior to his migration and also to emphasise that he actually enjoyed a superior lifestyle in East Africa. Karim's familiarity with Britain and his previous higher standard of living were core themes of his narrative and were resonant in other details which helped to define his identity. For instance, it was evident in references to his cultural capital, such as his British education, and his symbolic capital, like his car, which was a clear emblem of his status: 'we had good family Mercedes'.[20] This suggests that Karim was acutely aware of the racial stereotypes that a white interviewer may hold and constructed his life story to contest their prejudices. That is, the reference to food was one way of explaining that although anti-black immigration discourse defined Asians as 'strangers' and 'outsiders', they were, in effect already accustomed with British colonialism. Moreover, whilst racist discourses served to stigmatise Asians as 'backward peasants' and disregard their disparate and diverse histories, Karim's emphasis on his middle class status effectively debunked this stereotype and warned against any presumptions that all Asians migrated to Britain to escape poverty and privation. His dark skin colour did not denote a lower social standing.

Other food memories focused on consuming specific produce and this was evident in Singh's narrative. Singh's background was very different to Karim's. He originated from a landowning Jat family and this rural background was reflected in his childhood memories of growing up in a village in the Punjab in the 1960s. Like Karim, Singh emphasised the abundance of food, yet he focused on one particular memory: 'When I think of India and those times it brings back great memories, you know as soon as my mum would go down to milk cattle I would go down with a glass and put sugar in it and she would give me the first milk.'[21] At one level, Singh may have recalled this event because the consumption of fresh milk represented a daily ritual, one which he shared with his mother and that structured everyday life.[22] It represented a food regime; a habit of behaviour that was a vital element of his self-identity.[23] Yet Singh's memory also evokes a nurturing environment and relates to a phase in his life course when he was ultimately free of responsibilities, when his needs were met and pleasures and joys were simple. His cherished memory of drinking the milk was one way of idealising 'home'.

This perception of 'home' as an ideal land, coupled with the reminiscence of a more uncomplicated existence was also evident in Kapasi's narrative. Kapasi described the village where he grew up in Western Uganda, which was surrounded by wildlife and beautiful scenery. He remarked, 'It's funny, I mean every Sunday I still think of what I used to do every Sunday back at home, this is after twenty seven years of existence in England'. He explained,

> On a Sunday we used to go out for a long walk and we used to sit in a hotel, I used to have English cheddar and enjoy a ginger ale or any other drink with it, we just wanted to have that cheese you see 'cause cheese was something which was uncommon in that part of Uganda and it was fantastic having a piece of cheese [laughs].[24]

Cheese was uncommon and desired as a special luxurious treat because it was an expensive product, which like the smoked salmon in Kenya, was bought to Uganda for the British.[25] Kapasi's narrative, specifically the cheese and the hotel, signals his middle class status, yet the memory also encapsulates a sense of satisfaction and contentment and, coupled with the leisurely walk, the scene recreated by Kapasi, ultimately conveys a more relaxed and pleasurable life in Uganda.[26]

These food memories were not, therefore, simple anecdotes about the lives they left behind. They cannot be dismissed as mere nostalgia or a romanticisation of the 'good old days'. Rather, by presenting this idealised view of 'home' the men simultaneously expressed the unequivocal conviction that life was better before migration. The men's narratives were intimately tied to their feelings of living in Britain and can be read as a symptom of their dissatisfaction with their present lives. As other academics have noted, statements about 'back home' are fashioned by the circumstances of leaving and consequent experiences in Britain, most notably, experiences of exclusion.[27] Kapasi's story provides a prime example of this. Firstly, the conditions of Kapasi's departure were most significant. The sense of wellbeing that Kapasi recalled in Uganda contrasts sharply with his experience of having to flee Uganda. In his words,

> The trauma of it and also the anxiety and the suffering which you go through, there is no way words can describe those feelings because suddenly you realise that you have to leave your home and you're suddenly, homeless, stateless you don't know where your next meal is going to come from and you begin to hear stories as well and it was very widely known that Britain was a racist country and racism was rife in England and we asked ourselves 'are we going to the right country?'[28]

These feelings did not dissipate once in Britain and Kapasi claimed 'I think if you really think about it we are stateless or still remain homeless because we have been uprooted from a country'.[29]

Saddled with this, having settled in Leicester, Kapasi's narrative focused on the pervasiveness of racism in the 1970s including not only hostility on the streets which precipitated feelings of alienation and insecurity, but also exclusionary practices in the workplace, such as white businesses refusing to trade with his company. Other men's stories also focused on the endemic nature of racism in the workplace and how they initially endured physically demanding work in the factories and foundries. Many, particularly those from East Africa, stressed their frustration and acute sense of loss that they were unable to secure white collar jobs in Britain and were demoted socially. Hence Karim's insistence that his life had not improved in Britain. Within this context, utopian visions of 'back home' may have served as a vital coping strategy to counter feelings of disappointment, disillusionment and regret and functioned as an important source of respite, solace and self pride. Perhaps this sparked Kapasi's desire to routinely recreate his former life in Uganda.[30]

Gender and Work

References to food also offer an insight into the gendered dimension of narratives. The theme of food can be traced in several of the men's stories of their working life as entrepreneurs.[31] For instance, Khan migrated from Kashmir in 1952. He claimed he had difficulties obtaining halal produce as there were no halal meat shops, and so he would buy live chickens from Birmingham. To solve this problem he decided to leave his job working night shifts in a bakery and set up his own butchers in 1957. He then relayed how he acquired a grocery store and his story culminated in the establishment of his Turkish delight factory in 1970. His story stands as a chronological account of his economic achievements and portrays his skill and foresight to seize opportunities.[32]

Other men also detailed their progress within the food business and Patel's story was representative. Patel migrated from Nairobi, Kenya, in 1965 and the day after his arrival he saw an advert for some property. He purchased three houses and claimed,

> I started immediately, within two, three months I started the shop with English stuff, plus all Indian stuff and I rented that business for nearly twelve months and eventually I got another shop in Chester Street. I also started that and I asked my brother to run that shop then I brought another two ton truck which was a mobile shop and my son used to take that mobile shop through the city selling the goods and we had a big business at that time. There were only four Indian shops in the city of Leicester, only four. My shop was the fifth and at that time it was very difficult to find our foodstuff in this country. So first thing I started I imported some vegetables from Kenya, Nairobi for my shop and thus it was quite okay. I rented those three shops for twelve years.[33]

Like Khan, Patel's story is characterised by his series of advancements and the expansion of his business. Patel stressed the lack of other Indian shops in the city, and his insight in importing produce from Nairobi attests to his entrepreneurial drive and expertise. Clearly then, within his story, Patel plays the leading role of the dynamic pioneer. It is the familiar tale of the male immigrant's rise to success, whereby the men accentuate and affirm their status and influence within the public sphere.[34] Yet it is pertinent to note that whilst Patel recognised the help of other male relatives, namely his brother and son, the role of women is strikingly absent from these stories.

The women's stories serve as an important counterpoint to the men's narratives. They did not necessarily challenge the men's stories, but they provided an alternative perspective. Whilst the men's narratives tended to focus on their experiences within the workplace, the women's narratives, most notably from Sikh and Hindu women, centred on the difficulties they negotiated within the household. In one sense this was a reflection of the gendered nature of remembering, as other academics have noted the proclivity of women to situate their life stories within the context of the family.[35] Yet it was also grounded in the women's lived realities. It shows how the experience of migration was fundamentally different for men and women.

Food was also an important dimension of the women's everyday lives in Britain and this was anchored in their gendered roles. Put simply, women have typically been accorded the tasks of social reproduction and the preparation of food was a vital facet of this.[36] This role may have been accentuated in Britain as food was a key marker of ethnic identity and, as Yuval-Davis has contended, within multi-cultural societies it is women who have been responsible for symbolising, reproducing and preserving minority identities.[37] Some women were aware that they were socialised into this gendered role at an early age. Balbir grew up in a rural village in the Punjab and boasted her cooking proficiency. 'We were trained very very early. I was eleven when I came over from India and I could actually cook *subjee* curry and I could do the *atar* and I started washing up when I was in India when I was nine.'[38] Balbir claimed that her time after school was spent visiting relatives, and helping them in the kitchen and that the principal reason for her and her mother migrating to Britain was to relieve her father from the burden of cooking. She claimed, 'My dad was on his own. I think he found it very hard, you know getting up in the morning at three o'clock and cooking his food. Obviously he used to do all the curry and everything, cooking at night time'.[39] Integral to Balbir's narrative was the conception that cooking was as an important and valued skill. From this perspective, although Balbir and her mother 'followed' her father, they were not simply dependent on the men – a typical stereotype of migrant women. Rather, the men were reliant on them.[40]

This emphasis on the importance of their contribution within the household was evident in the narratives of other women. Sophina stressed the crucial help she provided as her family endeavoured to reconstruct their lives in Britain. Whilst her parents were primarily occupied with re-establishing her father's business, a significant part of Sophina's time was spent in the kitchen. She claimed, 'I helped my mum in the kitchen cooking, I was fifteen, sixteen, and did a lot of work in the house for her and in the shops you know, homework was last, you know, that wasn't a priority'.[41] Similarly, Devi's recollections of her initial years in Britain in the 1960s centred on her after-school duty of making chapattis for her family and the lodgers: an essential task as her mother was busy working full time. These stories were therefore one way for the women to expose the crucial and often hidden and unrecognised role they played in the migration process. That is, by helping in the smooth running of the household, and in Sophina's case, sacrificing her own concerns, they provided a vital means of support to their family and thus helped their parents adjust to their new lives in Britain.

The theme of preparing and cooking family meals was also used by the women to stress the hard work they endured when they assumed the role of wives and mothers. For instance, when Devi married she assumed full responsibility for family meals and when asked whether her husband contributed in the household she replied:

> Well Indian men they are coward they don't know. No. You have to do all the work. But then I didn't mind because I'm a woman and I always worked since I was little because I told you my father went to Singapore, my mother was on her own with my brothers, so I used to help my mum so I didn't mind. Even when I used to work full time, I used to come home and cook fresh dinner *every* evening. Yeah, yeah it's hard work, but I didn't mind because I enjoyed it.[42]

It would be easy to read Devi's narrative as evidence of the 'double burden', as her primary role as wife and mother was not displaced by her engagement in full time work. However, a closer reading reveals that Devi is attempting to communicate a different message. Whilst her narrative did not challenge the unequal gender division of labour within the household, by dismissing the men as cowardly and weak, she is marginalising their role and underscoring her tenacity and fortitude to maintain the household. Furthermore, although combining full-time employment and responsibility for cooking was defined as 'hard work', according to Devi, she did not subjectively experience it or perceive it as an added pressure because her upbringing had prepared her for this role. Her life story stressed the poverty and struggles which characterised life in Gujarat, India, where, in her words, 'the life was very hard'.[43] In one sense she was already accustomed to hardships.

This contrasts with many women from East Africa who voiced the immense difficulty they experienced when they shouldered the responsibility for providing household meals. For instance, Johan migrated from Nairobi in 1967 and she claimed,

> I used to get tired a lot, I just left school and came here and the work was so *hard* I used to work eight till eight and then come home

and cook dinner and everything and my father-in-law was with me as well as my husband, so there was three of us, and I was only seventeen so first I find it bit hard.[44]

Like Devi, Johan juggled full time employment with domestic duties yet unlike Devi, Johan had become accustomed to servants in East Africa – a privilege she instantaneously lost in Britain. As a result, she was not prepared for the arduous nature of housework. In Johan's narrative the new life in Britain was not presented as a continuous struggle; rather, she stressed the manifold adversities she experienced as she not only adjusted to a new class position but was expected to conform to new roles of responsibility. This is further illustrated in the context of her life story. To summarise, Johan had planned to study medicine at university. However, once in Britain she married at seventeen and then found unrewarding and monotonous work in a box factory. Her hopes and ambitions were irrevocably eradicated. Her emphasis on the hardships she experienced was one way of expressing the profound impact that migration had on the course of her life. It clearly underlined the sense of rupture and disjuncture she initially experienced.[45]

This theme was also resonant in Sue's narrative. Sue moved from Tanzania to India and then to Britain in 1976. Like many female respondents she married soon after migration and this was recalled as a particularly stressful and pressurised phase. According to Sue her in-laws expressed an unequivocal dislike to her based on her inability to pod peas efficiently and she stressed that her life in East Africa had not prepared her for the demanding role of daughter-in-law. She stated, 'So when I helped in the kitchen, cooking I wouldn't tidy the kitchen or the sink I would leave everything *messy* but it's not my fault because I was not trained to do that at all'.[46] The hardship she experienced was portrayed through various anecdotes. For instance, according to Sue, the family used physical force and expelled her from the house, to ensure her submission to their demands and in particular, that food be cooked to their preferences.

> I was thrown out so many times, out of the house because I'd argued or because I hadn't put enough salt in the curry or something like that you know, so it's like they'd throw me out then come and fetch me when they felt like it and you know I begged them for forgivingness and I cried and I said 'okay I'll never do it I'll make good curries from now on I'll make good chapattis'.[47]

This tale of suffering and hardship was also emphasised as she delineated the list of household tasks that punctured her daily routine.

> I used to cook, I used to make hot meals twice a day ... So I was like looking after my daughter, my new born daughter, doing all the shop work and doing all the house work and I was washing clothes and sounds like a Cinderella story but yes, I was hoovering the whole house it had to be done every day, polishing, cooking, washing clothes, washing up, everything you name it yeah? And then serve them hot food. It has to be hot served on the table for my father-in-law, my husband and my mother-in-law and then I was the last one to eat.[48]

These examples provide an insight into how many of the women's lives were governed by a hectic schedule, which revolved around balancing demanding household chores, childcare and responding to the needs of others. This labour was time consuming and had severe ramifications for other aspects of their lives. Consequently, many women lamented their lack of a social life during the initial years of resettlement. Nevertheless, this is not merely to suggest that these women were exploited by an oppressive patriarchal regime or were passive victims who should be pitied.[49] Rather, by giving precedence to these experiences, these women were exposing the ways in which their lives were constrained, but also demonstrating their strength and capacity to manage these difficulties. By stressing the demanding work they endured, they were simultaneously highlighting their resourcefulness and resilience to cope and adapt to different roles. It was, therefore, a way of defining themselves to show how they had lived through these struggles. Furthermore, the emphasis on hard work was a way of the women highlighting the importance of their contribution to the history of migrancy success. It served as a quiet protest, that their work and consequent sacrifices, albeit conducted 'behind the scenes', were not insignificant or of secondary importance to the men.[50] This is an important acknowledgement as women's work is often devalued and deemed trivial and insignificant.[51]

Notwithstanding this, it is important to note that the women's relationship to food was not uniformly associated with hard work. The narratives reveal that when the women reached middle age, cooking was not couched in terms of gruelling work, but was largely defined as a positive experience.[52] For instance, Sue felt proud that she was able to provide meals for her family.

> I still feel it is my duty to make sure that I've cooked for the family and managed to feed them on time if possible. The kind of work I do it doesn't always allow me to do that but as far as I can do that I

do that. I make a point to feed my family, to make it a priority once I walk into the house.[53]

This role was, therefore, an important source of identity and status and granted her respect from relatives, hence she added, 'in our family people take my example'.[54] For other women their knowledge of cooking gave them opportunities to pursue a 'cultural career' beyond the confines of the household. For instance, Devi described how after her children had grown up and left home she became involved in voluntary work within a local school. She reflected, 'I used to go and show cooking to Indian children, you know what is chapattis and all this. I used to love it, I used to love it'.[55] This highlights an important facet of the women's experiences: that they were not only gendered but were also fundamentally shaped by their stage within the life course. As a daughter-in-law a woman was expected to be deferential, yet this was a transient phase and in the course of her life she gained more authority within the household.[56]

Exclusion and Inclusion

The theme of food also featured in accounts of relationships with white people. In several cases, it featured in accounts of racism.[57] A typical recollection was of white neighbours complaining of the smell of food. Johan claimed, 'English people they used to say "oh do you eat garlic? Oh doesn't that smell?"'[58] Similarly, Singh, referring to the 1970s, asserted that:

> in those days because we were in a minority I think we were a little bit more picked on because we were different. I remember some of the neighbours didn't like the smell of our cooking and they came round and said 'can you close the doors or something when you're cooking? We don't like the smell of your cooking' and things like that that started irritating the white people.[59]

Singh was therefore conscious of how the smell of food marked him out as 'different' and as an 'other'. His experience was an encounter with cultural racism, whereby cultural characteristics were used to determine who belonged to the British nation. Here the street was a microcosm of the nation, thus the complaints of the white neighbours signalled that Asians and their cultural habits were incompatible with British lifestyles and were essentially an undesirable presence in the neighbourhood.[60] Singh's comment was also typical of other accounts whereby hostility was not remembered through accounts of verbal or physical abuse but was experienced as minor disturbances and petty conflicts at the local street level.

Despite this example, food was more commonly employed by the respondents to symbolise positive relations with the local white population and this was most apparent in the women's narratives. For instance, when Balbir first arrived in Leicester she described how her neighbour would offer her lollypops over the garden and another neighbour would bring round mince pies and jam tarts. She claimed, 'The *whole street* was so friendly you can't find neighbours like that nowadays. I just don't think you can, they were so friendly'.[61] In this case, food illustrated her inclusion into the neighbourhood and emphasised how she felt welcomed by the local white inhabitants. There were a multitude of other examples. For instance, Chitra described how she spent her lunchtimes eating ice cream in the park with her friend from work to illustrate the absence of hostility and show how she was unambiguously accepted. Hence she stressed, 'I honestly didn't have any problems *at all* when I started working'.[62]

Other women recalled more close friendships with white women. Devi claimed,

> There was a lady called Mabel and she taught me how to do overlocking how to do it and she became *such a good* friend she was old lady, *very nice,* very gentle. I used to go to her house and visit her at the hall but because she was older she passed away. Oh often I think about her, such a wonderful lady I used to go and visit her all the time. I remember she used to make banana jelly, frothy with milk and then she used to slice bananas on top, you know such a wonderful; I will never forget that bit.[63]

Mabel was more than a work colleague or neighbour to Devi, she was valued as a 'good friend'. The banana jelly was a tangible signifier of their friendship and of Mabel's hospitality. In the context of Devi's life story it is clear that Devi appreciated this friendship because of the initial social isolation she experienced during the early years of resettlement in Britain. Devi consistently emphasised the lack of other South Asian women and this was influenced by the timing of her arrival as she came to Britain in 1960. She claimed, 'there was no culture here at that time, not many Indians here. I tell you there were only three girls in whole school on Melbourne Road. Myself and I'm Hindu there was one Muslim girl and there was another Punjabi girl. Only three girls'. She reiterated '*Only three girls* in whole school. Three Indian girls in the whole school'.[64] She attended school for two years before finding work in a textile factory. Again she claimed, 'there was only one Indian girl I met [laughing] she was Punjabi and she got married very young she was I think only about seventeen or something. She went away and there was only me, only me in the whole factory again'.[65] Within this context, the friendship of Mabel may have helped to alleviate the isolation she experienced.

Devi's story was not unique and for other women relationships with elderly white women provided an important form of support and companionship. For instance, Ranjan described at great length her family's friendship with their white neighbour. Again food was a prominent theme as her sisters would offer the neighbour the dishes they had prepared at school. She explained, 'So they used to make these wonderful dishes which none of us would eat so we used to call her and ask her and she'd be delighted because she knew what they were, so I think we built up a really good rapport'.[66] Like Devi, Ranjan emphasised the initial feelings of isolation she experienced and she recalled the practical help the neighbour provided, for instance, in helping Ranjan with her washing. Perhaps these relationships were remembered because the gestures of aid from the white women also helped the newcomers adjust to their new situation in Britain. Furthermore, arguably the women preferred to recall these relationships because they represented a positive experience. Indeed, several women stated explicitly that focusing on the positive was a means of coping with the more negative aspects of living in Britain. According to Ranjan she recalled the friendship of her neighbour as a response to racism:

> but it was so nice to have that experience you know whenever we'd thought of a racist remark being made outside or you felt angry about something we always had somebody to compare to say all English people are not like that and I think that was what kept us sane for a long long time and I think it's nice to have that. [67]

Conclusion

This chapter has attempted to decipher the complex meanings of food within the respondents' life stories. This has shown the importance of the need to identify patterns and tropes as clues to interpret narratives that reveal both personal and collective experiences. Attending to these aspects of the narratives is most important in the cross-cultural interview, where the respondents intended meanings may be easily lost or misconstrued and the western interviewer may unwittingly misrepresent the respondents' perspective. Overall, despite the contrasting and diverse backgrounds of the respondents and the kaleidoscope of experiences, food was a common theme that was interwoven in the narratives. As a metaphor, food was used in multifaceted ways: to convey aspects of the respondents' identities, in particular, relating to gender and class: and to vocalise their feelings and emotions. The topic of food was, therefore, an accessible medium that gave the respondents the opportunity to express complicated issues and experiences that may have been difficult to articulate.

Food was most important in descriptions of 'back home'. The memory of food as an embodied experience helped the respondents to evoke and re-imagine the past, and food also played a significant role as a custom that punctuated and ordered their everyday lives. Moreover, food was used by the male respondents to stress their class identity in the pre-migration setting and was an integral part of their construction of a former 'golden age', when life was unequivocally better. This idealisation of 'home' can be construed as a coping mechanism that helped to alleviate the men's dismay with aspects of their lives in Britain, most notably, experiences of racism in the 1970s that blocked opportunities for employment.

Food was also prominent in stories of work in Britain. Several male respondents established firms within the food industry and typically emphasised their abilities and success. In these stories of the dynamic *male* pioneer who essentially made good in the new land, the input of the women's labour was rarely recognised. The women, however, were keen to make visible their vital contribution and show that their work was not peripheral but fundamental to the family's success. The interviews revealed how the women's experiences were shaped by their former class status and were also tied to their stage within the life course. Furthermore, the women's stories not only emphasised their active participation, but also illustrated their resilience and strength, and their stories were part of a wider genre of 'hard work' narratives, which structured and gave meaning to their life histories.

The third context that has been examined is memories of food and inter-ethnic relations with whites. Although there were some examples of whites stigmatising South Asian food and thus defining the newcomers as 'out of place', the female respondents preferred to remember more amicable relations and a time when food was shared and reciprocated between white work colleagues and neighbours. These friendships were clearly valued because they helped overcome initial feelings of social isolation and, echoing the male respondents' idealised versions of 'home', the interviews suggest that the women may have also idealised these relations to help them cope with problems of racial exclusion. Finally, this chapter has highlighted some of the disparities between the men's and women's stories and this reflects the importance of the gendered nature of migration. In particular, the women's stories were a crucial counterpoint to the dominant image in migration literature of the pioneering male immigrant. This reminds us of one of the strengths of oral history: to question conventional wisdom and popular conceptions and actually challenge what history is.[68]

9

A Journey Through the Material Geographies of Diaspora Cultures: Four Modes of Environmental Memory

Divya P. Tolia-Kelly

Material Geographies: Objects as Artefacts

In this chapter I want to examine the importance of researching visual and material cultures in the migrant home, as they operate as mechanisms for remembering geographies that contribute to British Asian social history. My approach to this research is located within the 'material geographies'[1] literature that has burgeoned in tune with new anthropological writings[2] that posit a new politics of the material. My premise here is that material cultures resonate with active connections with memories; constituting a source of collective social history and personal memory for the British Asian diaspora. Memories activated through these cultures in the home are considered as essential in discourses of heritage, which are significant for the South Asian diaspora, often marginalised from the formal record of British, Indian and East African history. The prismatic qualities of material cultures ensure that these cultures become nodes of connection to a network of people, places, and, more importantly, to a narration of past stories, histories and traditions. Solid materials situated within the home are charged with memories that activate common connections to pre-migratory landscapes and environments. These memories signify geographical nodes of connection which in turn, shape and shift contemporary social geographies in Britain, post-migration. This form of memory-history locates the post-colonial both geographically (through landscape memories) and historically, as they are meaningful after migration. These landscapes are neither simply bounded nationalistic landscapes or lived tangible everyday spaces; instead, these remembered locations situate the post-colonial migrant within matrices of social history and heritage cultures. This situation is a post-colonial space-time, unbounded by formal nation or national history, not usually mapped or recorded by the academy.

In this research I have mapped these postcolonial connections, through the positioning of domestic cultures as artefactual records of connections to other remembered landscapes, natures and lived environments. This research positions the home as a site where a history linked with past landscapes is refracted through the material artefacts in the domestic sphere.[3] This reflects a shift in the focus of British heritage work that disturbs partial and thin accounts of a national past, which have emerged more recently. However, questions of 'whose heritage?' and 'whose histories?' are continually significant in examining the relationship between memory and the materials of historical narration.[4] It is clear therefore that any British historical geography or British heritage programme of presenting a relevant inclusive heritage record should include an understanding of memory-work that occurs in the everyday landscapes of the British Asian home.

Home is the site of critical artefacts that impact on the ways that South Asians remember collectively, representing a body of materials relevant to British heritage. By linking the refraction of local, national and migrational memory-histories, embedded in the fabric of everyday life, it is possible to refocus on the significance of 'home' in the making of broader national discourses. The 'home' becomes the stage for emitting history.[5] Material cultures are not simply situated as mementoes of a bounded past but are precipitates of syncretised textures of remembered ecologies and landscapes. These solid precipitates are where memories of past accounts accrue. Signification of identity, history and heritage, through these material cultures, depends upon the continuing reliance on the past for sustenance in the present. These material cultures secrete an essence of security and stability. Ironically, these material foundations are sometimes transient, ephemeral things, which in turn fade, tear, fragment, dissolve and break. Individual objects relate to individual biographies, but are simultaneously significant in stories of identity on national scales of citizenship, and the intimate domestic scene left behind. The new site of home becomes the site of historical identification, and the materials of the domestic sphere are the points of signification of enfranchisement with landscapes of belonging, tradition, and self-identity.

Material cultures, through their installation in post-migration homes are critical in the formation of new political identities, carving out new landscapes of belonging. These new contexts for material artefacts refigure the narration of the past imbued within them. Memory is an important political tool, grounding both individual memory and collective cultural heritage stories. These processes are not exclusive to the South Asian population: in fact other writers have looked at different migrant communities and their valuing of domestic artefacts as stores of cultural narratives and memorialised biographical narratives.[6] The presence of these materials of heritage disturb and shift notions of *Britishness*. By looking at the collage of material cultures in the British Asian home as layered with aspects of memory, I have examined them as historical inscriptions within the domestic landscape. Material cultures are critical in relation to the new sites of identity-territory relations; memory-history is activated in relation to the new context of living. These domestic inscriptions record the post-colonial positioning that informs a politics of South Asianess within a multicultural landscape. Imbued within this political orientation is a geography of being, belonging and making home, linked directly with a post-colonial history. Within this analysis 'multiple provenances' emerge,[7] where the notion of 'home' and 'origin' are not fixed in one locus. Memory-history counters the bounded notions of 'Asian' ethnicity (biological) and nationality (cultural) through a system of collective logic that is a collectively remembered and valued memory-history.[8] The specific contexts of 'home' and origin are set out in the next section, along with some methodological contexts. This section introduces the substantive argument promoting the value of re-memory in the social geographies of British Asians.

My research has been with South Asian women in North-London. To examine the valency of social memory as inscribed within the materials of culture I designed a methodological approach to attend to collage of 'textures' of identification, that are present within British Asian homes. In previous writings I have demonstrated the value of memory-work in situating their identities within geographies that are mobile; the ways in which experience of a past geography or home resides with you as you traverse toward your next.[9] This route engages with other cultures. For example, British Asians when engaged with visual cultures such as film, reconnect with social testimony and multisensory body-memories as part of the process of engaging with the text.[10] In this chapter I will illustrate the process of memory as it contributes to post-colonial South Asian discourses of heritage, race and cultural identity. This is memory that is inscribed with a race-politics that is part of everyday social discourse.[11] As Leela Gandhi has notably expressed, there is difficulty in considering the post-colonial position as being truly post, as the struggles that these societies face are intrinsically linked to social, cultural, economic and political structures which are controlled and shaped by those ex-colonial powers.[12]

Methodological Matters

The research materials were gathered while working with groups of British Asian women in North-West London, over a period of twenty weeks. Other attempts at group work by geographers within the Asian community have failed because of the perceived reluctance of the British Asian groups to committing to a series of sessions with researchers and a lack of trust.[13] My history of working within the London Boroughs of Harrow and Brent enabled me to recruit mixed groups of British Asian women. The decision to limit the research to women was to enable women's voices (normally marginalised within and without the British Asian community) to be recorded in academic writing. Many feminist geographers have paved the way in conducting research with excluded members of society using reflexive and empowering research methods.[14] Mohammed is especially eloquent on the complex positioning of the Asian researcher working with Asian women.[15] Here, I do not claim any cultural authority, but to simply acknowledge that my positioning within the community which has allowed me access, and a sense of common ground in terms of diasporic identification. The nature of the group methods used to situate the women's geographical knowledge and values within their biographies allowed me to record intense, intimate, and emotional connections not normally engaged with. The in-depth group method in combination with a home interview effectively aimed to allow the women to become conscious creators of their own identification within a set of social spaces including their homes, which offered a material rather than abstract context. These contexts ensured that the transcripts formed a record of the groups' social understanding and values *in situ* (of their homes and community groups). Specific objects and their textures (visual, material, organic) held meaning through their presence in the home, and were not separate from the political, economic, and social negotiations of post-colonial identity in Britain. They were critical in enfranchising them to the new territory of citizenship.[16] The women's geographies that they are connected with through material cultures in their home are represented in the following four vignettes. I have positioned the vignettes as 'four modes' of memory. Each in turn illustrates the prismatic quality of material cultures; their role in connecting the women to 'other' landscapes and heritage stories and finally locates the importance of these in their citizenship in Britain.

Memory Mode I: A Myriad of Geographies: The Suitcase

In Autumn 1999 I interviewed Shilpa in her home. A woman with a rich biography, she was born in India and was currently living in Harlesden. I asked her to talk about her route to England and used this to access landscapes of 'home', transition and experiences of settlement, which provided a map of formal identification. Shilpa lived in India until she was married, when she left for her husband's residence in Kenya. This marriage failed and she moved back to India. Shilpa then remarried and moved to her second husband's home in Sudan where they lived happily for four years. After the birth of their daughter, she was given the opportunity by her husband to visit her parents in India. He bought plane tickets for her and she left without her daughter for a trip 'back home'. Whilst in India, Shilpa had a visit from her brother-in-law who informed her that the marriage was over and he handed her a suitcase with her belongings. She was consoled by her family who advised her to make a life in India. But Shilpa, then aged 27, soon made tracks to Sudan to 'retrieve' her daughter. Shilpa did regain care of her daughter and fled to England where she rented a small room; from this she was able to apply for Housing Association property. She has lived here for fifteen years without going back to India, Sudan, or Kenya. On a tour of her home, Shilpa showed me visual cultures that were important to her and her sense of 'home'. The first thing Shilpa showed me was a locked cupboard in her 'religious' room in which she kept things dear to her. She went through photographs of Kenya, some of her wedding, her husband and mostly of her daughter and their life in London. The richness and multiplicity of the stories and experiences that were locked away in that sacred space of memory, identification and social history cannot be represented here, but in the discussion of the value of material cultures to the South Asian population may, to some degree, explore the myriad ways in which south Asians are connecting with several nations, continents and cultures of being through the fabric, textures and natures held within their homes in Britain.

Next, Shilpa drew out a large, old, suitcase. It looked fragile; it was bamboo yellow with aluminium fittings. It was from another age and certainly another society, in which her treasured things are kept. She reverently laid out the contents in the living room. There were pieces of jewellery and toys, attached to which was the story of her younger sister's visit to Harlesden from India about eleven years ago. Shilpa described in detail the markets in her home town where her sister had purchased these items, the temples, shops, her father's clothing business, his sales routes through the local farms, his journeys to Kenya and Uganda, fruits and flowers, kitchens and bathrooms. Her sister had given her a model of an

Indian gas stove, an open fire design used in the back yard of her family home. Shilpa explained how she had used a similar stove in Kenya and Sudan. She described the heat in Sudan, the cold nights and the humidity. Through the materials within the suitcase, Shilpa created a collage of her migration history and reasserted a set of textures of connection to past lives, landscapes and senses of self. These were inserted within her British home to give stability post-mobility.

A second object that Shilpa became very animated at the sight of, was a metal bucket in the bathroom which she had bought three years ago in Harlesden. She was so pleased with this find, that she bought two: one to keep in case the other got damaged. She explained that she had used a bucket like this in her family home in India, and in her marital home in Sudan. It represented the morning ritual of getting up before dawn, filling the bucket with water for bathing, and setting it on a fire to heat for the whole family. Shilpa's family, and life in India, was evoked through this morning ritual. Since the day it was bought, she and her daughter had been using the bucket to wash in the mornings. Through this piece of metal Shilpa evoked many different lands and different relationships, the textures of her family home and the environment of Sudan became implanted in Britain. The bucket became a prism through which the intimate, domestic spaces of bathing, cooking and cleaning were evoked. In these refracted cultural landscapes were inscribed a set of aesthetics that connected Harlesden with India and Sudan. She had made reconnections with these places for her daughter; creating an identity, a citizenship, not in the national sense, but as a set of co-ordinates which allows her to map her mother's biography and in turn her family and her cultures of identification.

To think of these connections that are refracted as 'diasporic' enables a sense of connections, as elastic and constituted through time and space, that contribute to a mobile set of cultures that, as in Raymond Williams' term, operate as 'structures of feeling'.[17] My premise is that these connections signify pathways to identification through their textures. It is difficult, however, to define the signposts – the suitcase and bucket are simply 'material culture' because they are active visual metaphors for past lives and landscapes. 'Visuality' in this research has become slippery and intangible. The sight of these objects is privileged here, but this sight is informed by touch, smell, feel, and embodiment. In some senses a 'westnocentric' definition of visual culture is structured around media of expression that privilege sight; each medium in turn being governed by schools of art history and 'laws' of aesthetics. But in a world of memories and landscapes it is difficult to locate the way in which 'the mind's eye' becomes activated in relation to pieces of metal and plastic. The bucket and the suitcase operate as visual keys to a past but also incorporate multidimensional textures that exist in everyday objects. In terms of environmental relationships and citizenship the material and visual cultures in the home are pivotal in identity-making. They enable triangulations and *positionings*[18] that allow for the process of reterritorialising in Britain.

These cultures of *positioning* offer a sense of inclusion, which has aesthetic, sensual, and psycho-sociological dimensions. The landscapes refracted through these objects and texts of home are far from the women's place of residence and citizenship, indicating a sense of connectedness to places outside Britain at the same time as reflecting their relationship with or reaction to belonging within England. This examination of the group's relationship with visual media offers insights into what places are desired, safe and owned by this group, and which lead to the points of enfranchisement. These intimate knowledges and connections now contribute to the shaping and landscaping of the U.K.

Memory Mode II: Ecological Fragments: Splices of African Savannah

Many of the women in the study had migrated to Britain via East Africa: these were double-migrants[19] and thus reflect these connections in their narratives. A common vehicle for these narratives about the East African savannah and Rift Valley were touristic curios and craft objects. The touristic curios and craft objects that the women in the groups gather in the home, have been part of the commodity culture in the African tourist economy. Copper plates, ivory products and Masai Mara curios were all listed as valuable to the Kenyan women in their homes in London. These objects were not deadened remnants of holiday trips but vital[20] and enlivening and infused with the biography or cultural markers of the owner. This cultural value of the curios is shared amongst the groups rather than being purely an individual relationship. In Kenya, Malawi, Uganda, Tanzania or Zimbabwe, these objects were meaningful in very different ways to their contemporary situation in a British context. They signify Africaness in the form of a craft aesthetic which is kitsch. They are debris of a commodified ecosystem – elephant tusks, zebra skin, ivory necklaces, leopard skin handbags are all examples of the splicing of the African savannah into saleable touristic souvenirs: however, for the Asian women here, these were tangible moments of stability within a nation that they contributed to and were once citizens of. One of the most explicit slicings was in the form of an elephant's foot, used as a telephone seat in the home of Anju.

The sight of this foot was a source of many reactions from the women in the group – ridicule, mockery, laughter, and empathy were amongst the responses from the group to the sight of this tragic object. Anju herself as she talks about this object is tearful. Her sentiments well up at the thought of animals in the African National Parks slaughtered each day for profit:

> I felt sorry for whoever killed that animal that's why I bought it . . . I've seen loads of animal migration in Kenya. I'm fascinated by animals, all sorts of animals in Kenya. So I've travelled to lodges where you can see most of the animals . . . but I've been always fascinated by elephants . . . There are markets there they sell . . . in Nairobi there's the biggest market, and I was walking in that market and something just happened. That . . . whoever killed that, I felt just so sorry that I had to buy that . . . how old the elephant could be, but they couldn't tell me, because they didn't have any information. They just killed . . . It's funny . . . you never think that when you go and choose you always go and pick up these things. Why? Because it's built in you isn't it?

Anju describes the collection of items in her home including handcrafted Mvuli wood furniture, coasters of animals in the National Park, Copper etchings of elephants and ivory bracelets. She feels that the connection with these things is biological. She feels drawn to these textures and identifies with them as references to her home in Kenya and the importance of this connection there. For Anju the vicious cycle of poverty leading to the destruction of elephant herds is horrifying. The City Market in Nairobi is described vividly. It is huge. There are rows and rows of animal parts, animal skins, animal furniture, bags, and clothes of animal skin. She is empathetic with the fate of the elephant, maybe a young elephant, but also empathetic with the trader who kills because of poverty and a flagging economy. She is reconciled only by possessing the elephant foot stool. She owns the piece and is paternalistic in her response both toward the elephant and the trader. The trader is removed of agency but defined as an inevitable accomplice in the poaching and commodification of the precious flesh of the animal. This ownership and appropriation is translated as an act of charity, a soft-hearted response which sentimentalises the butchering of the elephant. The appropriation gives back some life to the object, in this new 'reconstruction of value'.[21]

In her home in England, the commodity of the dead elephant is reconstructed as a life-giving, and meaning-giving process. The reconstruction elevates the commodity to an iconographical reflection of 'Africa'. It also embodies the sentiments of loss, bitterness at the deterioration of African ecology, but also becomes an article of cultural signification, not a spiritual reverence but a relic to a lost landscape of belonging – Kenya. Other women in the group also had collected splices of animal made into domestic curios, but had disposed of them since. Bhanu recalled, 'I had a zebra skin as well, but I just gave it away because I couldn't keep it in the house'. Lalita stated: 'I had two ivory pieces, I just gave it away . . . And if they were God pictures, I just put it in the temple. Quietly wrapped it and left it in the temple.'

Shanta describes quite vividly the way that traders used to come door to door in Malawi. They used to be from Mozambique, who poached from the National Parks that surrounded Malawi. She used to turn them away, but realised that they had no other means of making a living. This is deemed as a trade of black Africans, who are responsible for killing the animals. The women rarely, as a group, accept their own responsibility in keeping the trade going through their purchases. This ties in with paternalism towards the *native* Africans, which is sometimes demonstrated as racial superiority; this is both moral and social. The social and economic positioning of the Asians in the Imperial race hierarchy within East Africa influences the way in which Africa is remembered. I observed a difference between those who came directly from India and those who came via East Africa. Africa is 'owned' in a different way to the Asian African relationship with India. For East Africans, India is described as a place of spiritual roots, and reference, but Africa is celebrated as a site of citizenship, with national pride. Kenya is regarded as home in both narratives of personal belonging as well as narratives of ownership and nationhood. This is emphasised in the way that language is used in their descriptions, 'we', 'our', and 'my', prefix place names and country names. The Indian women do the same with India. What is significant here is that this is constructed in the context of absence and loss. These are to secure a sense of stability in the context of migration. These new formations of relationships with 'India' or 'Africa' are figured post-mobility. Whilst in East Africa, owning these pieces had different meanings and purpose, in fact these were not desirable. The elephant's foot was purchased post-migration and is a material extract of the African savannah. It is a piece of the landscape, made sacred through its reverence by Anju.

The process of creating landscapes of enfranchisement through remembering lived landscapes is part of the process of positioning within a territory of culture that is secure and inclusive. Within the process of collecting this research, there was a sense that the Asian group had a set of common territories not bounded within a narrative of nation state or a singular territory, but a territory of culture. The mapping of the landscapes and the elephant footstool are not signifying a single nation but announce a relationship with a set of landscapes, which are resonating within the group as spaces of enfranchisement. These in fact are spaces that are significant because of the experience of mobility. The elephant stool is only valued as a slice of past nationalism post-mobility. It was not purchased in situ in East

Africa, it was secured in the home post-migration, representing the absence of the ecology of the African Rift Valley and the form of savannah landscape. However, in East Africa these landscapes were not 'owned' in a sense of citizenship, they were experienced as subjects of British rule. Experienced as a member of an imported cultural group, set aside as different from Kenyans, Ugandans and Zimbabweans.[22] Through mobility these landscapes are appropriated, literally through material ownership of splices of the landscape – wooden carvings, zebra skins and touristic curios. As a mobile group, British Asians are marginal to national discourses resulting in moments of disenfranchisement. In this situation the diaspora seeks to secure a sense of identity, belonging and new geographies of enfranchisement. The renewed, yet re-figured attachment to Kenya, India and other territories is made meaningful through a sense of exclusion, marginality and disenfranchisement experienced in England.

The attachments to past citizenship of 'other' nations, are sterilized, as the experience of being mobile, racialised, and ejected citizens of East Africa or colonial India evaporate through the new lens of Englishnesss. The experience of mobility is a catalyst for new mobile nationalisms. As mobile nationalisms, they are not embedded within firm nation states, but a set of cultural modes of identification. The diaspora responds with a vision of inclusion embedded in a cultural nationalism based in particular landscapes mobilised through cultures within the home. An inclusive formal, historical Englishness, and cultural nationalism outside Britain are considered utopian[23] yet the desire for an enfranchisement to land, culture and heritage at the site of residence continues. Cultural relationships with landscape are dialectically linked to the route of migration and a sense of continued diaspora, whilst being located within British landscapes. Mobility is central to the visions of enfranchisement and belonging as these sites of settlement are always in the process of being made in relation to moving away from other sites and locales. The role of visualised landscapes and material cultures as presented here, is that through their own mobility they enable a cultural vocabulary that communicates a mobile cultural citizenship, yet in their material presence they provide stability in the moment of being English and diasporic. These two modes are not mutually exclusive because an attunement to mobile cultural nationalisms are made possible through their presence and dynamism. However, I do not wish to promote the notion that all diasporas seek a bounded cultural nationalism, located within a single territory of citizenship, but argue that the desire for a sense of belonging and inclusion posits culture, nation, and/or a connection with a territory of culture as being a foundational mode of negotiating day-to-day living in Britain. A diasporic cultural nationalism then is a source of stability within discourses of cultural heritage structured through the experience of mobility, migration and a type of trans-nationalism not bounded through usual socio-cultural structures of nationalism. At some moments this is imagined as a bounded 'other' citizenship located in 'Africa' or 'India' and at other moments it is hybridised into new vernacular cultures of being English formulated through the diasporic imaginary.

Memory Mode III: Landscapes of Film: Memories and Cinematic Cultures of Dislocation

The experience of watching a film affects viewers in many ways, not least in that film cultures activate the social networks of viewers, 'imagined communities'[24] of viewers. The culture of the cinema complicates the analysis of visual cultures in relation to diaspora; in particular this bears on the way that body-memory and the visual together operate as points of triangulation for the new communities of South Asian settlers to England. Cultures of watching and viewing film are complicated by the commodification, marketing, and commercial politics of distribution, consumption and contexts of display. Despite these obstacles in analysing the relationships between text, viewer, and the social act of consumption, Bollywood plays an important role in socialisation and cultural history within the South Asian diaspora. The activities of cinema-going, video-watching or satellite-viewing are prioritised as real, everyday connections with cultures of language, religion, social mores and a re-inscribing of identity practices. The act of going to the cinema for the women has been part of their lives from a young age. The women talk about going to the cinema in groups, as a social occasion. The text of the film was not always primary, the gelling of social groupings was most often, more important. Film-going in East Africa and India is an example of the way that visual culture is multifaceted in terms of analysis. In this respect I regard film culture as a means of 'presencing' past geographies and contexts of viewing the film. This broadens the event from being explicitly about a text to the location of the cinema, whether in India or East Africa. What remain powerful as a body-memory in the women's recollection are sensory experiences; the smells, sights, and feel of the air, food and the society who had come to be part of the event; the recollection of a different crowd passing comments with girlfriends; the smell of the Indian cinema - musty, old and tired. As Lalita recalled, 'All those things you never think of when you are there! The smell and the darkness and the romance of the cinema is different, because it was in that auditorium it was different.'

The sensory evocation expressed by Lalita, is critical in understanding the way that new cultures of film-going in the U.K. recreate the sensual memories of the past. This is illustrated in the following quotes. Neela recalled: 'The effect is fantastic and I think we never used to have ordinary cinemas in Mombassa, we always used to go to these.' Similarly, Anju stated: 'It's because it's the open air, a young town watching a film together you know . . . it was like a little society.' Finally, Shazia asserted, 'It's like a picnic, but watching a movie sort of thing'.

Such trips are recreated here in the U.K. The act of going to the cinema is a group event, and up to thirty people will go together as part of one group. Eating, family togetherness, seeing the film and hearing each other's comments during the film, provide the multisensory experience which forms the memory of film going in East Africa and India. Shanta asserted:

> In Malawi we did the same . . . same thing with driving. We used to do the same thing, we go early, sit there. Tell your friends if you're coming out or not. They decide we leave at the same time, we park nearby children play and we bring pyjamas with us, so before the picture starts we put them on.

Manjula recalled,

> It used to be fun, it used to be a social place for everybody to meet. Everybody was in open space, people used to go early. Because the film started when it gets dark because it was outdoors, so people go at 5-5:30, while it's still daylight . . . and at 7 o'clock, everybody has good food. Everybody shares their food. And everybody tries to park near each other so kids can get together and watch the movie.

These descriptions are clearly evidence of the complete multisensory experience being an essential context to the film. The community is watching together, almost as an extended family. Chatting, eating and socialising is particularly a focus. The women describe the drive into the cinemas through jungle and open land. The cinemas are outside of the cityscape and they literally get there by entering into the 'wilderness'. The wildness of the journey and the exotic animal smells are heightened in the descriptions. One of the Indian women mocked the hyper-reality of the recalled memories in the extract below. The animals are described as magnified and more immediately present. The descriptions together form a diorama almost of African wilderness. When viewing films in the U.K., these landscapes become 'presenced' through the new viewing practices in auditorium and the narration of oral histories of these past events.

Manjula: It's not pretty because where we used to go driving, we used to go through a kind of jungle. Where I am saying was always a weird smell, before we entered the drive-in side.
Anju: You could hear the animals . . . because of the National Parks . . . and one a herd of elephants must have come out of the National Park and obviously you could hear ah . . . the noises.
Shazia: These people from Africa, as the fashion progresses, their stories will get wilder and wilder! (laughing) . . . next the lions will be walking in the cinema, you just wait!
Manjula: . . . a thousand cars coming out of the cinema. So there is always a craze, and everybody wants to get out quickly because once you pass a certain, you know, row of trees, you know it's very stinky, very bad smell because it's really outside . . . the outskirts of Kampala.

In this sequence, the two women are talking about two different cinemas, one on the outskirts of Kampala, the other on the outskirts of Nairobi. Cinemas in Mwanza are described as the same as those in Malawi, Mombassa is the same as Kampala. In the group discussions places are conflated through their descriptions. These conflations are quite often privileged over specific co-ordinates, places and events. Through memories, space-time is interwoven in a created memory where the specificities of smell, sound and sight are more important than actual geographies. These similarities and conflations signify the fact that these are constructed memories of sentiments, and sensory moments. The women remember the textures of the experience without acknowledging their change. The tense is always mixed and past often merges into present. This qualifies the moment as transferable, and mutable. But it is sure in its signification, the moment is mutable but the signified is a particular scene, a constructed landscape of cinema going through the animal noises, dry savannah and as a familial network of a homogeneous community. The heterogeneity of African society is absent; the heterogeneity of Asianess itself is absent from their descriptions. The memories are iconographical in their reverent privileging of the memory rather than the material and social structures of the moment.

The women's first experiences of cinema-going in Britain are significant after the experience of migration, and contribute to their re-settlement here. Cinema-going becomes a site of consolidation of the community and a creation of an un-alienating environment in England. Manjula below describes the first time she went to the Indian cinema in Ealing Road, Wembley. The act of going was as important as the sighting of a mass of Asian bodies, and related sights and smells.

Yeah it was a kind of get together because weekdays nobody could meet so this was like a social day out. Every Sunday, without fail we used to go for a movie . . . and it used to be amazing because there were no Indian shops (in Wembley), and you know like on the bus (smiling) on that particular day, you used to see so many Asian people coming out for the movie so everybody used to look.

Cinema is and was a cultural magnet for the Asian community. It galvanised the community socially, and empowered them culturally. The act of going gave a sense of community, and the solidarity it offered to the crowd was a means of giving confidence to the newly arrived communities. Seeing a physical presence of Asian bodies is an uplifting experience, and feelings of alienation and isolation are minimised through this creation of a new and real social network. Cinema-going altered the social geography of the U.K. but also ensured a reawakening of the memories of social geographies of East Africa and India. Women reflected constantly on the differences between cinema-going now, and then. These past memories were relived through the landscape of cinema-going being altered. Soon foods like the varieties available in East Africa and India would be available, along with the ethnic economic development in the cinema areas allowing for all sorts of cultural products to become available. Clothes, kitchen utensils, fruits and vegetables were sold alongside cassettes of film songs and jewellery. Manjula recalled:

Also the movies reminded us of home, like after coming here when we used to be reminded of home. Although I'd never been to India when I came here. I still felt as though it was part of me. I used to feel nice when I watched Indian films. You know I felt as if I'd come from there (India) you know. Although I knew I wasn't from there, but my parents were. Somehow I had some kind of attachment to that place.

The women remember the films with poignancy. Tears are shed as films which have been seen over and over again in India or East Africa, are reshown in the U.K. But for the women it is not the text of the film that is primary, but the actual display of aesthetics, which are social and cultural, which are important. Lalita describes her first sighting of an Indian movie after leaving India. It is 1972 in Montreal, Canada:

So he [husband] said 'what are you talking?', 'which one you want to see?' . . . [Lalita said] 'Both! . . . I don't want to come home. We'll have our lunch there, we'll have our dinner there and if they repeat the show I'll see that one also . . . even if it's the third time.' He said 'O.K. . . . Because I knew maybe we'll never see it again. It was already five months, six months I was already married and I hadn't seen an Indian wedding or any Indian kind of TV or anything, anything Hindi speaking. So after that again nothing for two months and then in August they showed one movie.'

The emotional response to an Asian event is significant. Lalita does not mind which film is shown, she enjoys the whole experience of the Indian film's language, aesthetics and of being in the cinema with other Asians. Each film is three hours long. She watches three showings in a row, demonstrating the power of the meanings of film going beyond the textual. The experience is symbolic of the broader cultural practices of Indianess. The senses are stimulated in relation to an appetite for a particular cultural production. The desire for these is fuelled through the absence of Indian aesthetics and language in the everyday. The satiation of desire is mediated through the film text, but only wholly addressed through the context of watching.

When talking about the film text itself, recollections centre on social and natural environments. Sometimes the landscape imagery is described as a powerful signifier of the whole pre-migration experience. Bollywood films become a site of memorialisation of home, this process of reverencing emerges out of symbolic and iconographical imagery and narrative within the text. Films become points of remembering sites of location, not actual lived places but iconographical images of India, Kenya, and Uganda. The films also allow a connection with certain textual cornerstones of culture such as literature, and language. The film songs are examples of this. Film texts also operate as a place through which the oral histories of migratory groups are refracted. The layers of film text, as one example, offers a parallel to the workings of memory in the sense that Toni Morrison argues that images are stores of memories for those who have no history. Memories themselves are not fixed and true, but are memories of stories and reflections; what she terms in her novel Beloved 'memories of a rememory'.[25]

The Indian film industry as a whole constitutes new non-localised ethnic projects, and constructions of ethnic identity. These are termed 'global ethnoscapes' by writers such as Appadurai.[26] The viewing of a film can trigger memories of a past history, fragments of which are lodged in the whole text. At the same time, the practice of watching can give new meanings to the location from which we view the film. I use the example of the film *Guide* as a film that was discussed by many of the women for its evocative effect on them as viewers. *Guide* was an enormously popular film, with high production values, based on a novel by R. K. Narayan, with an acclaimed musical score and choreography; all the ingredients necessary for a Bollywood blockbuster. The film, in its opening sequence, is a montage of landscapes across India. When the women view these scenes in the film, they trigger memories of India, but not necessarily first-hand experiences of India. Filmic landscape epics are superimposed with actual journeys remembered, memories of stories that are visualised but, most importantly, are reverently praised as representing a spiritual locatedness in a country that was not necessary a place of birth or residence. Sumita Chakravarty writes:

> the self enclosed romanticism of the gesture of recall, the metonymic substitution of the Hindi film for India, is generally a means of effecting closure of constructing rigid mental boundaries between past and present, parent culture and adopted culture, belonging and exile, nationality and naturalization.[27]

I would argue that the importance of this metonymical effect is that rather than 'effecting closure' through 'rigid mental boundaries', as Chakravarty shows, the films trigger multiple experiences, oral histories, and memories of memories. The metonymical effect of aesthetics, sound and iconography is to be an inclusionary set of sensory textures, which resonate a broad set of experiences, memories, life-histories and sensory experiences of the past. The scenes become icons of a multi-textual engagement with film as a visual culture that signifies a body-memory. The Bollywood film becomes the site of crystallisation of the processes of identification. This simultaneously offers fluidity and fixity, and it allows for a multidimensional relationship with images that are viewed through the eye but actually contextualise the practices of the body. Indian popular commercial cinema has come to represent a kind of psychic investment for migrants from India all over the world. It operates on many different levels. For all the women in the research, *Guide* had a special meaning. The film text on its own operates as a prism. It allows a connection between localities, spatial and temporal connections, which are stores for experiences and relationships. Landscapes in the film become icons of moral order and citizenship as well as aesthetic expressions of a cultural history. The journey that Raju (Dev Anand) the lead character takes, is more than a journey between two co-ordinates. It is a pilgrimage through the icons of Indian landscape, which trigger senses of connection with a Hindu spirituality, morality and understandings of individual citizenship. For others it holds more poignant memories. Bharti stated:

That clip to me reminds me of how we've all moved through different places . . . And when you leave, like you've got 24 hours to leave Uganda, what do you pack in your suitcase? What do you bring with you, to this new place? You've got all your memories, all your family . . . anything that's important to you in just one or two bags.

Shanta, meanwhile, asserted that 'this reminds me of the innocent life you know without any worries or anything . . . Say like he hasn't got any pressure, him and his mum enjoying life . . . free. . . . now, he's got his potli (knapsack) and that's it'. Hansa remembered 'scenery, going in the car and those Gulmer trees, because we used to go to Bombay to Gujarat by car. Not many people did at that time'.

For some women the film extract triggers a memory of actual journeys made through India, while others recognise landscapes within the sequence. They describe actual places in India, or routes through these. But when I asked 'when did you go?' or 'how did you like it?' most of the women had never visited these places, or had never even seen India. But somehow the film refracted memories of memories that their parents or family members had recounted. India was inscribed onto the film text. The film becomes a testimony to India through these inscriptions; the iconographies of home are witnesses through the act of watching the film. The film becomes like an archival record of the experience of Indianess as a means of fixing a cultural heritage in celluloid, and a personalised means of recalling re-memories of a notion of 'homeland'. This is a relationship with visual cultures in the public sphere, which is reverential but secular, different from the deep spiritual cultures of the shrine within the domestic and private sphere of home.

Memory Mode IV: Ecological Icons: The Palm

A sense of ownership is the core emotion which opens up the possibilities for the women to feel a connection to England. The everyday textures of their environments are a route toward understanding their connections to the broader context of England, and some sense of territorial citizenship. My aim here is to gain an understanding of these connections to environment, which reflect the women's feelings of belonging. The narratives that the women create are very much about expressing connections to nature and landscapes. As in previous sections, their narratives describe real, imaginary and symbolic relationships with natural textures. Growing plants as a part of home-making in the U.K. is important, some of which is connected to practices of planting abroad in places such as Kenya, India, Uganda. For others, the plants trigger body-memories which are multisensory; the scent of a jasmine flower has the power to transport them back to their teenage years where there may have been a flowering jasmine below their bedroom windows. There are narratives recalling direct experiences, re-creating other environments in England, but also to re-planting organic symbols of life in another place. Part of these narratives express the complexity of migration and dislocation, but others are a celebration of the pleasure that the women get from plants, trees and landscape in England. These cross-over so that, sometimes, English roses are reminders of roses in Uganda, while fuchsias trigger memories of bougainvilleas in Africa and India. There are particular landscape icons which emerge which are about the elevation of certain plants, trees, or ecologies over others which are then metonymical of the whole ecology of other countries, and experiences had within them.

Palms are particularly symbolic of colonial projects overseas. They are iconographical in that they signify much of the colonial discourses about the tropics. The tropics have always figured in European discourse as a means of signifying narratives of biological racism, of signifying geographically a cultural logic of European superiority, and a sense of the 'other'. The construction of the tropics, through colonial discourse, has a legacy in the contemporary imagination. Palms are a cliché within the tourist industry advertising to signify 'exotic' holidays, distant destinations, and an ultimately sensual experience. These are set against narratives about the urban, cities of cultural and intellectual stimulation, cool temperate destinations as hyper-modern and developed. Within the group's discussions, the palm was quite often recalled with pleasure as something that was special and missed. I used a painting by Melanie Carvalho's entitled 'Goan Palms'. In this session Melanie Carvalho was a member of the group.

On first glance, it represents an idyllic Goan seaside hut with palms. The women in the groups responded in different ways to Carvalho's painting. Many have tried to plant palms, mangoes, and guavas in their London gardens, trying to recreate the exotic in England. But these are rarely successful, as recalled by Bhanu: 'In Kenya I used to grow in my garden, not here. I tried once, a coconut tree. It doesn't grow very much. It grows up to there (12 inches) and after some time it dies off.' The re-planting of seeds and pods of pineapple, papaya, coconut and date palms are all commented on by English horticulturists, as part of the multicultural gardening techniques practiced here.[28] Lalita has the greatest geographical mobility, having travelled globally with her husband's multinational firm. Lalita tells her group that having a palm means so much to her that she has to take an artificial one with her everywhere she goes. The plant's presence makes it home wherever Lalita travels. It is an essential artefact. It does not matter whether it is real or 'fresh' as she describes it, but the look of it, the authentic

Goan Palms, by the artist Melanie Carvalho

texture of the palm tree has to be the same. The planting of the palm ensures safe settlement in the new home. It is part of the laying down of roots, and aesthetically provides a familiar corner. This 'landscaped' corner in the garden offers a respite from newness and strangeness. It is a symbol of constancy which stabilises and settles amongst the continued uprooting and moving. It also resonates with the soil of India, the layout of her father's garden and the greenness that she is used to. This re-planting of the symbol could reflect conservatism, but it also signifies a reverential relationship with the icon. The mini palm tree emanates homeliness, and it allows for some level of belonging and rooting and thus inscribes the new territory of the home, with the old values of home; it has a productive and reflective presence. As Lalita asserted:

> It's one Polynesian favourite and this is a tree, it's an artificial one, but this is a tree I used to have loads of in my father's farm and our house also. And wherever I went and I could put those trees fresh, Iput in my garden in the same corners, with the same red ferns border. And I made a similar corner in whichever house I could do ... It's a palm fern. You know a mini palm?

In reaction to the slide of Carvalho's painting other women recall relationships and episodes in their lives.

> Hansa: We had a tree, in Gujarati we call it Madaf, in Swahili, what do we call it? In our house everyone would gather there, and then whenever it rained all the children would say 'Ehh! A coconut has fallen! A coconut has fallen!'
> Puja: This is at the seaside, I've seen it in Bombay, Mumbai. At Juhu, (and) Chaupatti beach.
> Manjula: I remember Africa as well, in the villages, you see these kind of things.
> Lalita: In my house, in the back garden, we used to have 3-4 trees of coconut. And we used to have fresh coconut everyday . . . We used to be part of a green belt. So it is part of a landscape, tropical.
> Neela: I see Mombassa when I see a coconut tree. (laughing) Because the surroundings of Mombassa is full of coconut trees.
> Shanta: I think of Lake Malawi. Because there are coconuts because they don't pick much. Because it's hot there and it's right near the lakes. The huts, they have the same kind of huts.

On first glance at the image of the painting, the women in the groups recalled a love story with Jaya Badhuri, Kenyan coconut groves in *Eldoret*, Bombay's Chaupatti beach, the silver sands resort in *Mombassa, Dar es Salaam*, the Girna jungle in *Kutch* in India. The palm has direct resonance for the women. Real experiences and contact are recalled alongside descriptions of Africa, or Goa, or India. The trees symbolise the whole experience of the pleasures of the tropical ecology. The immediacy of the coconut fruit, the shade of the palm, and the intense heat of the tropical sun are all communicated through their stories. These stories are experiences of a variety of countries but symbolised through a single icon. The women are elevated into a sense of pleasure and heightened awareness of the multisensory memories recalled through the sight of the painting of the palms.

For Melanie Carvalho, the artist, this painting had its own story as she recounted to the group in her session. In her father's house she had been surrounded since childhood with pictures of palms and groves. She said that her father had recently removed a panel from the kitchen door and placed within the space a stained glass image of coconut palms. Melanie had never lived in Goa. She did not consider this her home or place of belonging, yet her father's stories over many years had instilled in her a sense of connectedness, with the landscape of Goa. The painting itself is 7 foot wide and 5 foot tall. It is actually a painting of a table lamp in her father's home.

Look at the image closely and it becomes clear that the scale is completely wrong. The trees would normally be about 60-80 feet tall, the hut about 10 feet. The coconuts are the size of the front door. The image is symbolic of a sense of place; it represents the processes involved in remembering places of the past. The reality becomes embroidered, more vivid, some things exaggerated, some things forgotten. Melanie describes the operation of memory as a subconscious infiltration of her father's connections to the territory of Goa, but which has been transmitted to her through his stories.

Conclusion: Artefacts and the *Portmanteau* of South Asian Geographical Memories

I have shown in this chapter how practices of the visual and material go beyond analyses of them as forms of representation. They are situated here as a *portmanteau*, a suitcase of memories of 'other' landscapes that are critical in creating a sense of inclusive citizenship in Britain. Practices of embodiment, mimicry, and processes of connecting with texts and textures allow a situatedness, a territory of belonging to be formed through a dynamic relationship with material and 'visual' cultures. This is not a reduced sense of folk culture or race culture or bio-culture but an expansive one which allows for a multiple number of self definitions and practices. Memory activates connections to the past through providing the testimonial record of a lived past, a body-memory of multisensory recollections, and a collage of rememories which constitute a set of co-ordinates for the process of identification and belonging. These multiple memories provide a sense of inclusion which has aesthetic, sensual, and psycho-sociological dimensions. Memories, form the basis of the new 'structures of feeling' relevant to the diasporic journey and essential to the forging of a new residency in a new territory of home. A new identity is figured through the lens of memory and uses the co-ordinates of migration to do so. Co-ordinates of home are situated away from the women's place of residence and citizenship, sometimes in real places or imaginary intangible places. But the women's sense of connectedness to places outside England, reflects their relationship with, or reaction to, belonging within England. This examination of the groups' relationship with visual media has offered insights into what places are desired, safe, and owned and, in turn, are the points of enfranchisement.

Remembering and reconnecting with biographical migration routes are an active part of daily living in the U.K., triggered by material objects and visual cultures in people's homes. The way that home is created through daily cultures of living is illustrated and shaped by the process of settlement in the U.K. By studying the cultures of living, the networks of migration already illustrated are revitalised and made a crucial part of establishing a settlement and meaningful identity politics in the U.K. Many of the women initially on arriving in Britain felt alienated from the *English* way of doing things, and felt very aware that they did not know what is expected of them. Buying clothes, food and travelling all became torture. Over the years these social cultures of food, religion, clothes, and others have become ways for the women to make life vital here in Britain. These cultures inform their recreating a culture of living and being for themselves and their families. It is through these inscriptions of cultural practice in daily life that they have struggled through and resettled. Feeling a sense of locatedness is important in creating a safe place of security. The home is a site of recording past homes and lands, as well as inscribing a meaningful identification through the materials of culture. The look of things, the aesthetics of materials are active in refracting different experiences and places. The refractive nature of these visual cultures in the home is significant in making place but, also, in figuring identity through places. This important sense of locatedness is shot through with real experiences, fantasy and memories. The idea of location itself is constantly plural in the way that the groups talk about their place of 'home' and their identification.

The women's descriptions of past places are referenced through many materials. Their relationships are realised through domestic materials such as kitchen utensils, clothes, food, and fabrics. Feelings of discordancy are mediated through the presence of these objects and materials of identification, to ensure that daily life here is shot through with the 'other' places of residency. Through these means of reconnecting, individuals make a collage of safety, security, familiarity and, above all, an affirmation of identity. Transience, multiplicity, and routes are inscribed into the location of home, by making the routes part of the fabric of daily environments. By transferring memories and feelings of belonging into a particular cultural aesthetic, belonging becomes transportable, accessible and mutable. The physical space at home becomes a place made up of other places, and the refraction of these other places of home become representative of a fragmented relationship with other territories and nation states. Exclusion is mediated through the creation of somewhere else which locates the body in a space of belonging. Every home can be considered to be an affirmation of identity. This is not necessarily specific to the South Asian diaspora, but what may be specific is the kind of textures of identification that are placed in the home. Residency is consolidated, and new citizenship is enabled, by the textures in the home.

10

Hidden Objects in the World of Cultural Migrants: Significant Objects Used by European Migrants to Layer Thoughts and Memories[1]

Caroline Attan

Introduction

Objects are involved in complex overlapping relations of significance. This paper examines how the choices and arrangement of significant objects articulates self-identity across discontinuity in life experience. In-depth interviews and observations of migrants and the descendants of migrants are used for this investigation. Some informants interviewed suffered traumatic life experiences due to persecution and loss of homeland and therefore the experience of discontinuity may appear extreme. The living room environment is chosen for the investigation of self-identity as it is used as a personal space and is shared with other family members and guests.

The interior of the home is filled with objects that are chosen, arranged and maintained by the inhabitants; these may be functional, decorative and have personal, cultural or religious significance. The living room is used both as a private and public domain to build social and familial relationships. It may be used to relax alone or in company and pursue leisure activities or to just collapse in front of the television; books, photographs, furniture and ornaments are in constant flux with those who occupy the home. My investigation concerns how individuals use the arrangement and display of objects and furniture to articulate their personal worlds. In particular the research demonstrates how relations of personal significance with certain objects play a role in the historical layering of experience and the re-integration of the self across major life transitions.

The reading and understanding of the organisation of the home environment and the choice and arrangement of objects and furniture exemplifies self-objectification; how the self is elaborated through object choice, arrangement and how this develops over time. The interior is constantly being re-shaped through physical interaction with those who inhabit it. The research shows how the furniture and objects in the living room become the vehicles of self-expression; they are placed by inhabitants and subsequently reflect their personal histories. Individuals are often aware that the objects express something of themselves to those who enter the room and that these objects are ultimately reassuring as they represent 'home'.

The investigation relates most closely to the work of David Parkin as he identifies significant objects that are taken from one cultural context to another and are used to establish new homes in new cultural environments.[2] This article explores the arrangement of significant objects in the construction of homes and lives of individuals in a new cultural environment. The concept of home is found to be both 'mental' and 'physical' and therefore always exists in the memories of those who have migrated, even when a physical home has not been established. Memories of the past find expression in objects and are used to recreate the past in the present as they are both literally and metaphorically taken from one cultural environment to another. The construction of a new home is central to how individuals adapt to living in a new, cultural environment, as a certain sense of 'home' is never really left behind but re-established.[3] As a result of in-depth interviews individuals are able to rise to a level of consciousness and articulate their relations with objects.

The interiors of the respondents' living rooms are furnished with objects and furniture that in some ways are displayed as an expression of personal experience; they are used to reflect their inner and outer selves. The objects themselves have the capacity to dictate lifestyles based on religious or cultural beliefs or may be indicative of the individual belonging to either a specific social group or are relevant to a particular generation. While Milena Veenis describes how objects cannot change people, although they may effect human reactions and responses, research discovers that as people change, so their relationship with material objects develops as layers of memories are attached to significant objects.[4]

This study considers the relationship between individuals and significant objects from two opposite perspectives. One departs from the physical structure of artefacts and what they communicate to individuals and the other focuses on the materialisation of individuals shown through placement and selection of objects and how artefacts are used to articulate personal histories. Basically, this considers the effect the object has on the individual and the effect the individual has on the object. The co-existence of people and objects is so natural and taken for granted that the process generally passes unnoticed. This research draws attention to this process but has investigated it through a human perspective for as far as we are aware objects do not have a 'consciousness'. This perspective also accounts for the way people use objects as a form of self-expression and communication expressed here as 'objectification'. People continually create objects and the process is continually re-defined. It is evident that although objects are inanimate they do have 'autonomy' that suggests that they may influence and affect people in different ways.[5]

The study is based on observations of the way objects and furniture is arranged by individuals in their living rooms and the dialogue concerning these objects. In-depth interviews with both migrants and non-migrants are used to reveal: the layers of meaning attached to significant objects; the complexity of their relationship with objects; the significance of the placement of the object; and the way the individual reacts with it are recorded.

Approximately thirty informants above the age of eighteen have been selected from a range of social, cultural and ethnic backgrounds. These migrants are predominantly from Czechoslovakia and Poland although migrants from other countries including South Africa, Germany, Cyprus, Guyana and Britain have been included in this research. Informants from Poland and Czechoslovakia are either Catholic or Jewish. The children and grandchildren of migrants were interviewed enabling me to focus on the effects of migration on the different generations of informants. Non migrants were interviewed as a control group. The programme of interviews was predicated on recognition that what respondents say concerning the choice and arrangement of objects is often ambiguous as conventions of display may overlay personal significance; therefore the significance of chosen objects cannot be taken at face value. The common characteristics of these informants chosen as suitable subjects for this investigation draws on the remaking of the habitus through the creation and production of personal significance.

Twenty out of the thirty informants interviewed for this research project are Czechoslovakian or Polish or are connected to these countries through parents or grandparents. The study is based in North London, which, since 1945, has been richly populated with migrants from the above-mentioned countries. Therefore informants from these two countries were selected for interviews through local availability.

Czechoslovakian and Polish migrants interviewed in this study predominantly came to London immediately before, during and after the 1950s and many are Jewish and had escaped to London during the Second

World War to avoid persecution from Hitler's invasion of Europe and annihilation of the Jewish race. Once the concentration camps of Europe were liberated, survivors tried to return to their homes in Poland and Czechoslovakia only to discover that they were the sole survivor of their entire family. Some of these informants were sent by their parents on the Kindertransport and hoped to be re-united with their families after the war, only to discover that their families had not managed to leave the Nazi invaded territory and therefore had perished in the Holocaust. All these informants lost their parents, siblings and family and are sole survivors of their families and therefore the point of migration was that of extreme dislocation and loss.

Areas in North London subsequently became richly populated with refugees who had become displaced in Europe and subsequently a culturally rich community was established. Musicians, writers, academics, medical practitioners, psychoanalysts among others established their home in North London and remain there today.

Both countries were chosen for this research because they are significantly different in language, history and culture and yet are both 'Middle European' so that it is possible to compare and explore the differences. They also share similarities and therefore it is possible to compare how individuals from these two countries display objects in the principal living room as they are among cultures that share the use of the room for significant display. Although the study consists of predominantly Jewish informants the sample was random and restricted to availability and the research predominantly focuses on experiences of 'displacement' and the effects on subsequent generations. The re-making of personal worlds for migrants underlies the character of their creative work and creates significance for successive generations in their creation of their personal habitat.

Informants initially completed a questionnaire to establish basic factual information concerning the life histories of informants before commencing the interviews. This allowed the interviews to focus on personal and emotional responses to the living room environment. Generally the informant referred to specific objects and the objects were described with reference to past memories. It is at this stage that the common meanings attached to objects become less relevant as personal significance is discussed. During the course of the two-hour interviews a relationship with informants was established, revealing more complicated relationships with objects that were often not present in the room but hidden or lost. Informant intonations during dialogue, body language, movement are explored to identify elements not verbally communicated during the interview.[6] These elements rely on the relationship between the interviewer and informant that requires a level of trust and friendship to be established.

Data was analysed to explore the patterns that emerged concerning different configurations of object and furniture that are used by different groups of informants and how the significance of objects changes according to their placement in the living room. The placement of the object in the living room defines the informants' relationship with the object and the way the individual wants to represent themselves to others.

Analysis of the evidence presented by these respondents shows that both the perceived qualities of the object itself and its placement by the subject are used to layer memories. The significance of those memories is defined by hiding or postponing interaction with objects that evoke complex emotions. By placing them aside, like secret letters kept in a hidden compartment in a bureau, the confrontation of difficult emotions can be postponed.

The Layers of Memory Attached to Significant Objects

Objects may be arranged in prominent positions in the living room to emphasise their importance to both the individual and a visitor, and these objects often conform to accepted social codes. For example, family portraits may be displayed in a prominent position on a shelf above the fireplace, to be seen by others.[7] Photographs may be used to disguise hidden meanings, as the image of the 'smiling family' may be far removed from the reality.[8] The 'making' of the objects is that which is displayed to others, the 'unmaking' is the individual's, often sub-conscious, continually changing and developing relationship and physical interaction with material things. Informant M displays one photograph among a cluster on a side table of herself, husband and two young sons taken just before the family returned to Poland. Her late husband was born in Poland and was forced to leave during the Second World War due to persecution against the Jewish population. He subsequently lived in Belgium and eventually settled in London where he married Informant M whose parents were Polish. They lived in a council flat and had sons but Informant M's husband did not believe in private ownership of property and subsequently since his death Informant M continues to live in this flat. He lost most of his family during the war but felt committed to his Polish identity and politics and this initiated his desire to live in Poland in the sixties. The family group with the husband and wife on either side of two young boys appear confident and happy. In reality, Informant M remembers her fear of her enforced migration to Poland, their failure at making a new life in Poland and subsequent return to London.

Jules didn't like houses so we lived in a flat and I loathed it, I was brought up in a house, in the summer it was claustrophobic. When we came back from Poland we were saving up to buy a house and then this flat cropped up and I knew I was never going to get my wish. I would have been much better off financially if we would have bought, but Jules felt that he'd rather not live in a house he could not afford, it's a silly thing to do, to pay rent all your life. In retrospect he was frightened to take on the responsibility, he was a very insecure person; you could easily shatter his confidence. He'd suffered, he'd lost his mother at six and been brought up mainly by an older sister who he adored and she died, perished in Poland. She was married, she had a little girl, I had a lock of her hair, I don't know what happened to it. His brother survived but his wife perished coming out of Belgium on a truck, but the men walked across at the time of Dunkirk, I mean all these terrible experiences, we can think how lucky we are.

The diversity of the objects brought from a different cultural environment show the complexity of the migrant's feelings towards the divergence of their past and present experiences. Although their life experiences are significantly divided they also merge into one, as objects and furniture may both refer to their childhoods in a different cultural environment whilst simultaneously providing more recent memories of events and relationships with people up to the present. The layering of memories attached to objects allows for the simultaneous recall of different memories through physical and visual interaction with specific objects.[9]

Hidden objects or objects that have hidden meanings attached to them may be found predominantly around the perimeters of the room: the exception being Persian rugs that have hidden meanings attached to them. These rugs are obviously placed centrally in the living room of the homes of older Czechoslovakian and Polish informants. An example of this can be seen in the experience of Informant D who is seventy years of age and lives alone in the same house in which she and her husband brought up their two children. She was born in Prague but her parents sent her to an aunt in Ireland on the Kindertransport to avoid Nazi persecution. Subsequently her family perished in a concentration camp and she eventually left her aunt's home in Ireland to marry and live in London. Informant D's Persian rug displayed in the centre of her living room reminds her of different stages in her past: her life with her late aunt who was like a mother to her, the gift of the rug from her aunt as a wedding present to her, her feelings of loss when her aunt died. The rug also reminds her of leaving Ireland, subsequently entering a new phase by moving to London, marrying and having a family and presently, during the interview, her concern that the rug needed repairing. Every time she walks into the living room not all these memories will surface, but the rug is the key to her memories, just like the title of a book evokes a sense of content and the memory of having read the book, without actually remembering every detail.

> I like the carpet. It's an old Persian one and we had old Persian ones at home. Somebody bought it for me, my aunt who brought me up, we bought it together, I lived with her. I lived in Ireland until I got married and moved to London when I got married, I hated it. I liked Ireland, I like the country, I didn't like London at all, terrible, I felt claustrophobic.

Religious artefacts that have been inherited by the individual may be hidden away in a cabinet because the informant does not actually like the physical appearance of these objects. If they have been inherited, they may serve to remind the informants of that which they may be trying to reject, their cultural or religious inheritance. They are displayed in a cabinet, because their physical structure signifies cultural and religious inheritance that may be used to hide layers of personal significance.[10]

Alternatively these objects are hidden because the real meanings attached to these objects are too painful for the individual to display in their living room and they do not wish to be constantly reminded. These objects are hidden so that the informant cannot be taken by surprise and therefore will consciously decide when interaction with the object is appropriate. For example, an elderly, male informant keeps the candlesticks he inherited from his late parents hidden in a cabinet. They were originally displayed and used by his late wife and himself, but now he lives alone he only brings them out occasionally because they remind him of a female dominated ritual which presently only serves to focus on his life alone in the house which he once shared with his wife and family.

As this previous example has shown, objects are often hidden because the informant has an ambivalent relationship with them and the hiding may act as an expression of denial. They are also hidden because they are not used to communicate to others: the dialogue with the hidden object is private and used for private moments to refer back to and remember deceased relatives or partners. Informant R keeps a book hidden in a cabinet in which he is able to trace his ancestry and connections to Scottish royalty. During the interview Informant R opened a glass cabinet full of books and brought out his most precious hidden object, opening the page at a genealogical chart that demonstrates his ancestral lineage.

It may have little to do with what I am like as an individual, but I spend time thinking about it so it must have some kind of effect. I think about Scottish things connected with the country and one thinks about one's name and so on and its connection with the country. It gives one too much confidence, pride in one's family and national connections, because the family were Scottish standard bearers and were present at all the Scottish battles.

The inherited religious or cultural artefact may be the only repository from the past to enable the children and grandchildren of migrants to try to piece together their ancestry through the objects that have survived. These inherited objects may be placed in a cupboard because the informant does not personally like these objects, but they are unable to let go of the past. The existence of the object may one day help them to understand more about themselves, the object acting as a key to enter past worlds.[11] While certain objects may concretise a relation between common cultural and biological inheritance and personal experience of migration, when the key objects/archetypes appear in the homes of the grandchildren of migrants who have no direct experience of their ancestors' cultural identity, they are defined anew, and may be used to refer to 'inherent' trans-generational experience. Inherited objects may be the only repositories of a lost cultural heritage linking the individual to deceased parents or grand parents. The relationship the individual establishes with inherited objects may be complicated by their inability to personally experience parent culture but also by their desire to establish their own personal cultural identity and create their own futures.

An inherited art deco china cabinet stands in the corner of the living room of the home that Informant S shares with her husband and young family. Most of the objects displayed within it belonged to deceased relatives, china, glass, old photograph albums and religious artefacts are displayed in the same way as they appeared in her late mother's home. A way of life, which belonged to the informant's childhood, is represented in the contents of the cabinet. Photograph albums are displayed, full of images of Russian relatives who have long since perished in several wars, including the Russian Revolution and Hitler's invasion of Poland. Objects that represent the early-married life of her late parents, china tea sets and cut glass cocktail glasses acknowledge a lifestyle that has disappeared. Inherited objects are not chosen but forced upon the informant and represent a cultural or religious inheritance behind which personal significance is usefully hidden. Informant S explained that objects are hidden in the cabinet because they provoke memories of the past that support a sense of identity linking the informant with their cultural or religious inheritance; they also provoke feelings of temporality and loss as the informant enters the void between deceased ancestors and the present.

The most significant example of the importance of the object as sustaining people through their lives, is that of refugees who are now elderly and continue to furnish their living rooms in the style of their lost childhood homes. They use objects, even if they are replaced objects, to enable them to continually remember and refer to the past in order to live comfortably in the present. Refugees often lose the language of their thoughts and may be lost in translation. Objects serve as a link between two cultures because they are a more abstract form of communication than words.[12]

Informant D displays her silver ornaments on a shelf above the radiator, not quite in view when entering the room. Her mother packed these objects into her suitcase when she left Prague forever on the Kindertransport and they are the only objects she has left from her lost family. They are slightly hidden because she is still anxious that they were brought into England illegally, the ornaments are 'sustaining' but they subconsciously make her feel uneasy, for she has lost her country of birth, her parents and family, and may never really feel 'at home' again. She expresses fear when describing these objects and asks me to turn the tape recorder off during the interview, as she is scared that somebody might discover that these objects were smuggled in illegally.

> That's my husband's clock, it was again a very old clock, brought from his house, he was an only child, those figurines were a wedding present from somebody, who knows? I brought nothing over, you couldn't on the children's transport, you couldn't carry anything. The silver came from home; most of it, it came from Prague, I had a trunk sent and I had better not talk about it (informant D became very nervous when describing how these objects came to England). That was amongst the cloths etc. ... managed to get quite a lot of (at this point she asked me to turn the tape off.)

The photographs of her family that are hidden in a drawer by her bed are so private and evoke such painful memories, that they cannot be displayed. In this respect the most important of these 'sustaining' objects is the one which is hidden. The object that is hidden need not be disguised, as the act of 'hiding' is a greater form of disguise. The hidden object cannot take the informant by surprise, the process of hiding enables the individual to refer to the object at a chosen, often private moment, and it serves as the catalyst for poignant memories.

Informants who have experienced loss will use the process of hiding as a way of communicating with the past and as a form of self-identity. Gradually they refer to the hidden object less as the period of bereavement moves further into the past; whereas the process of arranging and displaying objects plays a significant role in reflecting the way the individual appears to organise thoughts and memories. Objects on display denote meanings within their physical structure, which conotate layers of hidden meanings and significance; these denoted meanings form the basis of object choice and display. People use the arrangement of objects as a form of personal expression by allowing public meanings attached to chosen objects to disguise 'private' meaning.

Objects that symbolise loss are frequently hidden whereas objects that are an expression of happiness and success are displayed in primary positions. In this culture death is rarely seen and more frequently hidden. The ceremonies surrounding the rituals of burials provide flowers to symbolise the continuity of life and the reality of death: the dead body, is hidden in a coffin. Cultural influences dictate that the objects and images that surround death are hidden in the home. Family photographs are generally displayed in the living room to demonstrate the informants' relationship with family members and to memorialise happy events. Often the layers of memories attached to the image in the photograph may not always precipitate positive feelings but the images displayed are often conventionally acceptable. The following is an example of an exception as this specific photograph would not generally be displayed on the wall of the living room.

An unusual photograph that is displayed by one informant portrays her late husband holding his grandson during his ritual circumcision. The image is displayed in the living room because it supports an extraordinary story of survival; both the informant and her late husband were Auschwitz survivors and this image represents both their personal survival and the survival of an entire 'race'. Informant A was born in Krakow, Poland and as a child was forced to leave her home forever and spent the war in Auschwitz. She had been separated from her family and was unaware until the liberation of the camps and her return to Poland that her entire family had been murdered by the Nazis. In Poland she met her husband and they moved to Paris and decided to migrate to London to bring up a family in a religious, Jewish community. At a personal level, it is the last photograph of her late husband that replaces the lost images of her murdered family. This image, which under normal circumstances would never conventionally be displayed, represents that which is now present as well as the lost past. Informant A proudly indicated the personal significance of the photograph of her late husband holding her grandson during his ritual circumcision and the layers of memories this image evokes for her personally. 'With my husband, yes.

My son has to make a picture which he is very proud of. This is just before my husband died. My son tells his son all the time about it.' The hiding of the object separates the object type into public and private domains and the existence of the hidden object, which when discovered during in-depth interviews was the object that the individual would try to retrieve if they had to leave their house suddenly, proved that the object itself materially supports the self and the act of hiding was part of the process of separating and integrating a personal world.

One informant, who lost her home in a fire in which everything was destroyed, comments on how this loss affected her identity so profoundly that for many years she felt totally disorientated. She has now rebuilt her home and replaced objects and furniture, almost exactly as her original house appeared; but she will never replace the family albums, which record her sons as children. The loss is enormous, she can still see the images in her head but the absence of these albums means that there is always something missing in her living room.

Czechoslovakian refugees, over seventy five years of age, all hid photographs and letters from their parents who perished in concentration camps. These objects are often the only material evidence to survive their childhood. These hidden objects link them to a past and a point in time, the annihilation of their families, loss of homeland and subsequently their childhood. They have been traumatised by these events in a way which does not allow them to use these hidden objects as a way of rationalising the past in order to move forward, but instead leaves them with the residue of the past which they find incomprehensible. The existence of these objects and images is still used as a way of condensing their life experiences in order to retain a sense of self identity, even when informants find events in their past incomprehensible.[13]

Those informants whose partners/relatives died of natural causes (unlike those mentioned previously who suffered the devastation of knowing that their close ones were murdered) have established a relationship with these hidden images, objects which continually changes and develop. The deceased remain, as they were, locked in time, whereas the individual is constantly changing. Therefore the relationship they have with these objects is in constant flux; they often refer to these hidden objects with warmth and humour as if these objects (meaning the deceased) have found a permanent but comfortable place in their inner lives. They no longer represent bereavement but act as props for their personal growth.

Informant G came from a small village in Cyprus and left after her marriage to live in London although her husband returned to Cyprus for extended periods leaving her with a large family to care and provide for. After her husband's death she lived with her daughter, son-in-law and children and occupied a kitchen and an upstairs bedroom. Later, unable to physically manage the stairs, she lived in a room downstairs among all her photographs and possessions. She never learnt to speak English and therefore spent her time with family and friends. Informant G hides a lace curtain in her cupboard that she embroidered for her wedding. The curtain represents her gift at being excellent at needlework and symbolises her married life, her children. The curtain is not used, therefore, but put away and often reflected upon as the repository of her past life in a different cultural environment. It represents the loss of country of birth, but also serves to remind her of whom she is, her special gifts and where she comes from. These are all positive aspects of the role of the hidden object, that of self-enrichment and the object supporting the individual through the process of self-discovery and personal identity. Informant G took the curtain out of her cupboard and proudly held it up for me to photograph.

> This is something I got for my dowry. I made this before I was married. It's 55 years old. I did it myself; you hang it around your bed. It might have got stolen if I left it there. There is a sheet the same but I brought it all. When a couple are sleeping, these had to be out of silk, that was the fashion. It had to be very good silk. They wanted to sell this because they are expensive now. But I won't sell it ... I made this and my parents were very poor and it is important to me for that reason. It reminds me of my childhood and all the pain I went through doing all this, because I worked all day so that we could eat at night time. I made this for my dowry.

Informant G is now deceased and her daughter has placed all her mother's photographs and religious artefacts alongside the lace curtain in a cupboard. The process of hiding these objects is her daughter's way of dealing with the finality of death and to find meaning in her own past through the process of migration. The past is separated from the present through the act of 'hiding', just as her mother's personal history is now separated from her own. Personal enrichment through knowing the faces of ancestors is significant in contrast to those who do not possess photographs from the past and feel a profound sense of loss of family and identity. Informant A describes how her most terrible loss as she ages are the fading memories of the images of her murdered family as there are no photographs or portraits to act as a catalyst for memory.

The arrangement of objects in the living room environment is a self-conscious process in which objects are positioned for the effect they may have on the self and others. That which is hidden is significantly absent, therefore the objects displayed refer to a layer of meaning which can be physically integrated into a generally socially accepted home environment. Hiding is a conscious process of omission, hidden objects are delegated to a deeper internal layer, but are not sub-consciously hidden as the hiding of an object is a very conscious physical process: it does not happen by chance. In-depth interviews reveal that the informant is conscious of why they have displayed objects and talk extensively about the personal significance of individual objects but also reveal different layers of significance attached to objects. It becomes evident that the object that is hidden has the capacity to evoke experience.

Informant O displays two silver thimbles on a shelf, which were the only objects she has inherited from her mother. These are the objects of her childhood that should represent her dependency on her mother and a warm nurturing relationship; these are meanings we generally understand as representing memories of parents. The thimbles represent her father's trade as a tailor and how her mother used these thimbles to finish off seams on garments. The thimble is used by the informant to articulate her feelings of resentment towards her mother for her lack of mothering. Her mother pawned her wedding ring and all other objects because she needed money to spend on herself. It is also the reminder that she has no objects from her father who died when she was a child and who she loved deeply.

These thimbles ironically represent the lack of objects given to her by her mother, but prove that she succeeded in nurturing two sons and continues to do so even though she was not personally nurtured by a parent. These thimbles remind her that she never really loved her mother, although they are displayed because she misses her and wishes to remember her. They are placed between the photographs of her adult sons in some ways to prove that she is deeply involved in her children, which has ultimately given them confidence to succeed (defying her mother's lack of nurturing.)

Informant L now lives alone in a flat she once shared with her parents and husband who have subsequently passed away. Her family were religious Jews and she still carries on the traditions and her flat has not changed since the fifties. The rooms are full of furniture, china, and silverware and although she rarely uses the objects, they remind her of the life she has lost, with her husband and her mother living in this flat in the fifties. Her family were refugees from Germany and they constantly entertained all the young refugees who lived in the locality. The objects are preserved as they were but the liveliness of people eating and talking has long gone. The objects are repositories of the past but, in her memories, the objects incorporate hidden objects that come to life through her dialogue. The actual hidden object is one that is kept in the kitchen; a chopping board and knife would not conventionally be displayed. Informant L. brings it out of the cupboard to demonstrate her mother making noodles and rolling out dough. Through her interaction with these utensils, the sounds and smells of her mother busy cooking fills the silence of the living room as she describes her late mother. The object represents what was; it is hidden because she does not attempt to make it appear to look as though it refers in any way to the present. Informant L places the chopping board and knife on her Persian rug and emotionally describes her memories of her late mother.

> My mother was very, very house proud, she never stopped working at home. It was never clean enough, she was a great *balabusta*, you are talking and she has created a meal out of nothing, on Thursday she started to prepare for *shabbos*, she made *loction*, she made her own noodles and she rolled it out, and she had a white cloth and she used to put the cloth on the table and rolled out the dough, and then it got dried out she chopped the noodles, she made broad noodles, narrow noodles, squares. She made *challas* with six plaits, that was every week ... when she made chopped liver it was all hand chopped the fish the same, all the smells and the cakes, she loved cooking, I miss it all.

Some objects that have an obvious, figurative meaning, through their structure, for example Informant N's grand piano, may be displayed with the certain confidence that outsiders will not be able to access the hidden layers of meaning. His memories of his late wife playing the piano are evoked by the physical presence of the piano, not only through evoking memories of her music but memories of making the music occur. The grand piano belonged to Informant N's late wife and has not been played since; it evokes happy memories but also reminds him of his loneliness and loss. The piano stands in the room almost waiting for her return, the lid tightly closed on the keys. Only Informant N could conjure these precise memories which refer to his relationship with his deceased partner.

Conclusion

The hidden object may literally refer to the object that is missing, which has been lost in the past but remains in the informant's memory. The object that is missing may also affect the arrangement and choice of objects displayed in the physical world. Informants who lost their childhood homes and were displaced have furnished and arranged objects in their living rooms that almost exactly replicate their childhood homes before 1945. This is exemplified by Informants A, D and L who have replicated the living rooms of their lost childhoods in Czechoslovakia and Poland. Younger informants also display objects that refer to their childhood homes but these are often hidden or placed in a less prominent position in the living room. The china cabinet belonging to Informant S demonstrates the need to place objects that trigger complicated emotions slightly out of sight. Memories of objects affect the way individuals relate to the world of objects in adulthood as every interaction with the physicality of things is memorised in the body and subsequently re-enacted. [14]

The placement of the object in the living room defines the informants relationship with the object and therefore those placed in prominent positions are displayed for others to see. Informant A displays the photograph of her late husband holding her grandson during his ritual circumcision because she is proud of this significant event. The photograph is both public and private as she associates many layers of memories and significance with the image: whereas objects placed in cabinets on high shelves are not used as a focal point in the room. The reason for this varies, but often the emphasis is placed on uncertainty; the informant does not want to communicate something immediately to those entering the room, although that which is private is ultimately completely hidden.

The object that is physically hidden is that which has been de-materialised, so that the memories it represents are much more significant than the physicality of the object. Many informants who had lost close relatives or partners kept images and letters hidden for private contemplation. Informant D hides the photograph of her murdered family in a drawer by her bed and Informant N hides his late wife's passport and letters for private contemplation. The hidden object can also be found in the object that is present in the room, through layers of hidden meanings the hidden object emerges. Persian rugs displayed in the centre of the living rooms of Informants A, D and N all remind the informants of their childhood homes in different cultural environments. The layers of individual memory attached to these rugs weave unique personal histories that precipitate different layers of memories and emotions for each individual. The process of arranging objects in the living room mirrors the way memories and experiences are organized as sustaining a sense of 'self'. Although the process initially appears subconscious and self-defining, it is used as an expression of creative empowerment that each individual has over their immediate environment. This form of display may usefully disguise reality whereas objects that provoke ambiguous feelings are placed in less prominent positions and those that are used for private contemplation are often hidden.

Appendix - Short Synopsis of Informants' Life Histories.

Informant A

Informant A lives in her own home but only uses the top floor as a 'live-in' help lives on the ground floor. She is over 70 years of age and is presently recovering from heart surgery. Her husband died a few years ago and her married children and grandchildren live locally. Born in Krakow, Poland, she was forced to leave her home forever as a child. She spent the war in Auschwitz and after the liberation of the camps returned to Poland only to discover that she was the sole survivor of her family. In Poland she met her husband and they lived in Paris but later moved to London in order to bring up her children in a 'Jewish Community'.

Informant D

Informant D is 76 years of age, Jewish and lives alone in the same home in which her late husband and herself brought up two children. She was born in Prague but her parents sent her to Ireland as a child on the Kindertransport to avoid Nazi persecution. Subsequently all her family perished in camp and she eventually left her aunt's home in Ireland to marry and live in London. She worked as a medical secretary and is now retired but helps at the local hospice.

Informant G

Informant G was over 75 years of age when interviewed, she has now passed away. Subsequently I have spoken to her daughter concerning her own hidden objects that comprise of those she has inherited from her late mother. Informant G came from a small village in Cyprus, which she left after her marriage to live in London. Her husband often returned to Cyprus leaving her with a large family to look after. After her husband's death she lived with her daughter and son-in-law and grandchildren and occupied a kitchen and a bedroom upstairs. Later, unable to physically manage the stairs, she lived in a room downstairs among all her photographs and possessions. She never learnt to speak a word of English and therefore spent her time with family and friends.

Informant L

Informant L who is 79 years old was born in Germany but left with her parents to come to London after Kristallnacht due to Nazi persecution. She now lives alone in the flat she once shared with her parents and husband who have subsequently passed away. Her family were religious Jews and she still carries on the traditions and her flat has not changed since the fifties.

Informant M

Informant M was born in London, although her parents were Polish and her late husband was born in Poland. She is eighty years of age and lives alone in a council flat but enjoys good health and a busy social life. Her late husband and herself were Jewish by birth and she continues to practice Judaism whereas he rejected religion due to his communist beliefs. Both their sons have married Christian women and no longer practice any faith. Informant M has always enjoyed her cultural heritage and has subsequently been more involved in cultural and religious activities since her husband died.

Informant N

Informant N is 78 and was born in London just after his parents emigrated from Poland. Brought up in a traditional Jewish environment he continues to practice his inherited traditions. He has many children and grandchildren from two marriages, but lives alone in the house he shared with his second wife who is now deceased.

Informant O

Informant O is in her mid-seventies and lives alone with her husband in the same house in which they brought up their two sons who are now married and have families of their own. Her parents came from Poland but her father died when she was young and she virtually brought up her younger brother.

Informant R

Informant R is in his sixties and was born in Scotland and is very proud of his Scottish ancestry. He moved to London as a young adult and met and married his German wife and they have lived in the same house all their married life. They have four adult children who spasmodically return home to stay for extended periods of time.

Informant S

Informant S is 40, Jewish and shares the family home with her husband and three children. Her parents were born in London although her grandparents were born in Russia and Poland and came to Britain as young adults. Informant S continues Jewish customs and traditions that she experienced in her home as a child although some of these traditions have changed encompassing Middle Eastern traditions since her husband's parents were Syrian.

Informant T

Informant T is in her mid-forties and lives with her two sons and her husband. Her father was Polish and survived life in a concentration camp. Informant T has kept letters sent from her father from camp. The interview focuses on issues concerning her feelings of loss since a fire destroyed her old home and the memories of lost objects affect her profoundly.

Glossary of Terms

Balabusta (Yiddish) A woman capable of running her household effectively.
Shabbos (Hebrew) The Sabbath
Chollas (Hebrew) Bread made with eggs and sugar is especially baked for the arrival of the Sabbath on Friday night.

Part IV

Irish Remembrances and Representations

11

Passing Time: Irish Women Remembering and Re-Telling Stories of Migration to Britain

Louise Ryan

Introduction

> It was a small house, three rooms, and all cement floors, there was a big kitchen, and all the photographs ... we used to eat and cook and everything in the kitchen, we used to cook with turf because there was no such thing as gas or electric, we had to cook with the turf, turf fires and we used to have the griddle and a crane, and we used to pull it in and out, you see, and big black pots, we used to have all them. (Bridget describing her childhood home in Ireland).[1]

In this chapter I analyse aspects of the oral narratives of twelve elderly women who migrated from Ireland to Britain in the 1930s. I have previously published three academic articles and one newspaper article based on my oral history interviews with these twelve women. I have written about the women's negotiation of places and spaces[2], their descriptions of clothes as a metaphor of social transformation[3] and their accounts of kinship migratory networks.[4] It may seem that there is little left to say about these twelve women. In these previous articles I have used the women's narratives as a historical source, but I have said very little about the processes of memory. For the purpose of this chapter I have listened to the tapes again and re-read the transcripts paying close attention to the ways in which the women describe their memories of the distant past. In this chapter I analyse the narratives as pieces of memory work. Despite the differences in the ways the various women re-tell their memories, I have become aware of certain recurring themes and motifs that I will explore in this chapter.

I am interested in the processes of remembering and re-telling the past, acknowledging that those two processes are not always identical. Oral narrative involves not only memory work but also decisions about sharing and censoring. What is told is not necessarily all that is remembered. In her book *Age, Narrative and Migration*, Katy Gardner refers to the respondents' 'narratives' or 'stories' rather than their 'memories' because, she argues, we can never know for sure what someone remembers. We only know what they choose to tell us.[5] The narratives of the twelve Irish women discussed in this chapter are based on memory. Obviously, these narratives may not be complete memories, there may have been some element of censorship or selection in the way the narrative has been told to me. Thus when I refer to memories, memory work and remembrance I am referring to what was presented to me in the narratives rather than what the women may have actually been remembering in the privacy of their own minds. I am not concerned with the reliability or veracity of the memories but rather with the narratives as the products of memory work. As Mary Chamberlain argues:

> The narratives recounted provide not merely rich empirical data, but are important cultural constructions in themselves. What we remember and recall is not random ... Memory and narrative are shaped by social categories, by language and priorities, by experience and tense, by choice and context ... Memory not only recounts; it also explains as it measures and judges.[6]

As Alastair Thomson points out, 'we compose our memories to make sense of our past and present lives'. He goes on to say 'we "compose" memories which help us to feel relatively comfortable with our lives ... We seek composure, an alignment of our past, present and future lives'.[7] However, composure is never complete, there are always tensions and contradictions. The twelve women I interviewed had all made a similar decision at a young age that shaped the course of their lives. They had all decided to leave home and emigrate. Now, approaching ninety years of age, these women were looking back over their lives and remembering, reinterpreting, perhaps justifying, a decision made when they were just sixteen or seventeen years old. They had to 'compose' their past, in particular their emigration, in a way that felt comfortable and made sense of the seventy years they had spent as immigrants in Britain. Hence, the primary aim of this chapter is to discuss the strategies, themes and motifs that these women used to make sense of the past and seek some sort of composure between the past and present.

Andreea Ritivoi argues that narrating the past usually involves an attempt to structure events and actions into a coherent temporal sequence: 'lived experience – which is inevitably at times "messy" and hard to explain or categorize — becomes verbal experience, and hence, is made coherent and articulate.'[8] However, while this may be true of written narratives such as memoirs, in my experience, oral narratives of the past are not always clear, sequential or coherent. Few of the narratives in my study followed a clear chronological structure. In fact, there was circularity in many of the narratives. Stories were told through interconnections of places and people rather than neat sequences of time. Listening to the tapes again, I was struck by my active involvement in the memory process not simply through my questions and prompts but also through my reactions to the stories and my attempts to clarify a temporal sequence in circular oral narratives. Hence, a secondary aim of this chapter is to discuss the ways in which the dynamic relationship between the interviewer and interviewee may impact on the content and form of the narrative.

The Study in Context

Emigration has been a defining feature of Irish society throughout the nineteenth and much of the twentieth centuries. However, up to the 1920s, 84% of migrants from the southern 26 counties of Ireland had gone to the USA.[9] During the early 1930s emigration from the Irish Free State actually fell as the international economic depression meant that the numbers of people going to North America decreased dramatically.[10] But, by the mid-1930s, as the economic situation overseas began to improve, emigration began to increase once again. However, the majority of migrants were now going to Britain.[11] Official statistics suggest that 5,239 people migrated from the Irish Free State to Britain in 1931 and that by 1937 the figure had risen to 28,052.[12] These statistics, however, conceal a remarkable gender ratio. Women vastly outnumbered men migrants during this period by a ratio of 1,298 to 1,000.[13] While women had made up the majority of migrants for much of nineteenth and early twentieth centuries, the proportion of female to male migrants reached its highest peak during the inter-war years.[14] Irish women came to Britain primarily as workers.[15] In many instances women have been directly recruited from Ireland to fill specific vacancies within specific regions of the British labour market. Since the late nineteenth century the majority of Irish women have come to Britain as single, independent workers.

The Interviews

In 2000 while working at the Irish Studies Centre, University of North London, I began researching Irish women's emigration to Britain in the 1930s. I initially focused on documentary sources and I spent many happy months ensconced in the British Library, the Public Record Office and the British Newspaper Library at Colindale. While I grappled with dusty documents from the past, my colleague Mary Hickman suggested that it would be interesting and informative to undertake some oral history interviews. I began by contacting the Irish Elders Forum in London and was quickly put in touch with two women, Joan and Maureen, who had emigrated in the 1930s. I then sent a letter to the *Irish Post*,[16] as a result of which seven women (Tilda, Rita, Maggie, Annie, Kate, Gertie and Eileen) contacted me and agreed to be interviewed. I was put in touch with three other women through personal contacts (Bridget, Nora and Molly).

I make no claims for the representativeness of the women I spoke to. All but one of the women (Kate) came from working class or small farming backgrounds. All had come to Britain in their late teens or early twenties. They were all Catholic, all had been married and were now widowed and all of them had children. However, in these shared characteristics they probably reflect the experiences and backgrounds of many of the Irish women who migrated to Britain in the early twentieth century.[17] In any case, the women I interviewed shared many similarities with the Irish migrant women interviewed in Bolton by Bronwen Walter and the women interviewed by Sharon Lambert in her study of Irish women in Lancashire.[18]

I enjoyed all the interviews enormously and felt quite privileged to meet women who had lived through so much history. As Joanna Bornat has noted, reading historical documents in archives seems very dull in comparison with speaking to the actual participants in historical events.[19] Nonetheless, I was aware that these women were not offering me snap shots of the past. They were not living records of historical events. Memory is the raw material of oral history but remembering is not a passive process.[20] It may be tempting to think that the researcher arrives, tape recorder at the ready, to tap the rich source of recall that has lain buried for decades in the narrator's memory. However, as David Dunaway has warned, the process of remembering is actually collaborative and situational.[21] What is remembered and how it is re-told is influenced by a number of factors. For example, the process of remembering is not always spontaneous. People may have told these anecdotes and funny stories many times before, honing and polishing them in the process of retelling. In the course of the interviews I discovered that several of the women had been interviewed before and had been involved in memory work on more than one occasion.

For example, Molly talked in great detail and with considerable clarity about her life as an emigrant in London. I later discovered that she had previously been interviewed by the Irish national broadcasting company, RTE, for a programme about emigration. I have since found a copy of that Irish broadcast and found it quite an odd experience to watch someone else interviewing Molly. I was somewhat relieved to discover that the brief television interview did not explore the same level of detail as Molly's interview with me. David Dunaway argues that each oral history interview 'constitutes a unique performance'.[22] Nevertheless, if people have recorded their memories in autobiographical writing or in previous interviews they may present you with their rehearsed stories and it may be difficult to discuss anything beyond this carefully constructed script. For example, when I interviewed Rita I was very impressed with the way she remembered the exact detail of the nurse's uniform she had worn in the 1930s, down to the number of bottoms on her cuffs. However, as I was leaving she gave me some typed pages of autobiography that she had prepared for an evening class in life writing and there was the description of her nurse's uniform, word for word as she had told me moments earlier. Towards the end of our interview, Bridget showed me a project by a student from a local college. The student had interviewed Bridget about her long working life in London and her memories of Ireland. I was shocked to discover that this student had managed to record many of the same stories and details that Bridget had just shared with me. Perhaps the student and I had asked the same questions or perhaps Bridget simply had her stories well honed and rehearsed. The fact that Bridget had recently been interviewed and had her memories recorded in detail may explain some of the stock, apparently ready-made answers she initially gave to my questions. I was disappointed when the women gave me what I perceived as stock answers and I frequently probed for more detailed remembrance. In the sections that follow I will discuss how my questions and my reactions may have influenced the kinds of answers the women gave me.

Remembering and Re-Telling the Past

> By focusing on the pleasant experiences of the past, I get in touch with previous stages of myself and find a convenient evaluative stance with regard to myself.[23]

In her theorisation of memory and migration, Ritivoi uses the concept of nostalgia as a type of autobiographical memory that is triggered by a critical discrepancy between the past and the present. Nostalgia was originally defined as a form of home sickness, a painful longing for a distant time and place. But nostalgia does not necessarily imply that people want to return to an idealised past. On the contrary, we may remember the past in a way that helps to justify and explain our present experiences. For Ritivoi, nostalgia is a tool that helps us reconcile our need for continuity with the challenges posed by change and discontinuity. For the migrant, nostalgia may be a coping mechanism in the process of adjustment to the new environment. Nostalgia can help us to position ourselves in relation to the past, 'back home', and the present 'over here'. By contextualising and explaining the differences between now and then and here and there, nostalgia enables migrants to construct a coherent view of ourselves that can also accommodate change across time and locations. Hence, Ritivoi argues, our stories of the past are constructed not only in relation to the present time and present selves but also in relation to present location.[24]

In a similar way, Sinead McDermott argues that a person's narrative of the past 'changes its meanings in the present'.[25] Memory work is not simply about embalming the past as 'a perfect, irretrievable moment' but rather it creates new understandings of the past.[26] Instead of being dismissed as a conservative project, she argues that 'reflective nostalgia' can be seen as a radical tool for revisiting the past. Reflective or critical nostalgia does not seek to restore the past but rather to actively engage with both positive and negative aspects of the past. However, McDermott emphasises that there may be 'disjunctures' between the present and past that cannot be easily resolved into a seamless, coherent story. Aspects of our past and present self may conflict or not fit together and thus may not be easily reconciled into a coherent self. While acknowledging this, I want to explore some of the strategic tools that may be used to achieve coherence between the past and present, i.e. between then and now, there and here. Examining the narratives of the twelve Irish migrants, I illustrate the ways in which the women revisit, reflect upon and make sense of the past and position themselves as actors within stories of mobility and transition.

McDermott also notes that nostalgia can be a powerful tool in combating silence, invisibility and exclusion from a collective history. I am also interested in how Irish women migrants retell their narratives in relation to the collective history, i.e. the popular, received or established narratives of migration. What Mary Chamberlain has called the 'narrative repertoire of explanation and account' or the received genre of migration.[27] As noted by a number of other researchers, narratives of emigration often follow a particular format; a tale of the active, autonomous agent who succeeds against all the odds, however, the hero of this narrative is usually male.[28] As mentioned earlier, the established narrative of Irish emigration, especially in the historical context, is a particularly male narrative. Despite the fact that women outnumbered male emigrants for much of the twentieth century, the image of men who leave and women who are left behind is strongly depicted in traditional songs, literature and art.[29] Hence, Irish men have been defined by their active mobility, while Irish women have been defined by their passive immobility. All of the women I interviewed can be seen as challenging that limited representation of Irish women as well as challenging the dominant masculine representation of Irish emigrants. Thus, I am interested in the ways in which these women explained and justified their emigration in terms of activity, mobility, and economic necessity, characteristics that are usually more associated with male narratives of emigration.

Motifs of 'Good Old Days' and 'Bad Old Days'

Jane Moodie has referred to the ways in which constructions of 'the good old days' may impact on the memories of older people.[30] A similar observation was made by Katy Gardner in her research with older Bengali immigrants in the East End of London.[31] The elderly men she interviewed all described their early days in Britain in terms of their own youth and mobility. 'Their relationships to British places are predominantly articulated through themes of employment and money.'[32] As economic migrants this is not surprising and ties in very much with how the elderly Irish women present their stories of the past. They present themselves as mobile, economic actors who changed jobs frequently always trying to make more money. This relates to the 'good old days' when they were young and were able to move around with ease. Just like Gardner's respondents, many of the Irish women recalled not only their jobs but also their economic independence, the fun, excitement, friendships and pleasure of their early years in London.[33] This gave a rosy glow to their stories of immigration. Clearly, their narratives of the 1930s can be interpreted as intertwined with nostalgia for their lost youth, good health and autonomy. As Ritivoi suggests:

> As a repository of our previous success and achievements, the past acts as a powerful self-reinforcing tool. We derive from our nostalgic remembrance the comfort of identifying with ourselves.[34]

However, it is interesting that in many cases this nostalgia for the 'good old days' of success and achievement did not easily apply to Ireland. The 1930s were a time of particularly severe economic hardship in Ireland. Thus the women's stories about growing up in Ireland involved a negotiation of both positive and negative memories. The past may have been a time of childhood innocence but it was also a time of great economic deprivation. As a powerful self-reinforcing tool, I suggest that the past may equally serve as a repository of bad memories, the 'bad old days' that have been successfully escaped or overcome in some way. Thomson refers to the 'poor man made good' motif that is a feature of many migrant stories. For example, in their narratives of migration Pakistani men use this motif to illustrate their success in escaping poverty and finding economic security in Britain.[35] The twelve Irish women in my study had all been economically active migrants so it is not surprising that they also employ the motif of 'poor woman made good'.

The poverty they left behind in Ireland was clearly an important element of the women's stories. They all left their country of birth and, although several went back for extended visits, they would spend the rest of their lives in Britain. One could argue that their need to justify the decision to settle in Britain has influenced their negative memories of economic deprivation and poverty in Ireland. Most of the women describe Ireland as a country scarred by lack of hope and poor prospects in the bleak 1930s. Perhaps because they left Ireland at that time, despite frequent holiday visits, their image of 'home' is located in the distant past and is now viewed through the lens of almost seventy years living in Britain. As Gardner also found with Bengali elders, migration changes our relationship to home. Narratives of home tell us more about a person's experiences of life in Britain than about the reality of life at home. However, the women's stories of home were not simple narratives of poverty and despair, they were complex and multi-layered.

Stories of Childhood

Because the women had all left Ireland in their late teens or early twenties, it is hardly surprising that their memories of home were woven around their childhood. When I asked them about Ireland they described people and places they knew as children. For most of the women, childhood was depicted as a time of happiness, freedom, and close family relationships. However, as I will discuss below, there were some notable exceptions to the happy childhood motif. Although the women had experienced poverty, most emphasised the simple pleasures of childhood. Maureen recalled that:

> We'd look forward to Thursdays, my mother would go to the market in town and buy a big bag of apples for a few shillings and we'd have one every morning in our school bag.

Bridget also remembered food and the healthy lifestyle of the family farm:

> In them days you had fresh air, d'you know what I mean? Doors were always open, and you were practically out in the air all the time, continuously. If you were hungry you'd have a slice of bread and jam or an apple, you had plenty of fruit.

These themes are echoed in the narratives of Eileen:

> Well, we had such a lot of freedom, running through the fields and picking mushrooms and then we used to play hurling. We used to make our own swings, hanging out of the tree branches, playing in the river, and we used to play skittles and make slides when the weather was frosty.

Unlike most of the other women, Nora grew up in a city, but she too remembers her childhood through stories of outdoor games with friends and siblings:

> We lived in a small house up Gilabbey Street, and there was a big, empty garden across the road and we used to have a great time there, we all used to play house, we used to have good fun ... And then we'd go down playing in the river and if you were brave enough you could slip down the rocks into the river.

The motifs of childhood freedom, fresh air, playing outside, healthy living, simple pleasures and innocence were common to several of the narratives. The theme of food was also a common feature. Although I did not ask the women any questions about food, it is significant that so many of them described the food they ate as children. The emphasis on fresh, home-grown, healthy food was often contrasted with the unhealthy food children eat today. In addition, one could argue the childhood memories of food need to be understood in relation to the 'narrative repertoire', the received or established narrative about Ireland in the 1930s. The popular memory of the '30s' as a time of great poverty and hunger may help to explain why food was so important in the women's memories of childhood.[36]

Many of the women located their stories of Ireland in detailed descriptions of the places where they played as children. I was struck by how many of the women could also remember details such as the names of their primary school teacher and the names of the children in their class. Maureen commented upon this aspect of remembering and suggested that her memory of the distant past improved as she got older:

> I can remember back now to when I was little, I can remember going to school and everybody's name, things I couldn't remember a few years ago.

However, I am wary of making generalisations about the process of remembering and retelling the past. Even among these 12 women of similar age, ethnicity and background, there were marked differences in the extent to which they remembered or were willing to reveal the distant past. Some women gave precise details and dates of events that happened over 70 years ago, while other women were much more vague about specific dates. For instance, while Maureen could remember all the names of the children in her class at primary school, she could not recall whether she had emigrated in 1935 or '36. Annie told me 'my memory is very bad'. She could remember that she emigrated in October and described what the weather was like when she arrived in London but she could not recall which year that had been. As mentioned earlier, the women's narratives were often told through significant people and places, while specific dates and temporal sequences were often absent or confused. Although I wanted the women to tell their stories in their own words and intervened as little as possible in the narrative, I did become confused by the lack of dates. Listening to the tapes I was surprised by the number of times I had intervened to ask 'what year was that?', 'when was that?' 'how old were you then?'. The need to clarify a temporal sequence was partly an attempt on my part to avoid confusion as the narratives became more intricate and complex but also partly derived from the naïve assumption on my part that a life narrative should follow some chronological order. In her research with Barbadian migrants, Mary Chamberlain also notes that the oral narratives were not linear but 'mixed up' circular stories of family relationships often told without reference to specific years or dates.[37]

Obviously, the oral history interviews were dynamic processes framed by the interactions between myself (interviewer) and each woman (interviewee). In most of the interviews my interventions were very limited and many of the women talked at great length without any interruption from me. Nevertheless, my presence and reactions were all important aspects of the process. My smiling, nodding, eye contact, etc. were all crucial aspects of the interview but these silent physical reactions were not recorded on the tape or transcribed in the written text. My reactions, my body language, may well have contributed to the style of the interview and structure of the narrative. I was not merely the interviewer and an actor in a social encounter between two people but I was additionally the audience to a performance. My reactions encouraged the women to talk, to say more, to elaborate and perhaps in some cases to entertain me. I was very aware of the advanced age of the women and, as other researchers have noted, interviewing older people carries with it the added issues of respect and sensitivity.[38] I was wary of over tiring the women and looked out for signs that they were becoming fatigued. However, in most cases the women had a good deal of time on their hands and were very happy to continue the interviews for several hours. The interviews frequently lasted up to two hours and there was plenty of time, space and encouragement for the women to reminisce. Of course, the ways in which the women chose to use that time and space differed according to individual style and personality.

There was considerable variety in the style of the narratives. Some women spoke at great length without any prompting at all, while others waited to be asked specific questions. Some of these differences in style may be explained by the personalities of the women. For example, Gertie immediately launched into a very detailed and intricate description of her childhood through amusing anecdotes peopled by family, friends and neighbours. Her long narrative of childhood was not framed by a chronological sequence but by a series of interrelated characters. It was not always easy to follow this flow of talk and memory. There were few temporal or spatial signposts and the stories weaved back and forth between childhood and adolescence, siblings and school friends. What emerges most clearly from reading the transcript is Gertie's personality. She is a great character; an accomplished storyteller, used to entertaining family and friends with amusing anecdotes. Other women needed far more encouragement to talk about themselves and their lives. They gave details about their date of birth, the number of siblings in the family, the geographical location of their homes, but their accounts were initially stilted and lacked elaboration. As the interviewer, I felt a little disappointment by brief, somewhat stock answers to my prompts. This question and answer format fell short of my expectation and lacked the personal descriptions that I associated with 'authentic' reminiscences.

As Ritivoi notes, if the past is only re-told in a neat and factual way it is difficult to capture the feelings and emotions of past events, people and places. The narrative may lack the emotional content that adds a sense of authenticity. But when the speaker is seized by the past and is 'perceiving' rather than simply 'remembering' there appears to be a perfect connection to the past.[39] Listening to the tapes, it is apparent that I became more excited and animated when the narrator really seemed to have connected to the past. It is possible that my enthusiastic reaction encouraged the women to take centre stage and perhaps elaborate and develop on their remembrances.

Rita began by telling me that she had a very good memory. She seemed to connect to the past, to be 'perceiving the past', when she related a particular incident from her childhood:

> My sister was nine months old and I am three and a half years older than her. I remember her sitting on a stool or a chair, she was sitting up, she was nine months old and she was covered in chicken pox. I remember that distinctly.

The reason Rita can recall this particular day when she just four years of age is not because her sister had the chicken pox but because that was the day her mother left home. Rita describes her mother as 'mad', 'she could hear voices'. When Rita was four her mother spent some time in an asylum.

For Tilda the image that seemed to transport her back to childhood in Ireland was the memory of her mother washing clothes. Her widowed mother supported her young daughters by taking in laundry. Tilda's vivid description evokes a powerful image of her mother, hard work and the poverty that defined her childhood:

> She used to go out and collect the washing, she used to wash for most of the village. She used to boil it over the fire, you daren't breathe if she had white shirts drying by the fire, we'd say 'don't go in mammy's got shirts on'. 6 pence for each shirt ... She used to have a bath in the middle of the kitchen floor on two chairs and a washing board and a bucket of water and the blue and the starch. Oh we hated wash days.

To me as the listener, Tilda seemed to be really 'seized by' and connected to the past. However, David Dunaway warns that these exciting, elaborate and evocative aspects of oral narratives are likely to be 'set pieces' that are well rehearsed from re-telling.[40] It is equally important to pay attention to the silences, omissions and avoidance for these may reveal aspects of a story that is not being told.

Only two of the women, Kate and Molly, said they could not remember much about their childhood experiences. I will discuss Kate in more detail below. Molly talked at great length about her life in London but told me little about her memories of Ireland.

> LR: so tell me about growing up in Ireland. What do you remember?
> Molly: not an awful lot. I went to school and I came back and always had jobs to do because the farm was run by the children really.

I then asked Molly about her school days:

> LR: so how old were you when you left school, do you remember leaving school?

Molly: oh God, I never did much at school.
LR: so, did you like school?
Molly: no I hated it.

But Molly's lack of interest in discussing her childhood does not necessarily mean that she had an unhappy childhood:

LR: you were telling me about your family
Molly: we had a farm, not a big farm, but a very happy home. We were very happy.

She describes her mother in very warm and affectionate terms: 'she was a lovely personality, she was wonderful.' However, Molly appears to have been frustrated by life in rural Ireland, she says it was 'too slow', the wages were low and working conditions were hard. She had no intention of remaining in Ireland and as soon as she reached 16 she left to join her sister in London. Although Molly said she was 'very sad' to leave her mother, she was determined to emigrate and find a better way of life in London. Perhaps Molly's reluctance to remember or to discuss her childhood can be understood in terms of her decision to leave when she was 16 years of age. Her memories of Ireland may well be defined through her decision to leave it. As Thomson says, we compose our memories to make us feel comfortable with ourselves and to justify the decisions we have made in our lives.[41] Perhaps Molly did not wish to recall experiences that might have challenged or undermined her decision to leave. For example, Molly was not in Ireland when her mother unexpectedly died at a relatively young age. Molly's experiences of leaving Ireland in her mid-teens were not unique and led me to question how the other women reconciled their apparently happy childhood with the decision to leave their home and family at such a young age.

Stories of Leaving Home

As mentioned earlier, the past serves as a powerful self-reinforcing tool. Our memories of the past can enable us to reconcile our past and present selves. However, as McDermott reminds us, there may be 'disjunctures', uneasiness between the past and present.[42] A theme shared by several of the Irish women's narratives was the apparent need to reconcile a lifetime of emigration with memories of a happy childhood and loving parents. How can one reconcile a loving family with the decision to leave and live permanently in another country? Most of the women used family narratives to reconcile their happy childhood memories with their decision to emigrate. They emphasised economic pragmatism, lack of opportunities in Ireland, the importance of remittances and the financial benefits that emigration brought to the whole family. They also used kinship migratory networks to illustrate that family loyalty, ties and contact continued after emigration.

Most of the women emphasised that the only work available in Ireland was low paid and very exploitative. With the exception of Rita, who trained to be a nurse, all the women left school at a young age and took up employment locally before deciding to emigrate. For example, Joan left school at 14 and started work as a domestic servant. She vividly described her workload:

> You'd have to do everything, draw the coal and the turf on your back, milk the cow, milk the goat, keep the place clean, make the butter, it was hard work ... I think that was slavery.

Joan migrated in 1935 and joined her sister in London before taking up a hotel job in Eastbourne. Bridget's account of child labour in Ireland is very similar. She started working as a domestic servant on a farm near her home when she was just 12 years of age:

> There was no bath like there is now, and they used to have baths in the rooms, you know, tin baths and I used to drag all the water up the stairs in padded buckets to keep the water hot ... I used to do all that in Ireland before I came over here.

After enduring this work for several years Bridget decided to join her older sister in London in 1937. She describes migrating to London as 'a new lease of life'. She also underlines that migration enabled her to support her parents in Ireland. 'The money I earned I used to send it home to my father and mother.' In addition, she also sent home parcels of clothes and bed linen. 'I used to buy those things to make my mother and father happy, you know.' Several of the women underline how their migration enabled them to help their parents financially. For example, Annie worked in a hotel in central London and sent her entire wage packet home to her widowed father while she lived on her tips.

The overlapping discourses of economic necessity and family loyalty are most obvious in the narrative of Tilda. She left school at 14 and took local employment in the town near her home. She became a domestic servant for the local publican who had a family of six children. Her wage was 'half a crown a week' which she saw as a very poor payment for the amount of work she was expected to do.

LR: so you came to England when you were 16, why did you decide to come over?
Tilda: I wanted to come because I was only getting half a crown a week at home looking after these kids.
LR: so how did your mother feel about you coming to England?
Tilda: she didn't like it but there were no young people in our town once they were coming to 15 or 16 there were all going. I had relatives here. I used to say 'when I am old enough I am going to England' ... I knew I'd be better off and be able to help mam.

Tilda had an aunt in London who helped her to find a job as a domestic servant in Chelsea. She earned one pound, eight shillings and four pence per month and she sent one pound home to her widowed mother. Thus, for Tilda, emigration made sense financially. Domestic servants in London earned far more money than servants in Ireland. Her emigration was a family strategy enabled by her aunt in London and financially beneficial to her mother back home in Ireland. Economic narratives of emigration such as Tilda's and Bridget's underlined family loyalty and could be easily reconciled with happy memories of childhood and loving, self-sacrificing parents.

As mentioned above, we construct our memories of the past in relation to the 'narrative repertoire', i.e. the established, received or popular narrative. The dominant and established narrative of Irish emigration is largely economic and justifies leaving home through discourses of employment and finance. Thus economic necessity is a socially acceptable, taken for granted, and 'permissible motivation/ justification for emigration'.[43] However, this dominant discourse silences or renders invisible other, 'impermissible narratives of migration'.[44] Within this context it becomes difficult to articulate alternative motivations for wanting to leave one's home and homeland.

Indeed, as I have argued elsewhere, there have always been diverse and complex reasons for women's emigration.[45] Although most of the women I spoke to gave economic necessity as the primary motivation for emigration, as I will discuss below, this was not the case for all twelve women. Even within the narratives of those women who did use economic justifications, there were hints to other, more social, reasons for wanting to leave Ireland. For example, Molly said that she did not want to stay in Ireland because life was 'too slow', she found London a more interesting place to be. Maureen made a similar comparison between the lifestyle in London and at home in rural Ireland. Within one year of arriving in London, Maureen contracted diptheria and returned to Ireland for several months to recuperate. I asked if she considered remaining in Ireland at that time and she replied 'no, no I wanted to come back (to London)'. She said that life in the Irish countryside was very different to London. She described life as 'nicer' in London. Hence, although both Maureen and Molly, in common with most of the other women, used the dominant narrative of economic necessity to justify emigration, there are some suggestions in their stories that other social or cultural factors also impacted on their decision to choose London over Ireland.

But not all the women did re-tell their stories of emigration through the dominant economic discourse. Three women (Kate, Rita and Maggie) explained their decision to leave Ireland through narratives of unhappiness and escape to a more independent life in London. These narratives shared a common theme of family conflict and negative childhood memories.

Sad Stories of Childhood and Family Conflict

Unlike the other women, Kate, Rita and Maggie, described sad memories of unhappy childhoods and thus explained their migration in terms of an escape from the drudgery or tensions of their family home. Maggie says that she was 'fed up' with working 'like a slave' in Ireland. She was expected to give her parents all the money she earned and so she never had any money for herself. Maggie was the only woman who blamed her parents for the family's poverty. She criticised her parents for having 12 children, whom they could not support. 'My father only done casual work in the autumn and the spring for other farmers and yet they kept on having all those kids.' She described her parents as 'a hard crowd'.

Rita said that her home was not a happy environment because her mother was mentally ill and spent some time in a mental institution. Rita described her childhood as 'absolutely terrible'. She and her three little sisters 'had to more or less bring ourselves up, it was really awful'. Rita made plans to migrate as soon as she left school. Her younger sister soon joined her in Britain.

But while Maggie and Rita did occasionally visit their families in Ireland, Kate was unique among the women I interviewed because after leaving home she remained completely estranged from her family and never saw her parents again. Kate told me very bluntly that she 'ran away from home'. Kate's family was middle class and owned several shops and other property in Cork city. Kate said that her parents vehemently disapproved of her relationship with a local man whom they referred to as 'only a tramp' who was not worthy of their daughter. After many rows on the subject Kate finally decided to leave home and went to England with the help of a female friend who was working in London.

Kate told me very few stories about her childhood. There were many silences and omissions in her narrative and when I asked her questions about her family life in Ireland she avoided answering or simply changed the subject. She gave little information about her family or her experiences growing up in Ireland. After almost 70 years of estrangement from her family and her home, it is possible that Kate had forgotten much about her childhood. Unlike the other women, she did not have regular holiday visits back home to refresh her memory. It is also possible that she simply did not want to remember the family and home that she 'ran away' from and blotted out of her mind. When she spoke about her early years in London she said 'ah they were happy days', everything was so 'nice' and the 'people were very friendly'. She laughed a good deal when she remembered the fun times she had working in a large London department store and going to dances with her friends. Thus, Kate's migration narrative was presented to me as a simple narrative of escape.

The experience of migration, although often entangled with family relationships, meant that women had more choices and some level of autonomy over the contact they maintained with their families 'here' and 'there'. For Kate, Maggie and Rita, coming to Britain and getting jobs gave them the freedom to become independent of their families. All three women told their stories through notions of defiance, independence and autonomy. Maggie said that she was happy in England because 'I got nobody to tell me what to do, I've always been my own boss. That was my life, I think its been quite good really'. These three women describe their migration as an enabling process that empowered them to leave unhappy family homes and assert their independence.

Conclusion

Reflective nostalgia can be a powerful tool that allows us to engage critically with the past.[46] In remembering and re-telling the past we seek to reconcile our past and present selves through an interconnectedness of then and now. For migrants, in particular, there is a need to reconcile now and then with here and there. Ritivoi argues that remembering the past plays an important part in the process of adjusting and reconciling because it enables the migrant to focus on themselves as active agents, as protagonists in their own life stories.[47] However, the links between the past and present may not be seamless or straightforward. There may be discontinuities, 'disjunctures' or discrepancies between our past and present selves.

The twelve women whose life narratives are discussed in this chapter position themselves as active agents in their stories of migration. They made the decision to leave Ireland and while they frequently drew upon kinship migratory networks, they usually came to England as single, young migrants. In this chapter I have explored some of issues raised by their narratives. I suggest that all the women discussed their emigration through family narratives and, in addition, that there was a strong relationship between stories of childhood and the ways in which migration was justified and explained. I have focused in particular on their memories of childhood and young adulthood in Ireland and how these have framed their justifications or explanations of migration. I have suggested that the stories or in some cases the silences around childhood and family memories were used to make sense of their adult life as migrants. Many women used economic necessity and the lack of opportunities in Ireland to reconcile happy childhood memories with the decision to leave their parental home at a young age. Thus, I suggest that these women blended nostalgia for the 'good old days', i.e. a happy childhood, with the motif of the 'poor woman made good'. However, for some women unhappy childhood memories and family conflict were directly linked to emigration as a form of escape.

It is tempting to contrast images of a happy Irish childhood, the motif of freedom, fresh air, companionship and fun, with the constraints and responsibilities of adulthood as an economic emigrant in Britain. However, I believe that such a sharp contrast is somewhat misleading. The women's narratives are more complex, multi-layered and less polarised than such a simplistic contrast would allow. In many of the narratives the 'freedom' of childhood is contrasted to the 'slavery' of working conditions in Ireland. Thus, within this reflective nostalgia, Ireland is described as both a place of freedom and exploitation, happiness and poverty, love and hopelessness. These overlapping memories contain both the explanation of emigration and the reasons for continued family loyalty and sentimental attachment to childhood and home.

In this chapter I have also spoken about my role as interviewer, listener, audience and active participant in the memory process. Although at times the circularity of stories and the lack of chronological referencing were confusing, I found the deeply involved narratives evocative and fascinating. By comparison, aspects of the interviews that were apparently factual and gave precise dates often seemed stilted and a little disappointing. The question and answer format failed to live up to my expectation of genuine reminiscence. However, the silences contained within these responses may also be quite illuminating and require more careful consideration. In any case, whether the narratives took the format of long, uninterrupted reminiscences or short 'factual' answers, they were all situational performances. The women's childhood stories did not spring from some untapped well of memory but were narratives that evolved within the context of the interview and a lifetime of migration. This is not to undervalue these oral history interviews in any way, each interview says a great deal about the interviewee in particular the ways in which their memories of the past are mediated by and filtered through the experiences of the intervening years. The Ireland in their memory, the Ireland they describe from their childhood, is a country that no longer exists, but it is also a country constructed within the distancing of time and place. These childhood stories stand as a testimony to the separation of now and then and here and there. If memory is an attempt to make sense of the past from the standpoint of the present, these memories of home reveal a great deal about how home, family and childhood may be revisited, reflected upon and constructed through the experience of migration.

12

Family History and Memory in Irish Immigrant Families

John Herson

Irish Migrants, Exile and Memory

This essay seeks to explore aspects of the relationship between history, memory and identity amongst the contemporary descendants of Irish immigrants to Britain in the nineteenth century. This is done by reference to interviews carried out with people from the Irish families who settled in the town of Stafford in the English midlands between the Famine period and the Great War.

Kerby Miller has argued that

> millions of Irishmen and women, whatever their objective reasons for emigration, approached their departures and their experiences in North America with an outlook which characterized emigration as exile. Rooted in ancient culture and tradition, shaped by historical circumstances, and adapted to 'explain' the impersonal workings of the market economy, the Irish world view crossed the ocean to confront the most modern of all societies. From the standpoint of the emigrants' ability to adjust and prosper overseas, the consequent tensions between past and present, ideology and reality, may have had mixed results. However, both the exile motif and the worldview that sustained it ensured the survival of Irish identity and nationalism in the New World.[1]

Miller's perspective has been very influential in Irish migrant studies. It is, however, uncertain to what degree the exile motif is applicable to the Irish emigrants who settled in Britain. It might be argued that many of the Irish who settled in the land of the colonial oppressor were those, particularly amongst the Famine refugees, who were forced to take the cheapest, easiest option whatever its economic and cultural drawbacks. From this perspective Britain would remain a hated place of exile, and Irish identity, culture and memories might be transmitted to the succeeding generation(s). Alternatively, settlement in Britain might have been adopted by those less burdened by loyalty to a baggage of Irish cultural, religious and political identities and whose prime objective was to achieve positive individual and family advancement in a different society. Indeed, Donald Akenson has argued that the exile motif and what he calls the 'Gaelic-Catholic Disability variable' present a misleading paradigm for explaining the actual Irish emigrant experience down the generations.[2] Little attempt has been made, however, to explore the long-term trajectory of Irish immigrants to Britain and their descendants and the extent to which emigration and exile has left a permanent imprint on their attitudes, behaviour and relationships.

Irish emigrants had to endure an experience that was inherently traumatic. Most, though not all, had to cross a frontier that was not merely geographic but could involve a shift from rural to urban living within an environment that was radically different and frequently hostile in cultural, religious and social terms. Immigrants and their families had to make a new start in circumstances that were only partly of their own choosing. Negotiation of the emigrant frontier posed direct challenges to identity. Modern writing emphasises the complexity of individual identity with its multi-facetted nature and dynamic development. Identity was a phenomenon contested in an individual's diverse circumstances as well as through the policies and practices of institutions with which he or she came into contact.[3]

One of those institutions was the family of which the migrant was, or became, part. Family relationships could pose dilemmas of loyalty versus individual autonomy, but through the generations these relationships played a major role as the conduit down which memories, legends and attitudes might be transmitted. Assmann has suggested, however, that this communicative memory process about the meaning of the past is subject to dilution that limits its potency after eighty to one hundred years.[4] In family terms, this suggests a continuous process of memory decay beyond three or four generations back. A further factor diluting the potency of specific memories such as the trauma of migration might also be intermarriage across ethnic, cultural or religious boundaries down the generations. The children of such marriages would inherently be subject to competing identities, the results of which would be mediated by the cultural environment within which the child grew up as well as by his or her own personality.

Direct communicative memory may be subject to decay and can be infinitely variable since it is determined primarily by the information flows between countless individuals and families. The cultural memory of a specific group that 'consists of the objectified culture, that is the texts, rites, images, buildings and monuments which are designed to recall fateful events in the history of the collective'[5] may, however, be defined, redefined and strengthened over time. This can be the case particularly if, like the emigrant Irish, the group is seen to have experienced a collective trauma such as the Famine and its aftermath. The exile motif may be a long-term element in this collective trauma. The definition of the cultural memory is a collective social process that may be openly contested but may also be dominated by specific sub-groups or interests in pursuit of contemporary political or social agendas. Kansteiner has, in fact, argued in relation to the Holocaust and Vietnam that:

> Small groups whose members have directly experienced such traumatic events ... only have a chance to shape the national memory if they command the means to express their visions, and if their vision meets with compatible social or political objectives among other important social groups, for instance, political elites or parties. Past events can only be recalled in a collective setting 'if they fit within the framework of contemporary interests'.[6]

Miller's analysis illustrates this in relation to the Irish in his argument that the exile motif continued to be developed and sustained in the second half of the nineteenth century. This was done both by the rural poor who emigrated and by a mix of nationalists, Catholic clergy and middle class farmers and townsmen who were then doing well in Ireland but whose agendas coalesced around the continued need to blame British colonial rule for the ills of the country, including emigration.[7] The modern historiography of Irish migration and settlement has played a significant role in both reflecting but also arguably in defining the collective cultural memory of Irish-descended people worldwide who positively wish to identify and articulate their heritage. This process is linked to the identification of an Irish community or communities – both past and present – within the context of contemporary events and agendas. Hickman, for example, asserts that:

> The imagined community of being Irish in Britain ... is one that has been constituted by the sense of forced migration and the differences and boundaries which were immanent in the problematisation of Irish immigrants. The making of a sense of

community for this generation of migrants at some level has been secured through a common experience of loss. This is the concrete reality of a distinct (although not homogeneous) community.[8]

She argues that the communal identity of being Irish in Britain can be understood as, in part, an aspect of resistance to anti-Irish disadvantage, discrimination and 'a racist British nationalism for which the Irish were a specific Other'. This analysis particularly concentrates on modern Irish immigrants living in Britain during the time of the Northern Ireland troubles. It is counterposed, however, with a perspective that sees the descendants of the nineteenth century Irish in Britain as having lost much of their Irishness through a conscious process of incorporation and denationalisation spearheaded by an alliance between the British state and the English Catholic Church.[9] There is considerable broad evidence to support this perspective, but the specific impact of such processes in the past on individuals, families and local populations in terms of their behaviour, attitudes and identity is less easy to demonstrate.

There is a danger that modern collective cultural memory is used to impute attitudes and identities on people in the past who have left little or no direct testimony of their own. To offset this danger other sources need to be explored and one is to use the possibilities inherent in family history. It is feasible to explore whether faint echoes from the past are present in the communicated memories and legends current in the families of modern-day descendants of the nineteenth century immigrant Irish. This might reveal evidence about the trauma of emigration and the strength of the exile motif in the immigrant generation and their communication to descendants. It could also reveal attitudes and identities in Irish immigrant families from the nineteenth century to the present day, and the extent to which these were affected by the environment and institutions surrounding them. This essay now goes on to describe the results of an experiment designed to explore these issues. It forms part of a long-term study of Irish immigrant families in Stafford in the period from 1815 to 1919.

Lost Memories: Stafford's Irish Families, 1845-2000

Lying between the Potteries and the Black Country, the market town of Stafford grew from a population of 4,216 in 1801 to 27,481 in 1921. The main industry of the town in the nineteenth century was shoemaking, but by the 1900s this was being replaced by engineering. Irish soldiers were present in Stafford during the Napoleonic wars and the first permanent settlers arrived in the 1820s. From then on the town had a significant Irish-born population that peaked at 532 in 1861, or 4 per cent of the population. It declined thereafter, but the loss of Irish-born was counterbalanced by many of their Stafford-born descendants, and by the 1900s, 700 or more people in the town could probably claim Irish descent. I have documented elsewhere aspects of the economic and social history of the Stafford Irish,[10] and in this essay such issues will be discussed only inasmuch as they are relevant to the family histories and memories of the Irish.

Stafford contrasts with the major centres of Irish settlement like Liverpool, Manchester, London or Glasgow in that the town was small and the Irish population similarly small in absolute numbers. Relative or absolute numbers did not wholly determine the experience of the Irish, however. In some settlements with smaller numbers the Irish experienced overt hostility and violence that inevitably strengthened Irish solidarity and community identity.[11] In Stafford the reception of the host community seems to have been much more muted and there is little historical evidence of outright hostility and anti-Irish violence. There seem to have been a number of reasons for this. There was no single 'Irishtown' in Stafford to become the focus of hostility. The Victorian Irish were to be found scattered throughout the town's slums but with a minority of more secure and respectable Irish living amongst similar people in the more salubrious areas. The labour market, mainly in farmwork and the shoe trade, offered no obvious flashpoints for competition and hostility. The political and religious environment tended to incorporate the Irish rather than use them as a focus for host society hostility. The Catholic Church, in particular, was dominated by members of the town's elite and had a substantial working class English congregation with whom the Catholic Irish increasingly intermarried.[12] All of these factors combined to produce an environment in which those Irish who settled in Stafford tended to live relatively quiet lives that were increasingly within the local community rather than ethnically distinct from it. By the First World War there was no definable 'Irish community' in Stafford. Rather, the descendants of the Irish immigrants had become Staffordians with greater or lesser amounts of Irish ancestry. This phenomenon was to have considerable significance for the revealed memories and identities of *their* descendants who were interviewed in the early twenty-first century.

In studying the long-term history of the Irish in Stafford it is possible to reconstruct and study the families of immigrants and their descendants.[13] Although there was considerable turnover of individuals and families, particularly in the years following the Famine influx, over time a significant number of families settled down in Stafford, and it is possible to identify 163 Irish families who lived in the town for more than ten years. 104 of these families (64%) were ethnically Irish when they settled in the town, and some of these went on to form complex family units, but the remainder (59 or

36%) were already ethnically mixed families with one Irish and one English-born partner. From the start of Irish settlement, there was, therefore, significant potential dilution of Irish identity in the ethnically mixed families. Using the census, registration data, newspapers and other sources it is possible to reconstruct the family trees of Stafford's Irish families in the decades after their settlement. It is then possible to outline their family *histories* and produce a narrative of their development and experiences both in Stafford and, sometimes, in the diaspora beyond. The overall aim of the research is to produce a comprehensive account of the Irish and Irish-descended families who settled in Stafford in the century before 1919.

As the research developed a number of individuals heard about the work down the local grapevine and approached the author for information on their families. Although there was no intention to engage in contract family history research, there was clearly a demand for information that suggested a worthwhile exchange could take place with the descendants of Irish families. The author could give information and insights to the descendants and, indeed, to the local community as a whole in terms of knowledge of part of its heritage. In exchange it might be possible to gain further information about specific families. The aim became, therefore, to make contact with descendants of the Irish, both in Stafford, elsewhere in Britain and beyond. Contact was sought in a number of ways:

- The following-up of chance contacts.
- A web-site designed to unearth descendants on a world-wide basis.[14]
- A local newspaper article aimed at descendants still living in the Stafford area.
- Promotion in family history networks world-wide.

By August 2004 these methods had resulted in contact with fifty-two people who were, between them, descended from forty of Stafford's Irish families.[15] These people have, in many cases, provided important information on their families, particularly in terms of their history since 1919.

Correspondence by mail and e-mail with these people suggested it might be worthwhile to interview some descendants of the Irish about the extent and nature of their family memories, about their attitudes to their Irish heritage and on more general perspectives on their context. In the short term it did not prove feasible to interview people overseas and the concentration has been on a range of descendants who still live in the Stafford district or the wider midland area. Between May 2002 and March 2004 twelve interviews were carried out using open-ended questions with the following objectives:

- To amplify and correct errors in nineteenth century family trees and to link the pre-1919 information to the respondents' subsequent family history. It was made clear, however, that there is no intention to make public any post-1919 information.
- To see if the respondents had any family memorabilia relating to their Irish ancestors.
- To explore whether there were family memories, anecdotes, legends and myths about their Irish ancestors and their experiences as immigrants.
- To probe the attitudes of respondents to their Irish heritage and possible ways it may have influenced their identity. To find out what they knew about the attitudes and identity of their ancestors
- To document respondents' knowledge and views of the Stafford context – community, politics, religion, schooling and other Irish families.

The interviewees are summarised on Table 1. There was a total of twenty respondents at the twelve interviews and they were descended from twenty different Stafford Irish families. There were twelve women and eight men and the oldest person interviewed was born in 1917 and was the only person in the cohort who had 100% Irish ancestry. All the other respondents had some degree of mixed ancestry because of intermarriage down the generations. Clearly, in this case, the people with Victorian Irish ancestry who are available for interview in the early twenty-first century are inevitably the product of dynamic intermixing over the previous 150 years. There is no relict 'Irish Community' amongst such people. Potential bias is always present in interview-based research and in this case there was inevitably some bias towards people who positively wanted to discuss their ancestry. In four interviews this was not the case, however, since local contacts suggested certain people who might have Irish ancestry and they were approached directly to see if they would be willing to be interviewed. As will be seen, none of the respondents was motivated to respond by any desire to express and perhaps romanticise their Irish identity.

Almost all the people interviewed were descended from Catholic Irish families originating in the Connacht area, and most of the original immigrants had left Ireland during the Famine or the 1850s and had settled in Stafford immediately or relatively shortly thereafter. In six cases, however, the Irish ancestors had only arrived in Stafford after 1870, having previously lived elsewhere in England. Almost all the originating immigrants had worked in unskilled jobs – labouring and domestic service – after their arrival in Stafford. The respondents' families reflected the overwhelming majority of Stafford's Victorian Irish. The 10-15% of immigrants from Protestant backgrounds were not represented, although there has been some contact with the descendants of this group living elsewhere in Britain and overseas. This is a gap that remains to be filled.

Three factors complicated the interviews. The first was that a two-way dialogue inevitably occurred at the start of the interview about the respondents' family history since in almost all cases the author had information that was previously unknown to the respondents themselves. The reaction to this information was heart-warmingly positive but inevitably cut across a rigorous interviewing process. There was, secondly, the potential problem that the information presented by the author might itself influence the attitudes and even the identity of the interviewees. This is felt to be a largely theoretical risk, but it needs to be recorded. The final issue concerned interviews involving more than one person. These arose because a number of respondents' families were positively interested in the information exchange and asked if other descendants could be present, a request the author could hardly refuse. The reported results from these interviews therefore represent a degree of 'corporate' rather than individual response.

The first area to be discussed was what the respondents actually knew about their family history. In most cases their detailed and accurate knowledge stopped in the early 20th century and in only four interviews did information go back to their Irish immigrant ancestors. In one of these cases the immigrants had in fact been late-nineteenth century arrivals. Some respondents had little or no perception of their Irish ancestry before contact with the author. It is clear, then, that there has been a massive loss of knowledge amongst a majority of families about their origins.

Fitzpatrick, McBride and others[16] have enlightened Irish migrant studies through the use of contemporary testimony from the Irish themselves, and it was hoped that some of the Stafford interviewees might have physical memorabilia from their Irish ancestors. The results were, however, disappointing. No contemporary letters, diaries or other written materials have survived, and only four respondents had pre-1919 photographs of family members. It seems that the struggle for existence, inevitable moves of house together with family conflicts over possessions has resulted in a huge attrition of physical evidence from the past.

An attempt was made in the interviews to gain a picture of past relationships in the respondents' families – to see what were perceived as the key family dynamics and to place their Irish ancestry within a wider perspective of family realities. Respondents were asked what legends there were about family relationships, family problems and the marriages that had taken place. The responses indicated that Irish ethnicity was not generally the most significant element in the family legend but in three interviews respondents did nevertheless report that English ancestors had regarded ethnically Irish marriage partners as socially inferior. This related to marriages from widely spread dates – the 1860s, the 1890s and the 1930s. The hostility clearly reflected a mélange of attitudes towards the Irish because of their ethnicity, their Catholic religion and the perceived lower occupational status either of the marriage partners themselves or their families. Although the Stafford Irish intermarried extensively with the host population, this evidence does show it was not necessarily a smooth process of ethnic intermixing. Family hostilities could emerge related to the ethnic factor, but the evidence also highlighted the significance of family conflicts not linked to ethnicity. Half the respondents reported hostility and conflict that stemmed from squabbles over inheritance and/or from perceptions *within* Irish families that certain people or branches were either socially inferior or were (as it was put in one case) 'perfect snobs' trying to hide 'that they had come up from nothing'. In two cases interviewees reported that their ancestors had never really talked of their background, perhaps suggesting they wished to obscure or forget it or, in one case, 'that there was something not quite right' about it.[17] Drink was mentioned in two interviews. It is important to stress, therefore, that in these Stafford families Irish ethnicity was only one subsidiary element in the legends about their family history.

It is within this wider context that legends about their specifically Irish history need to be seen. It was important to know about any legends there might be about where their ancestors came from in Ireland, why and when they left and why they settled in Stafford, as well as their experiences in the town after arrival. In asking these questions at the beginning of the twenty-first century, we are clearly at or beyond the extreme boundary of communicative memory, and it is germane to question whether respondents might have been influenced by more stereotyped forms of cultural/collective memories of Irish migration and settlement. In terms of actual family legends, the results were very limited. In only three cases were people able to tell any story about their families' origins in Ireland. The most complete picture was painted in interview 7 by two respondents whose ancestor had come from Co. Roscommon in the 1880s. The family had had a smallholding in the county that was too small and had been taken over by a relative. The ancestor had then emigrated to Stafford, but a dispute over rights to the small-holding had carried on down the generations. The respondents reported that their father's failure to resolve the legal problems ultimately resulted in the evidence being destroyed some decades ago. They could not even identify where in Co. Roscommon their family had originated, and there was also a legend that they had been involved in 'fishing off the coast', something difficult to square with an origin in land-locked Roscommon. Family legend was also unclear about why they had settled in Stafford. Four rather conflicting explanations were offered. The first was that they had come to Liverpool and bought a train ticket to as far as they could afford, which happened to be Stafford. The second was that they came to Stafford because they already knew someone there, which is quite likely. The third was that they worked for a company building an extension to Stafford gasworks and then got a job in the retort house, whilst the final suggestion was that the ancestor had married an Irish woman working in the Walsall leather trade and the couple had moved to Stafford because of town's boot and shoe industry. The interesting feature about this evidence is that it came from two people who were only three generations away from the original immigrants, yet the family legends were extremely vague.

In two cases respondents reported family legends that their ancestors had originated in Knock, County Mayo and County Tipperary, legends whose truth is attested by census evidence previously unknown to the respondents. In two other cases vague family legends about the place of origin do not appear to be substantiated by the census. In only three cases did respondents make unprompted reference to the Famine as a factor in their families' migration, and it seems clear that this was to some degree influenced by general knowledge of the Famine tragedy rather than any specific family legend relating to it. In half the interviews there were no family legends at all about their Irish origins or why they settled in Stafford.

In most of the families there has, therefore, been a massive loss of knowledge, memory and legend about their Irish origins. There appears, in fact, to be a cut-off point of knowledge and legend around the second generation after immigration, almost as though a line had been drawn across the family's previous history. This applied both to knowledge of Ireland and of why the family had settled in Stafford. The conflicting range of reasons why the family in interview 7 settled in Stafford has already been outlined, but at least in this family some possible explanations exist. In no other case could respondents offer a specific and plausible reason why their ancestors had settled in Stafford of all places. One respondent suggested it was 'as far as they could go' but she also suggested it might be because they 'dug the canals', a clearly false view since the nearest canal to Stafford, the Staffordshire and Worcestershire[18], had been cut in the early 1770s, seventy years before the family in question had settled in the town. Even in the case of the latest family to arrive in Stafford, who settled in 1915, the respondent in interview 6 was unable to say why her father had moved to the town from Blackburn in Lancashire. It seems likely he came because of wartime building work at an army camp on Cannock Chase.

There are a number of possible reasons for this poverty of knowledge and legend about the families' Irish origins and settlement in Stafford. The first is that the Irish element is by now only being a minority proportion of the ancestry of people in seven out of the twelve interviews. The Irish, in other words, are just not that important in their family history anymore. This was undoubtedly a factor in some cases, but the correlation was by no means perfect. Some respondents with a minority of Irish blood had better knowledge of facts and legends than others with stronger ethnic ancestry. The second factor is obviously the general decay or dilution of family knowledge that is likely to occur after the third generation. The fact is that most families' knowledge and legends are likely to be sketchy beyond the grandparents' generation – there is superficially no reason why these families would be any different. Nevertheless, it might have been expected that the trauma of emigration and settlement, especially connected with the Famine, would have offset this – that it would have been a lurking shadow passed down the generations. The collective memory of the emigrant Irish, especially that articulated in the overseas diaspora, would suggest this to be the case, yet the evidence from Stafford suggests it has failed to be transmitted down the generations of those families who settled and intermarried in the town. It was also clear that the Stafford respondents showed no sign of being influenced by – or even being aware of – a collective memory of Irish exile or of definitions of Irishness in the world-wide diaspora.

The loss of family memories or legends about the emigration suggests a further possibility – that family ancestors in the generation after settlement in Stafford actively rejected or eliminated their previous family history in Ireland. Such a view contrasts with the perspective that the Irish in areas of denser settlement transmitted Irish identity to succeeding generations born in the country of settlement. In a town like Stafford, where the number of Irish was quite small, there was little incentive to maintain an Irish identity in the face of the need to survive and prosper in a new environment. That is not to say that all the Irish who came to the town found it an attractive place to live and quickly abandoned their Irish identity. In the nineteenth century several hundred Irish people and their descendants left Stafford for other places in Britain or abroad. Much of this out-migration will have reflected lack of job opportunities, but one can also speculate that many Irish people – particularly those keen to retain and express their Irish and Catholic identities – found Stafford a claustrophobic and unrewarding place.[19] Those who settled in the town, and their descendants, were a self-selected population who almost certainly decided – implicitly or explicitly – that their future lay in broadly conforming to the norms and values of the Stafford community as they found them. Unfashionable as it is to argue the point, it seems clear that such people sought integration and ultimate assimilation through their social life, working relationships and intermarriage. The descendants who are available for interview in the early 2000s reflect this fact.

A final factor in this loss of memory may have been the active socialisation processes of church and state. Hickman has argued that the Catholic Church and schooling acted, in concert with the state, to incorporate the Irish Catholics into English Catholicism, 'denationalising' the Irish in the process.[20] There is certainly evidence to substantiate this process in Stafford, and this is examined later.

The final element of legend and memory that was probed with respondents was the families' experiences of life in Stafford up to the end of the Great War. Were they positive or negative? Three respondents were unable to offer opinions on this, although in the case of interview 1 this was because the respondents were not now Staffordians and were descended from a family line that had left the town in the early twentieth century.[21] The general perspective amongst most other respondents was that their ancestors' lives had been hard and poor. In interview 9 one legend was of a grandmother who had a coal business and carried the coal sacks around on her shoulders, but the same respondent also reported the view that both Irish families from whom she was descended had worked hard, had succeeded and that Stafford had proved a positive place to settle. In interview 6, the oldest respondent interviewed was able to speak from experience of the hard life her family led in Snow's Yard in the 1920s, a slum court occupied by many Irish families down the decades. She described the landlords as cruel people who thought nothing of putting families and children out on the streets. Children from other neighbourhoods looked down on them and would not play with them. Respondents whose Irish ancestors lay farther back in the nineteenth century also emphasised poverty but suggested that memories of their experiences as specifically Irish families had probably been obscured by the basic struggle for existence. One respondent in interview 8 suggested their families had been 'typical working class stock'. Three respondents were, however, descended from Irish families whose members had mostly achieved a modest respectability by the end of the nineteenth century, and in these cases the family memory was more positive about the Stafford experience, emphasising how hard work and steady employment had avoided the extremes of poverty.

Interview 3 was unusual in that it involved descendants of an Irish family in which there was one well publicised but tragic event, one mentioned, in fact, by respondents in two other interviews and perhaps the one significant incident involving an Irish person that has passed into the collective memory of Staffordians. It concerned Edward O'Connor, born in 1879, the son of mixed Irish/English parents. In 1921 he was hanged for the murder of his son Thomas. Evidence suggests there was more to the case than met the eye and that O'Connor's actions were partly explained by long-term stresses within an ethnically Irish family. He failed to receive a proper legal defence and his appeal against the death penalty was rejected with the apparently flawed logic that 'he cut the throats of three or four of his children in a brutal and *mad* (sic) manner and there was no evidence of insanity in law'.[22] In November and December 1921 over 13,000 Stafford people signed a petition for his reprieve, about half the population of the town at that time. This remarkable response suggests there was a widespread contemporary belief that O'Connor deserved better than he got. Although there is a family legend that Edward O'Connor was abused as a 'drunken Irishman', it seems there was little or no general antipathy towards him on ethnic grounds when faced with the manifest imperfections of British justice. The communicated memory of the family involved in interview 3 therefore involves coping with a trauma far more significant than anything engendered by emigration. It illustrates in stark form the general point that a whole range of family relationships and historical incidents may serve to complicate the analysis of ethnic identity in communicated family memories.

Identities Among the Stafford Irish Families

Having explored the extent of memories, legends and myths in the respondents' families, the essay now turns to the significance of the past for contemporary descendants of the Stafford Irish. The interviews probed the attitudes of respondents to their Irish heritage and possible ways it may have influenced their identity. There was also an attempt to find out what they knew about the attitudes and identity of their ancestors.

The first issue was whether, before the author's contact, the respondents had been interested in their family history and how they saw themselves in ethnic terms. What was their attitude to their Irish background and heritage? Most, but not all, of the respondents had been interested in their family history but only four had done substantial work themselves on their family trees. In three cases other relatives had done some work. Only three of the interviews were with people who could be described as avid family historians, and in every case the information provided by the author added substantially to their factual knowledge of their Irish ancestors.

Respondents' views of their own identity were somewhat conflicting. When asked initially how they saw *themselves*, none of the respondents saw themselves as significantly – or at all – Irish. None was clearly motivated by any desire to assert an Irish identity. One respondent saw herself primarily as a Catholic and another mentioned a class identity – 'working class from Cheshire' – but all the rest described themselves as 'English' and/or

'Staffordian', often with the epithet 'born and bred'. When asked more generally about their attitude to their Irish background, the responses were more mixed. The 100%-Irish woman in interview 6 expressed her Irish pride most forcefully. She commented that it was 'nothing to be ashamed of – why reject it?' and went on to say she was 'proud of it even now' since 'Ireland was the land of saints and scholars'. Such poetic views were not to be found amongst the other ethnically mixed respondents. In four interviews a sort of defensive pride was expressed in their Irish roots, reflecting a clear awareness that the social environment in Britain could be hostile to the Irish. In interview 1 respondents commented that they were proud to be one quarter Irish, but that 'people can be derogatory' about it. At the other extreme, in five interviews respondents had never seen an Irish background as being of significance in their lives, either in their upbringing or now – 'interesting, but so what – it's nothing to do with me' was the comment in interview 9. There was, nevertheless, a hint in two cases that these attitudes were motivated by a desire to distance themselves from relatives perceived to conform to crude stereotypes of Irishness – drink, gambling and so on. In one case the respondents claimed they had been unaware of their Irish heritage when young but that they had developed an increasing awareness of it in later life, partly because of the Troubles. Carrying an Irish family name had led to hostile comments at work in the aftermath of the Birmingham pub bombings (1975).

All of these respondents were three or more generations away from their Irish immigrant ancestors and all but one was the product of varying degrees of mixed parentage. It is therefore to be expected that they would show evidence of hybrid identities reflecting their family history, upbringing and the wider social environment. None of them had any interest in participating in overt manifestations of Irish nationalism or identity, though, again, it must be remembered that some were influenced by nervousness about the position of the Irish in a potentially hostile British society. In modern parlance, the degree of 'ethnic fade' from Irishness amongst these people was very high and the respondent in interview 2 expressed it very cogently: 'the first generation immigrant looks to home, the second faces both ways, the third says "forget it".' This process of fade would have been occurring down the generations, and it was worth probing respondents' knowledge of how their *ancestors* saw their identity. What was their attitude to their Irish backgrounds, and did their ancestors retain any obvious Irish connections – links with Ireland, general or specific loyalties, behaviour, accent and so on?

Only the respondents in interview 7 could remember surviving Irish-born immigrants in their families and this was because the family emigrated in the later nineteenth century. In all the other cases time has now broken the link to the Famine emigrants and their mid-century successors, though the potential testimony that could have been relayed by people who had actually known ancestors from those generations has only disappeared in the past thirty years. It is unfortunate that oral history was not carried out in this field then. The respondent in interview 2 had been born the same year (1921) as two key Irish-born family members had died. His comment on one of these people – 'as Irish as they came – a full-blown Irishman' – implied a real personal memory, and it illustrates the need to check the veracity of statements against the hard evidence. In this case, he was clearly reporting family memories current in his childhood about someone who had died around the time he was born.

Although direct knowledge of the immigrant generation was lacking, in all but two interviews the respondents had known some second generation people born in England in the second half of the nineteenth century. The picture in relation to these second generation people was mixed. The strongest expression of Irish identity came in interview 6. Here the respondent reported that 'it was drilled into us by our father that we were Irish Catholics … Neither of my parents forgot their Irish roots'. The respondent's father had sung Irish rebel songs, although her mother's response to this was 'shurrup, Mick, you'll get us all hung'. This family had migrated from Blackburn to Stafford in 1915, and the survival of such a strong Irish identity in this family may have reflected the contrasting Irish environment in densely settled Lancashire as compared with the West Midlands.

The respondents in interview 7 reported that their father 'went to Ireland at the drop of a hat' when they were young, partly because of the continuing dispute over the family's lost small-holding in Co. Roscommon. They also said he was 'well spoken' when sober but 'as Irish as they came' after a drink. There was, in other words, some clear evidence of transmitted Irish identity to the second generation in this family, but very little from thence into the third. They also had memories of their Irish-born grandfather and his Walsall-born (but Irish) wife. Of the latter they commented that 'she was as Irish as they came'. The specific memory was that she used to frighten the people in Browning Street Co-op by arriving five minutes before closing and aggressively buying the goods being sold off cheap. They remembered her as having an Irish accent despite being born in Staffordshire. Their grandfather 'was a real old Irish gentleman – broad Irish'.

The two families discussed above showed the clearest signs of the survival of Irish identity and perhaps patterns of behaviour into succeeding generations, but the late arrival of these families in Stafford to some extent set them apart from the other Irish families in the interviews. The longer time scale since immigration in the other families would inevitably tend to produce more 'ethnic fade' from a twenty-first century vantage point, but even allowing for this, there is also evidence that in most other families there was greater rejection or obscuring of their Irish origins. Respondents in interviews 1, 2, 9, 10 and 11 all suggested that some of their ancestors or people in other branches of the family had done this at least in part in pursuit of respectability within the local Stafford community. Other respondents could provide no specific comments on this but their inability to point to known evidence of Irish identity in family ancestors is its own commentary. It seems to have waned quite quickly amongst most of the Stafford Irish.

Overall the lack of historical knowledge and legend in the families, as well as the general shift away from Irishness in the second and third generations, suggests again the fundamental discontinuity imposed by migration to England or its aftermath. This raises the question of the processes at work to produce such a result. One way in which Irishness is commonly held to have faded, or been 'denationalised' was through its transmutation into an English Catholic identity.[23] Many of the Stafford Irish families showed signs that in the second and third generations Irish identity was largely converted into a Catholic identity, in some cases very staunch, in others rather nominal. In one case (interview 4) this identity had clearly been contested and ultimately displaced by class identity through their ancestors' involvement in trade unionism and Labour politics. To discuss this further we need to return to the experiences of the respondents. In eleven out of the twelve interviews the respondents had been brought up in Stafford, and in ten cases they have lived most or all of their lives there. What did they think were the most influential factors in their upbringing? The answer was very clear. Although parental influence was mentioned, the impact of schooling and the church was paramount. Twelve of the twenty respondents had been to one or other of the three Catholic schools in Stafford, and half had been to St Patrick's in the town's traditionally poorer north end.[24] These people emphasised the importance of the schools, churches and their linked social activities – youth clubs, scouts/guides, soirées – in local Catholic peoples' lives when they were young. They were also clear that there was a total marginalising of Irish issues, particularly at school. St Patrick's day was normally celebrated, but no other aspect of Irish culture, history or current affairs was ever raised at school or church. The school was, however, strong on saluting the flag and other aspects of British national expression. Although the first priest at St Patrick's, Father O'Hanlon (1893-99), came from an Irish background and had shown some interest in Irish affairs, almost all the succeeding priests were English, and the priest most remembered by respondents, Father Bernard Kelly, was described as 'very English' despite his name. Opinions of him were mixed but one respondent described him as a snob who looked down on poor (often Irish-descended) families in the parish. Despite this, the church and school, both at St Patrick's and at the other church, St Austin's, were clearly seen as the focus of a very strong Catholic community in Stafford, based particularly in the Back Walls area and the north end. Until these interviews, none of the respondents had had any conscious awareness, however, that the basis for that community was *partly* an *Irish* Catholic heritage. Stafford had a significant English working class Catholic population and this, together with the long-term recusant history of Catholicism in the area, gave English Catholic influences greater strength than in many other areas of Irish Catholic settlement.[25] It is estimated, nevertheless, that about half St Patrick's congregation in the 1900s came from ethnically Irish backgrounds.[26]

It seems very clear that Mary Hickman's view of the incorporationist role of the church and catholic schooling was the experience of the Stafford respondents and their ancestors. These institutions operated to 'denationalise' the Irish families and at the extreme it might be argued that the institutions had served to eradicate all Irish identity amongst the immigrants' descendants. This, nevertheless, begs the question of whether the immigrants and their descendants who stayed in Stafford were positive participants in the incorporation process, and the reasons for this. The interviews themselves provide little direct evidence on this, but one respondent's comment that 'the first generation looks to home, the second looks both ways and the third says "forget it"' has already been noted. Ideally the research needs to explore evidence for the motivation of those who left the town, but little has so far been forthcoming despite some contact with worldwide descendants of the Stafford Irish through the web-site[27].

To what extent was the creation of this 'Catholic community' influenced by, or a reaction to, a hostile external environment? This raises the question of the extent to which anti-Irishness and anti-Catholicism might have played a role in identity creation and affirmation by reaction to perceived external threats. This issue was probed with interviewees in terms of their own experiences due to their Irish background and their views of the extent of anti-Irishness and anti-Catholicism in the town.

All but one of the interviewees had lived through the period of renewed Irish immigration during and after the Second World War. They might, therefore, have direct knowledge of attitudes to the Irish in this period, but this knowledge might also obscure their perception of the earlier period. In fact no respondent argued there had been strong and widespread anti-Irishness or anti-Catholicism in Stafford, though some cited individual incidents. They found it difficult to distinguish between incidents of anti-Irishness and anti-Catholicism, but the respondents in interview 7 were clear that they had experienced some anti-Catholicism rather than anti-Irishness.

The fact that they had Stafford accents they felt removed any threat of the latter. The older respondent in interview 6 did, however, express strong, though rather contradictory views on this. She said that 'people used to call the Irish everything – but not me. People could be hostile to the Irish in Stafford – they thought you were below them'. She said that 'Staffordians resented the Irish' in the generation that grew up in the 1920s and 1930s, but her niece, born in 1940, claimed not to have experienced such reactions. This lady grew up, however, with a local surname and a local accent, both of which would have affected her experiences. Thirteen of the respondents had grown up with an 'Irish' surname and four referred to problems they had experienced with it. In the case of interview 11 it was said that 'people's attitudes change when they know your name is Irish, not Scottish. Being Scottish is fine, Irish not so fine'. The respondent, though proud of his Irish heritage, admitted to being wary about people's reactions to his name and that if they took it to be Scottish he did not enlighten them.[28] Nine respondents claimed to have had no difficulties in Stafford with their 'Irish' names. In day-to-day life these people and their immediate ancestors had clearly blended in because they were white, indistinguishable from long-term Staffordians and spoke with Stafford accents. The general view was that Stafford was a tolerant town, but in one case it was described as 'cliquey'. This was a perspective linked to class attitudes. It was felt that middle and upper class people tended to belittle poor working class people. The majority of respondents who still lived in Stafford nevertheless tended to be positive about their experience of the town and they emphasised that in the past it was a community and that 'everyone knew everyone' (interview 2). The respondent in interview 2 emphasised the social significance of Roman Catholics amongst the town's professions and commercial classes.

The respondents' experiences were of life in Stafford since the 1920s, and the majority had been young in the 1930-1955 period. There were no family memories of anti-Irishness or anti-Catholicism being more or less in their ancestors' generations. This absence of comment is not conclusive, but the lack of documented anti-Irish conflict in Victorian Stafford tends to sustain the perspective that the phenomenon was not overt or widespread in the town[29].

Anti-Catholicism in Stafford was mild in comparison with experiences in other Victorian towns and cities[30] but the strength of views expressed by respondents on the role of the church was significant. Strong and partially successful efforts were made by the church to build a 'Catholic community', and one explanation for this was that the church was under threat even in the second half of the nineteenth century through social interaction, intermarriage and leakage.[31] All of the Stafford Irish interviewees were descended from Catholic families, but there was a complex picture of the strength of Catholicism amongst both the respondents and in their previous family histories. Six of the families had retained Catholicism in the ancestors' generations from the late nineteenth century to the 1940s, though in two cases the adherence appears to have become nominal on the male side. Respondents from five of these families themselves remain active Catholics. There were six families where respondents were descended from religiously mixed marriages in that earlier period,[32] and the Church's concerns about 'leakage' from mixed marriages were borne out in these families. In four cases it was clear that adherence to the Church had weakened in the Catholic partner of the mixed marriage and none of the respondents descended from these marriages is now Catholic, though in one case (interview 12) the respondent herself lapsed from the Church in adulthood. The case of interview 7 is interesting because in this mixed marriage one of the respondents was brought up as a Catholic (and has retained his Catholicism) whereas the other was not and has no connection with the church. In this case the children of a mixed marriage were 'split' between the parents on religious lines. In total, seven of the respondents remain active Catholics, but they formed a minority of those interviewed. Seven respondents were never Catholics and six had themselves lapsed from the Church. This evidence indicates the attrition of religious adherence that took place in the generations after immigration from Ireland as well as during the twentieth century. In the case of interview 8 the respondents rejected the Church when they were young because of bad experiences at St Austin's Catholic School. They felt they were picked on because they were the poor children of a religiously-mixed marriage, and their parents took them away from the school. The male child also joined the Boys' Brigade connected to the Baptist Church because it was more welcoming than St Austin's Church.

The evidence from these interviews suggests, therefore, that the environment of the Catholic Church and schooling was a force for 'denationalising' the descendants of the Irish immigrants who remained in Stafford, but that the immigrants themselves and their children may also have actively buried their Irish heritage. In the long term a majority of their descendants also lost or rejected their Catholic heritage.

Memory and Identity: The Stafford Experience

The Irish who settled in the nineteenth century substantially modified Britain's social character. They were the largest group of immigrants from outside the island and their social impact on Liverpool, Glasgow and certain other areas of dense settlement was undoubtedly profound. There has, however, been little study of the long-term development of the Irish-descended population in terms of their family structures, intermarriage and the extent to which they remained ethnically distinct down the generations. In the years of peak immigration during and after the Famine the Irish were particularly concentrated in certain areas of the country. By 1871 three-quarters of the Irish-born in England and Wales were to be found in just seven counties – Lancashire, Cheshire, Yorkshire, Durham and Middlesex, Surrey and Kent (in other words, London). Within these counties many, but not all, of the Irish were crammed into distinct localities – the so-called 'little Irelands' – within cities, towns and smaller settlements. This pattern of concentration has tended to influence perceptions of the Irish and, at worst, can lead to an historic picture of the Irish 'community' that is simplistic and lacks dynamism. Pooley has pointed out that even in Liverpool

> detailed analysis of the distribution of Irish migrants ... suggests that not only were many Irish dispersed throughout the residential structure and thus, presumably, reasonably well-integrated into British urban society, but also that poor Irish living in Irish-dominated residential areas would have had extensive opportunities to interact with their non-Irish neighbours.[33]

Pooley's analysis and that of Papworth both suggest the importance of studying the whole of a settlement's Irish and Irish-descended population, taking in those who dispersed into the wider urban area as well as the more easily found and distinctive people clustered in enclaves.[34]

If the Irish were quite widely distributed even in their areas of densest settlement, the picture was similar in the areas in the country that had smaller numbers of Irish immigrants. Dense concentrations of Irish could be found in particular localities after the Famine influx but over time the descendants of the Irish fanned out into the housing areas occupied by their equals in the class hierarchy. Intermarriage of the Irish and their descendants with people from the host society was almost certainly a major factor in this process but historians have not studied it in detail.[35]

The history of Stafford's nineteenth century Irish population and its descendants demonstrates these characteristics. It was a numerically small population that was distributed throughout the working and middle class areas of the town. It increasingly intermarried with the local population. By 1884 a majority of Catholic marriages in Stafford involving an Irish-descended person were ethnically mixed and by the 1900's the proportion was over ninety per cent.[36] This basic fact is reflected in the family histories of the people interviewed for this study but it must also apply to the majority of descendants of the immigrants from Ireland who came to Britain in the nineteenth century. These people do not form some relict Irish 'community' but are a complex ethnic intermixture of people descended from that period. Time and social processes have had an overwhelming impact on family history, memory and identity amongst these people.

The results of the interviews reflect these circumstances. We have seen that in general people's hard factual knowledge of their Irish family histories tended to go back no further than the beginning of the twentieth century. Almost none of the families possessed memorabilia from their Irish past. Photographs were thin on the ground for the period before 1900. More significantly, family memories and legends about their Irish origins, as well as of the process of emigration and settlement in Britain, were very limited. Only occasionally did the barest communicated memories breach Assmann's one hundred year barrier and there were no legends concerning the traumas of the Famine and emigration. These findings, or rather the lack of them, suggest the massive attrition of evidence about their past amongst the descendants of the Irish in Britain. Earlier discussion suggested this may have been due to the dilution of Irishness within the respondents' families, the 'denationalising' effects of Catholic education and the Church and also a possible desire amongst first and second generation immigrants to make a break with their Irish past. One response to the trauma of emigration and Irish history may have been to blank it out of the family record, a finding that contrasts with the more common view that these events left an indelible stain in the collective memory. The Stafford respondents showed no sign of being influenced by the popular collective memories of Ireland's political, social and economic sufferings. The exile motif in Irish history meant nothing to them.

To some degree these negative findings may reflect the presence of anti-Irishness in British society both in the respondents' lifetimes and those of their ancestors. A number of respondents were sensitive about possible reactions to their Irish connections, and none proclaimed an Irish identity despite evidence of some pride in the Irish element of their family history. It was less easy to discern the presence of such attitudes in earlier generations and they were counterbalanced in some cases by clear attachments to Irish links, speech and patterns of behaviour. Nevertheless, the respondents' family histories point to the fact that, for the majority of the Irish who settled in Victorian Britain, there was no advantage in continuing to proclaim a strongly Irish identity and considerable perceived disadvantages in doing so.

This study of Irish descendants in Stafford needs to be complemented by research carried out in the areas of denser Irish settlement in nineteenth century Britain as well as elsewhere in the Irish diaspora. This would be a small response to Kenny's call for historical inquiry into 'how the diasporic sensibilities of the Irish vary according to the places where they reside'.[37]

Such work would need to consider the significance of the family as the site and focus of communicated memories and the role of ethnic dilution through intermarriage in the survival of memorabilia, memories and legends over time. The research would inherently highlight the extent of Irish ethnic descent from the nineteenth century and raise questions about the survival of Irish communities and identities. How do we examine identity as an historical phenomenon and how is the phenomenon of hybrid identity documented? Finally work needs to probe the relationship between family communicative memory and the wider collective memory within the context of the locality, the nation state and the wider Irish diaspora.

Int.	Source	Date	No. of Resp.	DoB	% Irish	Sex	Gen	Family(ies)	Immig. GB	Arr. St.	Dir. St?
1	A	10/02	4	1935-41	25	2M2F	4	Corcoran, Goodman	1841/1850s?	1841/1858	Y/N?
2	B	5& 9/02	1	1921	25	M	4	Coleman/Curley/ Carroll/Cassidy	1847-51	1847-51	Y
3	A	10/02	2	1939/49	50	2F	4	Hand, O'Connor	c1850?/c1870	1871/1875	N
4	C	3/03	1	1963	50	F	5	Coghlan, Kenny	1851/1851	1851/1851	Y
5	C	4/03	1	1930	12.5	M	4	Kenny, Mannion	1851-1860	1851-1860	Y
6	C	5/03	2	1917/40	100	2F	3	Crosson, Dolan	c1850	1915	N
7	B	6/03	2	1930/33	50	2M	3	Ryan, Walsh	1860/1882?	1860/1882?	Y?
8	D	6/03	3	1940-45	12.5	1M2F	5	Concar, Kenny	1850/1851	1850/1851	Y
9	B	7/03	1	1938	50	F	4/5	Geoghegan, Mulrooney	c1850/c1870	1881/1879	N
10	B	9/03	1	1925	25	F	3-4	Coleman/Cassidy/ Curley	1847/1851	1847/1851	Y
11	D	11/03	1	1937	12.5	M	5	McTighe	1860	1860	Y
12	A	3/04	1	1940	12.5	F	4	Hingerty	1851-5	1851-5	Y

Table 1 Stafford Irish: Interviewees and Families

Key to Table 1

Int	Interview
Source	Source of interviewees:
	A: unsolicited contact made by respondent(s)
	B: through local contact
	C: contact stimulated by local newspaper article
	D: contact in response to web-site
No. of Resp.	Number of family respondents at the interview
%Irish	% of descent from ethnically Irish ancestors: 100% - both parents Irish; 50% - one parent Irish; 25% - one grandparent Irish; 12.5% - one great grandparent Irish.
Gen	Generation since original immigrant born in Ireland
Immig. GB	Estimated date of immigration to Britain
Arr. St	Probable date of arrival in Stafford
Dir. St?	Whether immigrants settled directly in Stafford from Ireland

13

Marginal Voices:
Football and Identity in a Contested Space

Joseph M. Bradley

At a conference held at the University of Stirling in January 1997, consideration was given to a number of pertinent social and political questions that focused on the historical and contemporary position of Catholics in Scotland.[1] Apart from a small number of indigenous Scots, and several thousand with origins in countries such as Poland, Lithuania and Italy, Catholics in Scotland largely originate from Ireland and relevant issues were expected to be a part of conference proceedings. Nevertheless, during the discussion, two academic speakers expressed the view that the Irish in Scotland could be referred to historically but not contemporaneously. Only after a number of exchanges did one concede that discussants could talk about 'the ex-Irish' in Scotland. The Chair of the conference, as well as his supporting professorial colleague, offered a view that talk of the Irish in contemporary Scotland was illusory and that the greatest single immigrant grouping in society had, 'ceased being Irish'.

This assertion is not surprising considering that comparatively few academic or popular books and articles address historical, cultural, economic and religious issues in relation to the Irish in Scotland, and that a significant amount of published sources do so only within the boundaries of a 'sectarian discourse'.[2] T. M. Devine states with some surprise that, 'Irish immigrants in Scotland have not until recent years been effectively integrated into the wider study of Scottish historical development'.[3] In a related sense, a member of the Irish diaspora, Scottish-born writer and novelist Andrew O'Hagan, has lamented the dearth of reflective works on Catholic or Irish Catholic life in Scotland in the 1970s. For him, this means that there are few realistic or supportive references which can assist the formulation and transmission of his ideas and experiences.[4] Likewise, a Dublin based interviewee stated that at school he learned of the Irish in the USA, Australia and England. Until he became interested in Celtic Football Club in Glasgow, he was unaware that a significant part of the Irish diaspora existed in Scotland.[5] Such perspectives constitute a view that Irishness in Scotland has been pushed to the periphery of social, cultural and political narratives pertaining to every day life.

However, despite the polemics engaged in by the relevant speakers at Stirling, the Economic and Social Research Council funded 'Irish 2 Project' demonstrates that contrary to the 'opinions' expressed at the 1997 Stirling Conference, Irishness and Irish identity remain relevant in the personal, social and community composition of people born in Scotland whose parents, grandparents or great grandparents migrated from Ireland during the nineteenth and twentieth centuries.[6]

Celtic: The Irish Football Club Born in Scotland

J. Hoberman, states that, 'sport has no intrinsic value structure, but it is a ready and flexible vehicle through which ideological associations can be reinforced'.[7] Eric Hobsbawm believes that, 'the identity of a nation of millions, seems more real as a team of eleven named people'.[8] In a related sense, M. Blain and R. Boyle state that, 'the complex nature of collective identity formations associated with Scottish sport parallels the complexity of Scotland as a political [and cultural] entity'.[9] These commentators recognise that football has the capacity to embody, actualise and express identity; national, cultural, ethnic, religious, social, political, economic and community, in a way few other social manifestations are able to. It is for these reasons that the institution of Celtic Football Club based in the east end of Glasgow, demonstrates the fallacy in the argument used at Stirling that the Irish in Scotland have 'ceased to exist'. Further, the existence of the Scottish born Irish in Scotland and their denial by other elements in society illustrates a significant aspect of the experience of the Irish diaspora in Scotland. This is also an indication of the exclusion and marginalisation of that community over a century and a half as alluded to by other observers.

However, as well as being a manifestation of Irishness and a factor of celebration for the diaspora in Scotland, the Irishness of Celtic Football Club and its supporting community has also been a matter of controversy and contestation. Despite becoming the most significant Irish team in Scotland, Celtic's presence and subsequent success has often been problematic. Through the problematisation of Irishness in Scottish society is to be found part of the rationale for denying the presence of the Irish as well the sectarianising of Irishness in Scottish society. Further, in the problematising and sectarianising of Irishness in Scottish society is to be found the explanations for the importance and central role of Celtic for those in Scotland who are of the Irish diaspora.

Background and Context

In 1896, several years after the birth of Celtic from amidst the Irish Catholic community in the west of Scotland, Celtic and Hibernian (an Edinburgh side which had also emerged from the local Irish community) were top of the Scottish league. This prompted the newspaper, *Scottish Sport*, to note the dominance in Scotland of two Irish teams and asked where was the Scottish team that could challenge the incomers.[10] In fact, a few years earlier, Hibernian had been refused entry to the Scottish League on the basis of the club's Irish identity. Such newspaper comment was a refined example of the antagonism faced by Irish clubs in Scotland, but the challenge by *Scottish Sport* explicitly reflects the ethnic nature of the Scottish game from its earliest years and is also reflective of later discourses concerning the Irish and Celtic in Scotland.

More significantly, in 1952, Celtic's Irishness and the traditional flying of the Irish national flag at Celtic Park came to threaten the life and very place of the Club in Scottish football. Celtic's official club historian in its centenary year, future Labour Government Minister, Brian Wilson, describes how an attempt was made by the Scottish Football Association 'to force Celtic out of business if they would not agree to remove the Irish flag from their home ground'.[11] Nonetheless, the authorities lacked recourse to legitimate means in enforcing its demand. Most clubs eventually waned in their attack on Celtic recognising that the income generated by the club and its support was a major factor in Scottish Football's vibrancy. The furore eventually died down and Celtic continued to fly the Irish flag. Nevertheless, the presence of the Irish flag at Celtic Park continues to invite antagonistic comment.[12]

A history of ethno-religious cleavage in Scotland has meant that opposition and prejudice towards the immigrant community has been widespread, and has clearly had a wider resonance in Scottish society which has not been restricted to the Irishness of Celtic or the club's followers. As late as 1938, the Church and Nation Committee of the Church of Scotland emphasised, 'the elementary right of a nation to control and select its immigrants'. The debate which had resulted in such a way of thinking was conducted solely with Irish Catholics in mind. In fact, Brown states that from around the time of the Education Act (Scotland) 1918, until the outbreak of the Second World War, there was an 'official' Presbyterian campaign against the Irish Catholic community in Scotland. This campaign was both institutional and popular, and is viewed by Brown as an attempt at 'marginalising, and even eliminating an ethnic minority whose presence was regarded as an evil, polluting the purity of Scottish race and culture'.[13]

The unacceptability of Irish-Catholics to the Orange community in Scotland is one of the most perceptible contemporary manifestations of this attitude.

> Study the [Irish-Catholic] names of some of the 'Labour' candidates elected ... What do Glasgow's Protestant clergymen think of this situation? What do the genuine patriots, in the SNP's rank-and-file, think about it? ... There isn't a Scoto-Eirishman in Scotland, a Lally, a Murphy, or a Gaffney, who is not Eirish under his skin. Scratch them and their Eirish bit comes out ...[14]

In a secular society which inter alia involves popular conceptions of 'liberalism', and given the social and political progress made by a substantial number of the offspring of the Irish in Scotland, most of the overt statements and activities of half a century ago are unlikely to gain the currency they once had. Today, society in Scotland is more complex: for some sections of the population, ethnic and religious identity is less significant than in the past. However, an exploration of the fan base that gives substance to Celtic demonstrates the ongoing problematic nature of Irishness within Scottish society as well as the central role that the football club plays to Irish identity in Scotland. In addition, the arguments of Hoberman, Hobsbawm, Blain and Boyle, who view football as a means to view the literal expression of the 'imagined community', are expressed concisely through the meaningfulness that is constituted by the Irish diasporic identity of Celtic Football Club in Scotland.

Asking the People: Celtic's Place in the Diaspora

In 2002, the Economic and Social Research Council funded a project focusing on second and third generation Irish people in Britain. This work centred on ideas of self, family, community and nation within a context of having a background indicating that some, most, or all of one's family originated from Ireland. This involved notions relating to history, religion, politics, health, work, social life, family and sport. The research in Scotland also afforded the opportunity to explore the historical and contemporary links between the Irish Catholic community in Scotland and Celtic Football Club, an institution conceived, sustained and supported in the main by the multi-generational Irish diasporic community since 1887.

The nature of Celtic's involvement in football as well as the contentiousness of supporting the club was suggested by numerous Irish 2 Project respondents in Scotland. The comments of the interviewees also give some indications into perceptions of 'sectarianism' in Scotland and its links to football. An early experience of Clydebank born Johnny Kiernan negatively linked his ethnicity and religion with support for Celtic.

> When I joined the Civil Service ... they said to me, 'What team do you support?' and I said, 'Celtic', and the guy looked at the address and said 'oh how come you don't support Clydebank?' I support Celtic! It was silly things like that thrown at you.

Being subjected to violence and verbal abuse can sometimes be a consequence of being a football follower in a variety of societies. Nonetheless, there are few if any other football clubs outside of Ireland that could be considered Irish and the context for such hostility in Scotland is specific and unique, containing as it does a religious and ethnic frame of reference. Hostility shown towards Celtic and its support was a recurring theme for a number of interviewees. Paul Cassidy stated that:

> My mum wouldn't want me when I was younger to go out to Celtic games wearing a Celtic top in case I got attacked for it or whatever ... If I went to the game with my dad, my dad would never wear a scarf because he's seen too many people attacked and stuff like that ...

Mary Brolly contributed to this discourse:

> My son wouldn't have been in any danger wearing the Celtic strip at that time, even although it was the early seventies. I mean it was Blairhill [in Coatbridge – a town of predominantly Catholic Irish origin]. It was nice wee boys he was going out to play with, but it was this, you didn't want to offend the neighbours ... I remember my son being given a Celtic sweatband and his father [Catholic of Irish decent] pulling it off his head, very cruel like and I thought, just again because he was wearing a Celtic sweatband.

The feelings experienced by Brolly with regards the conflictual nature of her family's relationship to Celtic took another dimension, although the parallels with their support for Celtic were clear, when talk turned to support for Ireland in international soccer.

It's a difficult one because I remember reading about two or three weeks ago, Scotland and Ireland were playing on the same day and in here my son had said to me, oh God, all the boys will be wondering, they'll know fine well the reason I'm no out there is because I'm watching Ireland and they're all be sitting watching Scotland, and he was uneasy about it. Just a bit uneasy but he knew he wanted to watch Ireland and he knew that they didn't fully understand why he didn't want to watch Scotland.

Margaret Murphy believed that there was more to the idea of 'hiding' and 'denying' support for Celtic because she argued, 'it's not protection when its about suppression'. Esther McMellon concurred:

... if you pedal back all the time you're the one that's going under. If you can't hold your head up high and be what you are.

James Haggerty spoke of possible consequences in being dissuaded from supporting Celtic (and possibly other things Irish?), but he also unintentionally raised the question of socialisation in Scottish society and a context for the formation of ideas, principles and identities. Haggerty believed that as a result of continual and hegemonic arguments against the wearing of Celtic colours and of expressing aspects of Irishness in Scotland you would 'eventually lose interest in your colours', thus indicating the importance of agency in such formations.

Philomena Donnelly also described how Celtic was an aspect of Irish Catholic cultural life in Scotland that is required to be dealt with sensitively:

There was times when they wouldn't [want to be identified by Celtic, Catholic and Irish popular labels], it wasn't as openly discussed I suppose, almost like the football wouldn't be discussed if people were coming round who you knew weren't Celtic fans.
Q: So you wouldn't bring up Celtic?
Yeah, I can remember once when I was very young, I was about 7 or 8 and I got a baby doll for Christmas and I fancied a guy at school at the time, I must have been a bit older, called John Paul, but I told my mum that I was naming this baby doll after the Pope and her friends were coming in and I remember her saying 'don't say that in front of them, just call it John in front of people, because that would be easier'... I know he [my Father] takes an awful lot of abuse for Celtic but whether it goes on to Irishness I don't know. It's like because there are only 3 of us in the house, so they expect Irish families to have 10 or 12 and I remember one night being at a

party, it was one of the neighbours and somebody made a ... comment to her that if she was that good a Catholic she would have had a lot more children, without even thinking and I always remember thinking that was weird but she got really upset by it. So I suppose they did but as you say just they just protect you from it

This perceived difficulty in the Catholic-Celtic-Irish cultural linkage in the context of Scottish society was also experienced by Joseph John Flanagan in the late 1960s:

When I started work, I got a job as an apprentice in the works my father was in, which was absolutely great. He was over the moon about this, an apprentice electrician, he was chuffed to bits ... I'm starting there as a sixteen year old and just going straight out of Glenboig into this environment here and I'd been through Our Lady & St Joseph's school and St Augustine's High School, so it was Catholic, Catholic, Catholic all the way up. Going into this environment which was very much not a Catholic environment, very much managed by the Scottish Protestant background. Now he hadn't spoken about that to me but when I went over there the guys were wearing their football colours and you had a hard hat to wear and that kind of stuff, so the Rangers stickers and all that. So I put the Celtic stickers on mine, he went ballistic. I had not to do that. That was just something that was private, you keep that and I would never get on if that was, you know if I was going to wear them. I'm saying, but all the rest of them ... It doesn't matter about all the rest, just you ... so didn't blow it from the rooftop. I don't suppose he would have denied anything about it but it was just I think common-sense prevailed and said, there's no point making things difficult for yourself, and that stuck for a wee while ... Didn't talk about your background, just didn't talk about that kind of stuff, just avoided the conversations ... I think probably I'd speak about it more now than I should because I can. Because it felt as though I couldn't then. It wasn't a conscious thing, you just didn't do it and you didn't realise that till ... it wouldn't be expected. You were almost expected to conform into a subservient role. Do your bit, go away home ... I was coming in with my labour to do my bit and go away home again and that was in other organisations as well.

The connection of Celtic to other aspects of second and third generation Irish Catholic life in Scotland and the subservient role mentioned by Flanagan, shaped partly by an emigrant consciousness that believed it was better to downplay heritage as well as country of origin and faith, was also alluded to by seventy year old, James Haggerty. When Haggerty embarked on a working life outside of his community, and in relation to being as open and relaxed as he had previously been, he said,

> I would say that [the working environment and mixing with strangers] cautioned me a bit, you know. That I wouldn't be too loud and shouting about Celtic or anything like that, you know. I tended to cover that up, reluctant to get involved. The Irish part of it that was the part, if you like, it sort of [was] on a back boiler, out of the road, used when I was with the Irish crowd back home, the Boys Guild and so on but I knew that I couldn't cope with that identity in work. It just wasn't on at that time, especially among the young ones, you know, that I was working with … I don't know about promotion and so on but if you know, the men above and so on were all probably Masons and so on and I think it could have … made life kind of miserable and as it was I got on fine with everybody.

For Francis Daly, the workplace also presented a site for potential conflict and for downplaying Irishness. Again Celtic was mentioned as part of a triangle of ethnic distinctiveness – Irish, Catholic and Celtic – that attracted perceived hostility, suspicion and the privatisation of identity.

> I've got a not bad job and I would have to be very careful, it's alright saying these things don't happen but they do happen, and I would be exposing myself if I were to be outspoken about Irish things or about being a Catholic or being a Celtic supporter even, you need to watch … I know it would go against me, it wouldn't do me any favours … I might have lost my job. I might just, sort of my boss would be … I've got a pretty good idea he's a free mason, he's alright with me but if I was to be too, if I was to be outspoken or not watch my language or how I phrase things in front of him it could cause me trouble … I really would be very careful, I wouldn't use that to anybody. See I wouldn't emphasise my Irishness either because it's just, it can be too, it's not worth it, because it opens up a can of worms for a lot of people and they can't accept it. People don't, there's a thing about, it's dangerous to be quite outspoken I think in Scottish society about your Irish background because, it won't do you any favours, it won't do you any favours in employment … Scottish society does not accept people of Irish origin, they don't like it.

Similarly, Rosaleen Ashling Gaffney noted the hostility within Scottish society to Irishness.

> ... a lot of people would comment on, especially they pick up on your name, you know, Rosaleen Ashling Gaffney, straightaway they pick up on your name, that you're Irish. A lot of people it's fine but then some people don't like it ... they would just make maybe fly comments about, you know, you being Irish or the fact that you would be a Celtic fan, things like that ... Yeah, a lot of people are seen to be, you know, wanting to be Irish when really a lot of people say you are not because you are born here, you are Scottish or British but most of those groups do like to stay with their identity. If you take, you know, the vast majority that support Celtic, like of the Irish sort of Catholic that's their way, in my opinion, their way of identifying with their culture.

This implied hostility in Scottish Society to Irishness, Catholics and Celtic, had numerous facets as revealed by the interviewees. In a situation where one female subject was in a strong relationship with a secular minded Scottish Protestant boyfriend, and where marriage was in the offing, Rosaleen Connolly offered the view that her Irish Catholic identity still provoked contention with her boyfriend.

> I don't just go to Ireland or love Ireland or support Celtic or go to church because I'm meant to do it, because I'm from Coatbridge and everyone else does it, it's because I want to now ... At first, it bugged him because as I said earlier that I supported Celtic and people from Ireland were all alike, just wee Paddies. Now he knows. He can understand how important it is to me, the culture and all the rest. What he doesn't like is when I say I'm Irish. It drives him round the bend. In fact we had this conversation again the other day. It's just something that is mentioned all the time. When we went to Barcelona this year, I had my Irish passport and he said he couldn't believe that it was an Irish passport. It bugs him a bit.

Joseph John Flanagan also made the connection with other aspects of his life as a third generation Irish Catholic living in Scotland. The inhibitions he had assumed in his lifestyle with regards to Celtic also permeated Flanagan's working environment and life generally outside of his Irish and Catholic place of upbringing. Flanagan connected to the discourse of Philomena

Donnelly in stating that he too experienced the notion of changing names to disguise identity and fashion another more acceptable one.

> Q Do you feel differently about your identity in different places? Do you feel it easier to be Irish in certain situations?
> In different situations, aye. Without a doubt ... I was like a split personality because at home and with family and friends I was Joseph John and then became Joe ... wasn't my choice, all of a sudden people started to refer to me as Joe and I hadn't the confidence to say, excuse me ... you just wouldn't do that. Even like signatures, 'Joseph J' and stuff like that the 'J' got kind of knocked off payroll things, just very, very strange. So therefore I not just subconsciously, I physically then, well not physically but literally became a different person. When I went to work with Scottish Power, or SSEB as it was, or when I went to work prior to that in the British Steel Corporation, I left home as Joseph John and I arrived at work as Joe ... As a kid, as a fourteen, fifteen, sixteen year old, like, in fact more than a lot of them my room was absolutely plastered with Celtic photos and all that stuff, you know. I was a fanatic, I didn't miss a game, I'd the Celtic rug. I've still got a load of the stuff, there's memorabilia up in the loft all boxed away. Course in that environment then on the way to work leaving 'Joe' somewhere and picking him up on the way home. Strange.

The sometimes confused but disguised nature of Joseph John's identity was also inferred when asked whether he would support Ireland or Scotland in international football:

> If I'm honest? I mean my next door neighbour's a great guy, old man, Scottish through and through ... if I was watching it in the house and he came in to watch it with me, for his sake I would be a Scottish fan. If I was watching it privately, with Peter or Mark [his sons], I would be supporting Ireland.

Flanagan expressed the view that he felt little affinity with the Scottish football side and viewed Celtic as his national team. He also indicated that this was a common view amongst numerous Celtic supporters.

> If I was looking for my national team it would be Celtic over the years, which is a strange thing to say. That's the family, everybody in there is sort of ... I remember my dad, the reason I didn't know he was a big Celtic fan, what he always did every two years, the Home

Internationals were on at the time and he used to go to Wembley. He ran a Wembley Fund. Every second year about twelve of them went in the minibus down to Wembley and I was harping and harping, and round about the same time, just after this in fact, my mother eventually I think nagged him as much to say, right it's about time you took that boy down. He took me down on this trip and I would go down there ... Mid 60s, aye. So I went down and, oh this is great. Going down to London seeing Scotland playing England at Wembley. Fantastic. When we got there we went into a pub and I got an orange and they boys were all sitting having a pint and stuff, this was the Friday night. It took us about fifteen or sixteen hours, maybe longer, so I was saying to my dad, what time do we leave for the football, and there was this silence and they all stared at me. None of them went to the football. They went down every year and my dad said to me, look, did you not notice in the alternate years when they're at Hampden I don't go to the games at Hampden. It hadn't twigged. He said I wouldn't go and watch Scotland if they were playing out the back garden, so they came down for a weekend in London, a weekend away, a bevy session, a guys weekend and I got presented with twelve tickets to go and do what I liked with them and I was flogging them, fourteen years of age. So I went to the game myself at fourteen ...None of them went to the game ... I went on my own, went on the Underground ...

Numerous other respondents also mentioned the privatised aspect of the constitution of Irish identity in Scotland referred to by Joseph John.

When I went to a primary school, maybe 95 – 98 percent of the kids at the primary school were of Irish descent. All of the teachers, with the exception of one, were of Irish descent, she was a Lithuanian. But it wasn't encouraged, anyone showing an Irish identity wasn't encouraged at all. It was encouraged in the house perhaps, in certain families, but it wasn't encouraged out with the house, out with the house at all.

Nevertheless, Francis Daly repeated the theme of an otherwise privatised Irish identity being publicly celebrated in the context of Celtic Football Club

It was the only place you were allowed to express ... to a certain extent it was a sort of an Irish identity. You were allowed to go see Celtic matches and express your Irish identity ... it's maybe a lot more important, it's not just the football club of course, it's a lot more. Celtic is all about attitude and that as well. You know you can express an Irish identity and there's safety at Celtic Park, whereas you wouldn't be able to express it out ...

In this setting respondents attest to the capacity of Celtic to allow expression of their Irish identity in a public space, in the company of many thousands of other like minded individuals, void of the hostility and suspicion often found in experiences out with a private environment. Interviewees who made connections between Celtic and other cultural, social and political aspects of their lives frequently referred to the significance of Celtic to Catholics of Irish descent. Second generation Glasgow Irishman Peadar McGrath opined that but for Celtic's Irishness he would have no interest in football at all:

... I find that whenever if you're talking to people and you say that you're Irish, they don't actually hear the word 'Irish', they hear you saying 'bigot', but they don't ... I don't know how many debates I've had with people actually ... even Catholic teachers in the school, when you start talking about it, they start talking about bigotry, about I can understand what you're saying maybe, that was what your parents experienced. I'm saying, I'm not talking about that, I'm talking about me being Irish and about a culture. But they can't see the culture, they just keep relating it back to bigotry and to do with Celtic and Rangers ... I don't go to see Celtic, I've no interest in football. I was the wee guy that was left standing against the wall when I was at school.
Q: If you had to choose a club team, which one would you support?
Celtic. When I say that, I don't watch football, but sometimes I'd turn the radio on and listen to the Celtic game hoping that Celtic would win but I don't go to see them ... the only way I've got any interest in Celtic at all is, I'm not actually interested in football, my interest in Celtic is I see them as the Irish team in Glasgow. I used to go to see Celtic up till I was about eighteen. I went to see Celtic because I felt everybody standing there in the Jungle was the same as me. But all these guys had the same views, sang the same songs and just thought the same as me. I mean I could be totally wrong, but standing there in that crowd, that was the feeling I got and it was the only time in the whole week I could get that feeling ... every week you could stand there and sing to your heart's content and it made me feel really Irish, it made me feel this is good, here's other guys who think the same as me.

Unless in the company of others from an Irish background, social isolation, being a stranger and of not being welcome, was frequently referred to by interviewees. As McGrath suggests, only in Celtic related social circles did he experience comfort in being the person he saw himself to be. Harry McGuigan referred to this 'unease' that many Celtic people encounter in negotiating their Irish identities in Scottish society. He stated that:

> They play a central part, they should do and they should continue to do. When Irish emigrant's children had nothing, the only thing they had to anchor themselves here was Celtic. Why should they apologise for that and why should Celtic? That gave them something to anchor their identity to. 1887/88 all of those years that gave Irish Catholics in this country something to identify, something to identify with. You can't just turn around and say you can't have that any more.

Francis Daly thought similarly about Celtic's connection to the Irish immigrant community.

> Celtic are a, for me personally, and you don't need to be an Irish Celtic supporter to identify with or to embrace this sort of Irish thing, but to me and to everybody that I know, and all the friends I've got in Bellshill and in Blantyre, Celtic are an integral part of their culture, and it's an integral part of an Irish culture in the West of Scotland, there are no two ways about it. It's integral, it's without, I mean, that's not to say it wouldn't survive without Celtic but Celtic are such a massive part of it, and everybody grows up in families that supported Celtic so they've all got a sort of understanding, or an insight into things where may be they wouldn't have if it wasn't for the football club. So I personally think seeing the football club as central to the whole issue or notion of identity and culture.

Paul Cassidy also referred to the family and community aspect of supporting Celtic.

> I view Celtic as part of my culture, to such an extent that even when my father died ... we scattered some of his ashes behind the goal at Celtic Park. As well as putting some over in Donegal, and I kinda view it as kinda family thing, it's hard to put it all into words, but I view it as a family.

Similarly, Pauline Rice raised issues of family, community, heritage, religion, politics, Irish history and the Irish in Scotland in relation to her support for Celtic.

> My identity with Celtic, again, is the underdog, whether my strength of feeling is it associates me with the injustices that have been attached to Celtic Football Club over the years. All these ... we never had a discriminatory policy at any time at Celtic, you know there was never a religious discrimination ... My strength of feeling for Celtic goes back to having to fight for where we've got and from the poverty that we've come from and what we've done from that. I see the Irish culture over here doing the exact same, getting to the top having had to struggle to get there and that would be my association with Ireland and Celtic but again I don't apologise for thinking we should be able to sing Irish songs if we wanted to because Irish men have been involved with Celtic from the start.

The role of Celtic as pivotal to the Irish in Scotland in relation to their sense of history, heritage, cultural Catholicism and ethnic identity was confirmed by a majority of interviewees. The principal role of Celtic to Irish identity in Scotland was summed up succinctly by James Brannigan.

> Celtic is at the centre of my cultural and ethnic identity in Scotland. Celtic is the team of the Irish in Scotland. They represent the Irish who had to leave Ireland. Celtic is one of the only places where people who are Irish or Irish minded have been able to express that with some comfort. Celtic is our standard bearer in Scotland. They've never been an Irish only or a Catholic only club because that would be wrong. But, Celtic is essentially about us – it's our team, our club and our community. It's a small place where we can be us and not be forced to be the same as them – whoever they might be. Celtic wouldn't be here without the Irish. Ireland's history helps explain the institution that is Celtic Football Club. Every time we win a big match it's a celebration for a community. We can come together and we can celebrate publicly. We are recognised and the rest of the country can see us even though many of them ignore or despise us. We're here and sometimes we're the best at this particular sport. Just to see the green and white hoops running out is evidence that we've survived despite what many have thrown at us. Seeing the tricolour and the shamrock somewhere publicly where we don't 'usually' – usually we have to keep them hidden, is the greatest thing about Celtic. Without the Irish in Scotland there is no Celtic and

without Celtic there is no Irish in Scotland. They're inextricably linked – spiritually at one.

Celtic's role amongst many of the Irish diaspora in Scotland is fundamental. Celtic draws the vast majority of its support from this segment of the Scottish population. In an often contested social setting, the club allows public space for the expression of community and ethnic identity. Even when a third generation Irish Glasgow based interviewee was asked about his sense of home, John Flynn's reply reflected the place of Celtic in an Irish diasporic setting.

> Home's where the heart is. Home's Glasgow. I tell you the last couple of weeks I've seen Johnny Crawley the Cork singer at the Riverside. I've seen Juno at the Citizens. I've seen the Ploughboy of the Western World at the Arches and we were at the Irish concert last night in the Concert Hall and we've got Celtic as well, so if we only had Old Ireland over here. I think we've got it. No I'm quite happy with that, you know. I do feel at home in Ireland … There's a lot of places I love in England, cause I've got a lot of friends too but I do feel particularly at home in Ireland too. I don't feel, and I think it's like when Ella goes to Italy [his Scots born Italian identifying wife], she still feels kind of comfortable there you know. But I do too, I don't think … in Ireland I definitely feel at home but if anybody said to me, where's your home, I'd say Glasgow.

Although Monica McKevitt did not specifically refer to diaspora, she alluded to the concept as being physically and culturally displaced from the place she felt she belonged and correlated this with Celtic and the Irish in Scotland:

> It's a big part of being Irish, and the association. Especially the West of Scotland in being over here. I think it's because, to me like you're away from Ireland so that kind of holds some of your Irishness to a certain extent.

Perspective

The links made by respondents between their ethnic origins in Ireland and Celtic Football Club demonstrates that not everyone born in Scotland wants to be imagined as a Scot.[15] Even if some or many of the diaspora have become Scottish, the nature of Scottishness amongst Scottish born people in Scotland can vary in relation to ethnicity, geography and religion among other influences. The Irish 2 Project shows that numerous second and third generation Irish in Scotland identify themselves as Irish or see Irishness as their primary or favoured identity.

Significantly, the Irish 2 Project testifies to the perceived difficulties in being Irish in Scotland, especially for those who are part of the multi-generational Irish community. The evidence demonstrates that supporting Celtic in Scottish society, the one football club in Britain where Irishness is a defining aspect of the club and its support, can invite opprobrium, invective, sectarian labelling, occasionally violence and the possibility of social and economic discrimination. This is important to understanding past and present Irish identities in Scotland while such hostility also links to Hickman's idea of the 'denationalising' of Irish people in Britain.[16]

The Irish 2 Project interviewees believe that hostility towards Irishness is not limited to Celtic but also extends beyond football. It is perceived by the respondents that this hostility can be manifest in the workplace, in general social life and in some instances, from other members of this community, thus reflecting the contested nature of Irishness within the diaspora in Scotland.[17] That is, those who argue that being Scottish is an 'obvious', 'natural', 'right' and 'better' choice and, being Irish is linked to sectarianism and atavistic identities that should have been diluted by the assumed 'neutral' factor of time to the point of irrelevance.

Despite the contestation over Irishness and the assimilative and conforming pressures perceived by many second and third generation Irish to become Scots or, more acceptable Scots by divesting themselves of their Irish identities, the Irish 2 Project as well as other research,[18] reflects that Irishness is significant and manifest in Scotland. Further, it might also be argued that the disregard and marginalisation of Irish identity and, over the course of many decades, its lack of recognition in Scottish society, lends to the creation and sustenance of sectarian attitudes towards Catholics of Irish descent in Scotland. This additionally confuses any issue perceived as being sectarian. That the Irishness of Celtic and its supporters is often treated as aberrant, alien and sectarian, or, as is evidenced in the comments made by the academic speakers at the Stirling conference, Irishness is ignored, marginalised and rendered invisible, is a constant feature of society and frequently exhibits itself most obviously throughout the Scottish media. The west of Scotland is a specific location where ethnic difference and the sustenance of Irish identity has been labelled as sectarian, notably through the media and in its reporting of matters relating to Celtic.

The Press as a Medium for Prejudice

Celtic's participation in the UEFA Cup Final in the Spanish city of Seville in May 2003 attracted a vast amount of television, radio and newspaper attention in Scotland. Some of the discourses around the event can be seen to demonstrate the contentiousness of the Club and its supporters' Irish identities as well as public displays of these in Scotland. Although reporting of events was generally positive, when issues related to the Club's and support's Irish or Catholic nature, the discourse ignored this aspect of the achievement or modified it as Scottishness became the more acceptable medium through which Celtic and its fans celebration and representation was recorded by the media. Such references have a long history in Scottish society and can be seen to constitute an ideological construction where sectarian and Scottish identity discourses prevail.

The dominant discourses that persist in relation to Celtic and its support was demonstrated by Scotland's best selling tabloid newspaper, the *Daily Record*, and one of Scotland's best well known football journalists. On the eve of Celtic's match in Spain the journalist wrote:

> Celtic, a Scottish team whether some of their fans are willing to admit it or not ... Celtic ARE Scottish so they belong to more than the supporters who follow them week in, week out ... This is Scotland against Portugal ... right now Celtic, albeit unwittingly, are flying our flag.[19]

Around the time of the final, various newspapers carried letters that demonstrated the contentiousness of Celtic and its support's Irishness amongst many people in Scotland. The journalist's view was a popular one and some letter writers reflected this

> I was absolutely appalled and disgusted when watching the UEFA Cup Final. I am sure I am not the only non-Celtic supporter who was urged to 'get behind' the Scottish team. How many Scottish flags were in the stadium? I counted one but maybe I couldn't see the others due to the sea of Irish Republican flags in display. Isn't it about time that people like this decided which nationality they are?[20]

> I could have sworn the UEFA Cup Final in Seville was between teams from Scotland and Portugal, but judging by the flags in the stadium I think it was actually Ireland against Portugal; there were more American, Canadian, or Australian flags than Scottish. How do you expect neutral football fans to support their Scottish team when

the fans make it very clear that they have no loyalty to Scotland and where their true allegiance lies? I can't imagine what the rest of the world thought as they watched this disgraceful sight which was attended by some of our politicians who supposedly abhor this type of behaviour. This was not a good reflection on our culture and a bad night for Scottish sport.[21]

This correspondent was criticised by several letters in subsequent editions of the *Herald*. Nevertheless, it is interesting to note the apparent linking of Celtic fans flying of the Irish flag with 'sectarianism', reviving the arguments and accusations of the SFA against Celtic in 1952, while this is also an ever present and contentious contemporary issue in Scottish society. The head of the Dundee United Supporter's Association said with regards Celtic: 'They need Scotland. I just wish you'd see a few more Saltires amongst their support, rather than tricolours.'[22]

On the basis of the news correspondence during May 2003, it might be argued that the Irish diaspora has traditionally formed the great 'other' in Scottish society. Scottish sports writers and journalists as well as letter writers to various newspapers question and marginalise Celtic and its fans' Irishness while pursuing a well established assimilationist strategy informing Celtic fans, as well as the rest of Scottish society, of the 'truth': the club and its fans are not Irish. This discourse often utilises the ideological abstraction of 'sectarianism', as a means to encourage people to see the obvious sense in this argument. This argument dominates in Scottish society and manifests itself in the discourses of the Irish 2 respondents.

Creating Visibility

The Irish 2 Project demonstrates that Celtic is of foremost cultural importance to the Irish diaspora in Scotland. The club functions as a socialising agent into a unique form of Irish cultural activity and it exists as a public space where many of those who esteem their Irishness in Scotland demonstrate and celebrate their identity. Celtic's Irish identity and the offspring of the Irish immigrant community that has sustained this as 'the' central component of the Club and its fans makes it a unique football club, not only in Scotland but beyond as well as the Club and its support constitute a unique representation of Irishness amongst the Irish diaspora worldwide.

In Scotland, football is bound up and inherently linked with the process of community construction. For those descended from Ireland in Scotland and who view Celtic as intrinsic to their Irishness, the club remains a site for the preservation of their cultural traditions, customs, political preferences and in the socialisation and sustenance of Irish identity in Scotland. It exists as a site for a sense of community born from the majority of these supporters sharing familial and kinship origins in Ireland. It constitutes a setting for friendship and association with people often inter-married, having experienced the same denominational school format, sharing similar geographical spaces in Scotland (frequently in the Glasgow and Lanarkshire areas, within a thirty mile radius of Celtic Park in Glasgow) and with a sense of belonging, to Ireland, Catholicism, Irish history and Irish culture. Celtic represents part of the history of the Irish in Ireland, of the Irish in Scotland and of part of the history of the Irish diaspora worldwide.

As demonstrated in the Irish 2 Project, in relation to the Irish in Scotland and Britain more generally, Celtic and its supporters' Irishness challenge notions of assimilation amongst the children and grandchildren of Irish migrants in Britain. As Hickman stresses, this points to the need for more nuanced understandings of 'white' diasporic identities, as well as Scottishness and Britishness.[23] Without the Irish diasporic community's sense of Irishness in Scotland, Celtic would not exist, have become established or have gained widespread recognition as one of the most significant institutions in world football. For the Irish in Scotland, Celtic Football Club has emerged as a definition of Irishness itself.

Notes and References

Chapter 1

1. Pierre Nora, 'General Introduction: Between Memory and History', in Pierre Nora (ed.), *Realms of Memory: Rethinking the French Past*, Volume 1, *Conflicts and Division* (New York, 1996), p. 3.
2. See more generally Raphael Samuel's highly influential work on the expansion of historical culture in Britain: Raphael Samuel, *Theatres of Memory*, Volume 1, *Past and Present in Contemporary Culture* (London, 1994).
3. For the role of history in identity see, for instance: David Lowenthal, *The Past is a Foreign Country* (Cambridge, 1985); Frank Furedi, *Mythical Past, Elusive Future: History and Society in an Anxious Age* (London, 1992); and two books by Anthony Smith in the form of *National Identity* (London, 1991) and *Myths and Memories of the Nation* (Oxford, 1999).
4. Stefan Berger, Mark Donovan and Kevin Passmore (eds), *Writing National Histories: Western Europe Since 1800* (London, 1999).
5. Discussed in Michael Billig, *Banal Nationalism* (London, 1995).
6. For a discussion of this, and the coinciding increased interest in popular memory see: Popular Memory Group, 'Popular Memory: Theory, Politics, Method' in Richard Johnson, Gregor McLennan, Bill Schwartz and David Sutton (eds), *Making Histories: Studies in History – Writing and Politics* (London, 1982), pp. 205-252.
7. An interesting critique of the proliferation of heritage projects can be found in Robert Hewison, *The Heritage Industry: Britain in a Climate of Decline* (London, 1987).
8. Herbert Butterfield, *The Whig Interpretation of History* (London, 1965).
9. His most important work, written with Raymond Postgate, is perhaps *The Common People* (London, 1938).
10. See, for instance, *The Skilled Labourer, 1760-1832* (London, 1919).
11. A good starting point for working class history is the *Labour History Review*, which reached its seventieth year of publication in 2005, having

previously appeared as the *Bulletin of the Society for the Study of Labour History*.

12. Michael Banton, *The Coloured Quarter: Negro Immigrants in a British City* (London, 1955).
13. Ruth Glass, *Newcomers: The West Indians in London* (London, 1960).
14. The titles of the books are: *The Irish in Scotland, 1798-1945* (Cork, 1943); and *The Irish in Modern Scotland* (Cork, 1947).
15. Patrick O'Sullivan (ed.), *The Irish World Wide: History, Heritage, Identity*, 6 Volumes (Leicester and London, 1992-7).
16. Roger Swift and Sheridan Gilley have edited three important books in the form of: *The Irish in the Victorian City* (London, 1985); *The Irish in Britain, 1815-1939* (London, 1989); and *The Irish in Victorian Britain: The Local Dimension* (Dublin, 1999).
17. Mary Hickman, *Religion, Class and Identity: The State, the Catholic Church and the Education of the Irish in Britain* (Aldershot, 1994).
18. Donald M. MacRaild, *Culture, Conflict and Migration: The Irish in Victorian Cumbria* (Liverpool, 1998); *Irish Immigrants in Modern Britain, 1750-1922* (Basingstoke, 1999); (ed.), *The Great Famine and Beyond: Irish Migrants in Britain in the Nineteenth and Twentieth Centuries* (Dublin, 2000).
19. See: http://www.liv.ac.uk/irish/
20. See: http://www.londonmet.ac.uk/pg-prospectus-2004/research/centres/isc.cfm
21. See: http://www.brad.ac.uk/acad/diaspora/
22. Moses Margoliouth, *The History of the Jews in Great Britain*, 3 Volumes (London, 1851); John Mills, *The British Jews* (London, 1863); A. M. Hyamson, *The History of the Jews in England* (London, 1908).
23. See: http://www.jhse.dircon.co.uk/html/about_us.html
24. Perhaps his most important work is *A History of the Jews in England* (Oxford, 1941).
25. Lloyd P. Gartner, *The Jewish Immigrant in England, 1870-1914* (London, 1960); John A. Garrard, *The English and Immigration, 1880-1910* (London, 1971); Bernard Gainer, *The Alien Invasion: The Origins of the Aliens Act of 1905* (London, 1972).
26. The most important books include: Geoffrey Alderman, *Modern British Jewry* (Oxford, 1992); David·Cesarani (ed.), *The Making of Modern Anglo-Jewry* (Oxford, 1990); Todd M Endelman, *The Jews of Britain, 1656-2000* (London, 2002); David Feldman, *Englishmen and Jews: Social Relations and Political Culture, 1840-1914* (London, 1994); Tony Kushner, *The Persistence of Prejudice: Anti-Semitism in British Society during the Second World War* (Manchester, 1989); W. D. Rubinstein, *A History of the Jews in the English Speaking World: Great Britain* (Basingstoke, 1996); Colin Holmes, *Anti-Semitism in British Society, 1876-1939* (London, 1979); Bill Williams,

The Making of Manchester Jewry, 1740-1875 (Manchester, 1976); and David S. Katz, *The Jews in the History of England, 1485-1850* (Oxford, 1994).
27. See: http://www.parkes.soton.ac.uk/
28. See: http://www.huguenotsociety.org.uk/
29. Recent publications include: Robin D. Gwynn, *Huguenot Heritage: The History and Contribution of the Huguenots in Britain* (London, 1988); and Bernard Cottret, *The Huguenots in England: Immigration and Settlement, c.1550-1700* (Cambridge, 1991).
30. Ian Colvin, *The Germans in England, 1066-1598* (London, 1915); C. R. Hennings, *Deutsche in England* (Stuttgart, 1923).
31. Rosemary Ashton, *Little Germany: Exile and Asylum in Victorian England* (Oxford, 1986); Panikos Panayi, *The Enemy in Our Midst: Germans in Britain during the First World War* (Oxford, 1991); Panikos Panayi, *German Immigrants in Britain during the Nineteenth Century, 1815-1914* (Oxford, 1995) Panikos Panayi (ed.), *Germans in Britain Since 1500* (London, 1996).
32. See, for instance, Ulrike Kirchberger, *Aspekte deutsch-britischer Expansion: Die Überseeinteressen der deutschen Migranten in Großbritannien in der Mitte des 19. Jahrhunderts* (Stuttgart, 1999); Johannes-Dieter Steinert and Inge Weber-Newth, *Labour & Love: Deutsche in Grossbritannien nach dem Zweiten Weltkrieg* (Osnabrück, 2000); Stefan Manz, *Migranten und Internierte: Deutsche in Glasgow, 1864-1918* (Stuttgart, 2003).
33. The seminal work on this subject is W. E. Mosse, et al. (eds), *Second Chance: Two Centuries of German-Speaking Jews in the United Kingdom* (Tübingen, 1991).
34. See: http://www.sas.ac.uk/igs/HPEXILECENTRE.htm
35. Lucio Sponza: *Divided Loyalties: Italians in Britain during the Second World War* (Frankfurt, 2000); *Italian Immigrants in Nineteenth Century Britain* (Leicester, 1988).
36. Terri Colpi, *The Italian Factor: The Italian Community in Great Britain* (Edinburgh, 1991), p. 5.
37. The most recent include: Azadeh Medaglia, *Patriarchal Structures and Ethnicity in the Italian Community in Britain* (Aldershot, 2001); Claudia Baldoli, *Exporting Fascism: Italian Fascists and Britain's Italians in the 1930s* (Oxford, 2003); Anne Marie Fortier, *Migrant Belongings: Memory, Space, Identity* (Oxford, 2000).
38. The most important work on Poles includes: Jreszy Zubrzycki, *Polish Immigrants in Britain: A Study of Adjustment* (The Hague, 1956); Keith Sword with Norman Davies and Jan Ciechanowski, *The Formation of the Polish Community in Great Britain, 1939-1950* (London, 1989); and Peter

D. Stachura (ed.), *The Poles in Britain, 1940-2000: From Betrayal to Assimilation* (London, 2004).

39. These include Peter Fyer, *Staying Power: The History of Black People in Britain* (London, 1984); David Killingray (ed.), *Africans in Britain* (London, 1993); Kenneth Little, *Negroes in Britain* (London, 1972); James Walvin, *Black and White: The Negro and English Society, 1555-1945* (London, 1973).

40. See, for instance, Jagdish S. Gundara, and Ian Duffield (eds), *Essays on the History of Blacks in Britain* (Aldershot, 1992); Ron Ramdin, *The Making of the Black Working Class in Britain* (Aldershot, 1987); Hakim Adi, *West Africans in Britain, 1900-1960: Nationalism, Pan-Africanism and Communism* (London, 1998); Mike Phillips and Trevor Phillips, *Windrush: The Irresistible Rise of Multi-Racial Britain* (London, 1998).

41. Rosina Visram, *Asians in Britain: 400 Years of History* (London, 2002).

42. Panikos Panayi, *The Impact of Immigration: A Documentary History of the Effects and Experiences of Immigrants and Refugees in Britain Since 1945* (Manchester, 1999).

43. http://www.statistics.gov.uk/cci/nugget.asp?id=273 [accessed 15 November 2004]. This figure only refers to non-white groups. European immigrants and their offspring, particularly the Irish, would probably bring the percentage to around 12 per cent.

44. One of the key themes of Robert Winder, *Bloody Foreigners: The Story of Immigration to Britain* (London, 2004).

45. Tony Kushner and Kenneth Lunn, 'Introduction', in Kushner and Lunn (eds), *The Politics of Marginality: Race, The Radical Right and Minorities in Twentieth Century Britain* (London, 1990); Panayi, *Impact of Immigration*, p. 29.

46. Immigrants are absent from David Cannadine, *Class in Britain* (London, 1998).

47. Paul Gilroy, *There Ain't No Black in the Union Jack: The Cultural Politics of Race and Nation* (London, 1987).

48. William Cunningham, *Alien Immigrants in Britain* (London, 1897).

49. See, most importantly: Jim Walvin, *Passage to Britain: Immigration in British History and Politics* (Harmondsworth, 1984); Colin Holmes, *John Bull's Island: Immigration and British Society, 1871-1971* (Basingstoke, 1988); Panikos Panayi, *Immigration, Ethnicity and Racism in Britain, 1815-1945* (Manchester, 1994); Panayi, *Impact of Immigration*; Tony Kushner and Katherine Knox, *Refugees in an Age of Genocide: Global, National and Local Perspectives During the Twentieth Century* (London, 1999); Winder, *Bloody Foreigners*.

NOTES AND REFERENCES 257

50. Kevin Myers, however, offers an important counter argument to this point, highlighting the problems with commandeering 'history' so freely as a tool of identity. See below, pp. 35-53.
51. See: Paul Connerton, *How Societies Remember* (Cambridge, 1989); and Immanuel Wallerstein, 'The Construction of Peoplehood: Racism, Nationalism, Ethnicity', in Étienne Balibar and Immanuel Wallerstein (eds), *Race, Class and Nation* (London, 1991), pp. 71-85.
52. Lowenathal, *The Past*; Furedi, *Mythical Past*; Samuel, *Theatres of Memory*.
53. Tony Kushner (ed.), *The Jewish Heritage in British History: Englishness and Jewishness* (London, 1992).
54. As a starting point see the following websites: http://www.family.research.gov.uk, a national government grouping; the Federation of Family History Societies at http://www.ffhs.org.uk; and a BBC website, http://www.bbc.co.uk/history/familyhistory. For an academic analysis of genealogy and identity see, for instance, Nikolas Rose, 'Identity, Genealogy, History', in Stuart Hall and Paul du Gay (eds), *Questions of Cultural Identity* (London, 1991), pp. 128-50.
55. See: http://www.art-science.com/agfhs/events.html
56. See: http://www.jgsgb.org.uk
57. See the list of Family History and Genealogy societies provided at: http://www.genuki.org.uk/Societies/index.html
58. The titles include: *Asian Voices: Life-Stories from the Indian Sub-Continent* (London, 1993); *The Motherland Calls: African Caribbean Experiences* (London, 1992); *Xeni: Greek Cypriots in London* (London, 1990); and *Passport to Exile: The Polish Way to London* (London, 1988).
59. See below, pp. 35-53.
60. http://westworld.dmu.ac.uk/fmp/web/highfields/mainmenu.html
61. Newham Monitoring Project/Campaign Against Racism and Fascism, *Newham: the Forging of a Black Community* (London, 1991).
62. See CASBAH, 'a pilot web site for research resources relating to Caribbean Studies and the history of Black and Asian Peoples in the UK', at http://www.casbah.ac.uk
63. http://www.movinghere.org.uk/default.htm
64. http://www.movinghere.org.uk/about/ambh.htm
65. See Nick Merriman (ed.), *The Peopling of London: 15,000 Years of Settlement from Overseas* (London, 1993).
66. See below, pp. 18-34.
67. http://www.black-history-month.co.uk/home.html. See Darcus Howe's view of this event in New Statesman, 25 October 2004, as well as the view of Tony Kushner below, pp. 18-34.

68. See John Gillis (ed.), *Commemorations: The Politics of National Identity* (Princeton, 1994); Josep Llobera, *The Role of Historical Memory in Nation-Building* (London, 1996)
69. See below, pp. 96-113.
70. As an introduction see: Steven Fielding, *Class and Ethnicity: Irish Catholics in England, 1880-1939* (Buckingham, 1993); Hickman, *Religion, Class and Identity*.
71. See, for instance, Eugene C. Black, *The Social Politics of Anglo-Jewry, 1880-1920* (Oxford, 1988).
72. See, for instance, Daniele Joly, *Britannia's Crescent: Making a Place for Muslims in British Society* (Aldershot, 1995).
73. Floya Anthias, *Ethnicity, Class, Gender and Migration: Greek Cypriots in Britain* (Aldershot, 1992).
74. See Kathy Burrell, *Moving Lives: Narratives of Nation and Migration among Europeans in Post-War Britain* (Aldershot, 2006).
75. See Connerton, *How Societies Remember*.
76. See, for instance: Black, *Social Politics*; and Daniel Gutwein, *The Divided Elite: Economics, Politics and Anglo-Jewry, 1882-1917* (Leiden, 1992).
77. Good studies of pre-war ethnicity include: Panayi, *German Immigrants*, pp. 145-99; and Fielding, *Class and Ethnicity*. A general account can be found in Panayi, *Immigration*, pp. 76-101. For the post-war years see, for example: Anthias, *Ethnicity*; Fortier, *Migrant Belongings*; and contributions to James L. Watson (ed.), *Between Two Cultures: Migrants and Minorities in Britain* (Oxford, 1977).
78. See Fortier, *Migrant Belongings*.
79. See particularly Keith H. Halfacree and Paul J. Boyle, 'The Challenge Facing Migration Research: The Case for a Biographical Approach', *Progress in Human Geography*, 17 (1993), 333-48; Rina Benmayor and Andor Skotnes (eds), *Migration and Identity: International Yearbook of Oral History and Life Stories*, Volume 3 (Oxford, 1994); Mary Chamberlain, *Narratives of Exile and Return* (London, 1997); Alistair Thomson, 'Moving Stories: Oral History and Migration Studies', *Oral History*, 27 (1999), 24-37.
80. Katy Gardner, for example, presents her respondents as active agents in 'Narrating Location: Space, Age and Gender among Bengali Elders in East London', *Oral History*, 27 (1999), 65-74.
81. This is discussed in Caroline B. Brettell and James F. Hollifield, 'Introduction: Migration Theory – Talking Across Disciplines' in Caroline B. Brettell and James F. Hollifield (eds), *Migration Theory: Talking Across Disciplines* (London, 2000), pp. 1-26.
82. See Brian Roberts, *Biographical Research* (Buckingham, 2002).
83. Roberts, *Biographical Research*, p. 106.

84. Allessandro Portelli, 'The Peculiarities of Oral History', *History Workshop Journal*, 12 (1981), p. 99.
85. This issue is discussed in Susannah Radstone, 'Working with Memory: an Introduction', in Susannah Radstone (ed.), *Memory and Methodology* (Oxford, 2000), pp. 1-22.
86. See Craig R. Barclay, 'Remembering Ourselves', in Graham M. Davies and Robert H. Logie (eds), *Memory in Everyday Life* (London, 1993), pp. 285-309; Alistair Thomson, 'Anzac Memories: Popular Memory Theory in Practice in Australia', in Robert Perks and Alistair Thomson (eds), *The Oral History Reader* (London, 1998), pp. 300-10; see also Lowenthal, *The Past*, p. 210.
87. See below, pp. 133-48, and pp. 191-209.
88. See below, pp. 149-70. Some experiences, however, cannot be reconciled in this way. Lawrence Langer's discussion of the testimonies of Holocaust survivors in *Holocaust Testimonies: The Ruins of Memory* (London, 1991) also has resonance for the survivors of traumatic migration, and perhaps even migrants more generally.
89. See, for instance, Linda Basch, Nina Glick Schiller and Cristina Szanton Blanc, *Nations Unbound: Transnational Projects, Post-Colonial Predicaments and Deterritorialized Nation-States* (Basel, 1994); Alejandro Portes, Luis Eduardo Guarnizo and Patricia Landolt (eds), 'Transnational Communities', special issue of *Ethnic and Racial Studies*, 22 (1996); Michael Peter Smith and Luis Eduardo Guarnizo (eds) *Transnationalism From Below* (London, 1998); Ludger Pries (ed.) *Migration and Transnational Social Spaces* (Aldershot, 1999).
90. See below, pp. 57-74 and pp. 114-30.
91. See Kathy Burrell: 'Small-Scale Transnationalism: Homeland Connections and the Polish 'Community' in Leicester', *International Journal of Population Geography*, 9 (2003), 323-35; 'Homeland Memories and the Polish Community in Leicester', in Peter D. Stachura (ed.) *The Poles in Britain, 1940-2000: From Betrayal to Assimilation* (London, 2004), pp. 69-84.
92. Burrell, 'Homeland Memories'. See also Bogusia Temple, 'Time Travels: Oral History and British-Polish Identities', *Time and Society*, 5 (1996), 85-96.
93. See below, pp. 171-88 and pp. 149-70.
94. An interesting account of the uses of history in everyday life more generally can be found in Roy Rosenzweig and David Thelen, *The Presence of the Past: Popular Uses of History in American Life* (New York, 1998).
95. See below, pp. 210-33.

Chapter 2

1. See Malise Ruthven, *A Satanic Affair: Salman Rushdie and the Rage of Islam* (London, 1990).
2. *Guardian*, 21 November 2002 for a report of the broadcast autopsy in the former Truman Brewery in Brick Lane by von Hagens.
3. Salman Rushdie, *The Satanic Verses* (Dover, DE, 1992), p. 292.
4. Chaim Bermant, *Point of Arrival: A Study of London's East End* (London, 1975) remains the only longitudinal study of immigration in the East End, but see Anne Kershen's contribution to the present volume. For imagery and an evocative commentary, see also William Fishman and Nicholas Breach, *The Streets of East London* (London, 1979), chapter 4 'Immigrants'.
5. Monica Ali, *Brick Lane* (London, 2003), p. 391.
6. John Allin and Arnold Wesker, *Say Goodbye: You May Never See Them Again* (London, 1974).
7. See, for example, Nick Merriman (ed.), *The Peopling of London: Fifteen Thousand Years of Settlement from Overseas* (London, 1993), plate 2. The quote is from Mayerlene Frow, *Roots of the Future: Ethnic Diversity in the Making of Britain* (London, 1996), p. .2. For an evocation of the building in its phase as the 'Spitalfields Great Synagogue', see John Allin's painting in Allin and Wesker, *Say Goodbye* (no page number).
8. Nicholas Deakin, 'The Vitality of a Tradition', in Colin Holmes (ed.), *Immigrants and Minorities in British Society* (London, 1978), pp. 158-85; Christopher Husbands, 'East End Racism 1900-1980: Geographical Continuities in Vigilantist and Extreme Right-Wing Behaviour', *London Journal*, 8 (1982), 3-26; Commission for Racial Equality, *Brick Lane & Beyond: An Enquiry into Racial Strife and Violence in Tower Hamlets* (London, 1979).
9. *Guardian*, 26 April 1999 and 6 June 2000.
10. Ali, *Brick Lane*, p. 209.
11. Prince Charles quoted in Charles Oulton and Mazheer Mahmood, 'The Real Eastenders', *Sunday Times*, 5 July 1987; restaurant owner in *Daily Telegraph*, 26 April 1999.
12. Information from Dan Jones, 'Exploring Banglatown and the Bengali East End' (Tower Hamlets Cultural Walk no.3, no date).
13. Doreen May, 'Brick Lane: A Community Police Station', *Police Review*, 27 November 1981.
14. Bethnal Green and Stepney Trades Council, *Blood on the Streets* (London, 1978).
15. Jones, 'Exploring Banglatown'.

NOTES AND REFERENCES

16. Peter Fryer, *Staying Power: The History of Black People in Britain* (London, 1984); Rozina Visram, *Ayahs, Lascars and Princes: The story of Indians in Britain 1700-1947* (London, 1986).
17. From the back covers of these books.
18. Sukhdev Sandhu, *London Calling: How Black and Asian Writers Imagined a City* (London, 2003), p. xxi.
19. See the articles by Cesarani, Katz and Kushner in Tony Kushner (ed.), *The Jewish Heritage in British History: Englishness and Jewishness* (London, 1992).
20. The fruits of this new research were gathered in David Cesarani (ed.), *The Making of Modern Anglo-Jewry* (Oxford, 1990).
21. Tony Kushner, 'Looking Back With Nostalgia? The Jewish Museums of Britain', *Immigrants & Minorities*, 6 (1987), 200-11.
22. Jane Morris, 'Remember the riots of 1919?', *Guardian*, 30 September 2004.
23. Yasmin Alibhai-Brown, 'Black History Should Never Be Safe History', *Independent*, 7 October 2002.
24. Alibhai-Brown, 'Black History'.
25. Alibhai-Brown, 'Black History'.
26. Simon Heffer, *Like The Roman: The Life of Enoch Powell* (London, 1998).
27. Simon Heffer, 'History Betrayed', *Daily Mail*, 23 November 2002.
28. *Daily Mail*, 20 November 2002.
29. See the special issue of *Patterns of Prejudice*, 37 (2003) on 'Racism and Asylum in Europe'.
30. 'The Distortion of a Proud History', *Daily Mail*, 30 November 2002.
31. *Sun*, 4 July 2003.
32. *Express*, 4 July 2004.
33. *Sun*, 18 August 2003.
34. Alibhai-Brown, 'Black History'.
35. 'Polling History: A Great British Television Idea', *Guardian*, 25 November 2002.
36. Gary Younge, 'Churchill – The Truth', *Guardian*, 30 September 2002.
37. 'Great Britons', BBC 2, 24 November 2002.
38. Michael Gilkes, 'The Dark Strangers', in Lesley Smith, *The Making of Britain: Echoes of Greatness* (Basingstoke, 1988), pp. 143-4.
39. Brian Viner, 'List, I Have Bones to Pick and Names to Chew!', *Jewish Chronicle*, 1 November 2002.
40. Sidney Salomon, *The Jews of Britain* (London, 1938).
41. Todd Endelman and Tony Kushner (eds), *Disraeli's Jewishness* (London, 2002).
42. See generally, Paul Breines, *Tough Jews: Political Fantasies and the Moral Dilemmas of American Jewry* (New York, 1990); Salomon, *Jews of Britain*.
43. *Jewish Chronicle*, 31 October 2003.

44. Jonathan Freedland, 'The Trailblazer', *Guardian*, 31 October 2003.
45. David Clark, 'Viewing the Past With Vision', *Jewish Renaissance* (Summer 2002), pp. 10-11.
46. David Cesarani, 'Dual Heritage or Duel of Heritages? Englishness and Jewishness in the Heritage Industry', in Kushner, *Jewish Heritage*, pp. 30-7.
47. David Katz, 'The Marginalization of Early Modern Anglo-Jewish History', in Kushner, *Jewish Heritage*, p. 61.
48. Cesarani, 'Dual Heritage', p. 32.
49. Clark, 'Viewing the Past', p. 10.
50. Kushner, 'Looking Back?', p. 201. As late as 1986 the acquisition policy of the Jewish Museum was that items were 'not normally accepted unless they are 100 years old'.
51. See the articles by Cesarani, Katz and Kushner in Kushner, *Jewish Heritage*. A reassessment of this analysis is explored in a PhD thesis by Elisa Lawson, University of Southampton, on the historiography and heritage world of Cecil Roth (2005).
52. Tony Kushner, 'A History of Jewish Archives in the United Kingdom', *Archives*, 20 (1992), 3-16.
53. Bill Williams, 'Heritage and Community: The Rescue of Manchester's Jewish Past', in Kushner, *Jewish Heritage*, pp. 128-46.
54. Bill Williams, 'The Anti-Semitism of Tolerance: Middle-Class Manchester and Jews: 1870-1900', in Alan J. Kidd and Ken W. Roberts (eds), *City, Class and Culture: Studies of Social Policy and Cultural Production in Victorian Manchester* (Manchester, 1985), pp. 74-102.
55. Bill Williams quoted by *Jewish Chronicle*, 30 March 1984; Kushner, 'Looking Back?', p. 207.
56. Tony Kushner, 'The End of the "Anglo-Jewish Progress Show": Representations of the Jewish East End, 1887-1987', in Kushner, *Jewish Heritage*, pp. 91-2.
57. See Hasia Diner, Jeffrey Shandler and Beth Wenger (eds), *Remembering the Lower East Side: American Jewish Reflections* (Bloomington, 2000).
58. Jack Kugelmass, 'Turfing the Slum: New York City's Tenement Museum and the Politics of Heritage', in Diner, Shandler and Wenger (eds), *Remembering the Lower East Side*, pp. 179-211.
59. *Oral History*, 19 (1991), p. 80.
60. See *Observer*, 7 July 2002.
61. Alan Rice, 'Exploring Inside the Invisible: An Interview with Lubaina Himid', *Wasafari*, 40 (Winter 2003), p. 24.
62. Lloyd Gartner, 'Notes on the Statistics of Jewish Immigrants to England, 1870-1914', *Jewish Social Studies*, 22 (1960), 97-102.
63. Kushner, 'End of the "Anglo-Jewish Progress Show"', pp. 94-9; David Mazower, *Yiddish Theatre in London* (London, 1997).

64. 'The Jews of Aden' exhibition took place in 1991 and 'By the Rivers of Babylon: The Story of the Jews of Iraq', November 2002 to April 2003.
65. 'Before the Holocaust', Manchester Jewish Museum, 1986; 'Refugee from Nazism' (1988) and 'The Last Goodbye' (1996) in the London Museum of Jewish Life.
66. 'Leon Greenman Auschwitz Survivor 98288' has become a permanent part of the Finchley exhibition.
67. This is part of the National Life Story Collection at the British Library.
68. Tony Kushner, '"Meaning Nothing But Good": Ethics, History and Asylum Seeker Phobia in Britain', *Patterns of Prejudice*, 37 (2003), 257-76.
69. See the catalogue, Anthony Grenville, *Continental Britons: Jewish Refugees from Nazi Europe* (London, 2002).
70. Grenville, *Continental Britons*, p. 40.
71. Kushner, 'Meaning Nothing But Good'; Tony Kushner and Katharine Knox, *Refugees in an Age of Genocide: Global, National and Local Perspectives during the Twentieth Century* (London, 1999).
72. Grenville, *Continental Britons*, p. 65.
73. Jean Medawar and David Pyke, *Hitler's Gift: Scientists Who Fled Nazi Germany* (London, 2000); Daniel Snowman, *The Hitler Emigres: The Cultural Impact on Britain of Refugees from Nazism* (London, 2002).
74. *Observer*, 7 July 1996; Frow, *Roots of the Future*, p. viii, comments of the then Chairman of the Commission for Racial Equality, Herman Ouseley, and part 2 of the book.
75. Alibhai-Brown, 'Black History'.
76. In John Cooper, *Great Britons: The Great Debate* (London, 2002), p. 12.
77. Morris, 'Remember the Riots of 1919?'.
78. Tom Lehrer, 'National Brotherhood Week', on the album *That Was the Year That Was* (Reprise, 1965).
79. Vanessa Walters, 'More than Martin Luther King', *Guardian*, 29 September 2003.
80. Michael Collins, *The Likes of Us: A Biography of the White Working Class* (London, 2004), p. 263.
81. Morris, 'Remember the Riots of 1919?'.
82. Martin Wainwright, 'Over-50s Nostalgic for High Tea and Rin Tin Tin', *Guardian*, 1 October 2004.
83. Colin Holmes, *A Tolerant Country? Immigrants, Refugees and Minorities in Britain* (London, 1991).
84. The poll was conducted by the website http://www.100greatblackbritons.com which generated 10,000 votes. See *Guardian*, 10 February 2004.
85. Natalie Zemon Davis, '"Women's History" in Transition' in Joan Scott (ed.), *Feminism and History* (Oxford, 1996), p. 88. See also Joan Scott, 'The

Problem of Invisibility' in S. Kleinberg (ed.), *Retrieving Women's History: Changing Perspectives of the Role of Women in Politics and Society* (Oxford, 1988), pp. 5-29.
86. Cooper, *Great Britons*, pp. 8-9.

Chapter 3

1. Ludmilla Jordanova, *History in Practice* (London, 2000), pp. 141-7.
2. Jill Liddington, 'What Is Public History? Publics And Their Pasts, Meanings And Practices', *Oral History*, 30 (2002), p. 84.
3. Liddington, 'What is Public History?'; Stephen Porter Benson, Stephen Brier and Roy Rosenzweig, 'Introduction' in Benson, Brier and Rosenzweig (eds), *Presenting the Past: Essays on History and the Public* (Philadephia, 1986), p. xix.
4. See, for example, the influential work of Bhikhu Parekh most recently in *Rethinking Multiculturalism* (London, 2000).
5. Frank Furedi, *Mythical Past, Elusive Future: History and Society in an Anxious Age* (London, 1992), p. 63.
6. Mary Fulbrook, *Historical Theory* (London, 2002), p. 175
7. Robert Colls, *Identity of England* (Oxford, 2002), p. 160 rightly cautions that the 'words meant just what the home secretary wanted them to mean'.
8. This section draws on Stuart Hall's acute overview that equates this North American liberalism with social democratic reformist programmes in Europe. See his 'Conclusion: The Multi-Cultural Question' in Barnor Hesse (ed.), *Un/settled Multiculturalisms: Diasporas, Entanglements, 'Transruptions'* (London, 2000), p. 231.
9. For an analysis of multicultural drift and its fragility see Stuart Hall, 'From Scarman to Stephen Lawrence', *History Workshop Journal*, 48 (1999), 187-97.
10. Home Office, *Race Relations (Amendment) Act 2000: New Laws for a Successful Multi-Racial Britain* (London, 2001).
11. David Goodhart, 'Too Diverse', *Prospect*, 95 (February 2004).
12. For the development of multiculturalism across Europe more generally see Tariq Modood and Pnina Werbner, *The Politics of Multiculturalism in the New Europe: Racism, Identity and Community* (London, 1997). For a critical view of these developments in Britain see Floya Anthias and Nira Yuval-Davis, *Racialized Boundaries: Race, Nation, Gender, Colour and Class and the Anti-Racist Struggle* (London, 1993), chapter 6.

13. Charles Taylor, *Multiculturalism and the Politics of Recognition* (Princeton, 1992).
14. Nancy Fraser, *Justice Interruptus: Critical Reflections on the Postsocialist Condition* (London, 1997), p. 4.
15. Robert Hewison, *The Heritage Industry: Britain in a Climate of Decline* (London, 1987); Patrick Wright, *On Living in an Old Country: The National Past in Contemporary Britain* (London, 1985).
16. Raphael Samuel, *Theatres of Memory*, Volume 1, *Past and Present in Contemporary Culture* (London, 1994), p. 260. For a more detailed analysis of local authority cultural strategies see H. Lim, 'Cultural Strategies for Revitalising the City: A Review and Evaluation', *Regional Studies*, 27 (1993) 589-95.
17. G. J. Ashworth and J. E. Tunbridge, *The Tourist-Historic City: Retrospect and the Prospect of Managing the Heritage City* (Oxford, 2000).
18. Brian Graham, 'Heritage as Knowledge: Capital or Culture?' *Urban Studies*, 39 (2002), p. 1008. More generally see: Brian Graham, G.J. Ashworth and J.E. Tunbridge, *A Geography of Heritage: Power, Culture and Economy* (London, 2000); and James Donald and Ali Rattansi (eds), *'Race', Culture and Difference* (London, 1992).
19. Raphael Samuel, *Patriotism: The Making and Unmaking of British National Identity* (London, 1989); John Gillis (ed.), *Commemorations: The Politics of National Identity* (Princeton, 1994).
20. Stuart Hall and Martin Jacques, *New Times: The Changing Face of Politics in the 1990s* (London, 1989).
21. John Clarke and Janet Newman, *The Managerial State: Power, Politics and Ideology in the Making of Social Welfare* (London, 1997), p. 134.
22. Hewison, *The Heritage Industry*; Wright, *On Living in an Old County*.
23. Malcolm Smith, *Britain and 1940: History, Myth and Popular Memory* (London, 2000), pp. 125-8; Furedi, *Mythical Past*, p. 4.
24. Gargi Bhattacharyya, 'Riding Multiculturalism' in David Bennett (ed.), *Multicultural States: Rethinking Difference and Identity* (Routledge, 1998), pp. 252-66.
25. From a wealth of policy documents the final report of the *Highbury 3: Dynamic, Diverse, Different* (Birmingham, 2001) convention is particularly interesting, available at http://www.birmingham.gov.uk [accessed May 2004]. For marginalised community histories see Ted Rudge, *Brumroamin: Birmingham and Midland Romany Gypsy and Traveller Culture* (Birmingham, 2003); Carl Chinn, *Birmingham Irish: Making Our Mark* (Birmingham, 2003); Ian Grosvenor, Rita McLean and Sian Roberts, *Making Connections: Birmingham Black International History* (Birmingham, 2002); Yousef Choudry and Peter Drake *From Bangladesh to Birmingham: The History of Bangladeshis in Birmingham* (Birmingham, 2001); Malcolm

Dick, *Celebrating Sanctuary: Birmingham and the Refugee Experience* (Birmingham, 2001); George Makin and Phil Lea, *People Like Us: The Irish Community in Birmingham* (Birmingham, 1997); Dorren Hopwood and Margaret Dilloway, *Bella Brum: A History of Birmingham's Italian Community* (Birmingham, 1996).

26. See Ian Grosvenor and Kevin Myers 'Engaging with History after Macpherson', *Curriculum Journal*, 12 (2001), 275-89.
27. Malcolm Dick, 'Travelling Through Time: Migration and the Black Experience', in Grosvenor, McLean and Roberts, *Making Connections*, p. 37. See also Carl Chinn, *Birmingham: The Great Working City* (Birmingham, 1994).
28. Barnor Hesse, 'Introduction: Un/settled Multiculturalisms' in Hesse (ed.), *Un/settled Multiculturalisms*, p. 10.
29. David Parker and Paul Long, 'Reimagining Birmingham: Public History, Selective Memory and the Narration of Urban Change', *European Journal of Cultural Studies*, 6 (2003), pp. 160, 169.
30. A. Sivanandan, *Communities of Resistance: Writings on Black Struggles for Socialism* (London, 1990), pp. 65-66.
31. On tokenism see Michelynn Laflèche, *Runnymede Trust Bulletin* (March 2004), pp. 7-8. For an example of a more critical engagement with British history see Marika Sherwood, 'Race, Empire and Education: Teaching Racism', *Race and Class*, 42 (2001), 1-28.
32. Catherine Hall, 'Histories, Empires and the Post-Colonial Moment', in Iain Chambers and Lidia Curti (eds), *The Post-Colonial Question: Common Skies, Divided Horizons* (London, 1996), pp. 65-77; Bill Schwarz (ed.), *The Expansion of England: Race, Ethnicity and Cultural History* (London, 1996).
33. Lawrence Stone, *The Past and Present Revisited* (London, 1987), p. 74.
34. Eric Hobsbawm, *Interesting Times: A Twentieth Century Life* (London, 2002), p. 296.
35. Grosvenor and Myers, 'Engaging with History'.
36. Dilip Hiro, *Black British, White British* (London, 1971), p. 298.
37. Elizabeth Tonkin, Maryon McDonald and Malcolm Chapman (eds), *History and Ethnicity* (London, 1989).
38. Jagdish Gundara and Ian Duffied, 'Introduction', in Gundara and Duffield (eds), *Essays on the History of Blacks in Britain: From Roman Times to the Mid-Twentieth Century* (London, 1992), p.2. For a similarly loose view of community see Carl Chinn, 'The Irish in Early Victorian Birmingham', in Roger Swift and Sheridan Gilley (eds), *The Irish in Victorian Britain: The Local Dimension* (Dublin, 1999).
39. In a discussion on the historiography of slavery Clarence E. Walker also takes up the problems of community and argues that 'community

formed in response to oppression does not automatically become the constructive community historians assume'. See his *Deromanticizing Black History: Critical Essays and Appraisals* (Knoxville, 1991), p. xviii.

40. Brian Alleyne, 'An Idea of Community and its Discontents: Towards a More Reflexive Sense of Belonging in Multicultural Britain', *Ethnic and Racial Studies*, 25 (2000), 607-27.

41. Bob Carter, *Realism and Racism: Concepts of Race in Sociological Research* (London, 2000), p. 46.

42. Katya G. Azoulay, 'Experience, Empathy and Strategic Essentialism', *Cultural Studies*, 11 (1997), 89-110. This is the same challenge explored by Stuart Hall, 'New ethnicities' in Rattansi and Donald (eds), *Race, Culture and Difference*, and Paul Gilroy, *There Ain't No Black in the Union Jack* (London, 1987) over the past two decades. For an illuminating discussion of their analyses see Carter, *Realism and Racism*, pp. 40-54.

43. For an interesting discussion and practical illustration of this see James Duncan, 'Representing Empire at the National Maritime Museum', in Robert Shannan Peckham, *Rethinking Heritage: Cultures and Politics in Europe* (London, 2003), pp. 17-28.

44. Colls, *Identity of England*, p.153.

45. See Yasmin Alibhah-Brown, *True Colours: Public Attitudes to Multiculturalism and the Role of the Government* (London, 1999), p. 92; and, *Who Do We Think We Are? Imagining the New Britain* (London, 2001), pp. 115, 182-3.

46. 'Prince's Plea to Teach Children about the Empire', *Daily Telegraph*, 28 June 2003.

47. 'Opinion', *BBC History Magazine*, March 2002, p. 8.

48. 'They Come Not to Praise England But to Bury It', *Sunday Times*, 27 August 2000.

49. Richard Weight, *Patriots: National Identity in Britain 1940-2000* (London, 2002). An eclectic and necessarily selective list of national identity texts might include Colls, *Identity of England*; Maureen Duffy, *England: The Making of the Myth* (London, 2001); Roger Scruton, *England: An Elegy* (London, 2000); Kevin Davey, *English Imaginaries: Six Studies in Anglo-British Modernity* (London, 1999); S. Gikandi, *Maps of Englishness: Writing Identity in the Culture of Colonialism* (New York, 1996).

50. Simon Schama, *A History of Britain: At the Edge of the World?* (London, 2000), pp. 15-17.

51. Ian Craib, *Experiencing Identity* (London, 1998), p. 31

52. Weight, *Patriots*, p. 734.

53. Carolyn Steedman, *Dust* (Manchester, 2001), pp. 76-7.

54. Hall, 'Histories', p. 66. This is certainly a misreading of her actual historical practice that, as Edward Said pointed out, implicitly draws

on Gramsci's notion of common sense to indicate just how the past shapes but does not determine identities. See Edward Said, 'Always on Top', *London Review of Books*, 25 (June 2003), 3-6.

55. Bill Schwarz, 'The Communist Party Historians' Group, 1946-1956', in Centre for Contemporary Cultural Studies, *Making Histories: Studies in History-Writing and Politics* (London, 1982), p. 95.

56. Birmingham Libraries, Library and Information Services Divisional Plan 2003-04, pp. 3-4. For some policy background to this see Local Government Association, *Place at the Table? Culture and Leisure in Modern Local Government* (London, 2002).

57. Chinn, *Birmingham Irish*, pp. 118, 119, 122, 131.

58. Chinn, *Birmingham Irish*, p. 180.

59. For an illuminating analysis of how migration stories are told see Alistair Thomson, 'Moving Stories: Oral History and Migration Studies', *Oral History*, 27 (1999), 24-37.

60. It is worth noting in passing the historical contest between competing definitions of 'useful knowledge'. Nineteenth century radicals saw useful knowledge as that which anticipated liberation, and conservatives as that which promised subjection. Richard Johnson, 'Really Useful Knowledge: Radical Education and Working Class Culture, 1790-1848' in John Clarke, Chas Critcher and Richard Johnson (eds), *Working Class Culture: Studies in History and Theory* (London, 1979), pp. 75-102.

61. Heritage Lottery Fund, *Broadening the Horizons of Heritage* (London, 2002).

62. Hayton Associates, *Young Roots: Evaluation Report Stage Two* (London, 2003), available at: http://www.hlf.org.uk/dimages/policy/Young_roots_evaluation.pdf

63. Of particular interest is the Migrations project based in Kirklees. As 'a documentary history of racial diversity', the project director was keen to recognise that 'heritage isn't all about celebration'. Heritage Lottery Fund, *Broadening the Horizons*, p. 17.

64. Andrew Taylor, 'Arm's Length But Hands On: Mapping the New Governance: The Department of National Heritage and Cultural Politics in Britain', *Public Administration*, 75 (1997), 441-66.

65. Young Roots, 'Celebrating Diversity', p. 3; Hayton Associates, *Young Roots: Evaluation Report Stage Two*, p.11 provides the following figures: 22% of projects have explored the cultural heritage of ethnic minority communities and 18.5% of young participants were drawn from black and minority ethnic communities.

66. David Buckingham and Ken Jones, 'New Labour's Cultural Turn: Some Tensions in Contemporary Educational and Cultural Policy',

Journal of Education Policy, 16 (2001), 1-14.
67. Hayton Associates, *Young Roots: Evaluation Report Stage Two*, pp. 14, 25.
68. Graham Carr, 'War, History and the Education of (Canadian) Memory' in Katherine Hodgkin and Susannah Radstone (eds), *Contested Pasts: The Politics of Memory* (London, 2003), p. 68.
69. 'National Launch of Young Roots', Official Press Release, 29 October 2002, available at: http://www.hlf.org.uk
70. Furedi, *Mythical Past*, chapter 9.
71. Colls, *Identity of England*, p. 27, note 47.
72. The term comes from Antonio Gramsci, *Selections from the Prison Notebooks*, edited and translated by Quintin Hoare and Geoffrey Nowell-Smith (London, 1971), pp. 242-76.
73. Chris Haylett, 'Illegitimate Subjects?: Abject Whites, Neoliberal Modernisation and Middle-class Multiculturalism', *Environment and Planning D: Society and Space*, 19 (2001), p. 365.
74. 'Future Looks Rosy for England and St. George', *Birmingham Post*, 23 April 2004.
75. 'The Need to Belong But With a Strong Faith', *Guardian*, 17 June 2002.
76. Anne Holohan, *Working Lives: The Irish in Britain* (London, 1995), p. 8.
77. Ellis Cashmore, 'The Impure Strikes Back', *British Journal of Sociology*, 54, (2003), 407-14; Albert Moreiras, 'Hybridity and Double Consciousness', *Cultural Studies*, 13 (1999), 373-407.
78. Kenan Malik, 'Race, Pluralism and the Meaning of Difference', *New Formations*, 33 (1998), 125-41.
79. Bob Rowthorn, 'Migration Limits', *Prospect*, 83 (2003), 24-31.
80. For further comment on Goodhart see *Runnymede Trust Bulletin*, March 2004.
81. Christopher Hill, *Intellectual Origins of the English Revolution* (London, 1965), p. 203. Schwarz, 'Communist Party Historians' Group', has an interesting and early discussion of the relationships between history and memory. From a distance of twenty years in which the distinctive educational practices of the Labour movement have all but disappeared, it makes salutary and disturbing reading.

Chapter 4

1. For a general history of Italians in Britain see Terri Colpi, *The Italian Factor: The Italian Community in Great Britain* (Edinburgh, 1991). On the Italians in Britain during the nineteenth century, see my *Italian Immigrants in Nineteenth Century Britain: Realities and Images* (Leicester, 1988).

2. Both categories of skilled and semi-skilled artisans employed young apprentices and street vendors; the latter were unskilled.
3. See Lucio Sponza, *Divided Loyalties: Italians in Britain during the Second World War* (Bern, 2000).
4. On the early post-war arrival of Italians see my 'Italians in War and Post-War Britain', in Johannes Dieter Steinert and Inge Weber-Newth (eds), *European Immigrants in Britain, 1933-1950* (Munich, 2003), pp. 185-99.
5. Mario Menghini (ed.), *Edizione nazionale degli scritti di Giuseppe Mazzini* [henceforth, *Ediz. Naz.*] volume 23 (Imola, 1915), letter to Quirina Mocenni Magiotti, Florence, 14 November 1842, p. 329. My translation, as will be all others hereafter from Italian sources.
6. Some ten years after Mazzini opened his school, Henry Mayhew came across several Italians during his investigations into the 'London Poor'. In particular, he met five street musicians and two street exhibitors. When he asked them where they were from, only one said he was from Italy, before adding that he came from Genoa; all the others said they were either from around Parma (four of them) or from around Naples (but more likely from the Liri Valley). See Henry Mayhew, *London Labour and the London Poor*, 4 volumes (London, 1861), volume 3, pp. 77-9, 155-8, 174-7, 177-9, 179-81, 181-2.
7. Letter to the *Morning Chronicle*, signed 'A lover of Italy', 26 April 1842.
8. *Ediz. Naz.*, volume 20 (Imola, 1914), letter to Pietro Rolandi, London, 26 November 1841, p. 376.
9. 'La scuola gratuita italiana e la Cappella Sarda', *Apostolato Popolare*, 15 August 1942, pp. 49–51. *Apostolato Popolare* was the newspaper that Mazzini published in London in the early 1840s.
10. 'Priestly insolence, injustice and cruelty', *Weekly Dispatch*, 1 May 1842, p. 210.
11. *City Mission Magazine*, November 1844, p. 165.
12. 'The Leather Lane tragedy', *North Londoner and St. Pancras and Holborn Guardian*, 9 January 1875. The following week the murder scene and the judicial decision were reported in the newspaper thus: 'It was a scene of a party of angry Italians of both sexes fighting promiscuously in a dark underground kitchen, where it [was] impossible to distinguish what really occurred...the prisoner was accordingly discharged', *North Londoner and St. Pancras and Holborn Guardian*, 16 January 1875.
13. See my 'Italian "Penny-Ice men" in Victorian London', in Anne J. Kershen (ed.), *Food in the Migrant Experience* (Aldershot, 2002), pp. 17–41.
14. I have dealt with this perception of Italians in *Italian Immigrants*, pp. 241–51.

NOTES AND REFERENCES

15. At the 'infamous' address of 17 Eyre Street Hill, three families lived in 1891, according to the census taken in that year; there were no boarders or lodgers; two of the 'heads' were ice-cream vendors; the third was a bricklayer. Altogether: six adults and three children under ten.
16. 'Foreign Colonies in London – Italians: I', *St. James's Gazette*, 22 June 1891.
17. W. H. Wilkins, 'The Italian Aspect', in Arnold White (ed.), *The Destitute Alien in Great Britain* (London, 1892), pp. 149–50.
18. White (ed.), *The Destitute Alien*, p. 148.
19. See Pietro Dipaola, 'Italian Anarchists in London (1870–1914)', Unpublished PhD thesis (Goldsmiths' College, University of London, 2004).
20. See my *Italian Immigrants*, pp. 259-65.
21. There is a vast Italian language literature on the image of southern Italians in the second half of the nineteenth century. A concise survey of these views can be found in John Dickie, 'Stereotypes of the Italian South, 1860-1900', in Robert Lumley and Jonathan Morris (eds), *The New History of the Italian South* (Exeter, 1997), pp. 114-77.
22. Denis Mack Smith, *Mussolini* (London, 1983), p. 229.
23. See Claudia Baldoli, *Exporting Fascism: Italian Fascists and Britain's Italians in the 1930s* (Oxford, 2003), pp. 11–12.
24. 'Una gloria d'Italia', *Guida Generale degli Italiani a Londra* (London, 1933), p. 119.
25. Philip Morgan, *Italian Fascism, 1919–1945* (Basingstoke, 1995), p. 96.
26. Callisto Cavalli, *Ricordi di un emigrato* (London, 1973), pp. 68-9.
27. See F. H. Hinsley and C. A. G. Simkins, *British Intelligence in the Second World War: Volume 4, Security and Counter-Intelligence* (London, 1990), pp. 47–64.
28. 'Memo to the Home Office', *Daily Mirror*, 27 April 1940.
29. *New Statesman and Nation*, 24 June 1940.
30. Mass-Observation, *File Reports*, 194, 'Report on attitudes to Italy' (12 June 1940), p. 1.
31. Mass-Observation, *File Reports*, 194, p. 4.
32. The National Archives [NA], Ministry of Information 1/920, *Propaganda to Italy, Dec.1940–Aug.1941*, 'Standing directive on British propaganda towards Italy', 15 August 1941, p. 5.
33. Ministry of Information 1/920, *Propaganda to Italy*, p. 6.
34. Mass-Observation, *File Reports*, 541, 'A particular study of subjective feelings about various racial groups' (9 January 1941).
35. Mass-Observation, *File Reports*, 1669Q, 'Attitudes to foreigners' (April 1943), pp. 10–11.

36. Joe Pieri, *Isle of the Displaced: An Italian-Scot's Memoirs of Internment in the Second World War* (Glasgow, 1997), p. 8.
37. NA, Ministry of Labour 8/102, 'Employment of German ex-POWs in agriculture, 1948–49', K.B. Paice (Home Office) to M. A. Bevan (Ministry of Labour), 10 March 1948.
38. Ministry of Labour 8/102, Sir A. Maxwell (Home Office) to Sir G.H. Ince (Ministry of Labour), 12 August 1948.
39. Ministry of Labour 8/102, Ince to Maxwell, 27 August 1948.
40. 'Ho cambiato il cielo ma non il cuore' [The sky I've changed, but not my heart], *La Voce degli Italiani*, January 1948, p. 1.
41. 'Circolo della famiglia' [Family Circle], *La Voce degli Italiani*, June 1948, p. 5.
42. See my essay 'Italian Propaganda Abroad: The Case of the Surrogate "Voice of Italians" in Post-war Britain', in Luciano Cheles and Lucio Sponza (eds), *The Art of Persuasion: Political Communication in Italy from 1945 to the 1990s* (Manchester, 2001), pp. 62–73.
43. Cited in Colpi, *Italian Factor*, p. 199.

Chapter 5

1. BHRU [Bradford Heritage Recording Unit], B0104 Yugoslav male.
2. PRO [Public Record Office] FO [Foreign Office] 371/64379, 25-9-1947.
3. For detailed information on Displaced Persons in post-war Germany see particularly: Wolfgang Jacobmeyer, *Vom Zwangsarbeiter zum Heimatlosen Ausländer: Die Displaced Persons in Westdeutschland 1945-1951* (Göttingen, 1985); and Malcolm J. Proudfoot, *European Refugees, 1939-1952* (London, 1957).
4. Diana Kay and Robert Miles, *Refugees or Migrant Workers? European Workers in Britain 1946-1951* (London, 1992).
5. Elisabeth Stadulis, 'The Resettlement of Displaced Persons in the United Kingdom', *Population Studies*, 5 (1952), 207-237.
6. Cited in Diana Kay, 'Westward Ho!: The Recruitment of Displaced Persons for British Industries', in Johannes-Dieter Steinert and Inge Weber-Newth (eds), *European Immigrants in Britain, 1933-1950* (Munich, 2003), p. 160.
7. Colin Holmes, *John Bull's Island: Immigration and British Society 1871-1971* (London, 1988), pp. 199-206.
8. Kay and Miles, *Refugees*, pp. 56-9.
9. David Cesarani, *Justice Delayed: How Britain Became a Refuge for Nazi War Criminals* (London, 1992).

10. Cesarani, *Justice Delayed*, particularly pp. 102-33.
11. John A. Tannahill, *European Volunteer Workers in Britain* (Manchester, 1958), pp. 31-3.
12. A number of articles published by professionals who dealt with EVWs provide very useful insights into specialised aspects, particularly Maud Bülbring, 'Post-War Refugees in Britain', *Population Studies*, 7 (1954), 99-112; Stadulis, 'Resettlement', 207-37; Maud Bülbring and E. Nagy, 'The Receiving Community in Great Britain', 113-23, and H. B. M. Murphy, 'Refugee Psychoses in Great Britain: Admissions to Mental Hospitals', 173-94, both in: H. B. M. Murphy, *Flight and Resettlement*, volume 5 (Paris, 1955).
13. Kay and Miles, *Refugees*; Tannahill, *Volunteer Workers*; Johannes-Dieter Steinert and Inge Weber-Newth, *Labour & Love: Deutsche in Großbritannien nach dem Zweiten Weltkrieg* (Osnabrück, 2000). Revised edition in English: Johannes-Dieter Steinert and Inge Weber-Newth, *German Migrants in Post-War Britain: An Enemy Embrace* (London, 2005). The last publication includes an analyis of the experience of German immigrants in post-war Britain.
14. Kirklees Sound Archive, Central Library (Huddersfield, 1986).
15. Specifically on the BHRU project: Robert Perks, 'A Feeling of Not Belonging: Interviewing European Immigrants in Bradford', *Oral History*, 12 (1984), 64-7; Perks, 'Immigration to Bradford: The Oral Testimony', *Immigrants and Minorities*, 6 (1987), 362-9.
16. Steinert and Weber-Newth, *Labour & Love*.
17. Fees for shared accommodation including an evening meal ranged from approximately £1.75-£2.50, the average wage being about £4.50-£5.50.
18. BHRU interview B0121.
19. BHRU interview B0041.
20. BHRU interview B0019.
21. BHRU interview B0105.
22. Kirklees Sound Archive interview no. 031 PL.
23. Kay and Miles, *Refugees*, p. 137.
24. PRO LAB 26/193, Minute by Parliamentary Secretary, Ministry of Labour and National Service, 6 January 1948.
25. Kay and Miles, *Refugees*, p. 129.
26. BHRU interview B0088.
27. Cited in Kay and Miles, *Refugees*, p. 138.
28. Tannahill, *Volunteer Workers*, p. 87.
29. F. F. Kino, 'Refugee Psychosis in Great Britain: Aliens Paranoid Reactions', in H. B. M. Murphy, *Flight and Resettlement*, volume 2 (Paris, 1955), p. 201.

30. Kay and Miles, *Refugees*, p. 139.
31. Cited in Tim Edensor and Mij Kelly (eds), *Moving Worlds* (Edinburgh, 1989), p. 140.
32. Tannahill, *Volunteer Workers*, Appendix H.
33. Interview with Hilde C. in Steinert and Weber-Newth, *Labour & Love*, p. 178.
34. BHRU interview B0016; and Howard Olive (ed.), *Textile Voices: Mill Life this Century* (Bradford, 1989).
35. BHRU interview B0104.
36. BHRU interview B0033.
37. Kay and Miles, *Refugees*, p. 145.
38. BHRU interview B0121.
39. BHRU interview B0050.
40. BHRU interview B0016.
41. BHRU interview B0121.
42. Olive (ed.), *Textile Voices*.
43. Olive (ed.), *Textile Voices*.
44. Olive (ed.), *Textile Voices*.
45. BHRU interview B0031.
46. BHRU interview B0002.
47. BHRU interview A0144.
48. BHRU interview B0121.
49. BHRU interviews A0144, A0046.
50. BHRU interview B0041.
51. Kirklees interview 031; BHRU interviews B0086, B0002.
52. BHRU interview B0104, BHRU interview B0088.
53. *Picture Post*, 31 May 1947.
54. *Picture Post*, 17 January, 1948.
55. *Yorkshire Observer*, 26, 27, 30 July, 1951.
56. Ministry of Labour and National Service, *Workers from Abroad* (London, 1948).
57. Tannahill, *Volunteer Workers*, p. 96.
58. *Oldham Evening Chronicle*, 11 January 1949.
59. Tannahill, *Volunteer Workers*, pp. 70, 100.
60. BHRU interview B0010.
61. Kirklees interview 031; BHRU interview B00041
62. Steinert and Weber-Newth, *Labour & Love*, pp. 261-264.
63. BHRU interview B0010.
64. BHRU interview B0016.
65. Bülbring and Nagy, 'Community', pp. 113-23.
66. *Bolton Evening News*, 15 January 1949; *Halifax Daily Courier and Guardian*, 5 December 1949.

67. *Oldham Evening Chronicle*, 2 January 1950.
68. BHRU interview B0121.
69. *Yorkshire Observer*, 27 July 1951.
70. BHRU interview B0050.
71. For example, interviews B0121, B0041, B0002.
72. BHRU interview B0002.
73. Perks Robert, 'Ukraine's Forbidden History: Memory and Nationalism', *Oral History*, 21 (1993), p. 50.
74. Around 5,000 Italians, predominantly young women from the 'Mezzogiorno' region, were privately recruited for the textile industry at the same period.
75. Perks, 'Ukraine's Forbidden History', p. 51.
76. Tannahill, *Volunteer Workers*, p. 90.
77. Tannahill, *Volunteer Workers*, p. 90.
78. Interview with Elly G., in Steinert and Weber-Newth, *Labour & Love*, p. 249.
79. Interview with Gerlinde D., in Steinert and Weber-Newth, *Labour & Love*, p. 249.
80. Interview with Irmgard L., in Steinert and Weber-Newth, *Labour & Love*, p. 272.
81. BHRU interview B0105.
82. Interview with Irmgard L, and Elly G., in Steinert and Weber-Newth, *Labour & Love*, p. 272.
83. BHRU interview B0031.
84. BHRU interview B0010.
85. BHRU interview B0031.
86. BHRU interview B0031.
87. Interview with Elly G., in Steinert and Weber-Newth, *Labour & Love*, p. 254.
88. BHRU interview B0105.
89. Tannahill, *Volunteer Workers*, p. 93.
90. Tannahill, *Volunteer Workers*, pp. 97-8.
91. BHRU interview B0019.
92. BHRU interview B0046.
93. Tannahill, *Volunteer Workers*, Appendix.
94. BHRU interview B0086.
95. BHRU interview B0016.
96. BHRU interview B0004.
97. BHRU interview B0090.
98. BHRU interview B0009.
99. BHRU interview B0019.
100. BHRU interview B0016.

101. BHRU interview B0016.
102. BHRU interview B0031.
103. BHRU interview B0016.
104. BHRU interview B0016.
105. BHRU interview B0016.
106. BHRU interview B0025.
107. Tannahill, *Volunteer Workers*, p. 97.
108. For contemporary use of the term 'assimilation' see Steinert and Weber-Newth, *Labour & Love*, pp. 68-76.

Chapter 6

1. A detailed study of the settlement and integration of Huguenots, Eastern European Jews and Bangladeshis appears in Anne J. Kershen, *Strangers, Aliens and Asians: Huguenots, Jews and Bangladeshis in Spitalfields 1660-2000* (Abingdon, 2005).
2. Autumn, 2004.
3. The Bangladeshis are the most recent large-scale immigrants to Spitalfields. Since their arrival, there has been a small number of eastern European immigrants settling in the area. However, it is doubtful that they will ever reach the same volume or have the same impact as the Huguenots, Jews and Bangladeshis that came before.
4. See John Rex, *Race, Colonialism and the City* (London, 1973), p. 12.
5. The American writer and reporter Jack London visited the East End of London at the beginning of 1903. His impression of the area was of a jungle as he recorded in his disturbing monograph, *The People of the Abyss* (London, 1903).
6. Later Flower and Dean Street.
7. Quoted in Roy Porter, *London: A Social History* (London, 1994), p. 118.
8. Brick Lane was so named because the land around it was used for brick earth. The bricks were fired locally and either used to build local properties or transported to the river southwards down the track that became known as Brick Lane.
9. It is possible that Wren was referring to the southern most end of Brick Lane which, in the map of 1686 does appear as nothing more than a narrow lane, whilst further to the north the 'Lane' is more clearly defined as a thoroughfare.
10. See Anne J. Kershen, *Uniting the Tailors: Trade Unionism Amongst the Clothing Workers of London and Leeds 1870-1939* (Ilford, 1995), chapter 1.
11. In reality the immigrants that arrived prior to 1971 were Pakistanis as the nation state of Bangladesh was not created until 1971. However, it

has become common practice, and one preferred by Bangladeshis themselves, to call the immigrants who originate from, what was, East Pakistan, by the name of the country they fought a civil war to achieve.

12. Evidence of the impact of the Bangladeshi community on the district can be seen by the renaming of the electoral ward known as Spitalfields and Banglatown. The total size of the Bangladeshi community of Tower Hamlets was recorded as 65,553 in the 2001 census. Statistics supplied by the Census Customer Service 13 November 2003, from ONS, Table Population: All People, Geographical Level England and Wales to Ward; Table S101 Sex and Age by Ethnic Group.
13. For a discourse on memory and narrative see Katy Gardner, *Age, Narrative and Migration: The Life Course and Life Histories of Bengali Elders in London* (Oxford, 2002), pp. 27-33.
14. See Wendy Webster, *Imagining Home: Gender, 'Race' and National Identity, 1945-64* (London, 1998).
15. Katy Gardner and Abdus Shukur, 'I'm Bengali, I'm Asian and I'm Living Here: The Changing Identity of British Bengalis', in Roger Ballard (ed.), *Desh Pardesh: The South Asian Presence in Britain* (London, 1994), p. 150.
16. David Garbin, 'Migration, territoires diasporiques et politiques identitaires: Bengalis musulmans entre 'Banglatown' (Londres) et Sylhet (Bangladesh)', Unpublished PhD thesis (Université François Rabelais de Tours, 2004), p. 154.
17. Nigel Rapport and Andrew Dawson (eds), *Migrants of Identity: Perceptions of Home in a World of Movement* (Oxford, 1998), p. 7.
18. See, *Shorter Oxford English Dictionary* (Oxford, 2002), pp. 1258-9.
19. Danièle Joly and Robin Cohen, *Reluctant Host: Europe and its Refugees* (Aldershot, 1989), p. 6.
20. Unlike the English, Yiddish (derived clearly from the Hebrew/German) and Bengali there is no one French word for home, the writer or speaker thus chooses the one most relevant to the sense of the conversation/theme.
21. Mark Zborowski and Elizabeth Herzog, *Life is with People: The Culture of the Shtetl* (New York, 1970), p. 158.
22. Home or homeland
23. Abroad
24. Sarah C. White, Arguing with the Crocodile: Gender and Class in Bangladesh (London, 1992), p. 53.
25. Muhammad Anwar, *The Myth of Return: Pakistanis in Britain* (London, 1979).
26. Anwar, *The Myth of Return*, p. 21.

27. In 1995 it was estimated that Bangladesh was receiving one billion dollars per annum in remittances, see Katy Gardner, *Global Migrants, Local Lives: Travel and Transformation in Rural Bangladesh* (Oxford, 1995), p. 23.
28. French Calvinists began fleeing France in the 1570s, following the Massacre of St. Bartholomew's Day in 1572. A number settled in England, in towns such as Norwich and Canterbury as well as in London. The capital was an ideal location as it offered both religious freedom and economic opportunity. The Edict of Nantes, which was pronounced in 1598, promised the Huguenots freedom to worship as they chose. As result, a number of those who had crossed the channel returned to France. The period of religious tolerance lasted until the 1670s when crippling restrictions were imposed on all French Calvinists, culminating in the Revocation of the Edict of Nantes in 1685.
29. It needs to be pointed out that though the Jews were 'readmitted' to England in 1656 it was not until the last half of the eighteenth century that their 'presence' reached significant numbers, estimated to be between eight and ten thousand. By the mid-nineteenth there were between 35,000 to 50,000. It is estimated that between 16 and 20 thousand Huguenots settled in the Spitalfields district between 1675 and the first quarter of the eighteenth century.
30. It has been suggested that the cockney 'lingo', is a fusion of the old Huguenot patois and 'working man's' English. However Gareth Stedman Jones suggests that it derives from Middle English *Cokeney*, meaning cock's egg, a misshapen egg. According to Edwin Pugh the word originally meant townee, a Londoner '…the supreme type of Englishman'; by the early twentieth century the cockney had become associated with the East End, and as such could mean 'jingoistic Londoner'. See Gareth Stedman Jones, 'The "Cockney" and the Nation', in David Feldman and Gareth Stedman Jones (eds), *Metropolis London* (London, 1989), pp. 272-324.
31. Robin Gwynn, *The Huguenot Heritage* (Brighton, 2001), p. 260.
32. Daniel Statt, *Foreigners and Englishmen: The Controversy over Immigration and Population 1660-1760* (London, 1995), p. 31.
33. *Report of the Select Commission on the State of the Handloom Weavers II* (London, 1840), pp. 213-84.
34. Gwynn, *Huguenot*, p. 212.
35. W. M. Beaufort, *Records of the French Protestant School* (Lymington, 1894), p. 2.

36. Although the large-scale immigration of Huguenots took place in the fifty years between 1675 and 1725, Calvinists continued to arrive until the year before the French revolution.
37. See Anne J. Kershen, 'Mother Tongue as a Bridge to Assimilation', in Anne J. Kershen (ed.), *Language, Labour and Migration* (Aldershot, 2000), pp. 11-38.
38. Yiddish for 'the home'.
39. Nancy Green (ed.), *Jewish Workers in the Modern Diaspora* (London, 1998), p. 194.
40. Ironically, 'Bollywood films tend to be made in Hindi or Urdhu, never in Sylheti and only occasionally in Bengali.
41. See Kershen, 'Mother Tongue'.
42. Department of Education and Skills, *Aiming High: Raising the Achievement of Minority Ethnic Pupils* (London, 2003), p. 28.
43. Meeting with a group of Bangladeshi undergraduate students, 23 March 2000.
44. Statement made at a meeting of young Bangladeshi professionals to discuss their attitude towards mother tongue, Queen Mary, University of London, February 2000.
45. Kershen, 'Mother Tongue', p. 6.
46. Statt, *Foreigners*, p. 189.
47. *Jewish Year Book* (London, 1896), pp. 62-3.
48. The shop's ownership is recorded in Kelly's Street Directory for 1896 and is confirmation that, contrary to popular belief, Jewish married women carry out economic activities.
49. See Kershen, *Strangers*, chapters 3 and 7.
50. Angela Donkin and Elizabeth Dowler, 'Equal Access to Health Foods for Ethnic Minorities?', in Anne J. Kershen (ed.), *Food in the Migrant Experience* (Aldershot, 2002), p. 211.
51. The author counted some 45 'Indian' Restaurants in Brick Lane, November 2003.
52. See Anne J. Kershen, 'Introduction: Food in the Migrant Experience', in Kershen, *Food in the Migrant Experience*, p. 7.
53. For a detailed account of the religious activities of Huguenots, Jews and Bangladeshis in Spitalfields see Kershen, *Strangers*, chapter 4.
54. Anne J. Kershen, 'Huguenots, Jews and Bangladeshis and the Spirit of Capitalism in Spitalfields', in Anne J. Kershen (ed.), *London the Promised Land? The Migrant Experience in a Capital City* (Aldershot, 1997), p. 70.
55. For details about the French churches, Synagogues and mosques in Spitalfields, see Kershen, *Strangers*, chapter 4.

56. Few families were able to afford the luxury of a young bird that could be roasted, so the meal was composed of the chicken soup and the chicken that had been boiled in its making.
57. A *chevra* was a small synagogue as opposed to the more imposing places of worship to be found in Rectory Square, Sandys Row etc.
58. By the middle of the nineteenth century the Calvinist community no longer maintained a church in Spitalfields or Threadneedle Street. The bulk of the community had moved either to more salubrious areas or north-east to Bethnal Green. From the middle of the nineteenth century the French Church was located in Soho.
59. I am grateful to Martin Paisner for allowing me access to the files which provided this information.
60. Katy Gardner, 'Identity, Age and Masaculinity amongst Bengali Elders in East London', in Anne J Kershen (ed.), *A Question of Identity* (Aldershot, 1998), p. 165.
61. Caroline Adams, *Across Seven Seas and Thirteen Rivers* (London, 1987), p. 160
62. Author's meeting with ten Bangladeshi graduates and two undergraduates, 3 June 1999.
63. Yasmin Alibhai-Brown, '*Some of my Best Friends are…*', Channel 4, 17 August 2003; and Sarah Glynn, 'Bengali Muslims: The New East End Radicals', *Ethnic and Racial Studies*, 23 (2002), p. 280.
64. Iain Chambers, *Migrancy, Culture and Identity* (London, 1994), p. 9.
65. Monica Ali, *Brick Lane* (London, 2003), p. 44.
66. Zborowski and Herzog, *Life*.

Chapter 7

1. Antonino di Sparti, *Lingue a Metà. Plurilinguismo e Emigrazione di Ritorno in Sicilia* (Palermo, 1993), p. 38.
2. Francesco Cerase, 'Expectations and Reality: A Case Study of Return Migration from the United States to Southern Italy', *International Migration Review*, 8 (1974), 245-62; Mirjana Morokvasic, 'Birds of Passage Are Also Women…', *International Migration Review*, 18 (1984), 886-907; Amalia Signorelli, Maria Clara Trittico and Sara Rossi, *Scelte senza Potere. Il Ritorno degli Emigranti dalle Zone dell'Esodo* (Rome, 1977).
3. Mario Bolognari, 'Il rientro degli emigrati fra tradizione e trasformazione: ipotesi per un'indagine', *Sudi Emigrazione*, 79 (1985), 393-8.
4. Stephen Castles, *Here For Good: Western Europe's New Ethnic Minorities* (London, 1984).

5. Christian Dustmann, 'Return Migration, Wage Differentials, and the Optimal Migration Duration', *European Economic Review*, 47 (2003), 353-69; Oded Stark, Christian Helmenstein and Yury Yegorov, 'Migrants' Savings, Purchasing Power Parity, and the Optimal Duration of Migration', *International Tax and Public Finance*, 4 (1997), 307-24.
6. Castles, *Here for Good*; John Salt and Hugh Clout (eds), *Migration in Post-War Europe: Geographical Essays*, (London, 1976); Paul White, 'International Migration in the 1970s: Revolution or Evolution?', in Allan Findlay and Paul White (eds), *West European Population Change*, (London, 1986), pp. 50-80.
7. Castles, *Here for Good*, p. 41.
8. Colin Holmes, *John Bull's Island: Immigration and British Society, 1871-1971* (Basingstoke, 1988), p. 41.
9. John Briggs, *An Italian Passage: Immigrants to Three American Cities, 1890-1930* (London, 1978).
10. Terri Colpi, *The Italian Factor: The Italian Community in Great Britain* (Edinburgh, 1991), p. 134.
11. The names used in this chapter are pseudonyms.
12. Castles, *Here for Good*; Lucio Sponza and Arturo Tosi (eds), *A Century of Italian Immigration to Britain: Five Essays* (Reading, 1993).
13. Castles, *Here for Good*; Colpi, *Italian Factor*.
14. Colpi, *Italian Factor*.
15. Sara Ahmed, 'Home and Away: Narratives of Migration and Estrangement', *International Journal of Cultural Studies*, 2 (1999), 329-47; Loretta Baldassar, *Visits Home: Migration Experiences Between Italy and Australia* (Melbourne, 2001); Theodora Lam and Brenda Yeoh, 'Negotiating "Home" and "National Identity": Chinese-Malaysian Transmigrants in Singapore', *Asia Pacific Viewpoint*, 2 (2004), 141-64.
16. Ahmed, 'Home and Away', p. 341.
17. Baldassar, *Visits Home*.
18. Lam and Yeoh, 'Negotiating "Home"'.
19. Riva Kastoryano, 'Settlement, Transnational Communities and Citizenship', *International Social Science Journal*, 52 (2000), 307-12.
20. Louise Ryan, 'Family Matters: (E)migration, Familial Networks and Irish Women in Britain', *Sociological Review*, 52 (2004), p. 364.
21. Andreas Huber and Karen O'Reilly, 'The Construction of *Heimat* Under Conditions of Individualised Modernity: Swiss and British Elderly Migrants in Spain', *Ageing and Society*, 24 (2004), 327-51.
22. Lee Cuba and David Hummon, 'A Place to Call Home: Identification with Dwelling, Community and Region', *Sociological Quarterly*, 34, (1993), 111-31.

23. Michael Piore, *Birds of Passage: Migrant Labour and Industrial Societies* (Cambridge, 1979).
24. Claudio Bolzman, Rosita Fibbi and Marie Vial, 'Dove abitare dopo la pensione? Le logiche di decisione dei migranti di fronte ai rischi di povertà', in Velleda Bolognari and Klaus Kühne (eds), *Povertà, migrazione, razzismo* (Bergamo, 1997), pp. 3-114; Castles, *Here for Good*; Rosemarie Rogers (ed.), *Guests Come to Stay: The Effect of European Labour Migration on Sending and Receiving Countries* (Boulder, CO, 1985).
25. Signorelli, Trittico and Rossi, *Scelte senza Potere*, pp. 107-8.
26. Claudio Bolzman, Rosita Fibbi and Marie Vial, 'Espagnols et Italiens proches de la retraite: Structures et fonctionnement du réseau familial', in Pierrette Béday and Claudio Bolzman (eds), *On est né quelque part mais on peut vivre ailleurs: Familles, migrations, cultures, travail social* (Geneva, 1997), pp. 159-183 ; Bolzman, Fibbi and Vial, 'Dove abitare dopo la pensione?'; Claudio Bolzman, Raffaella Poncioni-Derigo, Marie Vial and Rosita Fibbi, 'Older Labour Migrants' Wellbeing in Europe: The Case of Switzerland', *Ageing and Society*, 24 (2004), 411-30.
27. Bolzman, Poncioni-Derigo, Vial and Fibbi, 'Dove abitare dopo la pensione?'.
28. Claudio Bolzman, Jean El-Sombati, Rosita Fibbi and Marie Vial, 'Liens intergénérationnels et formes de solidarité chez les immigrés: quelles implications pour le travail social?' in Claudio Bolzman and Jean-Pierre Tabin (eds), *Populations immigrées: quelle insertion? quel travail social?* (Geneva, 1999), pp. 77-90.
29. Salvatore Castorina and Giuseppina Mendorla, *Il Mito del 'ritorno': Il Disagio Psichico di Donne e Bambini che Rientrano dal Paese di Emigrazione* (Catania, 1989); Thomas Emmenegger, 'Malattia e migrazione: Problemi dell'adattamento e del ritorno', *Studi Emigrazione*, 89 (1988), 127-36; Gilberto Marselli, 'Un ritorno doloroso, un'occasione da non perdere', *Studi Emigrazione*, 63 (1981), 305-36.
30. Saskia Sassen, 'The De Facto Transnationalization of Immigration Policy', in Christian Joppke (ed.), *Challenge to the Nation-State: Immigration in Western Europe and the United States*. (Oxford, 1998).
31. Steven Vertovec, 'Transnationalism and identity', *Journal of Ethnic and Migration Studies*, 27 (2001), p. 575.
32. Bolzman, El-Sombati, Fibbi and Vial, 'Liens intergénérationnels', p. 107.
33. Anne Marie Fortier, *Migrant Belongings: Memory, Space, Identity* (Oxford, 2000), p. 88.
34. Baldassar, *Visits Home*.
35. Lloyd Wong, '"Home Away from Home?": Transnationalism and the Canadian Citizenship Regime', in Paul Kennedy and Victor

Roudometof (eds), *Communities Across Borders: New Immigrants and Transnational Cultures* (London, 2002), p. 169.

36. María Ángeles Casado-Díaz, Claudia Kaiser and Anthony Warnes, 'Northern European Retired Residents in Nine Southern European Areas: Characteristics, Motivations and Adjustment', *Ageing and Society*, 24 (2004), pp. 368-9; Huber and O'Reilly, 'Construction of *Heimat*', p. 340.
37. David Timothy Duval, 'Linking Return Visits and Return Migration Among Commonwealth Eastern Caribbean Migrants in Toronto', *Global Networks*, 4 (2004), 51-67.
38. Karen O'Reilly, 'A New Trend in European Migration: Contemporary British Migration to Fuengirola, Costa del Sol: A Response to King and Warnes', *Geographical Viewpoint*, 23 (1995), 25-36.
39. O'Reilly, 'A New Trend in European Migration'.
40. Russell King, Anthony Warnes and Allan Williams, *Sunset Lives: British Retirement Migration to the Mediterranean* (Oxford, 2000), p. 110.

Chapter 8

1. Alessandro Portelli, 'The Peculiarities of Oral History', *History Workshop Journal*, 12 (1981), 96-107.
2. For a discussion of genre see Mary Chamberlain and Paul Thompson (eds), *Narrative and Genre* (London, 1997), in particular, Alessandro Portelli, 'Oral History as Genre', pp. 23-45. See also Elizabeth Tonkin, *Narrating Our Pasts: The Social Construction of Oral History* (Cambridge, 1992).
3. For an overview see Alistair Thomson, 'Moving Stories: Oral History and Migration Studies', *Oral History*, 27 (1999), 24-37. For the use of metaphors see p. 34. Louise Ryan discusses the use of clothes as a metaphor in oral histories of Irish women: Louise Ryan, '"I'm Going to England": Women's Narratives of Leaving Ireland in the 1930's', *Oral History*, 30 (2002), 42-53.
4. South Asian is used as shorthand throughout this paper to describe collectively those who can trace their ancestry to the Indian subcontinent, namely, India, Pakistan, Bangladesh and Kashmir.
5. For research into the cultural meanings of food in South Asia see *South Asia Research*, 24 (2004).
6. This paper draws on the British Library National Sound Archive (BLNSA), Millennium Memory Bank collection (MMB). These interviews were conducted in 1999. For further details see Rob Perks,

'The Century Speaks: A Public History Partnership', *Oral History*, 29 (2001), 95-105.
7. 2,530 were from the Caribbean, and 3,023 from the rest of Europe. Leicester City Council, *Survey of Leicester 1983: Initial Report of Survey* (Leicester, 1984), p. 20. Leicester was second only to London in terms of the numbers of East African Asians it received. Rosemary A. Hill, 'Housing Characteristics and Aspirations of Leicester's Inner City Asian Community', Unpublished PhD thesis (University of Leicester, 1987), p. 60.
8. See Parminder Bhachu, *Twice Migrants: East African Sikh Settlers in Britain* (London, 1985).
9. Muhammad Anwar, *The Myth of Return: Pakistanis in Britain* (London, 1979).
10. For a discussion on the use of life documents, including life histories see Ken Plummer, *Documents of Life* (London, 2000).
11. Raphael Samuel and Paul Thompson (eds), *The Myths We Live By* (London, 1990).
12. Mary Chamberlain and Selma Leydesdorff, 'Transnational Families: Memories and Narratives', *Global Networks*, 4 (2004), p. 229.
13. Alessandro Portelli, 'Unchronic Dreams: Working-Class Memory and Possible Worlds', in Samuel and Thompson (eds), *Myths We Live By*; Elinor Ochs and Lisa Capps, 'Narrating the Self', *Annual Review of Anthropology*, 25 (1996), 19-43.
14. Anthony Giddens, *Modernity and Self-Identity* (Oxford, 1991), p. 54.
15. See for instance, Michele Langfield and Pam Maclean, '"But Pineapple I'm Still a Bit Weary of": Sensory Memories of Jewish Women Who Migrated to Australia as Children, 1938-9', in A. James Hammerton and Eric Richards (eds), *Speaking to Immigrants: Oral Testimony and the History of Australian Migration* (Adelaide, 2002), pp. 83-109. For the importance of food in experiences of migration see Anne J. Kershen, (ed.), *Food in the Migrant Experience* (Aldershot, 2002). Paritaa Mukta, *Shards of Memory, Woven Lives in Four Generations* (London, 2002), provides an interesting discussion of the multiple meanings embedded in narratives of food.
16. Interview with Sophina, 3 April 2004. Born in 1949.
17. Barbara A. Misztal, *Theories of Social Remembering* (Buckingham, 2003), p. 77.
18. Avtar Brah, *Cartographies of Diaspora* (London, 1996), p. 192. For further discussion on the concept of 'home' see Shelley Mallett, 'Understanding Home: A Critical Review of the Literature', *Sociological Review*, 52 (2004), 62-89.
19. Interview with Karim, 13 June 2002. Born in 1941.

20. Karim, 13 June 2002. See also Pierre Bourdieu, 'The Forms of Capital', in Allbert H. Halsey, et al. (eds), *Education, Culture, Economy, Society* (Oxford, 1998).
21. BLNSA, MMB, C900/00005, S. Singh. Born in 1964.
22. For the link between food and ritual see David E. Sutton, *Remembrance of Repasts* (Oxford, 2001), pp. 19-42.
23. Giddens, *Modernity and Self-Identity*, pp. 61-2. For the link between the consumption of food and identity and belonging see Katy Gardner, 'Desh-Bidesh: Sylheti Images of Home and Away', *Man*, 28 (1993), 1-15.
24. BLNSA, MMB, C900/09135B, J. Kapasi. Born in 1950.
25. Mukta, *Shards of Memory*, pp. 85, 99.
26. For further discussion of how types of food function as important classifiers of status see Pierre Bourdieu, 'Social Space and Symbolic Power', *Sociological Theory*, 7 (1988), 18-26.
27. Brah, *Cartographies*.
28. BLNSA, MMB, C900/09135B, J. Kapasi.
29. BLNSA, MMB, C900/09135B, J. Kapasi.
30. For a similar interpretation see Dwaine Plaza, 'Strategies and Strategizing: The Struggle for Upward Mobility Among University Education Black Caribbean-Born Men in Canada', in Mary Chamberlain (ed.), *Caribbean Migration: Globalised Identities* (London, 1998), pp. 248-66.
31. For further details of the development of Asian food in Leicester see Panikos Panayi, 'The Spicing up of English Provincial Life: The History of Curry in Leicester', in Kershen (ed.), *Food in the Migrant Experience*, pp. 42-76. For the development of Asian retailing in Leicester see Howard Aldrich, et al., 'Business Development and Self Segregation: Asian Enterprise in Three British Cities', in Ceri Peach, Vaughan Robinson and Susan Smith (eds), *Ethnic Segregation in Cities* (London, 1981).
32. Interview with Khan, 4 July 2002. Born in 1928.
33. Interview with Patel, 3 July 2002. Born in 1927.
34. Pnina Werbner, 'Rich Man, Poor Man – Or a Community of Suffering', *Oral History*, 8 (1980), 43-8.
35. Joan Sangster, 'Telling Our Stories: Feminist Debates and the Use of Oral History', in Robert Perks and Alistair Thompson (eds), *The Oral History Reader* (London, 1998); Isabelle Bertaux-Wiame, 'The Life Story Approach to the Study of Internal Migration', *Oral History*, 7 (1979), 26-32.
36. For the various explanations for this see Jane Pilcher, *Women in Contemporary Britain* (London, 1999), pp. 54-74.

37. Nira Yuval-Davis, *Gender and Nation* (London, 1997), p. 46.
38. BLNSA, MMB C900/00009, B. Kaur. Born in 1956.
39. BLNSA, MMB C900/00009, B. Kaur.
40. For further discussion see Eleonare Kofman, 'Female "Birds of Passage" a Decade Later: Gender and Immigration in the European Union', *International Migration Review*, 33 (1999), 269-90.
41. Sophina, 3 April 2004.
42. Interview with Devi, 24 June 2002. Born in 1948.
43. Devi, 24 June 2002.
44. Interview with Johan, 8 March 2002. Date of birth not known.
45. Johan, 8 March 2002.
46. Interview with Sue, 10 July 2002. Born in 1957.
47. Sue, 10 July 2002.
48. Sue, 10 July 2002.
49. Nirmal Puwar, 'Melodramatic Postures and Constructions', in Nirmal Puwar and Parvati Raghuram (eds), *South Asian Women in the Diaspora* (Oxford, 2003).
50. The genre of hard work was also noted in: Dhooleka S. Raj, *Where Are You From?* (Oxford, 2000); and Katy Gardner, *Age, Narrative and Migration: The Life Course and Life Histories of Bengali Elders in London* (Oxford, 2002).
51. Patricia Madoo Lengermann and Jill Niebrugge-Brantley, 'Contemporary Feminist Theory', in George Ritzer (ed.), *Sociological Theory* (London, 2000).
52. This compares to Westwood's study whereby the Asian women who worked in a garment firm in Leicester saw their work in the domestic domain as 'emotionally fulfilling'. Sallie Westwood, *All Day Everyday: Factory and Family in the Making of Women's Lives* (London, 1984), p. 187.
53. Sue, 10 July 2002.
54. Sue, 10 July 2002.
55. Devi, 24 June 2002.
56. See Roger Ballard, 'South Asian Families', in Robert Rapoport, Michael P. Fogarty and Rhona Rapoport (eds), *Families in Britain* (London, 1982). For further discussion of the honourable role women can occupy in the household see Haleh Afshar and Mary Maynard, 'Gender and Ethnicity at the Millennium: From Margin to Centre', *Ethnic and Racial Studies*, 23 (2000), 805-19.
57. Kershen, *Food in the Migrant Experience*.
58. Johan, 8 March 2002.
59. BLNSA, MMB, C900/00005, S. Singh.
60. Cultural habits were often a source of complaints by whites in the 1960s. See for instance, 'A House Divided', *Leicester Mercury*, 18 July

1968.
61. BLNSA, MMB C900/00009, B. Kaur.
62. Interview with Chitra, 22 May 2002. Born in 1957.
63. Devi, 24 June 2002.
64. Devi, 24 June 2002.
65. Devi, 24 June 2002.
66. BLNSA, MMB C900/00011, R. Saujani. Born in 1953.
67. BLNSA, MMB C900/00011, R. Saujani.
68. For the role and purpose of oral history see: Paul Thompson, *The Voice of the Past* (Oxford, 2000); and Michael Frisch, *A Shared Authority: Essays on the Craft and Meaning of Oral and Public History* (New York, 1990).

Chapter 9

1. Ben Anderson and Divya P. Tolia-Kelly, 'Matter(s) in Social and Cultural Geography', *Geoforum*, 35 (2004), 669-74.
2. Daniel Miller (ed.), *Home Possessions: Material Culture Behind Closed Doors* (Oxford, 2001).
3. Raphael Samuel, *Theatres of Memory*, Volume 1, *Past and Present in Contemporary Culture* (London, 1994).
4. Stuart Hall, 'Whose Heritage? Unsettling "The Heritage", Re-imagining the Post-nation', *Third Text*, 49 (2000), 3-13.
5. Samuel, *Theatres of Memory*.
6. See, for example, Svetlana Boym, 'On Diasporic Intimacy: Ilya Kabakov's Instalation and Immigrant Homes', *Critical Enquiry*, 24 (1998), 498-527; Mihaly Csikszentmihalyi and Eugene Rochberg-Halton, *The Meaning of Things: Domestic Symbols and the Self* (Cambridge, 1981); Raj Mehta and Russell W Belk, 'Artifacts, Identity and Transition: Favourite Possessions of Indians and Indian Immigrants to the United States', *Journal of Consumer Research*, 17 (1991), 398-411.
7. David Parkin, 'Mementoes as Transitional Objects in Human Displacement', *Journal of Material Cultural*, 43 (1999), p. 309.
8. See Divya P. Tolia-Kelly, 'Processes of Identification: Precipitates of Re-Memory in the South Asian Home', *Transactions of the Institute of British Geographers*, 29 (2004), 314-29; Divya P. Tolia-Kelly, 'Landscape, Race and Memory: Biographical Mapping of the Routes of British Asian Landscape Values', *Landscape Research*, 29 (2004), 277-92.
9. Divya P. Tolia-Kelly, 'Materializing Post-Colonial Geographies: Examining the Textural Landscapes of Migration in the South Asian Home', *Geoforum*, 35 (2004), 675-88.

10. Divya P. Tolia-Kelly, 'Iconographies of Identity: Visual Cultures of the Everyday in the South Asian Diaspora', *Visual Culture in Britain*, 2 (2001), 49-67.
11. Avtar Brah, 'The Scent of Memory: Strangers, Our Own and Others', *Feminist Review*, 61 (1999), 4-26.
12. Leela Gandhi, *Postcolonial Theory: A Critical Introduction* (New York, 1998).
13. Jacquelin Burgess, 'Focusing on Fear: The Use of Focus Groups in a Project for the Community Forest Unit Countryside Commission', *Area*, 28 (1996), p. 2.
14. Rosaline S. Barbour, 'Are Focus Groups an Appropriate Tool for Studying Organisational Change?', in Rosaline Barbour and Jenny Kitzinger (eds), *Developing Focus Group Research: Politics, Theory and Practice* (London, 1999), pp. 113-26; Sue Wilkinson, 'How Useful are Focus Groups in Feminist Research?', in Barbour and Kitzinger, *Developing Focus Group Research*, p. 215; Gillian Rose, 'Situating Knowledges: Positionality, Reflexivities and Other Tactics', *Progress in Human Geography*, 21 (1997), 305-20.
15. Robina Mohammed, '"Insiders" and/or "Outsiders": Positionality, Theory and Praxis', in Melanie Limb and Claire Dwyer (eds), *Qualitative Methodologies for Geographers* (London, 2002), pp. 101-17.
16. Csikszentmihalyi and Rochberg-Halton, *Meaning of Things*; Mehta and Belk, 'Artefacts'.
17. Raymond Williams, *The Country and the City* (London, 1973), p. 335.
18. Stuart Hall, 'Cultural Identity and Diaspora', in Jonathon Rutherford (ed.), *Identity: Community, Culture, Difference* (London, 1990), pp. 222-37.
19. Parminder Bhachu, *Twice Migrants: East African Sikh Settlers in Britain* (London, 1985).
20. Alfred Gell, 'Newcomers to the World of Goods: Consumption among the Muria Gonds', in Arjun Appadurai (ed.), *The Social Life of Things: Commodities in Cultural Perspective* (Cambridge, 1986), p. 114.
21. Patrick Geary, 'Sacred Commodities: The Circulation of Medieval Relics', in Appadurai, *The Social Life of Things*, pp. 169-91.
22. Muhammed Anwar, *The Myth of Return: Pakistanis in Britain* (London, 1979); Bhachu, *Twice Migrants*; Brah, 'Scent of Memory'.
23. William Safran, 'Diasporas in Modern Societies: Myths of Homeland and Return', *Diaspora*, 2 (1991), 83-99; Brah, 'Scent of Memory'.
24. Benedict Anderson, *Imagined Communities: Reflections on the Origins and Spread of Nationalism* (London, 1983).
25. Toni Morrison, *Beloved* (London, 1987).
26. Arjun Appadurai, *Modernity at Large: Cultural Dimensions of Globalisation* (Minnesota, 1997).

27. Sumita Chakravarty, *National Identity in Indian Popular Cinema, 1947-1987* (Delhi, 1993), p. 3.
28. C. Thomas 'Community Centre', *Gardeners' World* (September 1998), pp. 50-53.

Chapter 10

1. For much of the information in this article I am grateful to the people I interviewed living in North London; for access to the objects and furniture displayed in their living rooms; and for sharing their precious and unique memories. The research refers to thirty in-depth interviews with migrants and the children and grandchildren of migrants. Many, but not all people interviewed, are of Polish or Czechoslovakian extraction. The information produced comes from a much larger research project concerning 'significant objects and migrants' experiences'. All in-depth interviews have been recorded and produced in the form of transcripts. An archive of photographs has been collected documenting the interiors of the living rooms and focusing on specific objects.
2. David Parkin, 'Momentos as Transitional Objects in Human Displacement', *Journal of Material Culture*, 4 (1999), 3-75.
3. Jean-Claude Kauffman, *Dirty Linen: Couples and Their Laundry* (London, 1989). Kauffman interviews couples concerning how they organise their laundry and discovers that habits are often inherited from parent generations.
4. Milena Veenis, 'Consumption in East Germany: The Seduction and Betrayal of Things', *Journal of Material Culture*, 4 (1999), 79-112.
5. Elaine Scarry, *The Body in Pain* (Oxford, 1985), pp. 290-2. Scarry describes how objects are made by humans for human comfort: 'The chair is therefore the materialized structure of a perception; it is sentient awareness materialized into a free standing design'. In this way once the chair has been created by a human the physical object can independently provide comfort for another person and therefore has autonomy.
6. Jean-Pierre Warnier, 'Material Memories: Design and Evocation', *Journal of Design History*, 13 (2000), p. 264: 'In her prologue on the role played by the senses in building material memories, Susan Stewart deals with five senses, seemingly forgetting that there are actually seven of them including kinaesthesia, briefly mentioned only once, and the vestibular sense of balance and movement. Now, the first five senses, especially touch and sight, allow perception of an object. The

last two allow us to perceive our own sensory-motor behavior, in particular when it is geared to material objects and their attached wealth of sensations. Sensations are never disconnected from all others., especially kinaethesia and the vestibular sense, and that is why material memories reach deep into the human subject'.
7. David Halle, *Inside Culture* (Chicago, 1993), pp. 87-118.
8. Jo Spence and Patricia Holland, *Family Snaps: The Meaning of Domestic Photography* (London, 1996), p. 10.
9. Edward Casey, *Remembering* (Bloomington, 1987), pp. 102-305. Casey describes how memory can be divided into primary and secondary remembering and therefore layers of memory may be accessed simultaneously, even though this is often a subconscious process.
10. Roland Barthes, *Mythologies* (London, 1981).
11. Jean Baudrillard, *The System of Objects* (London, 1996), pp. 13-65.
12. Eva Hoffman, *Lost in Translation* (London, 1991). Hoffman describes how she emigrated as a child from Poland to Canada and found that the thoughts and language of her childhood could not be adequately described in Canadian English. In order to adapt she needed to make the transition from thinking in Polish to thinking in American English. It was only later, as a young adult attending University in America that she began to feel truly accepted as an American. Her thoughts had changed into English and therefore her identity had left Poland in the land of her childhood.
13. Primo Levi, *If Not Now, When?* (London, 1986).
14. Warnier, 'Material Memories', p. 264: 'When Proust entered the "Madeleine" in his own archives of sensations and emotions, his aunt and he were engaged in the bodily motion of sitting down for tea, eating and drinking. His aunt would dip the biscuit into her cup, and hand it over for him to eat'.

Chapter 11

1. The names of all participants have been changed.
2. Louise Ryan, 'Moving Spaces and Changing Places: Irish women's Memories of Emigration to Britain in the 1930s', *Journal of Ethnic and Migration Studies*, 29 (2003), 67-82.
3. Louise Ryan, '"I'm going to England": Women's Narratives of Leaving Ireland in the 1930s', *Oral History*, 30 (2002), 42-53.
4. Louise Ryan, 'Family Matters: (E)migration, Familial Networks and Irish Women in Britain', *Sociological Review*, 52 (2004), 351-70.

5. Katy Gardner, *Age, Narrative and Migration: Life Course and Life Histories of Bengali Elders in London* (Oxford, 2002), p. 31.
6. Mary Chamberlain, 'Gender and the Narratives of Migration', *History Workshop Journal*, 43 (1997), 87-108.
7. Alistair Thomson, 'Anzac Memories', in Robert Perks and Alistair Thomson (eds), *The Oral History Reader* (London 1998), p. 301.
8. Andreea Ritivoi, *Yesterday's Self: Nostalgia and the Immigrant Identity* (Lanham, MD, 2002), p. 61.
9. Robert Kennedy, *The Irish: Emigration, Marriage and Fertility* (Berkeley 1973).
10. John Archer Jackson, *The Irish in Britain* (London, 1963).
11. Steven Fielding, *Class and Ethnicity: Irish Catholics in England, 1880-1939* (Buckingham, 1993), p. 21.
12. *Commission on Seasonal Migration to Great Britain* (Dublin, 1938), p. 63.
13. *Commission on Emigration and Other Population Problems* (Dublin, 1955), p. 115.
14. Pauric Travers, 'There Was Nothing There for Me: Irish Female Emigration, 1922-72', in P. O'Sullivan (ed.), *Irish Women and Irish Migration* (Leicester, 1995).
15. Bronwen Walter, *Outsiders Inside: Whiteness, Place and Irish Women* (London, 2001), p. 119.
16. The *Irish Post* is the biggest selling newspaper for the Irish community in Britain.
17. Travers, 'Irish Female Emigration'.
18. Sharon Lambert, *Irish Women in Lancashire, 1922-1960* (Lancaster, 2001). The majority of the women in both Walter's *Outsiders Inside* and Lambert's *Irish Women in Lancashire* were post-world war II migrants and were thus considerably younger than the women in my study.
19. Joanna Bornat, 'Oral History as a Social Movement: Reminiscence and Older People', *Oral History*, 17 (1989), 16-24.
20. David Dunaway, 'Method and Theory in the Oral Biography', *Oral History*, 20 (1992), 40-44.
21. Dunaway, 'Method and Theory'.
22. Dunaway, 'Method and Theory', p.43.
23. Ritivoi, *Yesterday's Self*, p. 30.
24. Ritivoi, *Yesterday's Self*, p. 66.
25. Sinead McDermott, 'Memory, Nostalgia and Gender in A Thousand Acres', *Signs*, 28 (2002), p. 406.
26. McDermott, 'Memory, Nostalgia', p. 390.
27. Chamberlain, 'Gender', p. 11.

28. See Chamberlain, 'Gender' and Katy Gardner, 'Narrating Location: Space, Age and Gender among Bengali Elders in East London', *Oral History*, 27 (1999), 65-74.
29. Breda Gray, 'Gendering the Irish Diaspora: Questions of Enrichment, Hybridization and Return', *Women's Studies International Forum*, 23 (2000), 167-85.
30. Jane Moodie, 'Preparing the Waste Places for Future Prosperity? New Zealand's Pioneering Myth and Gendered Memories of Place', *Oral History*, 28 (2000), 54-64.
31. Gardner, 'Narrating Location', pp. 65-74.
32. Gardner, 'Narrating Location', p. 67.
33. A few of the women I interviewed had recently been mugged in the street. For example, Molly had her pension money stolen outside the Post Office. These experiences had clearly affected their self-confidence and their mobility and may add to their sense of nostalgia for the past.
34. Ritivoi, *Yesterday's Self*, p. 30.
35. Alistair Thomson, 'Moving Stories: Oral History and Migration Studies', *Oral History*, 27 (1999), p. 28.
36. Although she was born in the 1940s, my mother often invokes the folk memory of the 1930s as the 'Hungry '30s'.
37. Chamberlain, 'Gender', p. 109.
38. Ann Marie Turnbull, 'Collaboration and Censorship in the Oral History Interview', *International Journal of Social Research Methodology*, 3 (2000), 15-34.
39. Ritivoi, *Yesterday's Self*.
40. Dunaway, 'Method and Theory'.
41. Thomson, *Anzac Memories*.
42. McDermott, 'Memory, Nostalgia'.
43. Breda Gray, *Irish Women and Diaspora* (London, 2004), p. 93.
44. Gray, *Irish Women*, p. 91.
45. Ryan, 'Family Matters'.
46. McDermott, 'Memory, Nostalgia'.
47. Ritivoi, *Yesterday's Self*.

Chapter 12

1. Kerby Miller, *Emigrants and Exiles: Ireland and the Irish Exodus to North America* (New York, 1985), p. 8.
2. Donald Akenson, 'The Historiography of the Irish in the United States of America', in Patrick O'Sullivan (ed.), *The Irish in the New Communities*

[Volume 2 of the Irish World Wide series] (Leicester, 1992), pp. 115-21; Donald Akenson, *The Irish Diaspora: A Primer* (Toronto, 1993), pp. 237-8. A useful summary of arguments is contained in Kevin Kenny, 'Diaspora and Comparison: The Global Irish as a Case Study', *Journal of American History*, 90 (2003), pp. 137-40.

3. Perhaps best explored in relation to the Irish in Steven Fielding, *Class and Ethnicity: Irish Catholics in England, 1880-1939* (Buckingham, 1993).
4. Jan Assmann, 'Collective Memory and Cultural Identity', *New German Critique*, 65 (1995), p. 132.
5. Wulf Kansteiner, 'Finding Meaning in Memory: A Methodological Critique of Collective Memory Studies', *History and Theory*, 41 (2002), p. 182.
6. Kansteiner, 'Finding Meaning', pp. 187-8. The final quotation comes from Liliane Weissberg, 'Introduction', in Dan Ben-Amos and Liliane Weissberg, *Cultural Memory and the Construction of Identity* (Detroit, 1999), p. 15.
7. Miller, *Emigrants and Exiles*, pp. 427-92.
8. Mary J. Hickman, 'Differences, Boundaries, Community: The Irish in Britain', available from: http://www.zonezero.com/magazine/essays/distant/zdife2.html
9. Mary J. Hickman, *Religion, Class and Identity: State, the Catholic Church and the Education of the Irish in Britain* (Aldershot, 1997), chapters 3-5.
10. John Herson, 'Irish Migration and Settlement in Victorian Britain: A Small Town Perspective', in Roger Swift and Sheridan Gilley (eds), *The Irish in Britain, 1815-1939* (London, 1989), pp. 84-103; John Herson, 'Migration, "Community" or Integration? Irish Families in Victorian Stafford', in Roger Swift and Sheridan Gilley (eds), *The Irish in Victorian Britain: The Local Dimension* (Dublin, 1999), pp. 156-89; John Herson, 'Irish Immigrant families in the English West Midlands: A Long-Term View, 1830-1914', in John Belchem and Klaus Tenfelde (eds), *Irish and Polish Migration in Comparative Perspective* (Essen, 2003), pp. 75-92.
11. For example, Tredegar as described in Louise Miskell, 'Reassessing the Anti-Irish Riot: Popular Protest and the Irish in South Wales, c.1826-1882', in Paul O'Leary (ed.), *Irish Migrants in Modern Wales* (Liverpool, 2004), pp. 101-18.
12. John Herson, 'The Irish, the English and the Catholic Church in Stafford, 1815-1919', unpublished conference paper, 'Ireland and the Victorians' Conference, University College, Chester, July 2004.
13. Herson, 'Migration, "Community" or Integration?', pp. 167-89.
14. See: http://cwis.livjm.ac.uk/soc/families/ (URL may be subject to change)

15. Thirteen other contacts proved not to be descendants of the Stafford Irish. Of the total of 65 contacts, 48 were from the UK (fifteen from the Stafford area), eight from the USA, four from Australia, three from New Zealand and one each from Ireland and Canada.
16. David Fitzpatrick, *Oceans of Consolation: Personal Accounts of Irish Migration to Australia* (Cork, 1994); Lawrence W. McBride (ed.), *The Reynolds Letters: An Irish Emigrant Family in Late Victorian Manchester* (Cork, 1999); Kerby Miller, Arnold Schrier, Bruce Boling and David N. Doyle (eds), *Irish Immigrants in the Land of Canaan: Letters and Memoirs from Colonial and Revolutionary America, 1675-1815* (New York, 2003).
17. The historical evidence in this case does not support this perception.
18. The canal passes about two miles east of the town and was served by a short branch from it.
19. The one clear example of this was the Walsh family. John Walsh was a bricklayer's labourer who came to Stafford from Co. Galway around 1862 with his wife Mary Mannion and child. They had five more children in Stafford. Walsh was involved in trade union activity, and in 1881 he chaired a 'numerously attended' meeting to protest against the Coercion Bill. Resolutions were passed referring to 'the Irish electors of Stafford' and it was unanimously agreed to form a branch of the Irish National Land League in the town (*Staffordshire Advertiser* [*SA*], 19 February 1881). It is not known whether this was done, but there were no more reports. John Walsh and his family seem to have left Stafford shortly afterwards.
20. Hickman, *Religion*, chapters 3-5.
21. These respondents did, nevertheless, have one of the best photographic records of their Stafford Irish family.
22. *SA*, 19 December 1921.
23. Hickman, *Religion*, chapters 3-5.
24. St Patrick's school had been founded in 1868 and was linked to St Patrick's Church which was established as a separate mission in 1893. St Austin's school was founded in 1818 and was linked to its eponymous Catholic church founded in 1791. One person had been to the Convent run by the Sisters of St Joseph of Cluny who set up in Stafford in 1903.
25. M.W. Greenslade, *St Austin's, Stafford* (Birmingham, 2004), pp. 3-9.
26. Herson, 'The Irish, the English and the Catholic Church'.
27. See: http://cwis.livjm.ac.uk/soc/families
28. This respondent had not lived in Stafford since 1968, so his comments were not specifically about reactions in the town.
29. Herson, 'Migration, "Community" or Integration', p. 182; Herson, 'Irish Immigrant Families', pp. 103-4.

NOTES AND REFERENCES

30. Herson, 'The Irish'.
31. Herson, 'The Irish'.
32. The families in interviews 1, 7, 11 and 12.
33. Colin Pooley, 'Segregation or Integration? The Residential Experience of the Irish in Mid-Victorian Britain', in Swift and Gilley, *The Irish in Britain, 1815-1939*, p. 80. The essay reports a detailed study of Liverpool and Lancaster.
34. John D. Papworth, 'The Irish in Liverpool, 1835-1871: Segregation and Dispersal', Unpublished PhD thesis (University of Liverpool, 1981), chapter 4. Another unresolved problem is whether absolute numbers of Irish-born or their proportion in the population was more significant in terms of the retention of Irish identity and ethnic fade. Liverpool had both high absolute numbers of Irish-born and a high proportion in the population, though by 1871 this had already dropped to 15.6% of the city's people. Despite Pooley's analysis, it is clear that elements of Irish ethnicity survived more strongly in Liverpool than elsewhere, although even here it was increasingly transmuted into a Liverpool Catholic (or Protestant) identity. London on the other hand had high numbers of Irish-born - 78,422 in 1871, almost the same as Liverpool - but they constituted only 2.8% of the population. Although viable Irish institutions could clearly survive in such a population, the pressures towards intermingling were stronger, and in the longer-term the descendants of London's Victorian Irish generally merged with the wider population.
35. Trainor argued that in the Black Country anti-Catholicism dwindled in the late nineteenth century because of the overall decline in the Irish-born population and because of frequent intermarriage with local people. Richard H. Trainor, 'Anti-Catholicism and the Priesthood in the Nineteenth Century Black Country', *Staffordshire Catholic History*, 16 (1976), p. 19.
36. Herson, 'Migration, "Community" or Integration?', p. 173.
37. Kenny, 'Diaspora and Comparison', p. 162.

Chapter 13

1. 'Out of the Ghetto? The Catholic Community in Modern Scotland', University of Stirling, 24 January 1997.
2. Such discourses characterise much Scottish press reporting regarding matters connected to Irishness in Scotland.

3. Thomas M. Devine, 'Introduction', in Thomas M. Devine (ed.), *Irish Immigrants and Scottish Society in the Nineteenth and Twentieth Centuries* (Edinburgh, 1991).
4. M. Tierney on Andrew O'Hagan in 'Leaving Caledonia', *Herald*, 9 October 1999.
5. Interview with Mark Burke, secretary, Naomh Padraig Celtic Supporters Club, Dublin, 3 December 1999.
6. This project was financed by the Government sponsored Economic and Social Research Council in 2001/02 and essentially looked at questions and issues of identity focusing on people born in Britain of at least one Irish born parent or grandparent. Interviewees have been given pseudonyms for the purpose of reporting findings. The work was carried out by Dr J Bradley, Dr S Morgan, Professor M. Hickman and Professor B. Walter. For further references see http://www.anglia.ac.uk/geography/progress/irish2/
7. John Hoberman in John Sugden and Alan Bairner, *Sport, Sectarianism and Society in a Divided Ireland* (Leicester, 1993), p. 10.
8. Eric Hobsbawm, *Nations and Nationalism Since 1780: Programme, Myth, Reality* (Cambridge, 1990), p. 4.
9. Neil Blain and Raymond Boyle, 'Battling Along the Boundaries: The Marking of Scottish Identity in Sports Journalism', in Grant Jarvie and Graham Walker (eds), *Scottish Sport in the Making of the Nation* (Leicester, 1994), pp. 125-41.
10. See Gerry Finn, 'Racism, Religion and Social Prejudice: Irish Catholic Clubs, Soccer and Scottish Society – 1, The Historical Roots of Prejudice', *International Journal of the History of Sport*, 8 (1991), 72-95; and 'Racism, Religion and Social Prejudice: Irish Catholic Clubs, Soccer and Scottish Society – 2, Social Identities and Conspiracy Theories', *International Journal of the History of Sport*, 8 (1991), 370-97.
11. Brian Wilson, *Celtic: A Century with Honour* (Glasgow, 1988), p. 94.
12. For example, see comments by sports columnist, G. McNee, Radio Clyde, 13 January 1996.
13. Stewart J. Brown, 'Outside the Covenant: The Scottish Presbyterian Churches and Irish Immigration, 1922-1938', *Innes Review*, 13 (1991), 19-45.
14. *Orange Torch*, June 1984.
15. See Joseph M. Bradley, 'Images of Scottishness and Otherness in International Football', *Social Identities*, 9 (2003), 7-23.
16. Mary J. Hickman, *Religion, Class and Identity: State, the Catholic Church and the Education of the Irish in Britain* (Aldershot, 1994).
17. See *Daily Record* and letter from Celtic supporter of Irish descent 20 May 2003, p. 47.

18. This also reflects in current and ongoing research supported by the Carnegie Trust and the British Academy.
19. J. Traynor, *Daily Record*, 19 May 2003.
20. *Daily Star*, 26 May 2003.
21. *Herald*, 23 May 2003.
22. See S. Fisher, *Sunday Herald, Sport*, 18 May 2003.
23. See Mary J. Hickman, 'Reconstructing Deconstructing "Race": British Political Discourses about the Irish in Britain', *Ethnic and Racial Studies*, 21 (1998), 288-307.

Notes on Contributors

Caroline Attan is presently carrying out research on 'What the Body Remembers' focusing on kinaesthesia through in-depth interviews with Holocaust survivors and their descendants originating from Poland and Czechoslovakia and currently living in north London. This research extends her PhD thesis 'Significant Objects in Migrants' Experiences' awarded by the University of Portsmouth. The study used in-depth interviews concerning the significant objects in the living rooms of the homes of the above mentioned informants. She currently lectures in Contextual and Historical Studies (Art and Design) at Barnet College and is a visiting Lecturer at University of London (MA Cultural Memory).

Joseph M. Bradley is Lecturer in Sports Studies at the University of Stirling, Scotland. He has published widely on sporting matters in relation to religion, ethnicity, diaspora and politics. Along with several colleagues he is co-ordinator of an ESRC funded study, 'The Irish 2 Project' which looks at 2nd and 3rd generation Irish identities in Britain.

Kathy Burrell is Lecturer in Modern History at De Montfort University and is the list owner for the mailing list 'immigration-history-uk@jiscmail.ac.uk'. Her main research interest is in the field of migration, specifically forced migration, memory and narratives, national identity, transnationalism and community networks. She has published articles on Polish immigrants in the United Kingdom and is currently preparing *Moving Lives: Narratives of Nation and Migration among Europeans in Post-war Britain*, a monograph from her thesis on the Polish, Italian and Greek-Cypriot communities in the UK, for publication by Ashgate. She is also continuing new research into more recent migration from Poland to Britain.

Deianira Ganga has been investigating intergenerational processes of identity construction of individuals of immigrant origin. Through her PhD research, she focussed on the role played by the family of origin in the negotiation of the identity of the children and grandchildren of Italian immigrants who moved to Nottingham. She is currently working on the ESF 'Ethnicity in the Labour Market' project, which involves several different institutions and explores the relationship between ethnicity and employment. She is also one of the founding members of HERMES (European Researchers for Migration and Ethnic Studies: www.hermes.euro.st), an international non-profit organisation, promoting comparative research on migration and ethnic relations across European academic institutions.

Joanna Herbert is a Research Fellow in the Department of Geography, Queen Mary University of London. The research for this paper was conducted whilst she was an ESRC Postdoctoral Research Fellow at the Centre for Urban History, University of Leicester. Her book *Negotiating Boundaries in the City: Migration, Ethnicity, and Gender in Britain* (Ashgate) is forthcoming. Her main areas of interest include the gendered nature of migratory experiences, the role of memory in life histories and constructions of whiteness and racisms.

John Herson is Head of History at Liverpool John Moores University. His prime area of interest is in Irish migration and he has published a number of previous essays relating to the Irish who settled in nineteenth century Stafford. He is currently writing a book on the subject that places the local experiences of the Irish within the wider diaspora context. His research interests also include urban history, planning and transport history and he has produced a number of publications in these fields.

Anne J. Kershen is Director of the Centre for the Study of Migration at Queen Mary, University of London and Barnet Shine Senior Research Fellow in the Department of Politics. She has published widely on topics relating to migrants and migration. Her latest publication is *Strangers, Aliens and Asians: Huguenots, Jews and Bangladeshis in Spitalfields 1660-2000* (London, 2005).

Tony Kushner is Professor of History and director of the AHRB Parkes Centre for the Study of Jewish/non-Jewish relations at the University of Southampton. His most recent books are *We Europeans? Mass-Observation, 'Race' and British Identity in the Twentieth Century* (Aldershot, 2004), a study of ordinary people and their responses to and experiences of ethnic diversity, and, with Donald Bloxham, *The Holocaust: Critical Historical Approaches* (Manchester, 2005).

Kevin Myers teaches social history and education in the School of Education at the University of Birmingham. His doctoral thesis examined the settlement and education of refugee children in Britain between 1937 and 1945. He has research interests in heritage and the politics of public history.

Panikos Panayi is Professor of European History at De Montfort University. He has published twelve books on themes including the history of Germans in Britain, racial violence in Britain and war and minorities. His articles have appeared in some of the leading history and ethnic relations journals including *Ethnic and Racial Studies*, the *Journal of Contemporary History* and *Social History*. He is currently completing a book on ethnic majorities and minorities in the German town of Osnabrück between 1929 and 1949 and is carrying out research for a volume on the multiculturalisation of food in England.

Louise Ryan is a sociologist based at the Social Policy Research Centre, Middlesex University. Her main research interests are migration, gender and national identity, and social movements. She has published articles in various journals such as the *Sociological Review*, *Immigrants and Minorities*, *Journal of Ethnic and Migration Studies*, *Oral History* and *Feminist Review*. Louise's latest book is *Women and Irish Nationalism* (co-edited with Margaret Ward) published by Irish Academic Press, 2004. Louise is currently researching migrant women's negotiations of motherhood, employment and support networks.

Lucio Sponza is Professor Emeritus of Italian Studies at the University of Westminster, London. His publications include: *Italian Immigrants in Nineteenth Century Britain: Realities and Images* (Leicester, 1988); *Divided Loyalties: Italians in Britain during the Second World War* (Frankfurt, 2000); and, as co-editor with L. Cheles, *The Art of Persuasion: Political Communication in Italy from 1945 to the 1980s* (Manchester, 2001).

Divya P. Tolia-Kelly is a Lecturer in Social and Cultural Geography at the University of Durham. She is interested in post-colonial memory as manifested in the everyday lives of migrant communities in Britain. Her work has appeared in a variety of journals including *Visual Culture in Britain*, *Transactions of the Institute of British Geographers* and *Geoforum*.

Inge Weber-Newth is Principal Lecturer in Applied Language Studies and a member of the Research Institute for the Study of European Transformations (ISET) at London Metropolitan University. Her main research interests are in the areas of migration and ethnic minorities, language and identity, biographical and collective memory. Recent publications include: *Labour & Love, Deutsche in Grossbritannien nach dem Zweiten Weltkrieg* (co-author) (Osnabrück, 2000) and *European Immigrants in Britain 1933-1950* (co-editor) (Munich, 2003).

Index

Abrahams, Harold 25, 26
Abyssinian War 68, 71
Acts
   Education (1944) 5
   Education (Scotland) (1918) 236
   National Heritage (1980) 38
Akenson, Donald 211
Alderman, Geoffrey 6
Ali, Altab 21
Ali, Monica 11, 19–20
   Brick Lane 11, 19–20
Alibhai-Brown, Yasmin 22–3, 24, 25, 32, 45
Allin, John 19
Anderson, Benedict 46
   Imagined Communities 46
Anti-Demolition League 27
Anwar, Muhammad 101
Appadurai, Arjun 163
Arandora Star 59
Argentina 58
Assmann, Jan 211, 230
Attan, Caroline xiv, 16
Australia 59, 76, 234, 250
Austria 87
   Vienna 27
Austrians in Britain 87

Baldacconi, Luigi 61
Bangladesh 101, 106, 107
Bangladeshis in Britain *see* Bengalis
Banton, Michael 5
Barnsley 85
Bayliss, Lilian 26
BBC 22, 24, 69
Beaufort, W. M. 103
Bedford 73, 117
Bedfordshire Times 73
Belgium 76, 175, 176
Belorussians in Britain 92
Bengalis in London xiii, 19, 20, 21, 96, 98, 99, 101, 102, 104–5, 106–7, 108, 109–13, 197, 198
Berlin, Isaiah 26
Bhattacharyya, Gargi 40, 41
Birmingham xii, 10, 11, 40, 41, 45, 47–8, 73, 139, 223
Blackburn 219, 224
Black Cultural Archives 10
Black History Month xii, 11, 12, 22, 23, 24, 33, 44
Black people in Britain 7, 8, 10, 21, 22, 24, 34, 42–3, 73, 77, 200
Blain, Neil 235, 237
Blair, Tony 22, 23
'Bollywood' 104, 159–65
   Guide 163–4
Bolton 194
Bornat, Joanna 194
Bolzmann, Claudio 122
Boswell, John 68

Bourdin, Martial 65
Boyle, Raymond 235, 237
Bradford 79, 84, 90, 93, 117
    Heritage Recording Unit, 78–9, 87
    Telegraph and Argus 93
    University Irish Diaspora Research Unit 6
Bradley, Joseph M. xv
Brazil 58
Briggs, John 117
Bristol 73
British Brothers League 19
British Library 194
    National Sound Archive 31
    Newspaper Library 194
British Union of Fascists 19
British National Party 19
Brown, Stewart J. 237
Brunel, Isambard Kingdom 26
Buckingham, David 49
Burke, Edmund 51
Burman, Ricky 28–9
Burrell, Kathy xi

Calcutta 102
Canada 50, 59, 76, 83, 90, 162, 250
    Montreal 162
Cannadine, David 8
Captive Nations Association 92–3
Carno, Sedi 65
Carr, Graham 50
Carvalho, Melanie 166–9
    'Goan Palms' 166–9
Celtic Football Club xv 235–52
Cesarani, David 6
Chakravarty, Sumita 164
Chamberlain, Mary 192, 196, 197, 200
Chesterfield 117
Chinn, Carl 44–5, 47–8
    Birmingham Irish 45, 47–8

Churchill, Winston 23, 25, 26
Clark, David 27
Clarke, John 39
Clydebank 238
Coatbridge 238, 242
Cohen, Jack 26
Cohen, Robin 100
Cold War 72
Cole, G. D. H. 5
Collins, Michael 32
    The Likes of Us 32
Colls, Robert 44
Colpi, Terri 7
Commission for Racial Equality 32
Conservative Party 26
Copeland, David 19–20
Craib, Ian 46
Crimea 18
Crispi, Francesco 65
Cuba, Lee 119
Cyprus 173, 181, 186
Czechoslovakia 76, 173, 174, 184
    Prague 176, 179, 186
Czechs in Britain 85, 173, 174, 176, 181

Daily Mail 23, 24, 68
Daily Mirror 69
Daily Record 250
Danzig 27
Davis, Natalie Zemon 34
Defoe, Daniel 97
    Tour of England and Wales 97
Denmark 68
Denvir, John 5–6
    The Irish in Britain 5–6
Derby 117
Devine, T. M. 234
Diana Princess of Wales 23, 34
Dick, Malcolm 40
'Displaced Persons' xiii, 71–2, 75–95
Disraeli, Benjamin 26

INDEX

Duffield, Ian 43
Dunaway, David 194, 195, 202
Dundee United 251

Eastbourne 204
Economic and Social Research Council 235, 237
Edinburgh 236
Empire Windrush 73
Endelman, Todd 6
Estonians in Britain 85, 90, 92
Ethiopia 66
European Economic Community 59
'European Volunteer Workers' xiii, 75–95
    'Balt Cygnet' scheme 75, 78
    'Westward Ho!' scheme 75, 78, 80
Examiner 61
Express 24

Feldman, David 6
Figi 24
First World War 6, 7, 98, 211, 214, 221
Fishman, Bill 28–9
Fitzpatrick, David 217
food xiii, xiv, 88, 105–7, 133–48, 162, 199
football as a signifier of identity xv, 234–52
Fornara, Giuseppe 65
Forgan, Liz 50
France 3, 22, 58, 65, 76, 99, 100, 105
    Dunkirk 176
    Paris 27
    Revolution 51
Fraser, Nancy 38
Freud, Lucien 25, 26
Fulbrook, Mary 36
Furedi, Frank 36, 51
Fryer, Peter 21
Staying Power 21

Gandhi, Leela 151
Ganga, Deianira xiii, 15
Gardner, Katy 7, 99, 192, 198
    Age, Narrative and Migration 7–8, 192
Germans in Britain 7, 71–2, 77, 78, 80, 87, 88, 89, 173, 187
    Anglo-German Family History Society 9
Germany 15, 23, 68, 70, 76, 78, 80, 84, 87, 91, 93, 94, 173, 183
    Nazism 7, 26, 28, 30, 31, 76, 78, 91, 94, 176, 180, 186
Giddens, Anthony 135
Gilley, Sheridan 6
Gilroy, Paul 8
    There Ain't No Black in the Union Jack 8
Gladstone, William Ewart 23
Glasgow xv, 214, 228, 235–52
    Herald 251
Glass, Ruth 5
Goodhart, David 53
Grade, Lew 25
Graham, Brian 39
Grandi, Dino 71
Great Britons xii, 12, 22–34
Greek Cypriots in Britain 12, 173, 181–2, 186
Greenman, Leon 30
Guardian 24–5, 33
Gundara, Jagdish 43
Guyana 173

Halifax 90
Hall, Catherine 47
Hammond, J. L and L. B. 5
Handley, J. E. 6
Harrison, Mark 32
Haylett, Chris 51

Heffer, Simon 22–3, 24
Hennings, C. R. 7
Herbert, A. P. 68
Herbert, Joanna, xiii 14
Herson, John xv, 16
Herzl, Theodor 100
Hesse, Barnor 41
Hibernian Football Club 236
Hickman, Mary 6, 212–13, 221, 226
Hill, Christopher 53
Himid, Lubaina 29
Hiro, Dilip 42
Hitler, Adolf 178
Hoberman, John 235, 237
Hobsbawm, Eric 41–2, 235, 237
Holland 76
Holmes, Colin 6
Holohan, A. 52
Home Office 71
Hore-Belisha, Leslie 26
Howard, Michael 26
Huber, Andreas 110
Huguenots in Britain xiii, 7, 19, 20, 96, 97, 98, 99–100, 101–2, 103, 105, 107, 108–13
   French Protestant School 103
   London 96, 97, 98, 99–100, 103, 105, 107, 108–13
   Huguenot Society of Great Britain and Ireland 7
   Proceedings 7
Hummon, David 119
Hungarians in Britain 92

immigration history in Britain xi, xii, xv, 3–17
Ince, Sir Godfrey H. 72
India 134, 137, 140, 141, 142, 149, 153, 154, 157, 158, 159, 160, 162, 163, 164, 165, 166, 168
   Bombay 165, 168
Indians in Britain
   see South Asians
industrialisation 5
internment xiii, 59, 70, 77
Ireland 65, 176–7, 186, 193, 197–9, 202–9, 210–33, 234, 235, 237, 238, 239, 242, 243
   Dublin 234
   Cork 206
   Famine 210, 211, 212, 216, 219, 223, 230
   IRA 48
   RTE 195
Irish in America 193, 234
Irish in Australia 234
Irish in Britain xii, xiv–xv, 5–6, 7, 10, 11, 12, 19, 42, 45, 47–8, 52, 191–209, 210–33, 234–52
   Birmingham xii, 11, 47–8
   Blackburn 219, 224
   Bolton 194
   Eastbourne 204
   Glasgow xv, 214, 228, 235–52
   Liverpool 214, 219, 228, 229
   London 19, 194–209, 214, 229
   Manchester 214
   Stafford xv, 16, 210–33
   Walsall 219, 224
Israel, 12
Italians in Britain, xii–xiii, xiii, 7, 57–74, 77, 87, 114–30, 234
   Bedford, 73, 117
   Birmingham 73
   Bradford 117
   Bristol 73
   Chesterfield 117
   Derby 117
   Edinburgh 66
   Glasgow 66
   internment of xiii, 59, 70, 77
   Leicester 73, 117
   Liverpool 66
   London 58, 60–71, 72–3

INDEX

Fascio di Londra 66, 67
La Voce degli Italiani 72, 74
Manchester 66, 93
Mazzini's Free School 57, 60–2, 65
Nottingham xiii, 73, 114–30
Peterborough 73, 117
Swindon 73
Italians in Switzerland 122
Italy, xiii, 15, 57–74, 87, 116, 119, 120–30, 234
   Bologna 58
   Fascism 66–8
   Florence 60, 125
   Milan 58, 121
   Naples 58, 64, 65–6
   Parma 58, 60, 64
   Piacenza 58
   Rome 58
   Turin 121
   Venice 7
   Victor Emanuel 69

Jackson J. A. 6
   The Irish in Britain 6
Jewish Chronicle 25, 26
Jewish 'Displaced Persons' 76
Jewish history in Britain xi, xii, xiii, 6–7, 9, 25–34
   Jewish Historical Society of England 6, 27–8
     Transactions 6
   Jewish Genealogical Society of Britain 9
Jews in Britain xiii, xiv, 5, 6–7, 10, 11, 12, 13, 24, 25–31, 65, 77, 96, 98, 99–101, 102, 103–4, 105–6, 107, 108, 109–13, 173–4, 175–6, 183–4, 186–7, 188
   antisemitism 6, 25, 28
   Board of Deputies 26

London 19, 20, 26–30, 96, 98, 99–101, 103–4, 105–6, 107, 108, 109–13, 173–4, 175–6, 183–4, 186–7, 188
Joly, Daniele, 100
Jones, Grace 18
Jones, Ken 49

Kansteiner, Wulf 212
Karim, Abdul 18
Katz, David S. 6, 27
Kay, Diana 81
Kennedy, John F. 25
Kenny, Kevin 230
Kenya xiv, 134, 136, 139, 153, 154, 155, 156, 158, 161, 163, 164, 166
   Mombassa 160, 161, 168
   Nairobi 136, 139, 141, 156, 157
Kershen, Anne J. xiii, 12, 13
Khan, Noor-un-Nisa Inayat 22
King, Russell 129
King George IV 18
Kino, F. F. 81
Korean War 82
Kruschev, Nikita 93
Kushner, Tony xii, 6, 9, 11, 12

Lahiri, Shompa 7
   Indians in Britain 7
Lambert, Sharon 194
Laski, Harold 25
Latvians in Britain 85, 89, 92
League of Nations, 66
Lehrer, Tom 32
Leicester xiv, 10, 73, 117, 133–48
   De Montfort University xi, 10
   Highfields Remembered project, 10
   Leicestershire Libraries 10
   Multicultural Oral and Pictorial Archive Project 10

Lenin, Vladimir Ilych 93
Levy, Andrea 11
  Small Island 11
Lipman, V. D. 6
  Social History of the Jews in England 6
Libya 70
Lithuania 234
Lithuanians in Britain 85, 89, 90, 92, 234
Liverpool 33, 214, 219, 228, 229
  University Irish Studies Institute 6
London xiii, xiv, 11, 19, 26–30, 33, 58, 60–71, 72–3, 97–113, 151–70, 173–88, 194–209, 214, 229, 244
  Bethnal Green 20, 97
  Brent 152
  Brixton 19
  Chelsea 205
  Greater London Council 22
  Hammersmith and Fulham Council Ethnic Communities Oral History Project 9–10
  Harlesden 153–4
  Harrow 152
  Holborn 58
  Inner London Education Authority 22
  Jewish Museums 11, 22, 26–30, 31
  Metropolitan Archives 29
  Metropolitan University Irish Studies Centre 6, 194
  Museum of 10–11
  Newham Monitoring Project 10
  Shoreditch 97
  Soho 19
  Southwark 32
  Spitalfields xiii, 12, 29, 96–113

University Centre for German and Austrian Exile Studies at the University of London's Institute of German and Romance Studies 7
  Yearbook 7
  Wembley 161–2, 244
London City Mission 62
  City Mission Magazine 62
Long, Paul 41
Louis XIV 108

MacRaild, Donald 6
McBride, Lawrence W. 217
McDermott, Sinead 196, 203
Malatesta, Errico 65
Malawi 134, 155, 157, 160, 161
Malik, Kenan 38
Manchester 29, 30, 73, 90, 214
  Jewish Museum 11, 22, 28–9, 30–1
  Studies Unit of Manchester Polytechnic 28
Marconi, Guglielmo 67
Margoliouth, Moses 6
Marxism 4, 46
Mass Observation 69–70
Maxwell, Sir Alexander 71–2
Mazower, David 30
Mazzini, Giussepe 60–2, 65
Miles, Robert 81
Miller, Kerby 210, 212
Milton, John 23
Ministry of Labour 71–2, 78, 81
Mohammed 18
Mohammed, Robina 152
Moodie, Jane 197
Morning Chronicle 61
Morris, Jane 33
Morrison, Toni 163
Mosley, Sir Oswald 19

INDEX

Moving Here website 10
Mozambique 157
Museums Journal 33
Muslims in Britain 12, 52
   see also Bengalis and South Asians
Mussolini, Benito 59, 66–8, 70, 71
Myers, Kevin xii, 10, 11

Napoleonic Wars 213
Narayan, R. K. 164
National Archives 10, 194
National Front 19, 20, 134
National Lottery 10, 23, 45, 48–9, 50
New Statesman and Nation 68
Newman, Janet 39
Niceforo, Alfredo 66
Nightingale, Florence 22, 34
Nora, Pierre 3
Norway 68
Nottingham xiii, 73, 114–30

Oldham 86, 90
O'Hagan, Andrew 234
oral history xii, xiii, xiv–xv, 9–10, 13–16, 114–30, 133–48, 171–88, 191–209, 238–52
O'Reilly, Karen 119, 129
O'Sullivan, Patrick 6

Paine, Tom 51
Pakistanis in Britain
   see South Asians
Panayi, Panikos xi
Papworth, John D. 229
Parker, David 41
Parkin, David 172
Perks, Rob 29
Peterborough 73, 117
Picture Post 84
Pieri, Joe 71
Pinter, Harold 25, 26

Poland 12, 15, 76, 94, 106, 173, 174, 175, 178, 180, 184, 186, 187, 234
   Auschwitz 180, 186
   Krakow 180, 186
   TV Polonia 15
   Warsaw 27
Poles in Britain 7, 12, 15, 71, 78, 85, 87, 88, 89, 92, 173, 174, 175–6, 187, 234
   Barnsley 85
   Bradford 79, 87
   London 173, 174, 175–6, 187
   Polish Resettlement Corps 78
Poles in Germany 15
Polti, Francesco 65
Pooley, Colin 229
Pope Pius XI 67
Portelli, Allessandro 14, 133
Portugal 250
Postmodernism 4
Powell, Enoch 19, 23, 25, 37
Prague 27
Prince Charles 20, 45
Prospect 52
Public Record Office
   see National Archives

Queen Elizabeth I 34
Queen Victoria 18, 21, 65
Quran 108

Ralegh, Sir Walter 53
Rangers Football Club 240, 245
Richard, Sir Cliff 25
Ritivoi, Andreea 192–3, 195–6, 201, 207
Roberts, Brian 14
Roth, Cecil 6, 27
Rouen 97
Rowthorn, Bob 52
Rubinstein, W. D. 6

Runnymede Trust 42
   The Future of Multiethnic Britain 42
Rushdie, Salman 18–19, 21, 22, 34
   The Satanic Verses 18–19
Russia 65, 106, 178, 187
   Revolution 178
Ryan, Louise xiv, 14

St James's Gazette 64
Salomon, Sidney, 26, 32
   The Jews of Britain 26, 32
Samuel, Raphael 38, 44
Sancho, Igantius 18
Sandhu, Sukhdev 21
   London Calling 21
Sassoon, Siegfried 25
Schaible, Karl Heinrich 7
   Geschichte der Deutschen in England 7
Schama, Simon 46
   History of Britain 46
Schwarz, Bill 47
Scottish Nation Party (SNP) 237
Scottish Sport 236
Seacole, Mary 18, 22, 34
Second World War xiii, 7, 8, 13, 15, 19, 31, 57, 68–71, 73, 75, 98, 116, 174, 175, 226, 236
Serbs in Britain
   see Yugoslavs
Severus, Septimus 18
Shorter Oxford English Dictionary 100
Shukur, A., 99
Smith, Adam 23
Smith, Zadie 11
   White Teeth 11
Somalians in Britain 19
South Africa 24
South Asians in Britain, xiii–xiv, 7–8, 10, 21, 22, 24, 44, 73, 77, 85, 101, 133–48, 149–70, 198
   in Leicester 133–48

   in London 151–70
   see also Bengalis
Southampton University Parkes Centre for Jewish Non-Jewish Relations 6, 29
South Shields 33
Soviet Union 75, 76, 91–2, 94
Spain
   Barcelona 242
   Seville 250
Spaniards in Switzerland 122
Spanish Civil War 71
Sponza, Lucio, xii, 7, 15
Starkey, David 22, 45
Steedman, Carolyn 47
Stephen Lawrence Enquiry 21
Stirling University 234, 235
Stone, Lawrence 41
Stoppard, Tom 25
Strauss, Isaac 27
Sudan 153, 154
Sun 23–4, 61
Sunday Graphic 68
Swift, Roger 6
Swindon 73
Switzerland 122
Syal, Meera 11

Tannahill, J. A. 81, 87, 95
Tanzania 134, 135, 142, 155
Tate, Nick 45
Thatcher, Margaret 37, 40
Thompson, E. P. 5
   The Making of the English Working Classes 5
Thomson, Alistair 192, 203
Tolia-Kelly, Divya P. xiv, 15, 16
Tortolani, Mariana 62
Tovey, D'Blossiers 6
   Anglia Judaica 6
True Tablet 61
Tunbridge Wells 23

INDEX

Uganda 134, 137, 138, 153, 155, 163, 165, 166
   Kampala 161
Ukraine 76, 94
Ukrainians in Britain 71, 78, 82, 83, 85, 87, 88–9, 90, 91–2, 94
   Bradford 79, 90
   Halifax 90
   Oldham 90
   Manchester 90
United Nations 24
   International Refugee Organization 76, 81
   Relief and Rehabilitation Administration 76
USA 11, 22, 38, 58, 76, 83, 90, 117, 193, 234, 250
   New York 29

Valentina, Domenica 62, 63
Veenis, Milena 172
Vietnam War 212
Viner, Brian 25–6
Visram, Rosina 7, 21
   Ayahs, Lascars and Princes 21
von Hagen, Gunther 18
   Bodyworks Exhibition 18

Walsall 219, 224
Walter, Bronwen 194
Walters, Vanessa 33
War Office 78
Warnes, Anthony 129
Weber-Newth, Inge xiii
Weekly Dispatch 61
Weight, Richard 44, 45–7, 48
   Patriots 44, 45–7, 48
Wesker, Arnold 19
Whig tradition of history 5, 27
Wilkins, W. H. 64–5
Williams, Alan 129
Williams, Bill 6, 28
Williams, Raymond 154
Wilson, Brian 236
Wolf, Lucien 27
Wolfe, Alan 53
Women's Voluntary Service 81
Wren, Christopher 97

Yacoub, Magdi 22
Yorkshire Observer 84, 86
Young Roots 44, 45, 48–50
Yugoslavs in Britain, 81, 82, 86, 89, 90–1
   Bradford 79
Yugoslavia 76
Yuval-Davis, Nira 140

Zambia 134, 155
Zangwill, Israel 25